REAL WORLD
GLOBALIZATION

A READER IN ECONOMICS, BUSINESS, AND POLITICS FROM
DOLLARS&SENSE

EDITED BY RAVI BHANDARI, CHRIS STURR,

AND THE *DOLLARS & SENSE* COLLECTIVE

REAL WORLD GLOBALIZATION, 10th edition

ISBN: 978-1-878585-76-9

Published by:
Economic Affairs Bureau, Inc. d/b/a *Dollars & Sense*
29 Winter Street, Boston, MA 02108
617-447-2177; dollars@dollarsandsense.org.
For order information, contact Economic Affairs Bureau or visit: www.dollarsandsense.org.

Real World Globalization is edited by the *Dollars & Sense* Collective, which also publishes *Dollars & Sense* magazine and the classroom books *Real World Macro, Real World Micro, Current Economic Issues, Real World Labor, Real World Latin America, Real World Banking and Finance, The Wealth Inequality Reader, The Environment in Crisis, Introduction to Political Economy, Unlevel Playing Fields: Understanding Wage Inequality and Discrimination, Striking a Balance: Work, Family, Life,* and *Grassroots Journalism.*

The 2009 *Dollars & Sense* Collective:
Arpita Banerjee, Heather Boersma, Ben Collins, Amy Gluckman, Ben Greenberg, Daniel Fireside, Mary Jirmanus, James McBride, John Miller, Larry Peterson, Linda Pinkow, Paul Piwko, Smriti Rao, Alejandro Reuss, Dave Ryan, Bryan Snyder, Chris Sturr, Ramaa Vasudevan, and Jeanne Winner.

Co-editors of this volume: Ravi Bhandari, Chris Sturr
Editorial assistance: Hallie Acton, Arpita Banerjee, Elizabeth Cayouette-Gluckman, Jared Eisenberg, Amy Gluckman, Christopher Hearse, Linda Pinkow, Smriti Rao, and Jason Son.

Cover design: Chris Sturr, based on a design by David Garrett, dgcommunications.com.
Cover photo: © Alex Linghorn. All rights reserved. Used with permission.
Production: Chris Sturr and Katharine Davies.

Printed in U.S.A.

CONTENTS

Chapter 1

CRITICAL PERSPECTIVES ON GLOBALIZATION

Article 1.1

THE GOSPEL OF FREE TRADE
The New Evangelists

BY ARTHUR MacEWAN
November 1991, updated July 2009

Free trade! With the zeal of Christian missionaries, for decades the U.S. government has been preaching, advocating, pushing, and coercing around the globe for "free trade."

As the economic crisis emerged in 2007 and 2008 and rapidly became a global crisis, it was apparent that something was very wrong with the way the world economy was organized. Not surprisingly, as unemployment rose sharply in the United States, there were calls for protecting jobs by limiting imports and for the government to "buy American" in its economic stimulus program. Similarly, in many other countries, as unemployment jumped upwards, pressure emerged for protection—and some actual steps were taken. Yet, free trade missionaries did not retreat; they continued to preach the same gospel.

The free-traders were probably correct in claiming that protectionist policies would do more harm than good as a means to stem the rising unemployment generated by the economic crisis. Significant acts of protectionism in one country would lead to retaliation—or at least copying—by other countries, reducing world trade. The resulting loss of jobs from reduced trade would most likely outweigh any gains from protection.

Yet the argument over international economic policies should not be confined simply to what should be done in a crisis. Nor should it simply deal with trade in goods and services. The free-traders have advocated their program as one for long-

1

run economic growth and development, yet the evidence suggests that free trade is not a good economic development strategy. Furthermore, the free-traders preach the virtue of unrestricted global movement of finance as well as of goods and services. As it turns out, the free flow of finance has been a major factor in bringing about and spreading the economic crisis that began to appear in 2007—as well as earlier crises.

The Push

While the U.S. push for free trade goes back several decades, it has become more intense in recent years. In the 1990s, the U.S. government signed on to the North American Free Trade Agreement (NAFTA) and in 2005 established the Central American Free Trade Agreement (CAFTA). Both Republican and Democratic presidents, however, have pushed hard for a *global* free trade agenda. After the demise of the Soviet Union, U.S. advisers prescribed unfettered capitalism for Eastern and Central Europe, and ridiculed as unworkable any move toward a "third way." In low-income countries from Mexico to Malaysia, the prescription has been the same: open markets, deregulate business, don't restrict international investment, and let the free market flourish.

In the push for worldwide free trade, the World Trade Organization (WTO) has been the principal vehicle of change, establishing rules for commerce that assure markets are open and resources are available to those who can pay. And the International Monetary Fund (IMF) and World Bank, which provide loans to many governments, use their financial power to pressure countries around the world to accept the gospel and open their markets. In each of these international organizations, the United States—generally through the U.S. Treasury—plays a dominant role.

Of course, as with any gospel, the preachers often ignore their own sermons. While telling other countries to open their markets, the U.S. government continued, for instance, to limit imports of steel, cotton, sugar, textiles, and many other goods. But publicly at least, free-trade boosters insist that the path to true salvation—or economic expansion, which, in this day and age, seems to be the same thing—lies in opening our market to foreign goods. Get rid of trade barriers at home and abroad, allow business to go where it wants and do what it wants. We will all get rich.

Yet the history of the United States and other rich countries does not fit well with the free-trade gospel. Virtually all advanced capitalist countries found economic success through heavy government regulation of their international commerce, not in free trade. Likewise, a large role for government intervention has characterized those cases of rapid and sustained economic growth in recent decades—for example, Japan after World War II, South Korea in the 1970s through the 1990s, and China most recently.

Free trade does, however, have its uses. Highly developed nations can use free trade to extend their power and control of the world's wealth, and business can use it as a weapon against labor. Most important, free trade can limit efforts to redistribute income more equally, undermine social programs, and keep people from democratically controlling their economic lives.

A Day in the Park

At the beginning of the 19th century, Lowell, Massachusetts, became the premier site of the U.S. textile industry. Today, thanks to the Lowell National Historical Park, you can tour the huge mills, ride through the canals that redirected the Merrimack River's power to those mills, and learn the story of the textile workers, from the Yankee "mill girls" of the 1820s through the various waves of immigrant laborers who poured into the city over the next century.

During a day in the park, visitors get a graphic picture of the importance of 19th-century industry to the economic growth and prosperity of the United States. Lowell and the other mill towns of the era were centers of growth. They not only created a demand for Southern cotton, they also created a demand for new machinery, maintenance of old machinery, parts, dyes, *skills*, construction materials, construction machinery, *more skills*, equipment to move the raw materials and products, parts maintenance for that equipment, *and still more skills*. The mill towns also created markets—concentrated groups of wage earners who needed to buy products to sustain themselves. As centers of economic activity, Lowell and similar mill towns contributed to U.S. economic growth far beyond the value of the textiles they produced.

The U.S. textile industry emerged decades after the industrial revolution had spawned Britain's powerful textile industry. Nonetheless, it survived and prospered. British linens inundated markets throughout the world in the early 19th century, as the British navy nurtured free trade and kept ports open for commerce. In the United States, however, hostilities leading up to the War of 1812 and then a substantial tariff made British textiles relatively expensive. These limitations on trade allowed the Lowell mills to prosper, acting as a catalyst for other industries and helping to create the skilled work force at the center of U.S. economic expansion.

Beyond textiles, however, tariffs did not play a great role in the United States during the early 19th century. Southern planters had considerable power, and while they were willing to make some compromises, they opposed protecting manufacturing in general because that protection forced up the prices of the goods they purchased with their cotton revenues. The Civil War wiped out the planters' power to oppose protectionism, and from the 1860s through World War I, U.S. industry prospered behind considerable tariff barriers.

Different Countries, Similar Experiences

The story of the importance of protectionism in bringing economic growth has been repeated, with local variations, in other advanced capitalist countries. During the late 19th century, Germany entered the major league of international economic powers with substantial protection and government support for its industries. Likewise, in 19th-century France and Italy, national consolidation behind protectionist barriers was a key to economic development.

Britain—which entered the industrial era first—is often touted as the prime example of successful development without tariff protection. Yet, Britain embraced free trade only after its industrial base was well established; as in the U.S., the early and important textile industry was erected on a foundation of protectionism. In addition, Britain built its industry through the British navy and the expansion of empire, hardly prime ingredients in any recipe for free trade.

Japan provides an especially important case of successful government protection and support for industrial development. In the post-World War II era, when the Japanese established the foundations for their economic "miracle," the government rejected free trade and extensive foreign investment and instead promoted its national firms.

In the 1950s, for example, the government protected the country's fledgling auto firms from foreign competition. At first, quotas limited imports to $500,000 (in current dollars) each year; in the 1960s, prohibitively high tariffs replaced the quotas. Furthermore, the Japanese allowed foreign investment only insofar as it contributed to developing domestic industry. The government encouraged Japanese companies to import foreign technology, but required them to produce 90% of parts domestically within five years.

The Japanese also protected their computer industry. In the early 1970s, as the industry was developing, companies and individuals could only purchase a foreign machine if a suitable Japanese model was not available. IBM was allowed to produce within the country, but only when it licensed basic patents to Japanese firms. And IBM computers produced in Japan were treated as foreign-made machines.

In the 20th century, no other country matched Japan's economic success, as it moved in a few decades from a relative low-income country, through the devastation of war, to emerge as one of the world's economic leaders. Yet one looks back in vain to find a role for free trade in this success. The Japanese government provided an effective framework, support, and protection for the country's capitalist development.

Likewise, in many countries that have been late-comers to economic development, capitalism has generated high rates of economic growth where government involvement, and not free trade, played the central role. South Korea is a striking case. "Korea is an example of a country that grew very fast and yet violated the canons of conventional economic wisdom," writes Alice Amsden in *Asia's Next Giant: South Korea and Late Industrialization,* widely acclaimed as perhaps the most important analysis of the South Korean economic success. "In Korea, instead of the market mechanism allocating resources and guiding private entrepreneurship, the government made most of the pivotal investment decisions. Instead of firms operating in a competitive market structure, they each operated with an extraordinary degree of market control, protected from foreign competition."

Free trade, however, has had its impact in South Korea. In the 1990s, South Korea and other East Asian governments came under pressure from the U.S. government and the IMF to open their markets, including their financial markets. When they did so, the results were a veritable disaster. The East Asian financial crisis that began in 1997 was a major setback for the whole region, a major disruption of economic growth. After extremely rapid economic growth for three decades, with output expanding at 7% to 10% a year, South Korea's economy plummeted by 6.3% between 1997 and 1998.

Mexico and Its NAFTA Experience

While free trade in goods and services has its problems, which can be very serious, it is the free movement of capital, the opening of financial markets that has sharp, sudden impacts, sometimes wrecking havoc on national economies. Thus, virtually as soon as Mexico, the United States and Canada formed NAFTA at the beginning of 1994, Mexico was hit with a severe financial crisis. As the economy turned downward at the beginning of that year, capital rapidly left the country, greatly reducing the value of the Mexican peso. With this diminished value of the peso, the cost of servicing international debts and the costs of imports skyrocketed—and the downturn worsened.

Still, during the 1990s, before and after the financial crisis, free-traders extolled short periods of moderate economic growth in Mexico —3% to 4% per year—as evidence of success. Yet, compared to earlier years, Mexico's growth under free trade has been poor. From 1940 to 1990 (including the no-growth decade of the 1980s), when Mexico's market was highly protected and the state actively regulated economic affairs, output grew at an average annual rate of 5%.

Most important, Mexico's experience discredits the notion that free-market policies will improve living conditions for the masses of people in low-income countries. The Mexican government paved the way for free trade policies by reducing or eliminating social welfare programs, and for many Mexican workers wages declined sharply during the free trade era. The number of households living in poverty rose dramatically, with some 75% of Mexico's population below the poverty line at the beginning of the 21st century.

China and Its Impact

Part of Mexico's problem and its economy's relatively weak performance from the 1990s onward has been the full-scale entrance of China into the international economy. While the Mexican authorities thought they saw great possibilities in NAFTA, with the full opening of the U.S. market to goods produced with low-wage Mexican labor, China (and other Asian countries) had even cheaper labor. As China also gained access to the U.S. market, Mexican expectations were dashed.

The Chinese economy has surely gained in terms of economic growth as it has engaged more and more with the world market, and the absolute levels of incomes of millions of people have risen a great deal. However, China's rapid economic growth has come with a high degree of income inequality. Before its era of rapid growth, China was viewed as a country with a relatively equal distribution of income. By the beginning of the new millennium, however, it was much more unequal than any of the other most populace Asian countries (India, Indonesia, Bangladesh, Pakistan), and more in line with the high-inequality countries of Latin America. Furthermore, with the inequality has come a great deal of social conflict. Tens of thousands of "incidents" of conflict involving violence are reported each year, and most recently there have been the major conflicts involving Tibetans and Ouigers.

In any case, the Chinese trade and growth success should not be confused with "free trade." Foundations for China's surge of economic growth were established through state-sponsored infra-structure development and the vast expansion of the country's educational system. Even today, while private business, including foreign business, appears to have been given free rein in China, the government still plays a controlling role—including a central role in affecting foreign economic relations.

A central aspect of the government's role in the county's foreign commerce has been in the realm of finance. As Chinese-produced goods have virtually flooded international markets, the government has controlled the uses of the earnings from these exports. Instead of simply allowing those earnings to be used by Chinese firms and citizens to buy imports, the government has to a large extent held those earnings as reserves. Using those reserves, China's central bank has been the largest purchaser of U.S. government bonds, in effect becoming a major financer of the U.S. government's budget deficit of recent years.

China's reserves have been one large element in creating a giant pool of financial assets in the world economy. This "pool" has also been built up as the doubling of oil prices following the U.S. invasion of Iraq put huge amounts of funds in the pockets of oil-exporting countries and firm and individuals connected to the oil industry. Yet slow growth of the U.S. economy and extremely low interest rates, resulting from the Federal Reserve Bank's efforts to encourage more growth, limited the returns that could be obtained on these funds. One of the consequences—through a complex set of connections—was the development of the U.S. housing bubble, as financial firms, searching for higher returns, pushed funds into more and more risky mortgage loans.

It was not simply free trade and the unrestricted flow of international finance that generated the housing bubble and subsequent crisis in the U.S. economy. However, the generally unstable global economy—both in terms of trade and finance—that has emerged in the free trade era was certainly a factor bringing about the crisis. Moreover, as is widely recognized, it was not only the U.S. economy and U.S. financial institutions that were affected. The free international flow of finance has meant that banking has become more and more a global industry. So as the U.S. banks got in trouble in 2007 and 2008, their maladies spread to many other parts of the world.

The Uses of Free Trade

While free trade is not the best economic growth or development policy and, especially through the free flow of finance, can precipitate financial crises, the largest
and most powerful firms in many countries find it highly profitable. As Britain
preached the loudest sermons for free trade in the early 19th century, when its own
industry was already firmly established, so the United States—or at least many firms
based in the United States—find it a profitable policy at the beginning of the 21st
century. The Mexican experience provides an instructive illustration.

For U.S. firms, access to foreign markets is a high priority. Mexico may be relatively poor, but with a population of 105 million it provides a substantial market.
Furthermore, Mexican labor is cheap relative to U.S. labor; and using modern production techniques, Mexican workers can be as productive as workers in the United
States. For U.S. firms to obtain full access to the Mexican market, the United States
has to open its borders to Mexican goods. Also, if U.S. firms are to take full advantage of cheap foreign labor and sell the goods produced abroad to U.S. consumers,
the United States has to be open to imports.

On the other side of the border, wealthy Mexicans face a choice between
advancing their interests through national development or advancing their interests through ties to U.S. firms and access to U.S. markets. For many years, they
chose the former route. This led to some development of the Mexican economy but
also—due to corruption and the massive power of the ruling party, the PRI—huge
concentrations of wealth in the hands of a few small groups of firms and individuals. Eventually, these groups came into conflict with their own government over
regulation and taxation. Having benefited from government largesse, they came
to see their fortunes in greater freedom from government control and, particularly,
in greater access to foreign markets and partnerships with large foreign companies.
National development was a secondary concern when more involvement with international commerce would produce greater riches more quickly.

In addition, the old program of state-led development in Mexico ran into severe
problems. These problems came to the surface in the 1980s with the international
debt crisis. Owing huge amounts of money to foreign banks, the Mexican government was forced to respond to pressure from the IMF, the U.S. government, and
large international banks which sought to deregulate Mexico's trade and investment. That pressure meshed with the pressure from Mexico's own richest elites,
and the result was the move toward free trade and a greater opening of the Mexican
economy to foreign investment.

Since the early 1990s, these changes for Mexico and the United States (as well
as Canada) have been institutionalized in NAFTA. The U.S. government's agenda
since then has been to spread free trade policies to all of the Americas through more
regional agreements like CAFTA and ultimately through a Free Trade Area of the
Americas. On a broader scale, the U.S. government works through the WTO, the
IMF, and the World Bank to open markets and gain access to resources beyond

the Western Hemisphere. In fact, while markets remain important everywhere, low-wage manufacturing is increasingly concentrated in Asia—especially China— instead of Mexico or Latin America.

The Chinese experience involves many of the same advantages for U.S. business as does the Mexican—a vast market, low wages, and an increasingly productive labor force. However, the Chinese government, although it has liberalized the economy a great deal compared to the pre-1985 era, has not abdicated its major role in the economy. For better (growth) and for worse (inequality and repression), the Chinese government has not embraced free trade.

Who Gains, Who Loses?

Of course, in the United States, Mexico, China and elsewhere, advocates of free trade claim that their policies are in everyone's interest. Free trade, they point out, will mean cheaper products for all. Consumers in the United States, who are mostly workers, will be richer because their wages will buy more. In Mexico and China, on the one hand, and in the United States, on the other hand, they argue that rising trade will create more jobs. If some workers lose their jobs because cheaper imported goods are available, export industries will produce new jobs.

In recent years this argument has taken on a new dimension with the larger entrance of India into the world economy and with the burgeoning there of jobs based in information technology—programming and call centers, for example. This "out-sourcing" of service jobs has received a great deal of attention and concern in the United States. Yet free-traders have defended this development as good for the U.S. economy as well as for the Indian economy.

Such arguments obscure many of the most important issues in the free trade debate. Stated, as they usually are, as universal truths, these arguments are just plain silly. No one, for example, touring the Lowell National Historical Park could seriously argue that people in the United States would have been better off had there been no tariff on textiles. Yes, in 1820, they could have purchased textile goods more cheaply, but in the long run the result would have been less industrial advancement and a less wealthy nation. One could make the same point with the Japanese auto and computer industries, or indeed with numerous other examples from the last two centuries of capitalist development.

In the modern era, even though the United States already has a relatively developed economy with highly skilled workers, a freely open international economy does not serve the interests of most U.S. workers, though it will benefit large firms. U.S. workers today are in competition with workers around the globe. Many different workers in many different places can produce the same goods and services. Thus, an international economy governed by the free trade agenda will tend to bring down wages for many U.S. workers. This phenomenon has certainly been one of the factors leading to the substantial rise of income inequality in the United States during recent decades.

The problem is not simply that of workers in a few industries—such as auto and steel, or call-centers and computer programming—where import competition is an obvious and immediate issue. A country's openness to the international economy affects the entire structure of earnings in that country. Free trade forces down the general level of wages across the board, even of those workers not directly affected by imports. The simple fact is that when companies can produce the same products in several different places, it is owners who gain because they can move their factories and funds around much more easily than workers can move themselves around. Capital is mobile; labor is much less mobile. Businesses, more than workers, gain from having a larger territory in which to roam.

Control Over Our Economic Lives

But the difficulties with free trade do not end with wages. In both low-income and high-income parts of the world, free trade is a weapon in the hands of business when it opposes any progressive social programs. Efforts to place environmental restrictions on firms are met with the threat of moving production abroad. Higher taxes to improve the schools? Business threatens to go elsewhere. Better health and safety regulations? The same response.

Some might argue that the losses from free trade for people in the United States will be balanced by gains for most people in poor countries—lower wages in the United States, but higher wages in Mexico and China. Free trade, then, would bring about international equality. Not likely. In fact, as pointed out above, free trade reforms in Mexico have helped force down wages and reduce social welfare programs, processes rationalized by efforts to make Mexican goods competitive on international markets. China, while not embracing free trade, has seen its full-scale entrance into global commerce accompanied by increasing inequality.

Gains for Mexican or Chinese workers, like those for U.S. workers, depend on their power in relation to business. Free trade or simply the imperative of international "competitiveness" are just as much weapons in the hands of firms operating in Mexico and China as they are for firms operating in the United States. The great mobility of capital is business's best trump card in dealing with labor and popular demands for social change—in the United States, Mexico, China and elsewhere.

None of this means that people should demand that their economies operate as fortresses, protected from all foreign economic incursions. There are great gains that can be obtained from international economic relations—when a nation manages those relations in the interests of the great majority of the people. Protectionism often simply supports narrow vested interests, corrupt officials, and wealthy industrialists. In rejecting free trade, we should move beyond traditional protectionism.

Yet, at this time, rejecting free trade is an essential first step. Free trade places the cards in the hands of business. More than ever, free trade would subject us to the "bottom line," or at least the bottom line as calculated by those who own and run large companies.

Article 1.2

FREE MARKETS, INTERNATIONAL COMMERCE, AND ECONOMIC DEVELOPMENT

BY ARTHUR MacEWAN

November 2000

The essence of the neo-liberal position on international commerce is the proposition that economic growth will be most rapid when the movement of goods, services, and capital is unimpeded by government regulations. A simple logic lies at the basis of this free trade position. If, for whatever reasons, countries differ in their abilities to produce various goods, then they can all benefit if each specializes in the production of those items it produces most effectively (i.e., at least cost). They can then trade with one another to obtain the entire range of goods they need. In this manner, each country is using its resources to do what it can do best.

As an illustration of this logic, consider two countries, one with an abundance of good farmland and the other with a good supply of energy resources (hydro power, for example). It seems likely that each of these countries will gain from trade if the first specializes in the production of agricultural goods and the latter specializes in the production of manufactures. Moreover, if the governments impose no constraints on international trade, then this specialization is precisely what will occur. Without constraints on trade, people attempting to produce manufactured goods in the country with abundant good farmland will not be able to do so as cheaply as people in the country with a good supply of energy resources—and vice versa for people attempting to produce agricultural goods in the latter country.

The theory appears to run into trouble if one country produces everything more efficiently than the other. Yet the trouble is only apparent, not real. Under these circumstances, all will gain if each country specializes in the production of those goods where it has a *comparative advantage*. For example, let's assume that the country with abundant farmland produces agricultural goods at half what it costs to produce them in the other country. At the same time, this country with abundant farmland has a workforce with great capacity for industrial labor, and it therefore can produce manufactured goods at one-quarter of what it costs to produce them in the other country. Under these circumstances the country's skilled labor force gives it a greater advantage in the production of manufactures than the advantage that its abundant farmland gives it in the production of agricultural goods. Thus it has a *comparative* advantage in the production of manufactures. Similarly, the second country, even though it is less efficient in the production of both categories of goods, has a *comparative* advantage in the production of agricultural goods. To produce manufactures would cost four times as much in this country as in the other, whereas to produce agricultural goods would only cost twice as much. Consequently, both countries can gain if each specializes where it has a comparative advantage, and they then trade to obtain their full set of needs.

The theory of comparative advantage has played an important role in the history of economics, for it has provided an intellectual rationale for free trade policies. An intellectual rationale has been necessary because, whatever the larger efficacy of the policy, free trade is always costly to groups that have prospered under any prior trade restrictions.

Advocates of the neo-liberal position base their policy prescriptions as much on certain myths about history as on the internal coherence of their theory. They argue that their theory is validated by the history of successful economic growth, both in the longer experience of the relatively advanced economies and in the recent experience of successful growth in newly industrialized countries. They cite, in particular, the history of economic development in the United Kingdom, other countries of Western Europe, and the United States, and the more recent experiences of countries in East Asia.

An examination of these experiences, however, quickly demonstrates that the neo-liberal claims are but crude myths, having only a vague connection to reality.

Historical Experience: A Brief Sketch

Virtually all of our experience with economic development suggests that extensive regulation of foreign commerce by a country's government has been an essential foundation for successful economic growth. In the United Kingdom, perhaps the case most frequently cited to demonstrate the success of free trade, textile producers secured protection from import competition at the end of the 17th century, and high tariffs served British manufacturing well through the era of the country's rise to world economic preeminence. At the beginning of the 19th century, the average tariff rate on manufactures was 50%—high by almost any comparative standard. Later in the century, the United Kingdom did eliminate its tariffs on manufactures, but then it had passed the early stage of development and its industry was well established. Moreover, state support for industry in the United Kingdom came through the creation and maintenance of empire.

Tariff protection also played a large role in the emergence of U.S. industry. The textile industry, which was especially important in the country's economic development, got its start when the hostilities leading up to and through the War of 1812 provided implicit protection by limiting international shipping. After the war, the protection became explicit as a tariff was established. According to the World Bank, the average U.S. tariff on manufactures was 40% in 1820. In the last third of the 19th century, with tariff protection well established at an average of around 30% for most of the 1870 to 1910 period, the United States experienced a great industrial expansion. Only after World War II, when U.S. industry's dominant position in the world economy was secure, did a steady and lasting reduction of tariffs take place.

Countries that achieved their developmental advance at a later historical period were generally characterized by a significantly greater role for the state in the regulation of foreign commerce, both with regard to trade and investment. Japan's experience in joining the ranks of advanced capitalist countries provides the prime example and, insofar as any country has broken out of underdevelopment in more recent decades, South Korea would provide the most important case study. In broad terms, the South Korean experience is very similar to that of Japan. From the early 1960s, the South Korean state followed policies of protecting domestic markets, heavily favoring Korean-owned firms, and using state owned industries to develop national production in certain "strategic" sectors.

One of the important aspects of the South Korean experience is that, in protecting and supporting the development of national industry, the government did not by any means encourage Korean firms to abjure exports and follow an "inward looking" policy. On the contrary, the government used a firm's ability to compete in export markets as a measure of whether or not it was succeeding in becoming more efficient. The South Korean experience shows how economic policy can both regulate foreign commerce but at the same time make sure that national firms reap the many advantages associated with international commerce—including, especially, the transfer of knowledge and technology that come with foreign exposure.

Re-examining the Theory

So the neo-liberal theory of international commerce does not sit very well with historical experience, and this lack of congruence between theory and reality suggests that there are some problems with the theory. Indeed, there are several.

Technology in Economic Growth. The theory of free trade is fundamentally flawed because it fails to take account of the ways in which production itself affects technological change. "Learning-by-doing" is a particularly important form of the phenomenon. In a new activity, initial production may be very costly. Yet as time passes and experience accumulates, the people engaged in the activity learn. They change the way they do things, which is to say that they change the technology. Such an activity might never develop were it forced to compete with already established firms in other countries where the learning-by-doing had already taken place. Yet if the activity were protected from foreign competition during an initial phase in which experience could be accumulated, it could develop and become fully competitive.

Yet protection involves costs. Why should society in general bear the costs of protection in order to assure the development of any particular activity? The answer to these questions lies in the concept of *location specific technological externalities*. Different kinds of production activities tend to bring about different kinds of changes in the overall economic environment. In the 18th and 19th century, for example, manufacturing tended to generate new methods of production and a development of skills that had far reaching technological impacts. In the current era, "high tech" production appears to have similar far reaching impacts. Because the gains from these sorts of changes are not confined to the industry or firm where they originate, they are not reflected in the profits of that industry or firm and will not be taken into account as a basis for investment decisions. These positive technological impacts of particular production activity that do not affect the profits and are outside of—or external to—the purview of the people making decisions about that production are "technological externalities." When positive technological externalities exist for a particular activity, then the value of that activity to society will be greater than the private value. Technological externalities are often "location specific," having their greatest impact within relatively close geographic proximity to the site where they are originally generated—or at least having their principal impact within the same national unit.

The U.S. experience with the cotton textile industry, which I have cited above, provides a particularly good example of the generation of location specific technological externalities. The textile industry emerged in the early decades of the 19th century, prospering especially in the Northeastern part of the United States. Mill towns throughout southern New England became centers of growth. Not only did they create a demand for Southern cotton, but they also created a demand for new machinery, maintenance of old machinery, parts, dyes, *skills*, construction materials, construction machinery, *more skills*, equipment to move the raw materials and the products, parts and maintenance for that equipment, *and still more skills*. As centers of economic activity, innovation, and change, mill towns made a contribution to the economic growth of the United States that went far beyond the value of the textiles they produced.

Trade and Employment. The theory of comparative advantage and arguments for free trade rest on the assumption that full employment exists, or at least that the level of employment is independent of the *pattern* of trade and production. In addition, the theory assumes that when patterns of trade and production change, labor will move from one activity to another instantaneously—or at least sufficiently rapidly so as to cause no great welfare loss or disruption of overall demand. In reality, most low income countries are characterized by very high levels of unemployment and underemployment, the pattern of trade and production does affect employment levels (at least in the short run), and labor markets adjust to change relatively slowly.

An illustration of the problems is provided by experience in many low-income countries when trade restrictions on grain imports are lifted. In Mexico, where the internationalization of grain supply was proceeding apace in the 1980s, even before the establishment of the North American Free Trade Agreement (NAFTA), the replacement of peasant grain production by imports has not worked out so favorably. In fact, those parts of agriculture that have expanded in recent years—meat production and vegetable exports, for example—and export manufacturing use relatively small amounts of labor. Peasants displaced by the import of inexpensive U.S. and Canadian grain, instead of finding employment in these sectors, swell the ranks of the unemployed or underemployed, often in cities. Consequently, instead of labor resources being used more efficiently under the pressure of import competition, labor resources are wasted.

Free Trade and Large Firms. The neo-liberal argument for free trade is based on the assumption that if government did not intervene and regulate international commerce, then the economy would operate in a competitive manner with advantageous results... International commerce, however, is often dominated by a relatively small number of very large firms that operate in a monopolistic manner. Competition among them exists, and in some cases is very intense. It is, however, monopolistic competition, not simply the price competition that is assumed in the argument for free trade. The patterns of trade and production engaged in by very large firms are determined as part of their complex global strategies—with results that do not necessarily coincide with either the price competition model of the free trade argument or the long run development interests of a particular country.

Large firms are sensitive to price considerations, and they are often quick to re-locate production to take advantage of low cost resources. Yet resource costs, the foundation of the theory of comparative advantage, are only one element in the strategies of large, internationally integrated firms. The Japanese automobile companies, for example, established their leading role in the industry through a strategy of developing linkages to suppliers in close physical proximity to the central plant. Resource costs were secondary to the issue of strategic control, which had important impacts on technological change and the management of inventory. In the international textile industry, flexibility is a paramount concern in the strategy of large firms, and issues of market proximity and control over product supply stand along side of resource costs as factors determining the location of production. Similarly, in the semiconductor production of the electronics industry, many firms (particularly U.S. firms) have followed a strategy of vertical integration. When companies produce semiconductors for use in their own final products, their location decisions tend to be dominated by concerns about control of the technology and production process; concerns about least-cost siting tend to be secondary. In all of these examples, selected from industries that are both highly international in their operations and in which very large companies play central roles, monopolistic firms employ strategies of control that enhance their own long run profits. There is no reason to expect the outcomes to conform to those envisioned in the theoretical arguments for free trade.

Primary Product Problems. When the argument for free trade was developed in the 19th century, it was a rationalization for the particular character of the international division of labor that emerged so clearly at that time. That division of labor placed a few countries of Europe and North America in the position of specializing in the production and export of manufactured goods, while several other countries—many of which are today's low income countries—specialized in the production and export of primary products. Today, although the international division of labor has changed, there are still many low income countries characterized by primary product specialization.

Primary product specialization is problematic, first of all, because the prices of primary products are highly unstable. Primary products are, by definition, the raw materials that enter at an early stage into the production of other goods. Sugar, for example, is used largely in the manufacture of a great variety of sweets, and the cost of sugar plays a small role in affecting the final price of those sweets. Copper finds its demand as an input to houses, automobiles and other machinery. Like sugar, its cost plays a small role in determining the price of the final products of which it is a part. Grains, vanilla, cocoa, cotton, coffee and several other products fit this pattern. Consequently, the demand for such a product is very insensitive to its price (that is, the demand is very price inelastic). When the supply of a primary product increases—for example, because of good weather and a resulting good crop in some region of the world—prices will decline a great deal as producers compete with one another to unload their surpluses on the very limited market. Conversely, with a small decline in the supply—resulting, perhaps, from bad weather and a resulting crop failure—producers will be able to push up the price a great deal. Even when the average price of a primary product is in some sense "reasonable," price fluctuations create severe cyclical problems that, when the product is important, may disrupt the development of an entire national economy.

An additional problem of specialization in primary products is that in general the average prices of primary products are not "reasonable," in the sense that the demand for the products is subject to long-term downward pressure. Consider, for example, the case of foods—sugar, coffee, cocoa—exported from low income countries to the advanced economies of Europe and North America. As income rises in the advanced countries, the demand for food rises less rapidly. Under these circumstances, insofar as countries rely on primary product exports to the advanced countries for their national income, their national income must grow more slowly than income in those advanced countries.

International Commerce, Income Distribution, and Power

The deregulation of international commerce that is envisioned in the neo-liberal model is largely, if not entirely, a deregulation of business. By removing constraints on the operation of business, it necessarily would give more power to the owners of capital. It would allow business to seek out profits with fewer constraints—on the location of production, on its sources of supply, on characteristics of production, and so on. Power is largely a question of options, and by providing more options to the owners of capital, neo-liberal globalization would give them more power. Most clearly, within a deregulated international environment, owners of capital can resist labor's demands by exercising, or threatening to exercise, their option of shifting production to regions of the world where labor costs are lower. This is not only an option of moving from high wage to low wage countries, from Britain to Sri Lanka, for example. Owners of businesses in Sri Lanka may move, or threaten to move, operations to Britain if productivity is sufficiently higher in the latter country. So the power that business gains vis-a-vis labor by the deregulation of international commerce can be important in low wage and high wage countries.

Power in economic life means primarily an ability to shift more and more of the value produced by society into one's own hands. In this way, neo-liberal global-ization is a *de facto* formula for shifting income to the owners of capital, that is, for increasing inequality in the distribution of income. ❏

Excerpted from Chapter 2 of the Arthur MacEwan's Neo-Liberalism or Democracy? Economic Strategy, Markets, and Alternatives for the 21st Century, *Zed Books and St. Martin's Press, 1999.*

Article 1.3

WHAT'S WRONG WITH NEOLIBERALISM?
The Marx, Keynes, and Polanyi Problems

BY ROBERT POLLIN
May/June 2004

During the years of the Clinton administration, the term "Washington Consensus" began circulating to designate the common policy positions of the U.S. administration along with the International Monetary Fund (IMF) and World Bank. These positions, implemented in the United States and abroad, included free trade, a smaller government share of the economy, and the deregulation of financial markets. This policy approach has also become widely known as *neoliberalism*, a term which draws upon the classical meaning of the word *liberalism*.

Classical liberalism is the political philosophy that embraces the virtues of free-market capitalism and the corresponding minimal role for government interventions, especially as regards measures to promote economic equality within capitalist societies. Thus, a classical liberal would favor minimal levels of government spending and taxation, and minimal levels of government regulation over the economy, including financial and labor markets. According to the classical liberal view, businesses should be free to operate as they wish, and to succeed or fail as such in a competitive marketplace. Meanwhile, consumers rather than government should be responsible for deciding which businesses produce goods and services that are of sufficient quality as well as reasonably priced. Businesses that provide overexpensive or low-quality products will then be out-competed in the marketplace regardless of the regulatory standards established by governments. Similarly, if businesses offer workers a wage below what the worker is worth, then a competitor firm will offer this worker a higher wage. The firm unwilling to offer fair wages would not survive over time in the competitive marketplace.

This same reasoning also carries over to the international level. Classical liberals favor free trade between countries rather than countries operating with tariffs or other barriers to the free flow of goods and services between countries. They argue that restrictions on the free movement of products and money between countries only protects uncom-petitive firms from market competition, and thus holds back the economic development of countries that choose to erect such barriers.

Neoliberalism and the Washington Consensus are contemporary variants of this longstanding political and economic philosophy. The major difference between classical liberalism as a philosophy and contemporary neoliberalism as a set of policy measures is with implementation. Washington Consensus policy makers are committed to free-market policies when they support the interests of big business, as, for example, with lowering regulations at the workplace. But these same policy makers become far less insistent on free-market principles when invoking such principles might damage big business interests. Federal Reserve and IMF interventions to bail out wealthy asset holders during the frequent global financial crises in the 1990s are obvious violations of free-market precepts.

Broadly speaking, the effects of neoliberalism in the less developed countries over the 1990s reflected the experience of the Clinton years in the United States. A high proportion of less developed countries were successful, just in the manner of the United States under Clinton, in reducing inflation and government budget deficits, and creating a more welcoming climate for foreign trade, multinational corporations, and financial market investors. At the same time, most of Latin America, Africa, and Asia—with China being the one major exception—experienced deepening problems of poverty and inequality in the 1990s, along with slower growth and frequent financial market crises, which in turn produced still more poverty and inequality.

If free-market capitalism is a powerful mechanism for creating wealth, why does a neoliberal policy approach, whether pursued by Clinton, Bush, or the IMF, produce severe difficulties in terms of inequality and financial instability, which in turn diminish the market mechanism's ability to even promote economic growth? It will be helpful to consider this in terms of three fundamental problems that result from a free-market system, which I term "the Marx Problem," "the Keynes problem," and "the Polanyi problem." Let us take these up in turn.

The Marx Problem

Does someone in your family have a job and, if so, how much does it pay? For the majority of the world's population, how one answers these two questions determines, more than anything else, what one's standard of living will be. But how is it decided whether a person has a job and what their pay will be? Getting down to the most immediate level of decision-making, this occurs through various types of bargaining in labor markets between workers and employers. Karl Marx argued that, in a free-market economy generally, workers have less power than employers in this bargaining process because workers cannot fall back on other means of staying alive if they fail to get hired into a job. Capitalists gain higher profits through having this relatively stronger bargaining position. But Marx also stressed that workers' bargaining power diminishes further when unemployment and underemployment are high, since that means that employed workers can be more readily replaced by what Marx called "the reserve army" of the unemployed outside the office, mine, or factory gates.

Neoliberalism has brought increasing integration of the world's labor markets through reducing barriers to international trade and investment by multinationals. For workers in high-wage countries such as the United States, this effectively means that the reserve army of workers willing to accept jobs at lower pay than U.S. workers expands to include workers in less developed countries. It isn't the case that businesses will always move to less developed countries or that domestically produced goods will necessarily be supplanted by imports from low-wage countries. The point is that U.S. workers face an increased *credible* threat that they can be supplanted. If everything else were to remain the same in the U.S. labor market, this would then mean that global integration would erode the bargaining power of U.S. workers and thus tend to bring lower wages.

But even if this is true for workers in the United States and other rich countries, shouldn't it also mean that workers in poor countries have greater job opportunities and better bargaining positions? In fact, there are areas where workers in poor countries are gaining enhanced job opportunities through international trade and multinational investments. But these gains are generally quite limited. This is because a long-term transition out of agriculture in poor countries continues to expand the reserve army of unemployed and underemployed workers in these countries as well. Moreover, when neoliberal governments in poor countries reduce their support for agriculture—through cuts in both tariffs on imported food products and subsidies for domestic farmers—this makes it more difficult for poor farmers to compete with multinational agribusiness firms. This is especially so when the rich countries maintain or increase their own agricultural supports, as has been done in the United States under Bush. In addition, much of the growth in the recently developed export-oriented manufacturing sectors of poor countries has failed to significantly increase jobs even in this sector. This is because the new export-oriented production sites frequently do not represent net additions to the country's total supply of manufacturing firms. They rather replace older firms that were focused on supplying goods to domestic markets. The net result is that the number of people looking for jobs in the developing countries grows faster than the employers seeking new workers. Here again, workers' bargaining power diminishes.

This does not mean that global integration of labor markets must necessarily bring weakened bargaining power and lower wages for workers. But it does mean that unless some non-market forces in the economy, such as government regulations or effective labor unions, are able to counteract these market processes, workers will indeed continue to experience weakened bargaining strength and eroding living standards.

The Keynes Problem

In a free-market economy, investment spending by busi-nesses is the main driving force that produces economic growth, innovation, and jobs. But as John Maynard Keynes stressed, private investment decisions are also unavoidably risky ventures. Businesses have to put up money without knowing whether they will produce any profits in the future. As such, investment spending by business is likely to fluctuate far more than, say, decisions by households as to how much they will spend per week on groceries.

But investment fluctuations will also affect overall spending in the economy, including that of households. When investment spending declines, this means that businesses will hire fewer workers. Unemployment rises as a result, and this in turn will lead to cuts in household spending. Declines in business investment spending can therefore set off a vicious cycle: the investment decline leads to employment declines, then to cuts in household spending and corresponding increases in household financial problems, which then brings still more cuts in business investment and financial difficulties for the business sector. This is how capitalist economies produce mass unemployment, financial crises, and recessions.

Keynes also described a second major source of instability associated with private investment activity. Precisely because private investments are highly risky propositions, financial markets have evolved to make this risk more manageable for any given investor. Through financial markets, investors can sell off their investments if they need or want to, converting their office buildings, factories, and stock of machinery into cash much more readily than they could if they always had to find buyers on their own. But Keynes warned that when financial markets convert long-term assets into short-term commitments for investors, this also fosters a speculative mentality in the markets. What becomes central for investors is not whether a company's products will produce profits over a long term, but rather whether the short-term financial market investors *think* a company's fortunes will be strong enough in the present and immediate future to drive the stock price up. Or, to be more precise, what really matters for a speculative investor is not what they think about a given company's prospects per se, but rather what they think *other investors are thinking*, since that will be what determines where the stock price goes in the short term.

Because of this, the financial markets are highly susceptible to rumors, fads, and all sorts of deceptive accounting practices, since all of these can help drive the stock price up in the present, regardless of what they accomplish in the longer term. Thus, if U.S. stock traders are convinced that Alan Greenspan is a *maestro*, and if there is news that he is about to intervene with some kind of policy shift, then the rumor of Greenspan's policy shift can itself drive prices up, as the more nimble speculators try to keep one step ahead of the herd of Greenspan-philes.

Still, as with the Marx problem, it does not follow that the inherent instability of private investment and speculation in financial markets are uncontrollable, leading inevitably to persistent problems of mass unemployment and recession. But these social pathologies will become increasingly common through a neoliberal policy approach committed to minimizing government interventions to stabilize investment.

The Polanyi Problem

Karl Polanyi wrote his classic book *The Great Transformation* in the context of the 1930s depression, World War II, and the developing worldwide competition with Communist governments. He was also reflecting on the 1920s, dominated, as with our current epoch, by a free-market ethos. Polanyi wrote of the 1920s that "economic liberalism made a supreme bid to restore the self-regulation of the system by eliminating all interventionist policies which interfered with the freedom of markets."

Considering all of these experiences, Polanyi argued that for market economies to function with some modicum of fairness, they must be embedded in social norms and institutions that effectively promote broadly accepted notions of the common good. Otherwise, acquisitiveness and competition—the two driving forces of market economies—achieve overwhelming dominance as cultural forces, rendering life under capitalism a Hobbesian "war of all against all." This same idea is also central for Adam Smith. Smith showed how the invisible hand of self-interest and competition will yield higher levels of individual effort that increases the wealth of nations, but that it will also produce the corruption of our moral sentiments unless the market is itself governed at a fundamental level by norms of solidarity.

In the post-World War II period, various social democratic movements within the advanced capitalist economies adapted the Polanyi perspective. They argued in favor of government interventions to achieve three basic ends: stabilizing overall demand in the economy at a level that will provide for full employment; creating a financial market environment that is stable and conducive to the effective allocation of investment funds; and distributing equitably the rewards from high employment and a stable investment process. There were two basic means of achieving equitable distribution: relatively rapid wage growth, promoted by labor laws that were supportive of unions, minimum wage standards, and similar interventions in labor markets; and welfare state policies, including progressive taxation and redistributive programs such as Social Security. The political ascendancy of these ideas was the basis for a dramatic increase in the role of government in the post-World War II capitalist economies. As one indicator of this, total government expenditures in the United States rose from 8% of GDP in 1913, to 21% in 1950, then to 38% by 1992. The International Monetary Fund and World Bank were also formed in the mid-1940s to advance such policy ideas throughout the world—that is, to implement policies virtually the opposite of those they presently favor. John Maynard Keynes himself was a leading intellectual force contributing to the initial design of the International Monetary Fund and World Bank.

From Social Democracy to Neoliberalism

But the implementation of a social democratic capitalism, guided by a commitment to full employment and the welfare state, did also face serious and persistent difficulties, and we need to recognize them as part of a consideration of the Marx, Keynes, and Polanyi problems. In particular, many sectors of business opposed efforts to sustain full employment because, following the logic of the Marx problem, full employment provides greater bargaining power for workers in labor markets, even if it also increases the economy's total production of goods and services. Greater worker bargaining power can also create inflationary pressures because businesses will try to absorb their higher wage costs by raising prices. In addition, market-inhibiting financial regulations limit the capacity of financial market players to diversify their risk and speculate.

Corporations in the United States and Western Europe were experiencing some combination of these problems associated with social democratic capitalism. In particular, they were faced with rising labor costs associated with low unemployment rates, which then led to either inflation, when corporations had the ability to pass on their higher labor costs to consumers, or to a squeeze on profits, when competitive pressures prevented corporations from raising their prices in response to the rising labor costs. These pressures were compounded by the two oil price "shocks" initiated by the Oil Producing Exporting Countries (OPEC)—an initial fourfold increase in the world price of oil in 1973, then a second four-fold price spike in 1979.

These were the conditions that by the end of the 1970s led to the decline of social democratic approaches to policymaking and the ascendancy of neoliberalism. The two leading signposts of this historic transition were the election in 1979 of Margaret Thatcher as Prime Minister of the United Kingdom and in 1980 of Ronald Reagan as the President of the United States. Indeed, it was at this point that Mrs. Thatcher made her famous pronouncement that "there is no alternative" to neoliberalism.

This brings us to the contemporary era of smaller government, fiscal stringency and deregulation, i.e., to neoliberalism under Clinton, Bush, and throughout the less-developed world. The issue is not a simple juxtaposition between either regulating or deregulating markets. Rather it is that markets have become deregulated to support the interests of business and financial markets, even as these same groups still benefit greatly from many forms of government support, including investment subsidies, tax concessions, and rescue operations when financial crises get out of hand. At the same time, the deregulation of markets that favors business and finance is correspondingly the most powerful regulatory mechanism limiting the demands of workers, in that deregulation has been congruent with the worldwide expansion of the reserve army of labor and the declining capacity of national governments to implement full-employment and macroeconomic policies. In other words, deregulation has exacerbated both the Marx and Keynes problems.

Given the ways in which neoliberalism worsens the Marx, Keynes, and Polanyi problems, we should not be surprised by the wreckage that it has wrought since the late 1970s, when it became the ascendant policy model. Over the past generation, with neoliberals in the saddle almost everywhere in the world, the results have been straightforward: worsening inequality and poverty, along with slower economic growth and far more unstable financial markets. While Margaret Thatcher famously declared that "there is no alternative" to neoliberalism, there are in fact alternatives. The experience over the past generation demonstrates how important it is to develop them in the most workable and coherent ways possible. ❏

Article 1.4

DEBUNKING THE "INDEX OF ECONOMIC FREEDOM"

Economic freedom for corporations has little to do with either political freedom or economic growth.

BY JOHN MILLER
March/April 2005

"HAIL ESTONIA!"

For the first time in the 11 years that the Heritage Foundation and *The Wall Street Journal* have been publishing the Index of Economic Freedom, the U.S. has dropped out of the top 10 freest economies in the world. ...

The 2005 Index, released today, ranks Hong Kong once again as the world's freest economy, followed by Singapore and Luxembourg. But it is Estonia at No. 4 that makes the point. This former Soviet satellite is a model reformer, setting the standard for how fast countries can move ahead in the realm of economic liberalization. ...

The U.S. ... scores well. But worrying developments like Sarbanes-Oxley in the category of regulation and aggressive use of antidumping law in trade policy have kept it from keeping pace with the best performers in economic freedom. Most alarming is the U.S.'s fiscal burden, which imposes high marginal tax rates for individuals and very high marginal corporate tax rates. ...

Policy makers who pay lip service to fighting poverty would do well to grasp the link between economic freedom and prosperity. This year the Index finds that the freest economies have a per-capita income of $29,219, more than twice that of the "mostly free" at $12,839, and more than four times that of the "mostly unfree." Put simply, misery has a cure and its name is economic freedom.

> —*Wall Street Journal* op-ed by Mary Anastasia O'Grady,
> January 4, 2005

I must be confused. I somehow thought that an Index of Economic Freedom would showcase countries that are reducing the democratic deficits of the global economy by giving people more control over their economic lives and the institutions that govern them. In the hands of the *Wall Street Journal* and the Heritage Foundation, Washington's foremost right-wing think tank, however, an economic freedom index merely measures corporate and entrepreneurial freedom from accountability. Upon examination, the index turns out to be a poor barometer of either freedom more broadly construed or of prosperity.

The index does not even pretend that its definition of economic freedom has anything to do with political freedom. Take the two city-states, Hong Kong and Singapore, which top the index's list of free countries. Both are only "partially free" according to *Freedom in the World*, an annual country-by-country assessment published by the nonpartisan think tank Freedom House, which the *Journal*'s editors themselves have called "the Michelin Guide to democracy's development." Hong Kong is still without direct elections for its legislature or its chief executive, and a proposed internal security law threatens press and academic freedom as well as political dissent. In Singapore, freedom of the press and the right to demonstrate are limited; films, TV, and other media are censored; preventive detention is legal; and you can do jail time for littering.

Moving further down the list of "free" countries, the rankings are no better correlated with any ordinary definition of "freedom," as economic journalist Robert Kuttner pointed out when the index was first published in 1997. For instance, Bahrain (#20), where the king holds an effective veto over parliament and freedom of expression is limited, ranks higher than Norway (#29), whose comprehensive social insurance and strong environmental regulation drag down its score. Likewise, Kuwait, an emirship no one would term free or democratic, is tied (at #54) with Costa Rica, long the most vigorous democracy in Latin America.

These results are not surprising, however, given the index's premise: the less a government intervenes in the economy, the higher its freedom ranking. Specifically, the index breaks "economic freedom" down into 10 components: trade policy; fiscal burden of government; level of government intervention; monetary policy; financial liberalization; banking and finance policies; labor market policies; enforcement of property rights; business, labor, and environmental regulations; and size of the black market. In other words, minimum-wage laws, environmental regulations, or requirements for transparency in corporate accounting make a country less free, whereas low business taxes, harsh debtor laws, and little or no regulation of occupational health and safety make a country more free.

Consider that the index docks the United States' ranking for passing Sarbanes-Oxley, a law that seeks to improve corporate accounting practices and to make CEOs responsible for their corporations' profit reports. The segment of the U.S. population whose economic freedom this law erodes is tiny, but it's obviously that segment—not workers and not even shareholders—whose freedom counts for the folks at the *Journal* and at Heritage.

The rather objective-looking list that results from assessing the ten components ranks 155 countries from freest (Hong Kong and Singapore) to most repressive (Burma and North Korea). The index then becomes a tool its authors can use to hammer home their message: economic freedom (as they define it) brings prosperity. As they point out, "the freest economies have a per-capita income more than twice that of the 'mostly free' and more than four times that of the 'mostly unfree.'"

Not so fast. For one thing, the index's creators used some oddball methods that compromise its linkage of prosperity to economic freedom.

For instance, according to the index, the fiscal burden of the Swedish and Danish welfare states is smaller than that of the United States, even though U.S. government spending is more than 20 percentage points lower relative to Gross Domestic Product (GDP, or the size of the economy). This bizarre result comes about because the index uses the change in government spending, not its actual level, to calculate fiscal burden.

To measure the tax side of a country's fiscal burden, the index uses the top rate of the personal and corporate income taxes—and that's equally misleading. Besides ignoring the burden of other taxes, these two figures don't get at *effective* tax rates, which also depend on what share of corporate profits and personal income is actually taxed. On paper, U.S. corporate tax rates are higher than those in Europe, as the *Journal* is quick to point out. But nearly half of U.S. corporate profits go untaxed. The average rate of taxation on U.S. corporate profits currently stands at 15%, far below the top corporate tax rate of 35%. And relative to GDP, U.S. corporate income taxes are no more than half those of other OECD countries.

The index's treatment of government intervention is flawed as well, for it fails to count industrial policy as a form of intervention. This is a serious mistake: it means that the index overestimates the degree to which some of the fastest growing economies of the last few decades, such as in Taiwan and South Korea, relied on the market and underestimates the positive role that government played in directing economic development in those countries by guiding investment and protecting infant industries.

The treatment of informal markets is downright strange. The index considers a large informal sector to indicate less economic freedom because government restrictions must have driven that economic activity underground. (Of course, you could take the opposite view: since the informal sector is for the most part unregulated, countries with larger informal sectors are, by the index's definition, more free!) But this way of looking at it biases the index. Developing countries tend to have large informal sectors while developed economies usually have small informal sectors. That means the index systematically lowers the economic freedom index of developing countries while boosting the scores of developed countries, thus artificially correlating income levels with economic freedom. Even right-wing economist Stefan Karlsson of the libertarian Ludwig Von Mises Institute has criticized the index on this point. Thanks in part to this bias, Estonia, Chile, and Bahrain are the only middle-income countries to make it into the top 20.

Whatever the biases in the index do to cement a tight relationship between economic freedom and income, they can't produce a tight correlation between economic freedom and *growth*. The fastest-growing countries are mostly unfree. Take China, India, and Vietnam, three of the fastest-growing countries in the world. They are way down in the rankings, at #112, #118, and #137 respectively. While all three countries have adopted market reforms in recent years that have improved their standing in the index, their trade policies and regulations remain "repressive." And there are plenty of relatively slow growers among the countries high up in the index, including Estonia (#4), the *Journal*'s poster child for economic freedom. How free or unfree a country is according to the index seems to have little to do with how quickly it grows.

An "Index of Economic Freedom" that tells us little about economic growth or political freedom is a slipshod measure that would seem to have no other purpose other than to sell the neoliberal policies that stand in the way of most people gaining control over their economic lives and obtaining genuine economic freedom in today's global economy. ❑

Sources: Mary Anastasia O'Grady, "Hail Estonia!" *Wall Street Journal*, January 4, 2005; *The 2005 Index of Economic Freedom*, Heritage Foundation, 2005; Johan Fernandez, "Malaysia climbs up economic freedom index," *The Star Online*, January 25, 2005; "Freedom & Growth: No Siamese twins," *The Economic Times*, May 27, 2002; Robert Kuttner, "A Weird Set of Values," *The American Prospect*, December 7, 1997; Stefan M. I. Karlsson, "The Failings of the Economic Freedom Index," Ludwig Von Mises Institute, January 21, 2005; "Freedom in the World 2005: Civic Power and Electoral Politics," Freedom House, 2005, freedomhouse.org.

Article 1.5

THE WORLD IS NOT FLAT
How Thomas Friedman gets it wrong about globalization.

BY MARK ENGLER
May 2008

Turn on the TV and flip to a C-SPAN or CNN discussion of the global economy and you are likely to spot the square head and mustachioed face of *New York Times* columnist Thomas Friedman, who will probably be expressing enthusiasm for the business world's newest high-tech innovations. With his best-selling book *The Lexus and the Olive Tree*, Friedman stepped forward in the late 1990s as a leading cheerleader of neoliberal globalization. Then, in the wake of 9/11, he made common cause with White House militarists. He became a high-profile "liberal hawk" and supported the war in Iraq—only to distance himself later in the Bush era and return to championing corporate expansion with a second widely read book on globalization, *The World Is Flat*. For better or for worse, his punditry provides an indispensable guide to how mainstream commentators have tried to defend neoliberalism in the face of challenges from worldwide social movements. Moreover, Friedman's renewed emphasis on corporate globalization in the wake of the botched war in Iraq may also be a significant bellwether for how the Democratic Party—especially the more conservative "New Democrat" wing of the party—crafts a vision for international relations after Bush.

You Can't Stop the Dawn

In Friedman's view, the end of the Cold War left the world with a single, unassailable ideology. "Globalization," he wrote in *The Lexus and the Olive Tree*, "means the spread of free market capitalism to every country in the world." He saw this as an unmitigated good: "[T]he more you open your economy to free trade and competition, the more efficient and flourishing your economy will be." He marveled that "computerization, miniaturization, digitization, satellite communications, fiber optics, and the Internet" were bringing about untold wonders.

Friedman's conversion into the church of corporate expansion took place over many years. His academic training is not in economics, but in Middle Eastern studies. During the 1980s, Friedman was a respected *New York Times* correspondent in Israel and Lebanon, winning two Pulitzer Prizes for his reporting from the region. In 1994, just at the beginning of the Internet boom, he switched to a beat covering the intersection of politics and economics, and his excitement for globalization began to mount in earnest. By the time he became the *Times*' foreign affairs columnist the following year, he was perfectly positioned to evangelize about how unregulated markets and new technology were reshaping global affairs.

Aware that many people saw him as a modern-day Pangloss extolling the best of all possible worlds, Friedman contended in *The Lexus and the Olive Tree* that he was "not a salesman for globalization." But this is precisely what he was. More than any other public personality, he was responsible for portraying neoliberalism as an inevitable and laudable march of progress. "I feel about globalization a lot like I feel about the dawn," he wrote. "[E]ven if I didn't care much for the dawn there isn't much I could do about it. I didn't start globalization, I can't stop it—except at a huge cost to human development." By defining "globalization" as a broad, sweeping phenomenon—political, economic, technological, and cultural—he saw resistance as ridiculous. So when massive protests erupted at the World Trade Organization meetings in Seattle in late 1999, he disgustedly derided the demonstrators as "a Noah's ark of flat-earth advocates, protectionist trade unions and yuppies looking for their 1960s fix."

You might think that the deflating of the dot-com bubble that began in March 2000 would have quelled Friedman's fervor, but you would be wrong. In Friedman's view, the end of the 1990s boom only led to more advancement. "[T]he dot-com bust," he later wrote, "actually drove globalization into hypermode by forcing companies to outsource and offshore more and more functions in order to save on scarce capital." Friedman's cheerleading, too, would go into "hypermode," but not before the columnist took a detour to become one of the country's most prominent liberal hawks in the wake of 9/11. When Friedman did return to the subject of economic globalization with his 2005 book, *The World Is Flat*, he was once again wowed. Over the course of just a few years, he concluded, "we entered a whole new era: Globalization 3.0."

Fueled now by wireless technology and ever-smaller microchips, this wave of capitalism was "shrinking the world from a size small to a size tiny and flattening the playing field at the same time." Hospitals in the United States were sending CT scans to India for analysis; other corporations opened bustling call centers there to handle customer service calls, training their new South Asian employees to speak in American accents; globetrotting columnists could file their stories from the middle of a golf course in China by using their Blackberries. The march of progress was back on.

Friedman is known for conveying complicated ideas through the use of colorful metaphors. Yet his metaphors consistently get so mixed and muddled as to require delicate linguistic untangling. In the course of his two books on globalization, Friedman goes from seeing the world in 3-D to, remarkably enough, seeing it in at least six dimensions. Technological advance, he tells us, has now accelerated so much that we have gone through Globalization versions 1.0 and 2.0 and entered version 3.0. Friedman presents ten "flatteners," four "steroids," and a "triple convergence," plus at least seven releases of "DOScapital." Various steroids and flatteners are meant to have multiplied globalization's effects exponentially. Journalist Matt Taibbi, who has written the most cutting analysis of Friedman's peculiar language, notes, "Friedman's book is the first I have encountered, anywhere, in which the reader needs a calculator to figure the value of the author's metaphors."

If ever Orwell's warnings that "the slovenliness of our language makes it easier for us to have foolish thoughts" and that the world's "present political chaos is connected with the decay of language" apply to anyone, they apply to Friedman. The connection between Friedman's hazy writing and his suspect conclusions about the global economy shows up in the very premise of his second book on globalization. During a meeting between Friedman and Nandan Nilekani in Bangalore, the Infosys CEO offers that "the playing field is being leveled." For Friedman, the tired cliché is a revelation. He mulls it over for hours and then, suddenly, decides: "My God, he's telling me the world is flat!"

Now, it is quite a stretch to take a routine sports metaphor and superimpose it on the globe; there could be few worse metaphors for talking about a global system that is more integrated and networked than ever before. "Friedman is a person who not only speaks in malapropisms, he also hears malapropisms," Taibbi argues. Nilekani off-handedly mentions a level field and Friedman attributes to him the radical idea of a flat world. "This is the intellectual version of Far Out Space Nuts, when NASA repairman Bob Denver sets a whole sitcom in motion by pressing 'launch' instead of 'lunch' in a space capsule. And once he hits that button, the rocket takes off."

It would all be funny if it didn't mask a deeper political problem: For the world's poor, the playing field is far from level. Our world is not flat.

Putting on Reagan's Jacket

With the ideology of neoliberalism steadily losing ground in international discussion, it is important to see how a leading apologist mounts a defense. In Friedman's case, he does so by holding on to dogmatic assumptions, training his sights on high technology, conducting his interviews largely within the insular world of jet-setting corporate elites, and ignoring a world of evidence that would contradict his selective viewpoint.

Some reviewers have applauded Friedman for acknowledging negative aspects of globalization in his books. But for Friedman, this does not mean looking at the realities of exploitation or environmental destruction that have resulted from corporate expansion. Instead, his caveats boil down to two points: that terrorists, too, can use the Internet, and that many countries, especially in "unflat" Africa, are too backward to read the signs that would put them on the high tech, "free trade" superhighway to prosperity. With regard to the latter, it's not that anything is wrong really, only that the process has not gone far enough and fast enough for everyone to benefit yet.

Needless to say, Friedman's is hardly a biting exposé. In fact, it is virtually impossible to find any evidence that might make him skeptical about the fundamental greatness of corporate globalization. In 1999, even *BusinessWeek* argued "The Asian financial crisis of 1997–99 shows that unfettered liberalization of capital markets without proper regulation can lead the world to the brink of disaster." But for Friedman this crisis, too, was all for the best. He writes, "I believe globalization did us all a favor by melting down the economies of Thailand, Korea, Malaysia, Indonesia, Mexico, Russia and Brazil in the 1990s, because it laid bare a lot of the rotten practices and institutions in countries that had prematurely globalized." He slams the countries for corruption and cronyism, suggesting that they deserved their fates. But by "prematurely globalized" he does not mean that these countries should have been more cautious about linking their fates to speculative international markets. Rather, he believes that they had not done enough to "reduce the role of government" and "let markets more freely allocate resources." Friedman's solution to the dangers of unregulated markets is more deregulation, the remedy for the excesses of unfettered capitalism is even more excess. The argument is airtight.

Missing from this account, of course, is any sense of the social impact of the Asian crisis. In the end, wealthy foreign investors were bailed out by the International Monetary Fund and lost little. The real losers were an untold number of middle-class families in places like Thailand and Korea whose savings were wiped out overnight, as well as the poor in places like Indonesia who went hungry when the government cut food subsidies. It takes a very twisted viewpoint to say that the Asian financial crisis did these people a favor.

Friedman holds that the Internet age has created a "flat" world with opportunity for all. Yet he freely admits that the system he describes is founded on the Reagan-Thatcher model of extreme, "trickle down" neoliberalism—one of the most unequal methods of distributing social goods ever devised. Friedman writes: "Thatcher and Reagan combined to strip huge chunks of economic decision-making power from the state, from the advocates of the Great Society and from traditional Keynesian economics, and hand them over to the free market." Countries now have one choice for economic policy: neoliberalism. They must radically deregulate and privatize their economies. Friedman calls this the "Golden Straitjacket." It's "golden" because the model supposedly creates widespread affluence. But it's a "straitjacket" because it radically constricts democracy. Sounding a lot like Ralph Nader, Friedman writes:

Once your country puts [the Golden Straitjacket] on, its political choices get reduced to Pepsi or Coke—to slight nuances of taste, slight nuances of policy, slight alterations in design … but never any major deviation from the core golden rules. Governments—be they led by Democrats or Republicans, Conservatives or Labourites, Gaullists or Socialists, Christian Democrats or Social Democrats—that deviate too far away from the core rules will see their investors stampede away, interest rates rise, and stock market valuations fall.

The difference between Friedman and Nader is that the *New York Times* columnist approves of this situation. He does not condemn it as an assault on democracy; he says it's just the way things are. Of the Democrats, he writes, "Mr. Clinton effectively kidnapped the Democratic Party … moved it into the Republican economic agenda—including free trade, NAFTA and the WTO for China—while holding onto much of the Democrats' social agenda." Any Democrat who would try to move it back meets Friedman's wrath. In the new global age, all those to the left of Ronald Reagan on economic policy are simply out of luck.

Sitting On Top Of The World

Friedman's contention that everyone benefits when countries bind themselves into market fundamentalism is based less on a careful review of the evidence than on blind faith. In July of 2006, he made a startling admission during a CNBC interview with Tim Russert. He said:

> We got this free market, and I admit, I was speaking out in Minnesota—my hometown, in fact, and a guy stood up in the audience, said, "Mr. Friedman, is there any free trade agreement you'd oppose?" I said, "No, absolutely not." I said, "You know what, sir? I wrote a column supporting the CAFTA, the Caribbean Free Trade initiative. I didn't even know what was in it. I just knew two words: free trade."

That a nationally prominent columnist would gloat about such ignorance is a sad statement about the health of our political debate. "Free trade" is an incredibly politicized phrase, with little concrete meaning. For instance, CAFTA (which actually stands for the *Central American* Free Trade Agreement) includes provisions designed to protect the monopoly rights of giant pharmaceutical companies rather than to create "free" commerce.

But the larger point is that neoliberal globalization does not make winners of everyone. Its global track record for producing GDP growth is dismal. In fact, its main accomplishment may be to produce inequality. And Friedman's own position amid this global divide is telling. He regularly represents himself as just an average guy from Minnesota trying to make sense of the world. The real picture is far from average. In July 2006, *Washingtonian* magazine reported that in the 1970s Friedman married into one of the 100 richest families in the United States—the Bucksbaums—who have amassed a fortune worth some $2.7 billion, with origins in real estate development. The magazine noted that he lives in "a palatial 11,400-square-foot house, now valued at $9.3 million, on a 7.5-acre parcel just blocks from I-495 and the Bethesda Country Club." Given that the über-rich, those with huge stock portfolios and investments in multinational corporations, have benefited tremendously from corporate globalization, commentators like David Sirota have suggested that Friedman's vast wealth represents an undisclosed conflict of interest in his journalism. It is as if multimillionaire Richard Mellon Scaife were to write about the repeal of the estate tax without disclosing that he stands to profit handsomely from such a policy change.

Whether or not that is the case, Friedman's position at the very pinnacle of global prosperity is certainly reflected in his view of the world. In a telling admission, he relates in *The Lexus and the Olive Tree* that his "best intellectual sources" about globalization are hedge fund managers. Hedge funds are elite, largely unregulated investment pools that handle money for individuals of extremely high net worth. Their managers are among the highest paid individuals in the United States.

In 2006, the top 25 hedge fund managers in the country made in excess of $240 million each. This means they each pulled in $27,000 per hour, 24 hours per day, whether waking or sleeping, whether at the office or teeing off on the ninth hole. Corporate CEOs and hedge fund managers may indeed be well informed about certain aspects of the global economy. But if that is where you get your information, you end up with a very partial view of the world. You get the winner's view.

In an eloquent critique of *The World Is Flat*, Indian eco-feminist Vandana Shiva writes:

> Friedman has reduced the world to the friends he visits, the CEOs he knows, and the golf courses he plays at. From this microcosm of privilege, exclusion, blindness, he shuts out both the beauty of diversity and the brutality of exploitation and inequality …
>
> That is why he talks of 550 million Indian youth overtaking Americans in a flat world, when the entire information technology/outsourcing sector in India employs only a million out of 1.2 billion people. Food and farming, textiles and clothing, health and education are nowhere in Friedman's monoculture of mind locked into IT. Friedman presents a 0.1% picture and hides 99.9%. … In the eclipsed 99.9% are the 25 million women who disappeared in high growth areas of India because a commodified world has rendered women a dispensable sex. In the hidden 99.9% … are thousands of tribal children in Orissa, Maharashtra, Rajasthan who died of hunger because the public distribution system for food has been dismantled to create markets for agribusiness.

A Race to the Top?

The corporate globalization that Friedman champions has alarming changes in store not just for the poor of the global South, but also for working people in the United States and Europe. One of the things that Friedman particularly lauds about Reagan and Thatcher is their success in breaking unions. He writes: "it may turn out that one of the key turning points in American history, going into the millennium, was Ronald Reagan's decision to fire all the striking air traffic controllers in 1981." "No single event," he notes with satisfaction, "did more to alter the balance of power between management and workers." Everyone wins from this, he argues, since "[t]he easier it is to fire workers, the more incentive employers have to hire them." Because America busted its unions and Western European countries did not, he contends, the United States developed a more dynamic economy.

What Friedman fails to note is that real wages for working people in the United States have been largely stagnant since the early 1970s, while working hours have sky-rocketed. When compared with workers in Western Europe, the average American works 350 hours more per year, the equivalent of nine extra weeks. A study by the International Labor Organization reported that in 2000 the average U.S. worker put in 199 more hours than in 1973. Dramatizing such realities, a group of union and nonprofit activists now observe "Take Back Your Time Day" every October 24. On that day, if the U.S. workload were on par with the rest of the industrialized world, Americans would have the rest of the year off.

Friedman utters not a word of protest about the trend toward more work; in fact, he celebrates it. He argues that European social democracies are obsolete, even though they are successful capitalist countries. These nations are running on the wrong version of "DOScapital," Friedman contends, and need to shift to U.S. standards. Never mind that economies like Sweden's have performed very well over the past decade, all while maintaining a much higher quality of life for their citizens.

He has a special hatred for the French, who, he writes, "are trying to preserve a 35-hour work week in a world where Indian engineers are ready to work a 35-hour day." In what he calls a "race to the top," Friedman predicts a turbulent decade for Western Europe, as aging, inflexible economies—which have grown used to six-week vacations and unemployment insurance that is almost as good as having a job—become more intimately integrated with Eastern Europe, India and China in a flattening world. … The dirty little secret is that India is taking work from Europe or America not simply because of low wages. It is also because Indians are ready to work harder and can do anything from answering your phone to designing your next airplane or car. They are not racing us to the bottom. They are racing us to the top. … Yes, this is a bad time for France and friends to lose their appetite for hard work—just when India, China and Poland are rediscovering theirs.

It is unclear what Friedman sees as getting to the "top" if paid vacations, unemployment insurance, and retirement—benefits traditionally regarded as signs of a civilized economy—must be sacrificed. But, Friedman tells us, that is the new reality.

Ultimately, the "race to the top" is another of Friedman's botched metaphors. In the long-standing progressive argument that corporate globalization creates a "race to the bottom," it is not Indian or Chinese workers who are doing the racing at all. It's capital. Deregulation allows corporations to wander the globe in search of ever lower wages and laxer environmental standards. The moment workers stand up for their rights, refusing to tolerate a "35-hour day," a company can pick up and move elsewhere. The governments that might curb such abuses are in straitjackets. The unions that workers might have organized themselves into have been busted. All Friedman can offer is this cryptic and seemingly masochistic advice: "When the world goes flat—and you are feeling flattened—reach for a shovel and dig into yourself. Don't try to build walls."

Globalization from Below

An interesting aspect of Friedman's renewed focus on corporate globalization at the end of the Bush era is that governments and international financial institutions have faded from his picture of the integrating world. Even corporations are becoming less relevant. In his view, the new era of "Globalization 3.0" is all about *individuals*. Today, it is up to all people to pull themselves up by their bootstraps. He writes, "every person now must, and can, ask: Where do *I* as an individual fit into the global competition and opportunities of the day, and how can *I*, on my own, collaborate with others globally?"

Conveniently enough, accepting this idea makes it impossible to oppose neoliberalism. In a world of extreme individualism, no one in particular is responsible for setting the rules of the world order. It is pointless to protest governments or international financial institutions. Globalization is unstoppable because people want it.

These arguments are not new. With scant evidence, Friedman has long claimed that there is a "groundswell" of people throughout the developing world demanding corporate globalization. Of course, the massive protests of the past decade would seem to contradict his assertion. But he does not see this as a problem. He dismisses global justice activism by arguing, "from its origins, the movement that emerged in Seattle was primarily a Western-driven phenomenon." The backlash that does exist in poorer countries, he argues, is not rational politics but simple lawlessness: "what we have been seeing in many countries, instead of popular mass opposition to globalization, is wave after wave of crime—people just grabbing what they need, weaving their own social safety nets and not worrying about the theory or the ideology." In the end, Friedman seems ideologically incapable of accepting that people in the global South could organize their own movements or articulate a coherent politics of resistance.

Today, with much of the world in open rebellion against neoliberalism, this fiction is getting harder and harder to maintain. That Friedman has perpetually failed to spot the vibrant network of grassroots organizations that has built a worldwide campaign against the Washington Consensus is not a sign of widespread support for corporate globalization. It is an indictment of his reporting. Well before Seattle, there had been protests of millions of people throughout the global South against the "Golden Straitjacket."

These have continued into the new millennium. In their book *Globalization from Below*, Jeremy Brecher, Tim Costello, and Brendan Smith note that in just a two-month period, in May and June of 2000, there were six general strikes against the impact of neoliberalism. In India, as many as 20 million farmers and workers struck, protesting their government's involvement with the WTO and the IMF. Twelve million Argentineans went on strike in response to fiscal austerity policies imposed by the IMF. Nigeria was paralyzed by strikes against neoliberal price hikes on fuel. South Koreans demanded a shorter workweek and the full protection of part-time and temporary employees by the country's labor laws. Finally, general strikes in South Africa and Uruguay protested increasing unemployment rates, which resulted from IMF austerity policies. All of these escaped Friedman's notice.

In truth, they are only suggestions of wider resistance. The people of Latin America have certainly not joined the groundswell of support for neoliberal ideology. In country after country they have ousted conservative governments since 2000 and elected more progressive leaders, redrawing the region's political map. The columnist has yet to comment.

There is a way in which Friedman perfectly matches the politics of our times. "Like George Bush, he's in the reality-making business," Matt Taibbi argues. "You no longer have to worry about actually convincing anyone; the process ends when you make the case. Things are true because you say they are. The only thing that matters is how sure you sound when you say it."

As much as he might resemble Bush in this respect, however, Friedman also tells us something important about the post-Bush moment. As a new administration takes over, an increasing number of politicians will seek to move the United States away from the aggressive militarism of imperial globalization and back toward a softer approach to ruling the world. Following Friedman, many will look to revitalize corporate globalization as a model for international affairs. These "New Democrats" will promise a fresh approach to foreign affairs. But really, they will return to something old: a Clintonian model of corporate globalization. Like Friedman, many will proclaim it as the best of all possible worlds, a global order both exciting and unavoidable. It will be up to the world's citizens to demand something better. ❏

Sources: By Thomas Friedman: *The Lexus and the Olive Tree: Understanding Globalization* (Anchor Books, 2000); *The World Is Flat* (Farrar, Straus & Giroux, 2005); "Senseless in Seattle," *New York Times*, December 1, 1999; "Senseless in Seattle II," *New York Times*, December 8, 1999; "A Race To The Top," *New York Times*, June 3, 2005. Other sources: Matt Taibbi, "Flathead: The peculiar genius of Thomas L. Friedman," *New York Press*, April 27, 2005; "The Lessons of Seattle," *BusinessWeek*, December 13, 1999; Robin Broad and John Cavanagh, "The Hijacking of the Development Debate: How Friedman and Sachs Got It Wrong," *World Policy Journal*, Summer 2006; David Sirota, "Caught on Tape: Tom Friedman's Truly Shocking Admission," SirotaBlog, July 24, 2006; Garrett M. Graff, "Thomas Friedman is On Top of the World," *The Washingtonian*, July 2006; David Sirota, "Billionaire Scion Tom Friedman," DailyKos, July 31, 2006; Roger Lowenstein, "The Inequality Conundrum," *New York Times Magazine*, June 10, 2007; Vandana Shiva, "The Polarised World Of Globalisation," ZNet, May 27, 2005; Jeremy Brecher et al., *Globalization from Below* (South End Press, 2000).

Chapter 2

CORPORATE POWER AND THE GLOBAL ECONOMY

Article 2.1

U.S. BANKS AND THE DIRTY MONEY EMPIRE

BY JAMES PETRAS

September/October 2001

Washington and the mass media have portrayed the United States as being in the forefront of the struggle against narcotics trafficking, drug-money laundering, and political corruption. The image is of clean white hands fighting dirty money from the Third World (or the ex-Communist countries). The truth is exactly the opposite. U.S. banks have developed an elaborate set of policies for transferring illicit funds to the United States and "laundering" those funds by investing them in legitimate businesses or U.S. government bonds. The U.S. Congress has held numerous hearings, provided detailed exposés of the illicit practices of the banks, passed several anti-laundering laws, and called for stiffer enforcement by public regulators and private bankers. Yet the biggest banks continue their practices and the sums of dirty money grow exponentially. The $500 billion of criminal and dirty money flowing annually into and through the major U.S. banks far exceeds the net revenues of all the information technology companies in the United States. These yearly inflows surpass the net profits repatriated from abroad by the major U.S. oil producers, military industries, and airplane manufacturers combined. Neither the banks nor the government have the will or the interest to put an end to practices that provide such high profits and help maintain U.S. economic supremacy internationally.

Big U.S. Banks and Dirty Money Laundering

"Current estimates are that $500 billion to $1 trillion in illegal funds from organized crime, narcotics trafficking and other criminal misconduct are laundered through banks worldwide each year," according to Senator Carl Levin (D-Mich.), "with about half going through U.S. banks." The senator's statement, however, only covers proceeds from activities that are crimes under U.S. law. It does not include financial transfers by corrupt political leaders or tax evasion by overseas businesses, since in those cases any criminal activity takes place outside the United States. Raymond Baker, a leading U.S. expert on international finance and guest scholar in economic studies at the Brookings Institution, estimates the total "flow of corrupt money ... into Western coffers" from Third World or ex-Communist economies at $20 to $40 billion a year. He puts the "flow stemming from mis-priced trade" (the difference between the price quoted, for tax purposes, of goods sold abroad, and their real price) at a minimum of $80 billion a year. "My lowest estimate is $100 billion per year by these two means ... a trillion dollars in the decade, at least half to the United States," Baker concludes. "Including other elements of illegal flight capital would produce much higher figures."

The money laundering business, whether "criminal" or "corrupt," is carried out by the United States' most important banks. The bank officials involved in money laundering have backing from the highest levels of the banking institutions. These are not isolated offenses perpetrated by loose cannons. Take the case of Citibank's laundering of Raúl Salinas' $200 million account. The day after Salinas, the brother of Mexico's ex-President Carlos Salinas de Gortari, was arrested and his large-scale theft of government funds was exposed, his private bank manager at Citibank, Amy Elliott, said in a phone conversation with colleagues (the transcript of which was made available to Congressional investigators) that "this goes [on] in the very, very top of the corporation, this was known ... on the very top. We are little pawns in this whole thing."

Citibank is the United States' biggest bank, with 180,000 employees worldwide, operating in 100 countries, with $700 billion in known assets. It operates what are known as "private banking" offices in 30 countries, with over $100 billion in client assets. Private banking is the sector of a bank which caters to extremely wealthy clients, with deposits of $1 million or more. The big banks charge customers for managing their assets and for providing the specialized services of the private banks. These services go beyond routine banking services like check clearing and deposits, to include investment guidance, estate planning, tax assistance, off-shore accounts, and complicated schemes designed to secure the confidentiality of financial transactions. Private banks sell secrecy to their clients, making them ideal for money laundering. They routinely use code names for accounts. Their "concentration accounts" disguise the movement of client funds by co-mingling them with bank funds, cutting off paper trails for billions of dollars in wire transfers. And they locate offshore private investment corporations in countries such as the Cayman

Islands and the Bahamas, which have strict banking secrecy laws. These laws allow offshore banks and corporations to hide a depositor's name, nationality, the amount of funds deposited, and when they were deposited. They do not require any declarations from bank officials about sources of funds.

Private investment corporations (PICs) are one particulary tricky way that big banks hold and hide a client's assets. The nominal officers, trustees, and shareholders of these shell corporations are themselves shell corporations controlled by the private bank. The PIC then becomes the official holder of the client's accounts, while the client's identity is buried in so-called "records of jurisdiction" in countries with strict secrecy laws. The big banks keep pre-packaged PICs on the shelf awaiting activation when a private bank client wants one. The system works like Russian matryoshka dolls, shells within shells within shells, which in the end can be impenetrable to the legal process.

Hearings held in 1999 by the Senate's Permanent Subcommittee on Investigations (under the Governmental Affairs Committee) revealed that in the Salinas case, private banking personnel at Citibank—which has a larger global private banking operation than any other U.S. bank—helped Salinas transfer $90 to $100 million out of Mexico while disguising the funds' sources and destination. The bank set up a dummy offshore corporation, provided Salinas with a secret codename, provided an alias for a third party intermediary who deposited the money in a Citibank account in Mexico, transferred the money in a concentration account to New York, and finally moved it to Switzerland and London.

Instead of an account with the name "Raúl Salinas" attached, investigators found a Cayman Islands account held by a PIC called "Trocca, Ltd.," according to Minority Counsel Robert L. Roach of the Permanent Committee on Investigations. Three Panama shell companies formed Trocca, Ltd.'s board of directors and three Cayman shell companies were its officers and shareholders. "Citibank controls all six of these shell companies and routinely uses them to function as directors and officers of PICs that it makes available to private clients," says Roach. Salinas was only referred to in Citibank documents as "Confidential Client No. 2" or "CC-2."

Historically, big-bank money laundering has been investigated, audited, criticized, and subjected to legislation. The banks have written their own compliance procedures. But the big banks ignore the laws and procedures, and the government ignores their non-compliance. The Permanent Subcommittee on Investigations discovered that Citibank provided "services," moving a total of at least $360 million, for four major political swindlers, all of whom lost their protection when the political winds shifted in their home countries: Raúl Salinas, between $80 and $100 million; Asif Ali Zardari (husband of former Prime Minister of Pakistan), over $40 million; El Hadj Omar Bongo (dictator of Gabon since 1967), over $130 million; Mohammed, Ibrahim, and Abba Sani Abacha (sons of former Nigerian dictator General Sani Abacha), over $110 million. In all cases Citibank violated all of its own procedures and government guidelines: there was no review of the client's background (known as the "client profile"), no determination of the source of the funds, and no inquiry into any violations of the laws of the country where the money originated. On the contrary, the bank facilitated the outflow in its prepackaged format: shell corporations were established, code names were provided, funds were moved through concentration accounts, and the funds were invested in legitimate businesses or in U.S. bonds. In none of these cases did the banks practice "due diligence," taking the steps required by law to ensure that they do not facilitate money laundering. Yet top banking officials have never been brought to court and tried. Even after the arrest of its clients, Citibank continued to provide them with its services, including moving funds to secret accounts.

Another route that the big banks use to launder dirty money is "correspondent banking." Correspondent banking is the provision of banking services by one bank to another. It enables overseas banks to conduct business and provide services for their customers in jurisdictions where the bank has no physical presence. A bank that is licensed in a foreign country and has no office in the United States can use correspondent banking to attract and retain wealthy criminal or corrupt clients interested in laundering money in the United States. Instead of exposing itself to U.S. controls and incurring the high costs of locating in the U.S., the bank will open a correspondent account with an existing U.S. bank. By establishing such a relationship, the foreign bank (called the "respondent") and its customers can receive many or all of the services offered by the U.S. bank (called the "correspondent"). Today, all the big U.S. banks have established multiple correspondent relationships throughout the world so they may engage in international financial transactions for themselves and their clients in places where they do not have a physical presence. The largest U.S. and European banks, located in financial centers like New York or London, serve as correspondents for thousands of other banks. Most of the offshore banks laundering billions for criminal clients have accounts in the United States. Through June 1999, the top five correspondent bank holding companies in the United States held correspondent account balances exceeding $17 billion; the total correspondent balances of the 75 largest U.S. correspondent banks was $34.9 billion. For billionaire criminals an important feature of correspondent relationships is that they provide access to international transfer systems. The biggest banks specializing in international fund transfers (called "money center banks") can process up to $1 trillion in wire transfers a day.

The Damage Done

Hundreds of billions of dollars have been transferred, through the private-banking and correspondent-banking systems, from Africa, Asia, Latin America, and Eastern Europe to the biggest banks in the United States and Europe. In all these regions, liberalization and privatization of the economy have opened up lucrative opportunities for corruption and the easy movement of booty overseas. Authoritarian governments and close ties to Washington, meanwhile, have ensured impunity for most of the guilty parties. Russia alone has seen over $200 billion illegally transferred out of the country in the course of the 1990s. The massive flows of capital out of these regions—really the pillaging of these countries' wealth through the international banking system—is a major factor in their economic instability and mass impoverishment. The resulting economic crises, in turn, have made these countries more vulnerable to the prescriptions of the International Monetary Fund and the World Bank, including liberalized banking and financial systems that lead to further capital flight.

Even by an incomplete accounting (including both "criminal" and "corrupt" funds, but not other illicit capital transfers, such as illegal shifts of real estate or securities titles, wire fraud, etc.), the dirty money coming from abroad into U.S. banks amounted to $3.5 to $6.0 trillion during the 1990s. While this is not the whole picture, it gives us a basis for estimating the significance of the "dirty money factor" in the U.S. economy. The United States currently runs an annual trade deficit of over $400 billion. The gap has to be financed with inflows of funds from abroad—at least a third of which is "dirty money." Without the dirty money the U.S. economy's external accounts would be unsustainable. No wonder the biggest banks in the United States and Europe are actively involved, and the governments of these countries turn a blind eye. That is today's capitalism—built around pillage, criminality, corruption, and complicity. ❑

Sources: "Private Banking and Money Laundering: A Case Study of Opportunities and Vulnerabilities," Permanent Subcommittee on Investigations of the Committee on Governmental Affairs, United States Senate, One Hundred Sixth Congress, November 9-10, 1000; "Report on Correspondent Banking: A Gateway to Money Laundering," Minority Staff of the U.S. Senate Permanent Subcommittee on Investigations, February 2001.

Article 2.2

THE BUSINESS OF WAR IN THE DEMOCRATIC REPUBLIC OF CONGO

BY DENA MONTAGUE AND FRIDA BERRIGAN
July/August 2001

T his is all money," says a Western mining executive, his hand sweeping over a geological map toward the eastern Democratic Republic of Congo (DRC). He is explaining why, in 1997, he and planeloads of other businessmen were flocking to the impoverished country and vying for the attention of then-rebel leader Laurent Kabila. The executive could just as accurately have said, "This is all war."

The interplay among a seemingly endless supply of mineral resources, the greed of multinational corporations desperate to cash in on that wealth, and the provision of arms and military training to political tyrants has helped to produce the spiral of conflicts that have engulfed the continent—what many regard as "Africa's First World War."

When Westerners reach for their cell phones or pagers, turn on their computers, propose marriage with diamond rings, or board airplanes, few of them make the connection between their ability to use technology or buy luxury goods and a war raging in the DRC, half a world away. In what has been called the richest patch of earth on the planet, the DRC's wealth has also been its curse. The DRC holds millions of tons of diamonds, copper, cobalt, zinc, manganese, uranium (the atomic bombs dropped on Hiroshima and Nagasaki were built using Congolese uranium), niobium, and tantalum. Tantalum, also referred to as coltan, is a particularly valuable resource—used to make mobile phones, night vision goggles, fiber optics, and capacitors (the component that maintains the electrical charge in computer chips). In fact, a global shortage of coltan caused a wave of parental panic in the United States last Christmas when it resulted in the scarcity of the popular PlayStation 2. The DRC holds 80% of the world's coltan reserves, more than 60% of the world's cobalt, and the world's largest supply of high-grade copper.

These minerals are vital to maintaining U.S. military dominance, economic prosperity, and consumer satisfaction. Because the United States does not have a domestic supply of many essential minerals, the U.S. government identifies sources of strategic minerals, particularly in Third World countries, then encourages U.S. corporations to invest in and facilitate production of the needed materials. Historically, the DRC (formerly Zaire) has been an important source of strategic minerals for the United States. In the mid-1960s, the U.S. government installed the dictatorship of Mobutu Sese Seko, which ensured U.S. access to those minerals for more than 30 years.

Today, the United States claims that it has no interest in the DRC other than a peaceful resolution to the current war. Yet U.S. businessmen and politicians are still going to extreme lengths to gain and preserve sole access to the DRC's mineral resources. And to protect these economic interests, the U.S. government continues to provide millions of dollars in arms and military training to known human-rights abusers and undemocratic regimes. Thus, the DRC's mineral wealth is both an impetus for war and an impediment to stopping it.

Background to the War

Under colonialism, the Western countries perfected a system of divide-and-rule in Central Africa, callously dividing ancestral lands and orchestrating strife between ethnic groups. The current crisis represents a continuation of these insidious practices.

A flash point for the current war is the 1994 genocide in Rwanda, in which nearly one million people were killed. The U.S. government made every effort to block humanitarian intervention that could have stopped the slaughter of Rwandan Tutsis by the Hutu government, actively lobbying the United Nations to hold off on sending peacekeepers to the region. In the absence of U.N. forces, Paul Kagame, a U.S.-trained army commander, led the Rwandan Patriotic Front (RPF) in a military action that toppled the Hutu regime. After Kagame became Rwanda's vice president (a very powerful position) and defense minister, the United States sent $75 million in military aid to the new government. Additionally, U.S. Green Berets began to provide "humanitarian training" to Rwandan troops.

In October 1996, Kagame's RPF joined with members of Yoweri Museveni's Ugandan People's Defense Forces (UPDF) and Laurent Kabila, a Congolese rebel leader, in an invasion of Zaire. In 1997, they succeeded in toppling Mobutu. They also sought to dismantle camps controlled by the Hutu militia responsible for the Rwandan genocide. The coalition, known as the Democratic Forces for the Liberation of Congo-Zaire (AFDL), included U.S.-trained troops. Although Rwandan troops who participated in the AFDL invasion committed gross human-rights abuses that a U.N. report labeled "crimes against humanity," the U.S. government continued to provide military support to the Kagame regime.

During the conflict, U.S. corporations treated rebel-controlled Zaireian territory as open for business, even while Mobutu remained the internationally recognized leader of Zaire. Once the AFDL took control of Katanga (one of the DRC's richest mineral patches), Western friends and allies began negotiating with Kabila for access to mineral resources.

A SHORT CHRONOLOGY

October 1996 – AFDL movement begins
May 1997 – Mobutu flees Zaire; Laurent Kabila takes power in DRC
August 1998 – Rwandan and Ugandan troops invade DRC
July 1999 – Cease-fire agreement signed at Lusaka, Zambia
January 2001 – Laurent Kabila is killed; Joseph Kabila becomes President

Under rebel leadership, the method of exploiting these resources fundamentally changed. During Mobutu's reign, locally based Congolese strongmen had controlled the distribution of resources on the government's behalf, effectively limiting the potential for massive mining deals. But after the AFDL invasion, well-connected Western businessmen were able to secure much larger mining interests than in previous years.

For example, in May 1997, American Mineral Fields (AMF)—whose chair is Mike McMurrough, a personal friend of President Clinton—cut a $1 billion mining deal with Kabila. According to Kabila advisors and news reports, the negotiations began immediately after Kabila captured Goma (a city right across the border with Rwanda) in February 1997, and were handled by Kabila's U.S.-trained finance commissioner. The deal allowed AMF to perform feasibility studies on reactivating the Kipushi mine, a high-grade zinc and copper deposit. The company also landed exclusive exploration rights to an estimated 1.4 million tons of copper and 270,000 tons of cobalt (about ten times the volume of current world cobalt production). While AMF admits that political problems have slowed the pace of its DRC operations, the company continues to develop plans for the Kipushi mine.

Also in 1997, Bechtel, the engineering and construction company, established a strong relationship with Kabila. Bechtel—whose history of collaboration with the CIA is well-documented in Laton McCartney's 1989 book, *Friends in High Places*—drew up a master development plan and inventory of the country's mineral resources free of charge. Bechtel also commissioned and paid for NASA satellite studies of the

---

WHO'S WHO IN THE DRC CONFLICT

The Leaders

Mobutu Sese Seko – President of Zaire, 1966-1997
Paul Kagame – Vice President and Minister of Defense of Rwanda, 1994-2000;
    President of Rwanda, 2000-present
Yoweri Musevini – President of Uganda, 1986-present
Laurent Kabila – President of the DRC, 1997-2001
Joseph Kabila (son of Laurent Kabila) – President of the DRC, 2001-present

The Organizations

RPF – Rwandan Patriotic Front (led by Paul Kagame)
UPDF – Ugandan People's Defense Forces (led by Yoweri Museveni)
AFDL – Democratic Forces for the Liberation of Congo-Zaire (coalition of
    RPF, UPDF, and Kabila-led Congolese rebels)
RCD-Goma – Congolese Rally for Democracy (DRC rebels allied with Rwanda)
CLF – Congolese Liberation Front (DRC rebels allied with Uganda)

country for infrared maps of its mineral potential. Bechtel estimates that the DRC's mineral ores alone are worth $157 billion.

At the same time, Kabila enjoyed the support of Western military interests. Kabila was in frequent contact with Richard Orth, former deputy of the U.S. Defense Intelligence Agency for Africa. The agency, which operates as an arm of the Pentagon, supplies military intelligence to warfighters and weapons dealers around the world. During the Clinton administration, Orth was appointed U.S. military attaché to Kigali, the Rwandan capital, shortly before Kabila began his march across the DRC. Additionally, former Pentagon officials acted as military advisers to Kabila in Goma, producing a dangerous mix of business, politics, and military power.

Renewed War in the East

After Kabila's rise to power, the desire for mineral wealth helped to escalate conflict between the DRC on the one hand and Rwanda and Uganda on the other. In August 1998, after falling out with Kabila, Kagame of Rwanda and Museveni of Uganda launched a new invasion of the DRC. Both leaders claimed that they entered the DRC to undermine Kabila's power and protect their borders from rebel groups that threatened to destabilize their countries.

In the name of pursuing peace, Kabila's former allies have been able to advance their own mineral interests. During the AFDL war, top Rwandan and Ugandan military officials learned first-hand about the lucrative business of mining. Since the 1998 war began, territories controlled by Rwandan- and Ugandan-supported rebel groups have become *de facto* states where mining companies have openly expressed interest in investing. Rwanda is allied with Congolese Rally for Democracy (RCD-Goma), while the Ugandan government has formed a close relationship with leaders of the Congolese Liberation Front (CLF), a Mobutuist rebel movement. The RCD and the CLF now control the entire eastern region of the DRC, the wealthiest in terms of natural resources.

Both Rwanda and Uganda provide arms and training to their respective rebel allies and have set up extensive links to facilitate the exploitation of mineral resources. Along with their rebel allies, the two countries seized raw materials stockpiled in DRC territory and looted money from DRC banks. Rwanda and Uganda also set up colonial-style systems of governance, appointing local authorities to oversee their territories in the DRC. Meanwhile, high-ranking members of the Rwandan and Uganda military (including relatives of Kagame and Museveni) retain significant control over illegal mineral exploitation. Local Congolese, including children, are forced to work in the mines for little or no pay, under guard of Rwandan and Ugandan troops. Rwanda prisoners also participate in mining. To transport weapons to the rebels in the DRC, and to fly resources out of the DRC to Rwanda and Uganda, the authorities rely on private companies owned or controlled by Kagame's and Museveni's friends and relatives. They also utilize international connections made during the AFDL war.

The illegal mining has been a huge windfall for Rwanda and Uganda. The two countries have very few mineral reserves of their own. But since they began extracting the DRC's resources, their mineral exports have increased dramatically. For example, between 1996 and 1997, the volume of Rwanda's coltan production doubled, bringing the Rwandans and their rebel allies up to $20 million a month in revenue. Also, the volume of Rwanda's diamond exports rose from about 166 carats in 1998 to some 30,500 in 2000—a 184-fold increase! From 1997 to 1998, the annual volume of Uganda's diamond exports jumped from approximately 1,500 carats to about 11,300, or nearly eight-fold; since 1996, Ugandan gold exports have increased tenfold. The final destination for many of these minerals is the United States.

Western corporations and financial institutions have encouraged the exploitation. For example, in 1999, RCD-Goma's financial arm—known as SONEX—received $5 million in loans from Citibank New York. Additionally, a member of the U.S. Ambassador to the DRC's honorary council in Bukavu has been promoting deals between U.S. companies and coltan dealers in the eastern region. He is also acting chair of a group of coltan-exporting companies based in Bukavu. (Bukavu is located in RCD-held territory.)

U.S. military aid has contributed significantly to the crisis. During the Cold War, the U.S. government shipped $400 million in arms and training to Mobutu. After Mobutu was overthrown, the Clinton administration transferred its military allegiance to Rwanda and Uganda, although even the U.S. State Department has accused both countries of widespread corruption and human-rights abuses. During his historic visit to Africa in 1998, President Clinton praised Presidents Kagame and Musevini as leaders of the "African Renaissance," just a few months before they launched their deadly invasion of the DRC with U.S. weapons and training. The United States is not the only culprit; many other countries, including France, Serbia, North Korea, China, and Belgium, share responsibility. But the U.S. presence has helped to open networks and supply lines, providing an increased number of arms to the region.

The International Monetary Fund (IMF) and World Bank have knowingly contributed to the war effort. The international lending institutions praised both Rwanda and Uganda for increasing their gross domestic product (GDP), which resulted from the illegal mining of DRC resources. Although the IMF and World Bank were aware that the rise in GDP coincided with the DRC war, and that it was derived from exports of natural resources that neither country normally produced, they nonetheless touted both nations as economic success stories. Although Uganda in particular has made significant strides in improving access to education and reducing the rate of new AIDS infections, debt relief has also allowed it the space to appropriate more money for its military ventures.

Although rebels control half of the DRC's territory, deals with the Congolese government itself are still attractive. In January 2000, Chevron—the corporation that named an oil tanker after National Security Advisor Condoleezza Rice—announced a three-year, $75 million spending program in the DRC, thus challenging the notion that war discourages foreign investment. In 1999, the company, which has been present in the Congo for 40 years, was producing 17,700 barrels of oil a day. It hopes that, by 2002, production will increase to 21,000 barrels per day. The gamble seems to be paying off. When Joseph Kabila, Laurent Kabila's son and successor, visited the United States in 2001, he reassured Chevron officials that stability under his leadership would ensure a safe environment for investment.

Of course, because of war and ongoing political unrest, these deals may not endure. But considering the potential for billions of dollars in profits, many mining corporations believe the investment is worth the risk. As one investor put it, "It is a good moment to come: it is in difficult times that you can get the most advantage."

Prospects for Peace

In August 1999, Uganda, Rwanda, and their rebel allies, among others, signed a cease-fire agreement with the DRC at Lusaka, Zambia. The agreement, which the U.S. government heavily supported, gave the Rwandan- and Ugandan-backed rebels significant power in developing a new Congolese government. It also allowed them to collaborate with the Congolese army in monitoring the withdrawal of foreign troops. If implemented, the Lusaka accord could bring the peace and stability that some Western corporations prefer.

But the demand for mineral resources continues to drive the DRC conflict. In April 2001, a scathing U.N. report argued that Presidents Kagame and Museveni are "on the verge of becoming the godfathers of the illegal exploitation of natural resources and the continuation of the conflict in the Democratic Republic of Congo." The two leaders, the report alleged, have turned their armies into "armies of business."

In light of these findings, the U.N. report calls for sweeping restrictions on Uganda, Rwanda, and their Congolese-based rebel allies. These would include: embargoing the import or export of strategic minerals; embargoing the supply of weapons; freezing the financial assets of rebel movements and their leaders; and freezing the assets of companies or individuals who continue to illegally exploit the DRC's natural resources.

These proposals, however, would obstruct Western corporations' access to strategic minerals. Not surprisingly, the U.S. State Department has indicated that it is unlikely to recommend sanctions against its African allies. According to East African media reports, U.S. diplomats continue to view Rwanda and Uganda as "strategic allies in the Great Lakes region" and "would not want to upset relations with them at this time." Additionally, U.N. sources say that James Cunningham, the U.S. Ambassador to the U.N., has simply asked Uganda to "address in a constructive way" the U.N.'s findings. The IMF and World Bank have also indicated that their policies toward Rwanda and Uganda will remain unchanged.

Since 1994, close to four million people have perished in Rwanda and the eastern region of Congo. Many of the deaths are due to direct combat and torture by the belligerent parties, but most have been caused by starvation and malnutrition. Health services are practically nonexistent, and even where they do exist, many cannot reach them. Thousands of people hiding in the forest from soldiers have watched their villages burned to the ground and their families tortured. Soldiers have looted their possessions, their crops, and their life's savings. Foreign soldiers have manipulated ethnic tensions and encouraged neighbor killing neighbor. Oblivious to the suffering, many Westerners continue to reap the benefits of the rich Congolese soil.

Despite recent troop withdrawals, the illegal mining and trade continues unabated. The real party fueling the conflict is foreign capital investment by corporations, with the tacit support of their home countries' governments. This war of genocidal proportions cannot end until U.S. and other Western corporations and governments are forced to change their priorities. Amnesty International, Human Rights Watch, and other organizations have helped to raise international awareness about the urgency of the situation in the DRC, through campaigns against "blood diamonds," economic exploitation, and the massive humanitarian crisis the country faces.

But the DRC's future is in the hands of its youth, the next generation, the students and grassroots organizers who are dedicated to establishing peace and stability in their country. It remains to be seen whether the United States will encourage this hopeful spirit of change and democracy, or continue to enable the exploitation and destruction of the most resource-rich country on the African continent. ❑

Article 2.3

ENRON IN THE THIRD WORLD

BY THE INSTITUTE FOR POLICY STUDIES

July/August 2002, excerpted October 2003

The Institute for Policy Studies' (IPS) 2002 report, Enron's Pawns: How Public Institutions Bankrolled Enron's Globalization Game, *documents the extent to which Enron's ascendancy depended on public-sector financial assistance and governmental support for energy privatization policies worldwide. Since 1992, the U.S. government, the World Bank, and other government institutions have approved $7.2 billion in public financing for Enron's activities in 29 countries, with U.S. support totaling over $4 billion. These public actors also leveraged Enron's rise by actively promoting the deregulation of developing countries' energy sectors. The devastating consequences for these nations have included price hikes and blackouts more severe than California's and leading on numerous occasions to street rioting and state repression—and sometimes to protesters' deaths.*

The IPS report highlights Enron's misadventures in seven countries while detailing the role of public institutions in the company's activities in the United States and abroad. The excerpts below present the study's key findings and outline the efforts of the World Bank and Enron to forge a common agenda.

The full report can be found on IPS' Sustainable Energy and Economy Network website www.seen.org.

Many public officials have described Enron's demise as the product of corporate misbehavior. This perspective ignores a vital fact: Enron would not have scaled such grand global heights, nor fallen so dramatically, without its close financial relationships with government agencies.

Since 1992, at least 21 agencies, representing the U.S. government, multilateral development banks, and other national governments, helped leverage Enron's global reach by approving $7.219 billion in public financing toward 38 projects in 29 countries.

The now-fallen giant, until recently the country's seventh largest corporation, marched into risky projects abroad, backed by the "deep pockets" of government financing and with the firm, and at times forceful, assistance of U.S. officials and their counterparts in international organizations. Enron's overseas operations rewarded shareholders temporarily but often punished the people and governments of foreign countries with price hikes and blackouts worse than what California suffered in 2001, causing social unrest and riots that were sometimes brutally repressed. For example:

- In the Dominican Republic, eight people were killed when police were brought in to quell riots after blackouts lasting up to 20 hours followed a power price hike that Enron and other private firms initiated. The local population was further enraged by allegations that a local affiliate of Arthur Andersen had undervalued the newly privatized utility by almost $1 billion, reaping enormous profits for Enron.

- In India, police hired by the power consortium of which Enron was a part beat non-violent protesters who challenged the $30 billion agreement—the largest deal in Indian history—struck between local politicians and Enron.
- The president of Guatemala tried to dissolve the Congress and declare martial law after rioting ensued, following a price hike that the government deemed necessary after selling the power sector to Enron.
- In Panama, the man who negotiated the asking price for Enron's stake in power production was the brother-in-law of the head of the country's state-owned power company. Rioting followed suspicions of corruption, Enron's price hikes, and power outages.
- In Colombia, two politicians resigned amid accusations that one was trying to push a cut-rate deal for Enron on the state-owned power company.

While all this was occurring, the U.S. government and other public agencies continued to advocate on Enron's behalf, threatening poor countries like Mozambique with an end to aid if they did not accept Enron's bid on a natural gas field. So linked was Enron with the U.S. government in many people's minds that they assumed, as the late Croatian strongman Franjo Tjudman did, that pleasing Enron meant pleasing the White House. For Tjudman, he hoped that compliance with an overpriced Enron contract might parlay into an array of political favors, from softer treatment at The Hague's War Crimes Tribunal to the entry of his country into the World Trade Organization.

Only when Enron's scandals began to affect Americans did these same government officials and institutions hold the corporation at arm's length. And only when Enron leadership revealed its greed on home turf did it become the biggest corporate scandal in recent U.S. history.

The World Bank, India, and Enron in the 1990s

The history of the United States' experiments with power and energy supplies over the past century has proven that public, regulated power utilities tend to provide both cheaper and more reliable service than their private counterparts. Unregulated utilities not only tend to impose higher prices on household consumers; they also strip away transparency, accountability, and citizen oversight from their operations. Deregulation has proven disastrous in the United States—with the California energy crisis costing the state billions of dollars.

Nevertheless, in 1991, India was willing to take desperate measures to attract foreign investors. Capital was fleeing the country, while foreign exchange reserves were low. The World Bank's largest client at the time, India was getting heavy pressure from the lender to change its policies and allow private capital into certain sectors, particularly its petroleum sector. Prime Minister Narasimha Rao decided to bow to World Bank pressure and allowed foreign direct investment into the country after decades of economic protectionism. Power sector privatization plans drawn up by the World Bank soon followed.

It was shortly thereafter that Enron came calling. Claiming to be one of the "world's leading power companies" (though the company was only six years old and its actual production of power amounted to several hundred megawatts globally), Enron proposed to set up a natural gas power plant in the town of Dabhol, in the western Indian state of Maharashtra... The size of the Dabhol power plant, 2,500 megawatts, would more than double Enron's power production globally.

In the fine print of the memorandum of understanding Enron and General Electric signed with the Maharashtra State Electricity Board (MSEB) on June 20, 1992, was buried the fact that the MSEB would owe Enron $35 billion over the life of the contract, regardless of how much power the state consumed. This deal would have been the single largest purchase in the history of India. After learning of the deal, India's other branches of government began to object, and the squabbles began.

Meanwhile, Enron's Ken Lay and former CEO Rebecca Mark began courting the World Bank, lobbying the Bank for support of their Dabhol project in India. Though the Bank refused to support the project, citing [its] "adverse financial impact" on the MSEB, Enron succeeded in gaining financial backers at the Overseas Private Investment Corporation (OPIC), the Export-Import Bank, and elsewhere.

Lay and Mark also succeeded in garnering other favors, including a formal exchange of staff through the World Bank's Staff Exchange Program and other relationship-building exercises. At the 1996 World Bank annual meetings, NGOs [non-governmental organizations] observed, poverty and social development were not the focus of the meetings. Instead, they reported, "Special pleadings to the Annual Meeting [were] made by corporate presidents, such as Enron's Ken Lay, not by poor people or their representatives... Lay and other corporate representatives have also been pleading their case with the U.S. Congress through a task force on multilateral development banks chaired by Senator Bill Bradley and Representative John Kasich."

Though Lay gained access to top officials at the World Bank, he complained that World Bank officials were blocking guarantees for their projects. His efforts paid off here, too—with three Multilateral Investment Guarantee Agency (MIGA) guarantees in 1996, 1997 and 2001, totalling $80 million, for its power projects in Hainan Island, China; East Java, Indonesia; and Bahia las Minas, Panama.

However, the East Java project, joined at the hip with Suharto, shared the ruler's demise. Enron then filed the first-ever claim to MIGA. In 2000, MIGA paid Enron $15 million for its political risk insurance claim on the cancelled East Java 500-megawatt power plant in Indonesia. MIGA demanded—and received last year—reimbursement from the new Indonesian government, citing the dictates of "international law."

While the World Bank Group—the International Bank for Reconstruction and Development, the IDA, the International Finance Corporation, and MIGA—ultimately provided less financing for Enron-related projects—$761 million for 12 projects over the last decade—than OPIC [which provided $2.62 billion], they played a key role in Enron's global reach in other ways.

Deregulation, the World Bank, and Enron

Deregulation proved to be a more indirect, but extremely helpful, way in which the World Bank advanced Enron's global agenda. Here is how it worked: The World Bank would issue loans for privatization of the energy or the power sector in a developing country or make this a condition of further loans, and Enron would be amongst the first, and often the most successful, bidders to enter the country's newly privatized or deregulated energy markets.

Enron's activities in Argentina, Bolivia, Colombia, Dominican Republic, Guatemala, Mozambique, and Panama reveal ways in which the World Bank acted as a pawn for Enron, allowing the corporation entrée into some of the poorest countries in the world. As in Dabhol, India, the changes the two institutions introduced made things worse for the poor; protests and riots—even deaths—ensued as a result. But in almost all cases, Enron came out unscathed, paying no price in the form of restricted access to future capital, despite a growing list of dubious, and controversial practices. ❏

Article 2.4

STOP KILLER COKE!

BY MADELEINE BARAN
November/December 2003

O n the morning of December 5, 1996, two members of a paramilitary gang drove a motorcycle to the Carepa Coca-Cola bottling plant in northern Colombia. They fired 10 shots at worker and union activist Isidro Segundo Gil, killing him. Luis Adolso Cardona, a fellow worker, witnessed the assassination. "I was working and I heard the gun shots and then I saw Isidro Gil falling," he said in a recent interview. "I ran, but when I got there Isidro was already dead."

A few hours later, paramilitary officials detained Cardona, but he escaped, fleeing to the police office, where he received protection. Around midnight that night, the paramilitaries looted the local union office and set it on fire. "There was nothing left. Only the walls," said Cardona. The paramilitary group returned to the plant the next week, lined up the 60 unionized workers, and ordered them to sign a prepared letter of resignation from the union. Everyone did. Two months later, all the workers—including those who had never belonged to the union—were fired.

Gil, 27, had worked at the plant for eight years. His wife, Alcira Gil, protested her husband's killing and demanded reparations from Coca-Cola. She was killed by paramilitaries in 2000, leaving their two daughters orphaned. A Colombian judge later dropped the charges against Gil's alleged killers.

Paramilitaries, violent right-wing forces composed of professional soldiers and common thugs, maintain bases at several Coca-Cola bottling facilities in Colombia, allegedly to protect the bottlers from left-wing militants who might target the plants as symbols of globalization.

Activists say at least eight union activists have been killed by paramilitaries at Colombian Coca-Cola facilities since 1989. And plaintiffs in a recent series of lawsuits hold Coca-Cola and two of its bottlers responsible for the violence, alleging "systematic intimidation, kidnapping, detention, and murder of trade unionists in Colombia, South America at the hands of paramilitaries working as agents of corporations doing business in that country."

The murders of Coke bottling workers are part of a larger pattern of antiunion violence in Colombia. Since 1986, over 3,800 trade unionists have been murdered in the country, making it the most dangerous place to organize in the world. Three out of every five people killed worldwide for trade union activities are from Colombia.

Suing Coke and its Bottlers

The Washington, D.C.-based advocacy organization International Labor Rights Fund (ILRF) and the United Steel Workers of America filed four lawsuits in

Federal District Court in July 2001 on behalf of Sinaltrainal (a union representing food and beverage workers in Colombia), five individuals who have been tortured or unlawfully detained for union activities, and the estate of murdered union activist Isidro Gil. The plaintiffs contend Coca-Cola bottlers "contracted with or otherwise directed paramilitary security forces that utilized extreme violence and murdered, tortured, unlawfully detained, or otherwise silenced trade union leaders."

In addition to demanding that Coca-Cola take responsibility for the murder of Colombian union activists, the plaintiffs are asking for compensatory and punitive damages, which by some estimates could range from $50 million to $6 billion.

Coca-Cola's legal defense "is not that the murder and terrorism of trade unionists did not occur," according to an ILRF press release. The company argues that it cannot be held liable in a U.S. federal court for events outside the United States. "Coca-Cola also argues that it does not 'own,' and therefore does not control, the bottling plants in Colombia."

RAY ROGERS' CORPORATE CAMPAIGN STRATEGY

In the Corporate Campaign, Inc., offices near Union Square in Manhattan, Ray Rogers sits at a large table covered in binders detailing the investors, corporate structure, and finances of the Coca-Cola Company. Rogers, 59, is the founder of the progressive labor consulting company Corporate Campaign, Inc., and a veteran of dozens of battles against corporations like Hormel, Con Edison, and General Electric. His trademark strategy, the "corporate campaign," involves identifying and targeting a company's sources of power from as many angles as possible.

"If I'm representing a union and they're in a contract fight or some sort of organizing drive," Rogers said, "I'm going to find a whole series of sensitive issues as they relate to the company. What's their record on the environment? Do they have a bank tied into them? What's the record of the bank on redlining? How do they treat poor communities? What's the safety and health record of the company? Where are they lending their money? What right-wing groups are they tied into?"

Rogers famously used these tactics in 1980 to force the anti-union J.P. Stevens textile company to sign a collective bargaining agreement with the Amalgamated Clothing and Textile Workers Union. In that campaign, Rogers first publicized the textile company's exploitative workplace practices, then exposed its connections with other major corporations—most importantly, the Metropolitan Life Insurance Company. Top MetLife corporate officers who had business dealings with J.P. Stevens were forced to resign, and investor confidence in J.P. Stevens plummeted. Once the textile company realized the extent to which the campaign was hurting both its reputation and its profits, it agreed to union demands. The victory led many other unions and progressive groups to incorporate Rogers' tactics into their own struggles.

In late March, a judge dismissed Coca-Cola from the lawsuits—on grounds that the firm does not have control over the labor practices of its bottlers—but allowed the case against the bottlers to go forward. A request for an appeal is pending.

According to Daniel Kovalik, assistant general counsel for the United Steelworkers of America and co-counsel for the plaintiffs: "In the short run, [the court decision] means that we can't proceed against Coke, but it doesn't necessarily mean that in the long run. I am absolutely confident that we'll win the appeal."

Kovalik maintains that Coca-Cola is liable for its bottlers' actions. For one thing, the 20 Colombia bottlers are deeply entwined in Coke's core economic activities. Coca-Cola provides syrup to the bottlers, who mix, bottle, package, and ship the drinks to wholesalers and retailers throughout Colombia. The bottlers are integral to the beverage giant's operations in the country.

Moreover, Coca-Cola and its bottlers have deep financial links. In May, Coca-Cola FEMSA, a bottling company, acquired Pan American Beverages, Latin America's largest bottler and a defendant in the case. In the year before it was acquired, sales of Coca-Cola represented 89% of Pan American's $2.35 billion net

"You can't confront powerful institutions and expect to gain any meaningful concessions unless you're backed by significant force and power yourself," Rogers said. "The corporate campaign is really a mechanism to confront power with power."

Some dismiss Rogers' style as too uncompromising and say his tactics force him into polarizing positions—either total victory or total defeat, a style of campaigning that leaves no room for the compromises that are sometimes necessary in union battles. They say Rogers' brash tactics harm unions at the bargaining table. Former United Auto Workers organizer Jerry Tucker adds, "Ray doesn't have a lot of sense of the internal workings of unions."

Rogers acknowledges that collective bargaining is not his specialty, but states, "We go in there and back up the union leadership with publicity and resources. Bargaining does not go on when the union has no power behind it."

Rogers' defenders argue that opposition to the corporate campaign model stems from union leaders' rigid resistance to nontraditional strategies. Referring to Rogers' critics within the labor movement, labor historian Peter Rachleff said, "[they] hate people who are independent, who they can't control, who can walk out the door and get another job. They believe in organization from the top down."

Many have nothing but praise for Rogers' bold tactics. "Ray is a corporate-buster without peer," says Jim Guyette, who worked with Rogers during the 1985-1986 Hormel strike in Austin, Minn. Labor journalist Tom Robbins agrees. "He has a formula down," he says. Rogers sees that "there's a connection between the shareholders and the corporate responsibility to workers."

And according to Rogers, given the dominance of corporations worldwide, the need to analyze corporate structures and connections and to deploy that analysis in the growing battle against corporate power is more urgent than ever.

sales. The acquisition made Mexico-based Coca-Cola FEMSA the largest Coca-Cola bottler in Latin America. The Coca-Cola Company owns a 30% equity stake in Coca-Cola FEMSA, according to the bottling company, and several of its executives also work for Coke.

The plaintiffs are now considering whether to add Coca-Cola FEMSA as a defendant in the lawsuits. If they do, Coca-Cola will be put in the uncomfortable position of trying to prove that Coca-Cola FEMSA and the Coca-Cola Company—despite their shared name, shared executives, and Coke's part-ownership of FEMSA—are completely independent from one another.

Coca-Cola did not return calls for comment, but has stated in the past that Pan American Beverages was an independent company. More recently, Coca-Cola has denied allegations that its bottlers tolerate or assist in acts of violence against union activists. In a statement released in July, Coca-Cola said the allegations are "nothing more than a shameless effort to generate publicity using the name of our Company, its trademark and brands."

Kovalik argues that the corporation's communications with shareholders contradict these public statements and suggest that the firm in fact can, and should, investigate and put a stop to the killings. He plans to submit Coca-Cola documents as legal evidence, including a letter to a shareholder that reads: "We require that everyone within the Coca-Cola system abide by the laws and regulations of the countries in which they do business. We demand integrity and honesty in business at the Coca-Cola Company...."

"They can't be able to profit from these bottlers and say that they don't have control over these situations," says Kovalik.

Taking Down a Corporate Giant

The Stop Killer Coke campaign may prove to be the biggest test yet of the corporate campaign model pioneered by labor consultant Ray Rogers (see "Ray Rogers' Corporate Campaign Strategy"). As the public face of the ILRF lawsuits, the Stop Killer Coke campaign aims to put public pressure on Coca-Cola to acknowledge its role in the killings and to persuade the company to stop collaborating with violent paramilitary organizations.

It's one part of a massive coalition gearing up for a multi-front attack on Coca-Cola. The anti-Coke effort, launched by the lawsuits against Coca-Cola and its bottlers, has grown to include the Stop Killer Coke campaign, consumer and student groups, and labor organizations like the Teamsters and the AFL-CIO. These various groups share the same primary goal: to damage the soft-drink giant's reputation in order to force the company to acknowledge its role in the Colombian killings. With the launch of the Stop Killer Coke campaign this summer, the movement is picking up momentum.

Rogers plans to expand the campaign far beyond the plaintiffs' allegations to encompass "at least a dozen issues" including the lack of health care for Coca-Cola workers in Africa; the corporation's water use in India, which causes groundwater destruction; and more. He has spent the last several months researching Coke's corporate structure and intricate financial dealings.

Rogers often refers to his strategic style as "divide and conquer" because it aims to isolate companies from investors, creditors, politicians, and consumers. In the most successful corporate campaigns, the target corporation's relationship with the business world breaks down, as other companies, banks, and executives decide that the benefits of the business relationship are not worth the risk of being the target of a high-profile campaign. Eventually, the company, isolated and weak, caves in to the campaign's demands in order to end the media blitz and restore its position in the business world.

"A corporation is really nothing more than a coalition of individual and institutional economic and political interests, some more vital and vulnerable than others, that can be challenged and attacked, divided and conquered," Rogers said. "I know enough now to know exactly where the Achilles heel of Coca-Cola is. I'm so confident about where we're going with this thing."

That Achilles heel appears to be Coke's relationship with SunTrust Bank, its main creditor. Many of Coca-Cola's top shareholders own significant amounts of SunTrust stock, and their boards overlap—three current or former Coke CEOs sit on SunTrust's board of directors and two current or former SunTrust CEOs sit on Coke's board. "In almost 30 years of studying corporate structures, I have never seen a more intimate or incestuous relationship," said Rogers.

Rogers plans to expose the relations between SunTrust and Coca-Cola, then use information on Coke's human rights and environmental practices to drive SunTrust into a financial and public relations disaster. If the plan works, investors will lose confidence in SunTrust; key executives will resign rather than face negative media attention; and unions, progressive groups, and consumers will close their accounts. Given the deep ties between the two companies, whatever hurts SunTrust will hurt Coke. Backed into such a position, Coca-Cola would be forced to acknowledge and end its ties to paramilitaries in order to stabilize its main creditor and regain investor and consumer confidence.

The campaign faces an uphill battle. Coca-Cola has virtually unlimited resources to fight lawsuits and conduct its own media blitz. Also, Coca-Cola, like most major companies, now has years of experience fighting high-profile consumer campaigns. The beverage giant has a truly global reach, producing over 300 brands in more than 200 countries, with more than 70% of its income coming from outside the United States. If the campaign hopes to damage Coca-Cola financially, it will have to attract international support.

Despite these serious obstacles, Rogers is optimistic. "We're going to move very quickly on this thing," he said. "I think they're going to find themselves involved in something that they're going to find a total nightmare." Terry Collingsworth, executive director of the ILRF, is also confident. "Ray's like the classic pit bull," he said. "Once he bites into you, he won't let go. Ray's not going to walk away from this until he's won."

The battle is already heating up, with activists in Latin America, Turkey, Ireland, and Australia leading anti-Coke campaigns with Stop Killer Coke materials. Student organizations like United Students Against Sweatshops are starting campaigns to ban Coke from campuses. University College Dublin, Ireland's largest university, voted recently to remove all Coca-Cola products from the campus. Meanwhile, Bard College in New York has decided against renewing Coke's contract with the school when it expires in May. At Carnegie Mellon in Pittsburgh, students staged a "Coke dump," spilling soda into the streets to call attention to the plight of Colombian union activists. Union involvement is also growing. United Auto Workers Local 22 in Detroit, recently ordered 4,000 "Coke Float" flyers, which explain the campaign. The union will hand them out to workers as they leave their plant.

In the meantime, violence against union activists in Colombia continues. On September 10, 2003, David Jose Carranza Calle, the 15-year-old son of Sinaltrainal's national director, was kidnapped by paramilitaries. According to Sinaltrainal, four masked men forced the younger Carranza into a truck and tortured him, asking for the whereabouts of his father. At the same time, his father, Limberto Carranza, received a phone call from an unidentified individual who said, "Unionist son of a bitch, we are going to break you. And if you won't break, we will attack your home." The kidnappers freed Carranza Calle over three hours later. But unionists in Colombian bottling plants, including Coca-Cola facilities, are far from safe. ❏

For more information on the Coca-Cola campaign, go to www. killercoke.org.

Article 2.5

BLOOD ON THE PALMS

Afro-Colombians fight new plantations.

BY DAVID BACON

July/August 2007

On September 7, 2006, paramilitary gunmen invaded the home of Juan de Dios García, a community leader in the Colombian city of Buenaventura. García escaped, but the gunmen shot and killed seven members of his family.

The paramilitaries, linked to the government of President Alvaro Uribe and to the country's wealthy landholding elite, wanted to stop García and other activists from the *Proceso de Comunidades Negras* (Process of Black Communities, or PCN), who have been trying to recover land on which Afro-Colombians have lived for five centuries. The PCN is a network of over 140 organizations among Black Colombian communities.

García later told Radio Bemba, "when the *paras* [paramilitary soldiers] came looking for me, I could see they were using police and army vehicles. They operate with the direct and indirect participation of high government functionaries. So denouncing their crimes to the authorities actually puts you at an even greater risk."

South of Buenaventura along the Pacific, in the coastal lowlands of the department of Nariño, oil palm plantations are spreading through historically Afro-Colombian lands. The plantation owners' association, Fedepalma, plans to expand production to a million hectares (about 3,861 square miles), and the government has proposed that by 2020 seven million hectares will be used for export crops, including oil palms.

Helping planters reach their goal is the U.S. Agency for International Development (USAID). In what the agency describes as an effort to resettle right-wing paramilitary members who agree to be disarmed, USAID funds projects in which they are given land to cultivate. The land, however, is often located in historically Afro-Colombian areas.

On paper these resettlement projects may appear to be effective components of a national peace process. On the ground, however, what typically happens is that the paramilitaries take on the task of protecting the plantation owners' (and the government's) investment. And Afro-Colombian activists who get in the way pay a price in blood.

Growing Plantations

In the 1960s, only about 18,000 hectares were planted with the trees. By 2003 oil palm plantations occupied 188,000 hectares—and closer to 300,000 counting fields planted but not yet producing. Colombia has become the largest palm oil producer in the Americas, and 35% of its product is already exported as fuel. Palm oil used to be used just for cooking. But the global effort to shift away from petroleum has created a new market for biofuels, and one of the world's major sources is the kernel of the oil palm.

Oil palm planters take advantage of the growing depopulation of the Afro-Colombian countryside caused by poverty, internal migration, and the civil war. But they also drive people off the land directly using armed guards and paramilitaries, who often seem to be the same people. "When the companies are buying land, if a farmer sells only part of what he owns, but not his house, he'll be burned out the next day," said Jorge Ibañez, an activist involved in land recovery, whose name has been changed to protect him from retaliation.

Ibañez organizes urban committees in Tumaco, a coastal city where many of the displaced Afro-Colombians in Nariño now live. Displaced people have traveled to the department capital, Pasto, to protest and demand services for the communities of shacks they've built on the edge of Tumaco's mangrove swamps. "But the government says the problem of displacement has been solved," Ibañez says, "even while those same displaced people are camping out in the plaza in front of the offices of the authorities, because they have no place to go."

Other community activists charge that coca production follows the palms. Raul Alvarez explains that "we never consumed coca here, but now it's all over our schools and barrios." Residents accuse the newly arrived armed plantation guards of involvement in the traffic and suspect the planters themselves are its financial backers. The earliest and largest plantation owners have been the sugar barons of Cali, in the Valle de Cauca department, who for years have been suspected of involvement in the drug trade. Ibañez says the gunmen are "people who come here from other regions, go to work for these companies, and threaten people."

In Tumaco, among the shacks of the displaced, the network of armed guards runs loan sharking operations and pawnshops, keeping watch on community activity by monopolizing the tiny phone stores where residents go to make their calls.

"These people aren't a political force themselves," García says. "They're mercenaries. In an area like the Pacific coast, where the average income isn't even $500 a year, they offer $400 a month to join up. Even Black and indigenous people get bought, and then they use one group to commit massacres against the other—Blacks against indigenous, indigenous against Black."

Regaining Land Rights

In the face of the displacement and dispersal of their communities, Afro-Colombians have fought with the government for decades, trying to force recognition of their land rights. Those persistent efforts have produced important legal gains. As a result of Afro-Colombian and indigenous community pressure, the country's constitution, rewritten in 1991, finally validated their right to their historical territories. Law 70, passed in 1993, said these communities had to be consulted and had to give their approval prior to any new projects planned on their land. But having a law is one thing; enforcing it is another.

In Nariño's interior, displaced residents have joined forces with those still on the land. Together they've filed a series of legal challenges to regain title to land where their ancestors settled centuries ago. Francisco Hurtado, an Afro-Colombian leader who began the effort over a decade ago, was assassinated in 1998. Nevertheless, Afro-Colombians recovered their first collective territories in the department in 2005. Since the passage of Law 70, Afro-Colombians have gained title to 6.1 million hectares of land. Recovery is still far from complete, however.

Tiny communities in the jungle, like Bajo Pusbi, still live in fear of the various armed groups who walk their dirt streets with impunity. And Palmeira, the largest of the Nariño planters, has ceded land planted in palms, but not the roads that lead to or through that land. As a result, the territory's inhabitants still earn their living by collecting wood. Most people can't read or write. Deep in the *selva*, or jungle, Bajo Pusbi has neither a school nor a clinic .

President Uribe's response to this poverty is his plan to force Afro-Colombian communities to become the planters' junior partners, maintaining and harvesting the trees and turning over the product to the companies for refining. Further, he wants to take even more land for this monoculture. To support expanding palm oil production, conservative parties in the Colombian Congress—with encouragement from USAID—have promulgated new laws for forests, water and other resources that require their commercial exploitation. If a community doesn't exploit the resources, it can lose title to its land.

At Fedepalma's 2006 congress in Villavicencio, Uribe told the growers' organization that he would "lock up the businessmen of Tumaco with our Afro-Colombian compatriots, and not let them out of the office until they've reached an agreement on the use of these lands." Leaders from the Community Councils of the Black Communities of Kurrulao condemned the idea in a letter to the president, claiming "it would bring with it great environmental, social and cultural harm." They argue that more palm plantations would affect the ability to reproduce Afro-Colombian culture, and would replace one of the most biodiverse regions of the planet with monocrop cultivation.

"Afro-Colombian communities on the Pacific Coast," García told Radio Bemba, "use the land, and are the owners of what the land produces, but don't believe they own the land itself, which belongs to us all. We follow the concept of collective property. The fact that we've recovered some of our lands and now hold them in this way has infuriated powerful economic forces in our country, as well as transnational corporations."

The PCN was organized to push for land recovery and to address the extreme poverty Afro-Colombians suffer. Some of its leaders have traveled to Washington to denounce the project in meetings with U.S. Congress members, trying to convince them to vote no on the proposed U.S.-Colombia free trade agreement. That agreement would vastly expand palm oil production.

A History of Forced Labor

Development projects like the palm oil plantations threaten more than just a group of families or a single town. They endanger the territorial basis for maintaining the unique Afro-Colombian culture and society, developed over the course of nearly 500 years.

The first Spaniard landed at what would eventually become Colombia in 1500, finding a territory already inhabited by Carib and Chibchan people. Before the century was out, musket-bearing troops of the Spanish king had decimated these indigenous communities, forcing survivors away from the coast and deep into remote mountains. To replace their forced labor in plantations and mines, colonial administrators brought the first slaves from Africa. By 1521, a hundred years before slavery began in the Virginia colony, the first Africans had already started five centuries of labor in the Americas.

In Colombia, as in the U.S. South, Africans were not docile. They fled the plantations in huge numbers, traveling south and west to the Pacific coast and inland to the jungle-clad mountains of the interior. The runaways called their towns "*palenques*." By the time Simón Bolívar and Francisco de Paula Santander raised the flag of liberation from Spain in 1810, African rage was so great that slaves and ex-slaves made up three of every five soldiers in the anti-colonial army.

Yet emancipation was delayed another 40 years until 1851, a decade before Lincoln's Emancipation Proclamation freed slaves in the United States. By then, the rural Afro-Colombian communities founded by escaped slaves were as old as the great cities of Bogotá and Cartagena.

Poverty Polarized by Race

Today Colombia, a country of 44 million people, is the third largest in Latin America and one of the most economically polarized. Its Department of National Planning estimates that 49.2% of the people live below the poverty line (the National University says 66%). In the countryside, 68% are officially impoverished. And within rural areas, poverty is not evenly distributed.

The *Asociacion de Afro-Colombiano Desplazados* (the Association of Displaced Afro-Colombians) documents more than 10 million Black Colombians living on the Pacific Coast, making up 90% of the coastal population. Even in interior departments like Valle de Cauca and northern Cauca, they are a majority. In Afro-Colombian communities 86% of basic needs go unsatisfied, including basic public services from sewers to running water, according to a report given to the 23rd International Congress of the Latin American Studies Association. Most white and *mestizo* communities, by contrast, have such services.

The country's health care system, damaged by budget cuts to fund the government's counterinsurgency war, covers 40% of white Colombians. Only 10% of Black Colombians get health services, and a mere 3% of Afro-Colombian workers receive social security benefits. Black illiteracy is 45%; white illiteracy is 14%.

Approximately 120 of every 1000 Afro-Colombian infants die in their first year, compared to 20 white babies. And at the other end of life, Afro-Colombians live 54 years on average; whites, 70 years.

And while non-Black Colombians have an average annual income of $1,500, Afro-Colombian families make $500. Only 38% of Afro-Colombian young people go to high school, compared to 66% of non-Black Colombians. Just 2% go on to the university.

Institutionalized inequality has been reinforced by decades of internal displacement. From 1940 to 1990, the urban share of Colombia's population grew from 31% to 77%. Afro-Colombians joined this internal migration in hopes of gaining a better standard of living. But those hopes were dashed—instead, they joined the ranks of the urban poor, living in the marginal areas of cities like Tumaco, Cali, Medellín and Bogotá. Currently, most Afro-Colombians are living in urban areas, according to Luis Gilberto Murillo Urrutia, the former governor of Choco state. "Afro-Colombians make up 36-40% of Colombia's people," he says, "although the government says it's only 26% (or about 11 million people). Only 25%, approximately three million people, are still based on the land."

More Displacement Expected

The Colombian government's current development program will depress that number even further. Afro-Colombian communities are in greater danger of disappearance and displacement than at any previous time in their history, thanks to huge new government-backed development projects, pushed by the United States and international financial institutions.

Local communities do not control these large development projects. Palm oil refineries create dividends, but the only Colombians who benefit from them are a tiny handful of planters in Cali and Medellín. But the Colombian government, like many in the thrall of market-driven policies, sees foreign investment in these projects as the key to economic development, and thus revenue. It cuts the budget for public services needed by Afro-Colombian, indigenous and other poor communities, while increasing military spending.

Plan Colombia, the U.S. military aid program, underwrites much of that growing military budget. Both Plan Colombia and a new free trade treaty, expected to be ratified by Congress this year, will lead to further displacement of rural Afro-Colombian and indigenous communities. Leaders who stand in the way of foreign investment projects will disappear or die.

PCN activists estimate that the proposed free trade agreement will force approximately 80,000 families working in agriculture off the land. They say this will be just the beginning, and point to the 1.3 million farmers displaced in Mexico under the North American Free Trade Agreement.

And while most displaced Colombians become internal migrants in the country's growing urban slums, that migratory stream will eventually cross borders into those wealthy countries whose policies have set it into motion. Since 2002, over 200,000 Colombians have arrived in the United States.

Preserving Land and Culture

García points out that Afro-Colombian communities are the historic guardians of the country's biodiversity. "The whole Pacific coast is made up of rich mangrove forests, to which we owe our subsistence," he explains. "Afro-Colombian and indigenous culture sees that territory as a place to live, and not as a potential source of economic wealth. But this is the basis for planning these megaprojects, so they are now using their private armies, the paramilitaries, and have assassinated thousands of our movement's leaders and displaced millions of people. That includes one million Black Colombians who have had to leave the Pacific coast."

Afro-Colombian communities and their centuries-old culture have no place in the current megadevelopment plans. "They see Black people as objects that have no value," García emphasizes. "Therefore sacrificing us, even to the extent of a holocaust, doesn't matter. That's the kind of racism to which we're subjected. We believe all acts against a people's culture should be considered crimes against human rights, because there is no human life without culture."

García and others warn that continued funding of Plan Colombia will produce more conflict and more displacement. The government often accuses the guerrillas of the *Fuerzas Armadas Revolucionarias de Colombia* (FARC) of committing massacres, and in fact uses their activity as a pretext for maintaining an extremely heavy military presence in the countryside. On the other hand, it says it has forced the paramilitaries to demobilize. "But at the same time they make these commitments in the U.S. and Europe, the *paras* are massacring people here," García told Radio Bemba. "The government asks for money for the peace process, but what happens on the ground is the opposite of peace."

The U.S. Congress has appropriated $21 million to aid the resettlement of paramilitaries. Local people say the same *paras*, with the same guns, are doing the same killing. High officials of the Uribe administration have been forced to resign because their links to the paramilitaries were exposed.

"The displacement of our communities isn't a consequence of conflict," García points out. "The conflict itself is being used to displace us, to make us flee our territories. Then the land is expropriated, because the state says it's no longer being used productively. We have no arms to fight this, but we will resist politically, because to give up our land is to give up our life." ❑

Chapter 3

TRADE, INVESTMENT, AND DEBT

Article 3.1

WHAT CAUSES EXCHANGE-RATE FLUCTUATIONS?

BY ARTHUR MacEWAN
March/April 2001, updated August 2009

Dear Dr. Dollar:

What are the primary forces that cause foreign exchange rates to fluctuate, and what are the remedies to these forces?

—*Mario Anthony, West Palm Beach, Fla.*

A foreign exchange rate is the price, in terms of one currency, that is paid for another currency. For example, at the end of December 2000, in terms of the U.S. dollar, the price of a British pound was $1.50, the price of a Japanese yen was 0.9 cents, and the price of a Canadian dollar was 67 cents. Like any other prices, currency prices fluctuate due to a variety of forces that we loosely categorize as "supply and demand." And as with other prices, the forces of "supply and demand" can have severe economic impacts and nasty human consequences.

Two factors, however, make exchange rates especially problematic. One is that they are subject to a high degree of speculation. This is seldom a significant problem for countries with stable economies—the "developed" countries. But for low-income countries, where instability is endemic, small changes in economic conditions can lead speculators to move billions of dollars in the time it takes to press a button, resulting in very large changes in the prices of currencies. This can quickly and greatly magnify small changes in economic conditions. In 1997 in East Asia, this sort of speculation greatly worsened the economic crisis that arose first in Thailand

and then in several other countries. The speculators who drive such crises include bankers and the treasurers of multinational firms, as well as individuals and the operatives of investment companies that specialize in profiting off of the international movement of funds.

The second factor making exchange rates especially problematic is that they affect the prices of many other commodities. For a country that imports a great deal, a drop in the price of its currency relative to the currencies of the countries from which it imports means that a host of imported goods—everything from food to machinery—become more costly. When speculators moved funds out of East Asian countries in 1997, the price of foreign exchange (e.g., the price of the dollar in terms of local currencies) rose, imports became extremely expensive (in local currencies), and both living standards and investment fell dramatically. (Strong speculative movement of funds into a country can also create problems—driving up the price of the local currency, thereby hurting demand for the country's exports, and limiting economic growth.)

In the "normal" course of international trade, short-term exchange-rate fluctuations are seldom large. Consider, for example, trade between the United States and Canada. If people in the United States increasingly buy things from Canada—lumber, vacations in the Canadian Rockies, fish, minerals, auto parts—they will need Canadian dollars to do so. Thus these increased purchases of Canadian goods by people in the United States will mean an increased demand for Canadian dollars and a corresponding increased supply of U.S. dollars. If nothing else changes, the price of the Canadian dollar in terms of the U.S. dollar will tend to rise.

A great deal of the demand and supply of international currencies, however, is not for trade but for investment, often speculative investment. With the strong U.S. stock market in the late 1990s, investors in other countries bought a large amount of assets in the United States. To do so, they demanded U.S. dollars and supplied their own currencies. As a result, the price of the dollar in terms of the currencies of other countries rose substantially, by about 25% on average between the middle of 1995 and the end of 2000. One of the results has been to make imports to the U.S. relatively cheap, and this has been a factor holding down inflation in the United States. Also, as the cost of foreign currency dropped, the cost (in terms of dollars) of hiring foreign workers to supply goods also dropped. The result was more severe competition for many U.S. workers (including, for example, people employed in the production of auto parts, glass goods, textiles, and apparel) and, no surprise, their wages suffered.

There is little point in attempts by governments to constrain the "normal" fluctuations in foreign exchange rates that are associated with trade adjustments (as in the U.S.-Canada example above) or those associated with long-run investment movements (as in the case of the United States during the late 1990s). Although these fluctuations can create large problems—like their impact on U.S. wages—it would be very costly and very difficult, if not impossible, to eliminate them. There are other ways to deal with declining wages.

The experience of the East Asian countries in 1997 is another matter. Speculative investment drove huge exchange-rate changes and (along with other factors) severely disrupted these countries' economies. Between mid-1997 and early 1998, for example, the value of the Thai baht lost close to 60% of its value in terms of the U.S. dollar, and the Malaysian ringgit lost close to 50%. Governments can control such speculative swings by a variety of limits on the quick movement of capital into and out of countries. One mechanism would be a tax on short-term investments. Another would be direct limits on movements of funds. These sorts of controls are not easy to implement, but they have worked effectively in many cases—notably in Malaysia following the 1997 crisis.

It has become increasingly clear in recent years that effective development policies in low-income countries cannot be pursued in the absence of some sort of controls on the movement of funds in and out of those countries. Otherwise, any successful program—whatever its particular aims—can be disrupted and destroyed by the actions of international speculators.

Update, August 2009

The years leading into the economic crisis that appeared in 2007 and 2009 illustrate the way a variety of forces affect the value of the dollar relative to other currencies. Between 1995 and the end of the millennium, the value of the dollar relative to other currencies rose by almost 28%. Many factors were involved, but one important force was the demand by foreign interests for dollars to take part in the stock market boom of that period. After the dot-com stock market bubble of the late 1990s burst, however, the value of the dollar did not fall immediately. The value of the dollar was maintained (and even rose a bit through 2001) as the U.S. economy entered into the 2001 recession; with the recession, there was a fall off in demand for imports—which meant a reduction in the supply of dollars.

Then, however, the value of the dollar began to fall. By early 2008, it was back down to its 1995 level, more than 25% below the 2001 peak. Again, several factors account for the fall. In particular, the vary large trade deficit (imports greater than exports)—which more than doubled between 2001 and 2006—meant a growing supply of dollars relative to the demand for dollars. This was partly offset by the demand of foreign interests—for example, the central banks of China, Japan and other countries—for U.S. government bonds (which financed the growing federal budget deficit). But low interest rates in the United States kept the demand for U.S. assets from outweighing the huge supply of dollars generated by the trade deficit.

Ironically, from early 2008 through the beginning of 2009, as the U.S. economy plunged, the value of the dollar shot back up—rising by 14% between April 2008 and April 2009. The reason was simple: as the instability of world financial markets became increasingly apparent, there was a rush to security. That is, investors moved their money into U.S. government bonds, widely viewed as the most secure way to hold assets (in spite of the very low interest rates). This meant a strong demand for dollars.

These movements in the value of the dollar over the last two decades tell a story of instability in the world economy and in the economic relation of the United States to other countries. This instability in turn, can be extremely disruptive for a variety of industries—and for workers in those industries. ❑

[In this discussion of recent experience, the value of the dollar is the "trade-weighted value of the dollar"—that is the average value of the dollar relative to the values of the currencies of U.S. trading partners.]

Article 3.2

DISARMING THE DEBT TRAP

BY ELLEN FRANK
November/December 2000

Q UESTION: What if the IMF, World Bank and G-7 governments canceled the debts of the poorer countries right now, fully and with no strings attached?

ANSWER: Within five years, most would be up to their necks in debt again. While a Jubilee 2000 debt cancellation would provide short-term relief for heavily indebted countries, the bitter reality of the current global financing system is that poor countries are virtually doomed to be debtors.

When residents of Zambia or Zaire buy maize or medicine in America, they are required to pay in dollars. If they can't earn enough dollars through their own exports, they must borrow them—from the IMF, the World Bank, a Western government agency, or from a commercial lender. But foreign currency loans are problematic for poor countries. If CitiCorp loans funds to a U.S. business, it fully expects that the business will realize a stream of earnings from which the loan can be repaid. When the IMF or World Bank makes foreign currency loans to poor countries—to finance deficits or development projects—no such foreign currency revenue stream is generated and the debt becomes a burdensome obligation that can be met only by abandoning internal development goals in favor of export promotion.

Few poor countries can avoid the occasional trade deficit—of 93 low- and moderate-income countries, only 11 currently have trade surpluses—and most are heavily dependent on imports of food, oil, and manufactured goods. Even the most tightly managed economy is only an earthquake or crop failure away from a foreign currency debt. Once incurred, interest payments and other debt-servicing charges mount quickly. Because few countries can manage payment surpluses large enough to service the debt regularly, servicing charges are rolled over into new loans and the debt balloons. This is why, despite heroic efforts by many indebted less-developed countries (LDCs) to pump up exports and cut imports, the outstanding foreign currency debt of developing countries has more than tripled during the past two decades.

Many poorer nations, hoping to avoid borrowing, have attempted recently to attract foreign investor dollars with the bait of high interest rates or casino-style stock exchanges. But the global debt trap is not so easily eluded. An American financial firm that purchases shares on the Thai stock exchange with baht (the Thai currency) wants, eventually, to distribute gains to shareholders in dollars. Big banks and mutual funds are wary, therefore, of becoming ensnared in minor currencies and, to compensate against potential losses when local currencies are converted back into dollars, they demand sky-high interest rates on LDC bonds. Thailand, Brazil, Indonesia and many other countries recently discovered that speculative financial investors are quick to turn heel and flee, driving interest rates up and exchange rates down, and leaving debtor countries even deeper in the hole.

If plans to revamp the international "financial architecture" are to help anyone but the already rich, they must address these issues. Developing countries need many things from the rest of the world—manufactured goods, skilled advisors, technical know-how—but loans are not among them. A global payments system based on the borrowing and lending of foreign currencies is, for small and poor nations, a life sentence to debtor's prison.

There are alternatives. Rather than scrambling endlessly for the foreign currency they cannot print, do not control, and cannot earn in sufficient amounts through exporting, developing countries could be permitted to pay for foreign goods and services in their own currencies. Americans do this routinely, issuing dollars to cover a trade deficit that will exceed $300 billion this year. Europe, too, finances external deficits with issues of euro-denominated bonds and bank deposits. But private financial firms will generally not hold assets denominated in LDC currencies; when they do hold them, they frequently demand interest rates several times higher than those paid by rich countries. But the governments of the world could jointly agree to hold these minor currencies, even if private investors will not.

The world needs an international central bank, democratically structured and publicly controlled, that would allow countries to settle payment imbalances politically, without relying on loans of foreign currencies. The idea is not new. John Maynard Keynes had something similar in mind in the 1940s, when the International Monetary Fund was established. Cambridge economist Nicholas Kaldor toyed with the idea in the 1960s. Recently, Jane D'Arista of the Financial Markets Center and a number of other international financial specialists have revived this notion, calling for a global settlements bank that could act not as a lender of last resort to international banks (as the IMF does), but as a lender of first resort for payments imbalances between sovereign nations. Such a system would take the problems of debts, deficits, and development out of the marketplace and place them in the international political arena, where questions of fairness and equity could be squarely and openly addressed.

The idea is beguilingly simple, eminently practicable, and easy to implement. It would benefit poor and rich countries alike, since the advanced nations could export far more to developing countries if those countries were able to settle international payments on more advantageous terms. A global settlements bank, however, would dramatically shift the balance of power in the world economy and will be fiercely opposed by those who profit from the international debt trap. If developing countries were not so desperate for dollars, multinational corporations would find them less eager to sell their resources and citizens for a fistful of greenbacks. That nations rich in people and resources, like South Africa, can be deemed bankrupt and forced into debt peonage for lack of foreign exchange is not merely a shame. It is absurd, an unacceptable artifact of a global finance system that enriches the already rich. ❑

Article 3.3

WHERE DO U.S. DOLLARS GO WHEN THE UNITED STATES RUNS A TRADE DEFICIT?

BY ELLEN FRANK

March/April 2004

Dear Dr. Dollar:

Can you explain what trade deficits are? Who owes what to whom or is it just an accounting device?

—*Jack Miller, Indianapolis, Ind.*

I see that the United States has had a negative international trade balance for years. What happens to those dollars we've sent overseas?

—*Bill Clark, Chillicothe, Ohio*

If Americans collectively import more goods and services from foreigners than we export, we are said to have a trade deficit. Paying for the things we import accounts for most of the flow of dollars out of the United States. However, money flows out of the country for other reasons as well. The U.S. government provides foreign aid and supports overseas military bases; immigrants to the United States send dollars back to their families; foreigners who own U.S. businesses or financial assets take income out of the country.

When these factors are added to the trade deficit, the net outflow of dollars is called the *current account deficit*. In 2002, the U.S. trade deficit amounted to $418 billion, and the current account deficit totaled $480 billion. Data for 2003 is not yet available, but preliminary reports indicate the current account deficit will be at least $550 billion.

Once the dollars leave the country, three things can happen. First, foreigners can use dollars to purchase U.S. assets: stocks, bonds, bank deposits, government debt, real estate, businesses. When Toyota buys land and equipment for a factory in the United States, when a British investment fund buys stock in a U.S. corporation, when a German bank purchases U.S. Treasury bonds, then the United States is said to be "financing" its current account deficit by selling assets. In 2002, foreigners acquired $612 billion in U.S. assets.

The United States has run persistent and increasing current account deficits since the 1980s, and foreigners have used the dollars to stake significant claims on U.S. assets. At the end of 2002, the value of U.S. assets owned by foreigners exceeded the value of foreign assets owned by U.S. residents by $2.4 trillion. This is the reason the United States is often said to be a debtor nation, with a net debt to the rest of the world of $2.4 trillion. But this "debt" is denominated in our own currency. For that reason, it does not pose the same risks for the United States as developing countries with large debts—which must be repaid in dollars or euro—face.

Foreign central banks provide a second outlet for dollars that leave the United States. The dollar is the most widely used international currency, and many less-developed countries have sizable dollar-denominated debts. Governments sometimes hang on to whatever dollars fall into their hands, parking them in liquid assets like U.S. bank accounts or U.S. government bonds to earn interest. In 2002, foreign governments held almost $95 billion in dollar reserves, which they will use to cover future deficits, repay debts, intervene in financial markets, or simply to exert influence in negotiations with the United States.

If you've followed the arithmetic so far, you will have figured out that in 2002, on balance, more dollars flowed back into the United States to purchase assets then flowed out. This allowed U.S. companies to buy assets overseas, almost $200 billion worth.

As long as the country's large current account deficit is financed by these capital inflows, it is not necessarily a problem. But a third possible consequence of the massive U.S. current account deficit is that foreigners will lose confidence in the U.S. economy and stop purchasing U.S. assets. If this happens, the supply of dollars in the global banking system will exceed demand and the exchange value of the dollar will fall.

Some people believe this is already happening. Over the past few years, the dollar lost about one-third of its value relative to the euro. This could signify that foreigners are shifting from U.S. to euro-based assets. If the era of dollar supremacy is indeed coming to a close, the value of the dollar will continue to fall. What this would mean for the U.S. and world economies is difficult to predict. A sustained loss of confidence in the dollar could have many potentially serious ramifications.

Imports would grow more expensive, infuriating our trading partners, who depend on the U.S. market for their goods. With less foreign demand for U.S. assets, stock prices might tumble and interest rates rise. United States-based banks and corporations would find it harder to buy foreign assets and expand overseas. The dollar has been in trouble before and, in the past, the U.S. government pressured other countries to buy or hold dollars and prop up its value. Whether other countries agree to this will depend, ultimately, on whether the United States and other major economic powers are still talking to one another. ❏

Article 3.4

DOLLAR ANXIETY—REAL REASONS TO WORRY

The advantages of imperial finance have propped up the U.S. economy—but they may not last.

BY JOHN MILLER
January/February 2005

The value of the dollar is falling. Does that mean that our economic sky is falling as well? Not to sound like Chicken Little, but the answer may well be yes. If an economic collapse is not in our future, then at least economic storm clouds are gathering on the horizon.

It's what lies behind the slide of the dollar that has even many mainstream economists spooked: an unprecedented current account deficit—the difference between the country's income and its consumption and investment spending. The current account deficit, which primarily reflects the huge gap between the amount the United States imports and the amount it exports, is the best indicator of where the country stands in its financial relationship with the rest of the world.

At an estimated $670 billion, or 5.7% of gross domestic product (GDP), the 2004 current account deficit is the largest ever. An already huge trade deficit (the amount exports fall short of imports) made worse by high oil prices, along with rock bottom private savings and a gaping federal budget deficit, have helped push the U.S. current account deficit into uncharted territory. The last time it was above 4% of GDP was in 1816, and no other country has ever run a current account deficit that equals nearly 1% of the world's GDP. If current trends continue, the gap could reach 7.8% of U.S. GDP by 2008, according to Nouriel Roubini of New York University and Brad Setser of University College, Oxford, two well-known finance economists.

Most of the current account deficit stems from the U.S. trade deficit (about $610 billion). The rest reflects the remittances immigrants send home to their families plus U.S. foreign aid (together another $80 billion) less net investment income (a positive $20 billion because the United States still earns more from investments abroad than it pays out in interest on its borrowing from abroad).

The current account deficit represents the amount of money the United States must attract from abroad each year. Money comes from overseas in two ways: foreign investors can buy stock in U.S. corporations, or they can lend money to corporations or to the government by buying bonds. Currently, almost all of the money must come from loans because European and Japanese investors are no longer buying U.S. stocks. U.S. equity returns have been trivial since 2000 in dollar terms and actually negative in euro terms since the dollar has lost ground against the euro.

In essence, the U.S. economy racks up record current account deficits by spending more than its national income to feed its appetite for imports that are now half again exports. That increases the supply of dollars in foreign hands.

At the same time, the demand for dollars has diminished. Foreign investors are less interested in purchasing dollar-dominated assets as they hold more of them (and as the self-fulfilling expectation that the value of the dollar is likely to fall sets in). In October 2004 (the most recent data available), net foreign purchases of U.S. securities—stocks and bonds—dipped to their lowest level in a year and below what was necessary to offset the current account deficit. In addition, global investors' stock and bond portfolios are now overloaded with dollar-denominated assets, up to 50% from 30% in the early '90s.

Under the weight of the massive current account deficit, the dollar has already begun to give way. Since January 2002, the value of the dollar has fallen more than 20%, with much of that dropoff happening since August 2004. The greenback now stands at multiyear lows against the euro, the yen, and an index of major currencies.

Should foreign investors stop buying U.S. securities, then the dollar will crash, stock values plummet, and an economic downturn surely follow. But even if foreigners continue to purchase U.S. bonds—and they already hold 47% of U.S Treasury bonds—a current account deficit of this magnitude will be a costly drag on the economy. The Fed will have to boost interest rates, which determine the rate of return on U.S. bonds, to compensate for their lost value as the dollar slips in value and to keep foreigners coming back for more. In addition, a falling dollar makes imports cost more, pushing up U.S inflation rates. The Fed will either tolerate the uptick in inflation or attempt to counteract it by raising interest rates yet higher. Even in this more orderly scenario of decline, the current expansion will slow or perhaps come to a halt.

Imperial Finance

You can still find those who claim none of this is a problem. Recently, for example, the editors of the *Wall Street Journal* offered worried readers the following relaxation technique—a version of what former Treasury Secretary Larry Summers says is the sharpest argument you typically hear from a finance minister whose country is saddled with a large current account deficit.

First, recall that a large trade deficit requires a large surplus of capital flowing into your country to cover it. Then ask yourself, would you rather live in a country that continues to attract investment, or one that capital is trying to get out of? Finally, remind yourself that the monetary authorities control the value of currencies and are fully capable of halting the decline.

Feel better? You shouldn't. Arguments like these are unconvincing, a bravado borne not of postmodern cool so much as the old-fashioned, unilateral financial imperialism that underlies the muscular U.S. foreign policy we see today.

True, so far foreigners have been happy to purchase the gobs of debt issued by the U.S. Treasury and corporate America to cover the current account deficit. And that has kept U.S. interest rates low. If not for the flood of foreign money, Morgan

Stanley economist Stephen Roach figures, U.S. long-term interest rates would be between one and 1.5 percentage points higher today.

The ability to borrow without pushing up interest rates has paid off handsomely for the Bush administration. Now when the government spends more than it takes in to prosecute the war in Iraq and bestow tax cuts on the rich, savers from foreign shores finance those deficits at reduced rates. And cash-strapped U.S. consumers are more ready to swallow an upside-down economic recovery that has pushed up profit but neither created jobs nor lifted wages when they can borrow at low interest rates.

How can the United States get away with running up debt at low rates? Are other countries' central banks and private savers really the co-dependent "global enablers" Roach and others call them, who happily hold loads of low-yielding U.S.

IF THE UNITED STATES WERE AN EMERGING MARKET

If the United States were a small or less-developed country, financial alarm bells would already be ringing. The U.S. current account deficit is well above the 5%-of-GDP standard the IMF and others use to pronounce economies in the developing world vulnerable to financial crisis.

Just how crisis-prone depends on how the current account deficit affects the economy's spending. If the foreign funds flowing into the country are being invested in export-producing sectors of the economy, or the tradable goods sectors, such as manufacturing and some services, they are likely over time to generate revenues necessary to pay back the rest of the world. In that case, the shortfall is less of a problem. If those monies go to consumption or speculative investment in non-tradable (i.e., non-export producing) sectors such as a real estate, then they surely will be a problem.

By that standard, the U.S. current account deficit is highly problematic. Economists assess the impact of a current account deficit by comparing it to the difference between net national investment and net national savings. (Net here means less the money set aside to cover depreciation.) In the U.S. case, that difference has widened because saving has plummeted, not because investment has picked up. Last year, the United States registered its lowest net national savings rate ever, 1.5%, due to the return of large federal budget deficits and anemic personal savings. In addition, U.S. investment has shifted substantially away from tradable goods as manufacturing has come under heavy foreign competition toward the non-traded goods sector, such as residential real estate whose prices have soared in and around most major American cities.

Capital inflows that cover a decline in savings instead of a surge in investment are not a sign of economic health nor cause to stop worrying about the current account deficit.

assets? The truth is, the United States has taken advantage of the status of the dollar as the currency of the global economy to make others adjust to its spending patterns. Foreign central banks hold their reserves in dollars, and countries are billed in dollars for their oil imports, which requires them to buy dollars. That sustains the demand for the dollar and protects its value even as the current account imbalance widens.

The U.S. strong dollar policy in the face of its yawning current account deficit imposes a "shadow tax" on the rest of the world, at least in part to pay for its cost of empire. "But payment," as Robert Skidelsky, the British biographer of Keynes, reminds us, "is voluntary and depends at minimum on acquiescence in U.S. foreign policy." The geopolitical reason for the rest of the capitalist world to accept the "seignorage of the dollar"—in other words, the advantage the United States enjoys by virtue of minting the reserve currency of the international economy—became less compelling when the United States substituted a "puny war on terrorism" for the Cold War, Skidelsky adds.

The tax does not fall only on other industrialized countries. The U.S. economy has not just become a giant vacuum cleaner that sucks up "all the world's spare investible cash," in the words of University of California, Berkeley economist Brad DeLong, but about one-third of that money comes from the developing world. To put this contribution in perspective: DeLong calculates that $90 billion a year, or one-third of the average U.S. current account deficit over the last two decades, is equal to the income of the poorest 500 million people in India.

The rest of the world ought not to complain about these global imbalances, insist the strong dollar types. That the United States racks up debt while other countries rack up savings is not profligacy but a virtue. The United States, they argue, is the global economy's "consumer of last resort." Others, especially in Europe, according to U.S. policymakers, are guilty of "insufficient consumption": they hold back their economies and dampen the demand for U.S. exports, exacerbating the U.S. current account deficit. Last year U.S. consumers increased their spending three times as quickly as European consumers (excluding Britain), and the U.S. economy grew about two and half times as quickly.

Global Uprising

Not surprisingly, old Europe and newly industrializing Asia don't see it that way. They have grown weary from all their heavy lifting of U.S. securities. And while they have yet to throw them overboard, a revolt is brewing.

Those cranky French are especially indignant about the unfairness of it all. The editors of Le Monde, the French daily, complain that "The United States considers itself innocent: it refuses to admit that it lives beyond its means through weak savings and excessive consumption." On top of that, the drop of the dollar has led to a brutal rise in the value of the euro that is wiping out the demand for euro-zone exports and slowing their already sluggish economic recoveries.

Even in Blair's Britain *The Economist*, the newsweekly, ran an unusually tough-minded editorial warning: "The dollar's role as the leading international currency can no longer be taken for granted. … Imagine if you could write checks that were accepted as payment but never cashed. That is what [the privileged position of the dollar] amounts to. If you had been granted that ability, you might take care to hang to it. America is taking no such care. And may come to regret it."

But the real threat comes from Asia, especially Japan and China, the two largest holders of U.S. Treasury bonds. Asian central banks already hold most of their reserves in dollar-denominated assets, an enormous financial risk given that the value of the dollar will likely continue to fall at current low interest rates.

In late November, just the rumor that China's Central Bank threatened to reduce its purchases of U.S. Treasury bonds was enough to send the dollar tumbling.

No less than Alan Greenspan, chair of the Fed, seems to have come down with a case of dollar anxiety. In his November remarks to the European Banking Community, Greenspan warned of a "diminished appetite for adding to dollar balances" even if the current account deficit stops increasing. Greenspan believes that foreign investors are likely to realize they have put too many of their eggs in the dollar basket and will either unload their dollar-denominated investments or demand higher interest rates. After Greenspan spoke, the dollar fell to its lowest level against the Japanese yen in more than four years.

A Rough Ride From Here

The question that divides economists at this point is not whether the dollar will decline more, but whether the descent will be slow and orderly or quick and panicky. Either way, there is real reason to believe it will be a rough ride.

First, a controlled devaluation of the dollar won't be easy to accomplish. Several major Asian currencies are formally or informally pegged to the dollar, including the Chinese yuan. The United States faces a $160 billion trade deficit with China alone. U.S. financial authorities have exerted tremendous pressure on the Chinese to raise the value of their currency, in the hope of slowing the tide of Chinese imports into the United States and making U.S. exports more competitive. But the Chinese have yet to budge.

Beyond that, a fall in the dollar sufficient to close the current account deficit will slaughter large amounts of capital. The *Economist* warns that "[i]f the dollar falls by another 30%, as some predict, it would amount to the biggest default in history: not a conventional default on debt service, but default by stealth, wiping trillions off the value of foreigners' dollar assets."

Even a gradual decline in the value of dollar will bring tough economic consequences. Inflation will pick up, as imports cost more in this bid to make U.S. exports cheaper. The Fed will surely raise interest rates to counteract that inflationary pressure, slowing consumer borrowing and investment. Also, closing the current account deficit would require smaller government deficits. (Although not politically likely, repealing Bush's pro-rich tax cuts would help.)

What will happen is anyone's guess given the unprecedented size of the U.S. current account deficit. But there is a real possibility that the dollar's slide will be anything but slow or orderly. Should Asian central banks stop intervening on the scale needed to finance the U.S. deficit, then a crisis surely would follow. The dollar would drop through the floor; U.S. interest rates would skyrocket (on everything from Treasury bonds to mortgages to credit cards); the stock market and home values would collapse; consumer and investment spending would plunge; and a sharp recession would take hold here and abroad.

The Bush administration seems determined to make things worse. Should the Bush crew push through their plan to privatize Social Security and pay the trillion-dollar transition cost with massive borrowing, the consequences could be disastrous. The example of Argentina is instructive. Privatizing the country's retirement program, as economist Paul Krugman has pointed out, was a major source of the debt that brought on Argentina's crisis in 2001. Dismantling the U.S. welfare state's most successful program just might push the dollar-based financial system over the edge.

The U.S. economy is in a precarious situation held together so far by imperial privilege. Its prospects appear to fall into one of three categories: a dollar crisis; a long, slow, excruciating decline in value of the dollar; or a dollar propped up through repeated interest-rate hikes. That's real reason to worry. ❑

Sources: "Dollar Anxiety," editorial, *Wall Street Journal*, 11/11/04; D. Wessel, "Behind Big Drop in Currency: U.S. Soaks Up Asia's Output," *WSJ*, 12/2/04; J. B. DeLong, "Should We Still Support Untrammeled International Capital Mobility? Or are Capital Controls Less Evil than We Once Believed," *Economists' Voice*, 2004; R. Skidelsky, "U.S. Current Account Deficit and Future of the World Monetary System" and N. Roubini and B. Setser "The U.S. as A Net Debtor: The Sustainability of the U.S. External Imbalances," 11/04, Nouriel Roubini's Global Macroeconomic and Financial Policy site <www.stern.nyu.edu/globalmacro>; Rich Miller, "Why the Dollar is Giving Way," *BusinessWeek*, 12/6/04; Robert Barro, "Mysteries of the Gaping Current-Account Gap," *BusinessWeek*, 12/13/04; D. Streitford and J. Fleishman, "Greenspan Issues Warning on Dollar," *L.A. Times*, 11/20/04; S. Roach, "Global: What Happens If the Dollar Does Not Fall?" Global Economic Forum, Morgan Stanley, 11/22/04; L. Summers, "The U.S. Current Account Deficit and the Global Economy," The 2004 Per Jacobsson Lecture, 10/3/04; "The Dollar," editorial, *The Economist*, 12/3/04; "Mr. Gaymard and the Dollar," editorial, *Le Monde*, 11/30/04.

Article 3.5

HOT COMMODITIES, STUFFED MARKETS, AND EMPTY BELLIES

What's behind higher food prices?

BY BEN COLLINS
July/August 2008

Since 2003, prices of basic agricultural commodities such as corn, wheat, soybeans, and rice have skyrocketed worldwide, threatening to further impoverish hundreds of millions of the world's poor.

Shifts in fundamental supply and demand factors for food grains have undoubtedly contributed to higher food prices. Prominent among these shifts are the increasing diversion of food crops for biofuel production in the United States and Europe; sustained drought and water scarcity in Australia's wheat-growing regions; flooding in the U.S. grain belt; rising prices for oil and fertilizer worldwide; and the adoption of European and American meat-rich diets by the growing middle classes throughout Asia.

On top of these recent developments, long-term threats to worldwide agricultural output have eroded the world food system's resilience in the face of changing supply and demand. Although decades in the making, a loss of agricultural capacity worldwide caused by soil depletion, climate change, water scarcity, and urbanization has begun to take its toll on food production. Moreover, half a century of import restrictions and cheap agricultural exports by wealthy countries has devastated domestic food production capacity in poorer countries, forcing many countries that were once self-sufficient to rely on imported food from the world market.

At the same time, however, the growing presence of buy-and-hold investors in commodity markets has prompted heated debate among commodity traders, economists, and politicians over other possible causes of higher commodity prices apart from supply and demand shifts.

Since 2001, the declining value of the U.S. dollar, low U.S. interest rates, weak stock market returns, and accelerating inflation have drawn investment dollars away from stocks and into non-traditional investments such as commodities. This flight to perceived safety in commodity markets turned into a stampede in 2007 and early 2008, as a credit-induced financial crisis in the United States compounded these existing stresses on global financial markets.

Rising commodity prices and financial speculation on food are not new phenomena. The 1970s saw a similar rise in commodity prices in the United States, and in the 1920s, U.S. investors formed commodity pools to bet on commodity price movements. But the quantity and liquidity of money flowing through today's global markets is unprecedented in history. The current commodities boom could be a sign of looming agricultural scarcity, or it may prove to be a short-lived speculative bubble that will deflate over the next few months or years. But regardless of where agricultural commodity prices are headed, the boom has already begun to transform how food is financed, grown, and sold, and may dramatically change how people around the world eat (or don't).

Commodity Investment Goes Retail

Commodity exchanges exist as a mechanism for the producers and consumers of grains, energy, and livestock to transfer risk to financial institutions and other traders. For example, wheat farmers might seek to reduce the risk of price fluctuations by selling a contract for the future delivery of their wheat crop on a commodity exchange. This futures contract will guarantee a price for the farmer selling the contract, enabling them to pay for their planting costs, and avoid the risk that the price of wheat may decrease between the date they sell the contract and the date they agree to deliver the wheat. Food giants such as Kraft and Nabisco, as well as smaller bakers and grain consumers, typically purchase commodity futures contracts to avoid the opposite risk—that the price of their raw materials may increase in the future. (Commodity markets also trade "spot" contracts, which entitle the purchaser to the immediate delivery of a commodity.)

Because producers and consumers seek to reduce risk, they function as so-called hedgers in commodity markets. In contrast, commercial trading firms and other speculators bet on the price of a commodity rising or falling, buying and selling futures contracts frequently in order to profit from short-term changes in their prices.

Since 2001, commodity funds have gained in popularity as a mechanism for institutions and individuals to profit from increases in commodity prices. These funds purchase commodity futures contracts in order to simulate ownership of a commodity. By periodically rolling over commodity futures contracts prior to their maturity date and reinvesting the proceeds in new contracts, the funds allow investors to gain investment returns equivalent to the change in price of a single commodity, or an "index" of several commodities (hence the name "index investor").

Investors in these commodity index funds include public pension funds, university endowments, and even individual investors, through mutual funds, for example. Although these investors are similar to traditional commodity speculators in that both seek to profit from changes in price, traditional speculators zero in on short-term price shifts, while index investors are almost exclusively long-term buyers betting on higher commodity prices in the future.

Some observers have argued that index investors themselves may have pushed already-high prices of commodities even higher. Hedge fund manager Michael Masters testified to the U.S. Senate that the total holdings of commodity index investors on regulated U.S. exchanges have increased from $13 billion in 2003 to nearly $260 billion as of March 2008. And as of April 2008, index investors owned approximately 35% of all corn futures contracts on regulated exchanges in the United States, 42% of all soybean contracts, and 64% of all wheat contracts, compared to minimal holdings in 2001. As Masters emphasized, these are immense commodity holdings. The wheat contracts, for example, are good for the delivery of 1.3 billion bushels of wheat, equivalent to twice the United States' annual wheat consumption.

Index fund managers have defended against charges that commodity index investment contributes to higher prices, arguing that because index funds never take delivery on their futures contracts, they simulate commodity price shifts for their investors without affecting the price of the underlying commodity. Some economists have also expressed skepticism that investment demand has driven commodity prices higher. Paul Krugman of Princeton University has noted that there is no evidence of "the usual telltale signs of a speculative price boom" such as physical hoarding of commodities. Furthermore, Krugman and others have pointed to non-exchange traded commodities such as iron ore that have also experienced rapid price increases during recent years, arguing that fundamental supply and demand factors, not investors, are to blame for higher commodity prices.

Other economists and commodity market observers have argued that despite price increases in non-exchange traded commodities, and an absence of physical hoarding, the recent flood of money into commodity markets has altered the balance between speculators and hedgers, leading to higher prices and greater price volatility. Mack Frankfurter, a commodities trading advisor at Cervino Capital Management, suggests that the influx of commodity index investors has transformed commodity futures from tools for risk management to long-term investments, "causing a self-perpetuating feedback loop of ever higher prices."

One reason the precise impact of index investors on commodity prices is difficult to determine is that the U.S. commodity trading regulator, the Commodity Futures Trading Commission (CFTC), does not collect data on so-called "over-the-counter" commodity trading—that is, trading on unregulated markets—even though the agency estimated that 85% of commodity index investment takes place on these markets. Because Masters's data on the holdings of commodity index investors only include the 15% of index investor contracts that are held on CFTC-regulated exchanges, total commodity index investor holdings may be much higher than his estimates.

In testimony that warned of the influence of these unregulated markets on commodity prices, Michael Greenberger, the former head of the CFTC's Division of Trading and Markets, estimated that if unregulated trading of energy and agricultural commodities were eliminated, the price of oil would drop by 25% to 50% "overnight." If Greenberger is correct, the effect on food commodity prices would likely be similar. However, index investment is just one of many avenues through which money can enter commodity markets, making it difficult to assess the impact of index investors without taking into account the recent deregulation of U.S. commodity markets that has facilitated the current boom in food and energy investments.

Commodity Trading Regulation, Enron-Style

Commodity index investment is deeply intertwined with the growth of unregulated commodity trading authorized by the Commodity Futures Modernization Act of 2000. Before 2000, U.S. commodity futures contracts were traded exclusively on regulated exchanges under the oversight of the CFTC. Traders were required to disclose their holdings of each commodity and adhere to strict position limits, which set a maximum number of futures contracts that an individual institution could hold. These regulations were intended to prevent market manipulation by traders who might otherwise attempt to build up concentrated holdings of futures contracts in order to manipulate the price of a commodity.

The 2000 law effectively deregulated commodity trading in the United States by exempting over-the-counter commodity trading outside of regulated exchanges from CFTC oversight. Soon after the bill was passed, several unregulated commodity exchanges opened for trading, allowing investors, hedge funds, and investment banks to trade commodities futures contracts without any position limits, disclosure requirements, or regulatory oversight. Since then, unregulated over-the-counter commodity trading has grown exponentially. The total value of all over-the-counter commodity contracts was estimated to be $9 trillion at the end of 2007, or nearly twice the value of the $4.78 trillion in commodity contracts traded on regulated U.S. exchanges.

Once these unregulated commodity markets were created, energy traders and hedge funds began to use them to place massive bets on commodity prices. Enron famously exploited deregulated electricity markets in 2001, when the firm managed to generate unheard-of profits by using its trading operations to effectively withhold electricity and charge extortionate rates from power grids in California and other western states.

Although Enron went bankrupt later that year, the hedge fund Amaranth later exploited unregulated natural gas markets prior to its 2006 collapse. The fund had been heavily invested in complicated bets on the price of natural gas, borrowing eight times its assets to trade natural gas futures, and lost $6.5 billion when natural gas prices moved in the wrong direction. One month prior to Amaranth's collapse, the New York Mercantile Exchange (NYMEX), which is regulated by the CFTC, asked Amaranth to reduce its huge natural gas position. Amaranth reduced its position at NYMEX's request, but purchased identical positions on the unregulated InterContinental Exchange, where its transactions were invisible to regulators until the fund finally collapsed.

Amaranth's implosion demonstrated the ineffectiveness of regulating some commodity exchanges but not others. Thanks to the Commodity Futures Modernization Act, traders could flout position limits and disclosure rules with impunity, simply by re-routing trades to unregulated exchanges. Although index investment in commodities does not typically involve white-knuckle, leveraged bets on a single commodity's short-term performance, index investment was made possible by the same deregulated environment exploited by Amaranth and Enron. Like Amaranth, commodity index investors commonly purchase futures contracts on unregulated markets when they exceed CFTC position limits on futures contracts for a particular commodity. And other financial actors such as investment banks, hedge funds, or even the sovereign wealth funds of other countries may also be heavily invested in these over-the-counter commodity contracts, but since this trading is unregulated and unreported, the holders of these $9 trillion worth of contracts remain anonymous.

This year, the CFTC has faced intense scrutiny from investors, politicians, farmers, and agricultural traders over the unprecedented volatility and price increases of several agricultural and energy commodities traded on U.S. exchanges. A lively CFTC roundtable on commodity markets in April appeared to confirm arguments made by Frankfurter, Greenberger, Masters, and other critics of commodity index investment. Representatives for farmers, grain elevator operators, and commercial bankers at the hearing repeatedly stressed that commodity markets were "broken," while the only pleas for calm came from CFTC economists and representatives for index investors and the financial industry. Unlike index investors, farmers have not benefited greatly from higher commodity prices, because extremely high levels of market volatility have made it difficult for some farmers to finance crop planting. National Farmers Union president Tom Buis sounded a particularly dire warning about the consequences of tight commodity supplies and burgeoning index investment demand: "We've got a train wreck coming in agriculture that's bigger than anything else we've seen."

Following these warnings from farmers and food producers about the presence of index investors in commodity markets, the CFTC's acting chair publicly acknowledged the ongoing debate over "whether the massive amount of money coming into the markets is overwhelming the system." Despite this admission, Greenberger, the former CFTC official, remains skeptical of the agency's capacity and willingness to regulate commodity markets effectively. He urged Congress and the Federal Trade Commission to circumvent the CFTC's authority and eliminate unregulated over-the-counter commodity trading. Recently, faced with strong criticism from Congress, the CFTC retreated further from its claim that commodity markets are functioning normally. A CFTC commissioner admitted: "We didn't have the data that we needed to make the statements that we made, and the data we did have didn't support our declarative statements. If we were so right, why the heck are we doing a study now?"

The Consequences of Financializing Food

Facing political pressure by constituents over high oil and food prices, several members of Congress have sponsored legislation that would bar index investors from commodity markets. One bill proposed by Sen. Joseph Lieberman (Ind-Conn.) would prohibit public and private pension funds with more than $500 million in assets from trading in commodity futures, and other bills would limit the maximum number of futures contracts an index investor could hold. These bills may stem the flood of money from index investors into commodities, but comprehensive reform is needed to reverse the Commodity Futures Modernization Act's authorization of over-the-counter commodity trading. Absent an outright repeal of this so-called "Enron loophole," energy and agricultural commodities will continue to be traded outside the reach of government regulation, making future Enron- and Amaranth-style market disruptions inevitable.

Ultimately, eliminating unregulated commodity trading cannot address the fundamental causes of higher agricultural prices. Even if speculative buying is curtailed, supply and demand factors such as falling crop yields, destructive trade policies, and the growing use of biofuels have likely brought the age of cheap food to an end. However, if the critics of commodity index investment are correct, then these investors have amplified recent food price shocks and are needlessly contributing to the impoverishment of the world's poorest citizens. Even though commodity market transparency and regulatory oversight will not solve the global food crisis, eliminating unregulated commodity trading can help resolve the debate over the effects of index investors on commodity prices and restore the accountability of commodity markets to the social interests they were originally established to serve. ❏

Sources: Michael Masters, testimony before the Committee on Homeland Security and Government Affairs, United States Senate, May 20, 2008; Daniel P. Collins, "CFTC to up spec limits," *Futures,* May 1, 2005; Paul Krugman, "Fuels on the Hill," *New York Times,* June 27, 2008; Michael Frankfurter, *The Mysterious Case of the Commodity Conundrum, Securitization of Commodities, and Systemic Concerns,* Parts 1-3, www.marketoracle.co.uk; Michael Frankfurter and Davide Accomazzo, "Is Managed Futures an Asset Class? The Search for the Beta of Commodity Futures," December 31, 2007, *Graziadio Business Report;* "Regulator Admits to Futures Tracking Volatility," Associated Press, June 4, 2008; Commodity Futures Trading Commission, *CFTC Announces Agricultural Market Initiatives.* June 3, 2008; Michael Greenberger, testimony before the Committee on Commerce, Science, and Transportation, United States Senate, June 3, 2008; Sinclair Stewart and Paul Waldie. "Who is responsible for the global food crisis?" *Globe and Mail,* May 30, 2008; Commodity Futures Trading Commission, *Agricultural Markets Roundtable,* April 22, 2008; Ann Davis, "Commodities Regulator Under Fire—CFTC Scrutinized As Congress Looks Into Oil-Price Jump," *Wall Street Journal,* July 7, 2008; Ed Wallace, "ICE, ICE, Baby," *Houston Chronicle,* May 19, 2008; Laura Mandaro, "Lieberman plans would bar funds from commodities," *Marketwatch,* June 18, 2008; "Our Confusing Economy, Explained," *Fresh Air,* April 3, 2008, www.npr.org.

Chapter 4

INTERNATIONAL INSTITUTIONS AND TRADE AGREEMENTS

Article 4.1

THE ABCs OF THE GLOBAL ECONOMY

BY THE *DOLLARS & SENSE* COLLECTIVE

March/April 2000; updated December 2006 and August 2009

In the 1960s, U.S. corporations changed the way they went after profits in the international economy. Instead of producing goods in the United States to export, they moved more and more toward producing goods overseas to sell to consumers in those countries and at home. They had done some of this in the 1950s, but really sped up the process in the 1960s.

Before the mid-1960s, free trade probably helped workers and consumers in the United States while disadvantaging workers in poorer countries. Exporters invested their profits at home in the United States, creating new jobs and boosting incomes. The American Federation of Labor-Congress of Industrial Organizations (AFL-CIO) thought this was a good deal and backed free trade.

But when corporations changed strategies, they changed their alliances. By the late 1960s, the AFL-CIO began opposing free trade as it watched jobs go overseas. But unionists did not see that they had to start building alliances internationally. The union federation continued to take money secretly from the U.S. government to help break up red unions abroad, not a good tactic for producing solidarity. It took until the 1990s for the AFL-CIO to reduce (though not eliminate) its alliance with the U.S. State Department. In the 1990s, unions also forged their alliance with the environmental movement to oppose free trade.

But corporations were not standing still; in the 1980s and 1990s they were working to shift the architecture of international institutions created after World War II to work more effectively in the new global economy they were creating. More and more of their profits were coming from overseas—by the 1990s, 30% of U.S. corporate profits came from their direct investments overseas, up from 13% in the 1960s. This includes money made from the operations of their subsidiaries abroad. But the share of corporate profits earned overseas is even higher than that because the 30% figure doesn't include the interest companies earn on money they loan abroad. And the financial sector is an increasingly important player in the global economy.

Financial institutions and other global corporations without national ties now use governments to dissolve any national restraints on their activities. They are global, so they want their governments to be global too. And while trade used to be taken care of through its own organization (GATT) and money vaguely managed through another organization (the International Monetary Fund), the World Trade Organization has erased the divide between trade and investment in its efforts to deregulate investment worldwide.

In helping design some of the global institutions after World War II, John Maynard Keynes assumed companies and economies would operate within national bounds, with the IMF and others regulating exchanges across those borders. The instability created by ruptured borders is made worse by the deregulation sought by corporations, and especially, the financial sector. The most powerful governments of the world seem oblivious to the threat giving into this neoliberal corporate agenda poses to their ability to govern.

The current economic crisis presents us with a world-historical moment in which it is possible to stop the corporate offensive, a moment when the weaknesses of the neoliberal approach have been laid bare. In fact, even amidst the celebration of globalization pre-crisis, the further expansion of this model had already begun to meet with resistance. In the Americas, further progress on a continent-wide free-trade agreement stalled after 2003, although Central America did conclude a new free-trade deal with the United States in 2005. In the summer of 2006, the current round of World Trade Organization talks, launched in Doha, Qatar in 2001, collapsed for good in the face of European refusal to give up its farm supports and the growing recognition among developing countries that further trade liberalization had little to offer them. This economic crisis signals the end of the United States' ability and desire to enable the export-led growth that developing countries have been asked to pin their futures upon. Resistance to neoliberalism in developing countries is likely to increase even more. Amidst the economic rubble of the crisis there is some hope that global institutions just might be reshaped in a liberatory manner.

What follows is a primer on the most important of those institutions.

—*The* Dollars & Sense *collective*

THE WORLD BANK AND THE INTERNATIONAL MONETARY FUND (IMF)

The basic institutions of the postwar international capitalist economy were framed in 1944, at an international conference in Bretton Woods, New Hampshire, dominated by the United States and the United Kingdom. Among the institutions coming out of this conference were the World Bank and the International Monetary Fund (IMF).

At both the World Bank and the IMF, the number of votes a country receives is based on how much capital it contributes to the institution, so rich countries like the United States enjoy disproportionate voting power. At both, five powerful countries—the United States, the United Kingdom, France, Germany, and Japan—get to appoint their own representatives to the institution's executive board, with 19 other directors elected by the rest of the 150-odd member countries. The president of the World Bank is elected by the Board of Executive Directors, and traditionally nominated by the U.S. representative. The managing director of the IMF is traditionally a European.

Just after World War II, the World Bank mostly loaned money to Western European governments to help rebuild their countries. But during the long presidency (1968-1981) of former U.S. Defense Secretary Robert S. McNamara, the bank turned toward "development" loans to Third World countries. McNamara brought the same philosophy to development that he had used in the war against Vietnam: more is better. Ever since, the Bank has favored large, expensive projects regardless of their appropriateness to local conditions. Critics argue that the Bank pays little heed to the social and environmental impact of the projects it finances, that it creates dependence on imports and capital from rich countries, and that it often works through dictatorial elites that channel benefits to themselves rather than to those who need help. The poor are left to foot the bill later.

The most important function of the IMF is as a "lender of last resort" to member countries that cannot borrow money from other sources, usually when they are in danger of defaulting on previous loans from private banks. The IMF lends money on the condition that the country implement policy changes that are formally known as a "structural adjustment program" (SAP), but more often referred to as an "austerity plan." Typically, a government is told to devalue its currency, eliminate price controls and subsidies, and eliminate labor regulations like minimum wage laws—all changes that hurt the working class and the poor by cutting their real incomes.

The IMF and the World Bank wield power disproportionate to the size of the loans they give out because private lenders follow their lead in deciding which countries are credit-worthy. Both institutions have taken advantage of this leverage—and of debt crises in Latin America, Africa, and Asia—to impose a cookie-cutter model of "development" based on "free market" principles, against varying levels of resistance, on the people and governments of poor countries around the world.

THE MULTILATERAL AGREEMENT ON INVESTMENT (MAI) AND TRADE RELATED INVESTMENT MEASURES (TRIMS)

Where did they come from?

You're probably not the sort of person who would own a chemical plant or luxury hotel, but imagine you were. Imagine you built a chemical plant or luxury hotel in a foreign country, only to see a labor-friendly government take power and threaten your profits. This is the scenario which makes the CEOs of footloose global corporations wake up in the middle of the night in a cold sweat. To avert such threats, ministers of the richest countries met secretly at the Organization for Economic Cooperation and Development (OECD) in Paris in 1997 and tried to hammer out a bill of rights for international investors, the Multilateral Agreement on Investment (MAI).

When protests against the MAI broke out in the streets and the halls of government alike in 1998 and 1999, scuttling the agreement in that form, the corporations turned to the World Trade Organization to achieve their goal.

What are they up to?

Both the MAI and Trade Related Investment Measures (or TRIMs, the name of the WTO version) would force governments to compensate companies for any losses (or reductions in profits) they might suffer because of changes in public policy. Governments would be compelled to tax, regulate, and subsidize foreign businesses exactly as they do local businesses. Policies designed to protect fledgling national industries (a staple of industrial development strategies from the United States and Germany in the 19th century to Japan and Korea in the 20th) would be ruled out.

TRIMs would also be a crowning blow to the control of governments over the movement of capital into or out of their countries. Until fairly recently, most governments imposed controls on the buying and selling of their currencies for purposes other than trade. Known as capital controls, these curbs significantly impeded the mobility of capital. By simply outlawing conversion, governments could trap investors into keeping their holdings in the local currency. But since the 1980s, the IMF and the U.S. Treasury have pressured governments to lift these controls so that international companies can more easily move money around the globe. Corporations and wealthy individuals can now credibly threaten to pull liquid capital out of any country whose policies displease them.

Malaysia successfully imposed controls during the Asian crisis of 1997 and 1998, spurring broad interest among developing countries. The United States wants to establish a new international discussion group—the Group of 20 (G-20), consisting of ministers from 20 developing countries handpicked by the United States—to consider reforms. Meanwhile, it continues to push for the MAI-style liberation of capital from any control whatsoever.

Why should you care?

It is sometimes said that the widening chasm between the rich and poor is due to the fact that capital is so easily shifted around the globe while labor, bound to family and place, is not. But there is nothing natural in this. Human beings, after all, have wandered the earth for millennia—traversing oceans and continents, in search of food, land, and adventure—whereas a factory, shipyard, or office building, once built, is almost impossible to move in a cost effective way. Even liquid capital (money) is less mobile than it seems. To be sure, a Mexican can fill a suitcase with pesos, hop a plane and fly to California, but once she disembarks, who's to say what the pesos will be worth, or whether they'll be worth anything at all? For most of this century, however, capitalist governments have curbed labor's natural mobility through passports, migration laws, border checkpoints, and armed border patrols, while capital has been rendered movable by treaties and laws that harmonize the treatment of wealth around the world. The past three decades especially have seen a vast expansion in the legal rights of capital across borders. In other words, labor fights with the cuffs on, while capital takes the gloves off.

WORLD INTELLECTUAL PROPERTY ORGANIZATION (WIPO) AND TRADE-RELATED ASPECTS OF INTELLECTUAL PROPERTY RIGHTS (TRIPS)

One of the less familiar members of the "alphabet soup" of international economic institutions, the World Intellectual Property Organization (WIPO) has governed "intellectual property" issues since its founding in 1970. In the old days, "intellectual property" only covered property rights over inventions, industrial designs, trademarks, and artistic and literary works. But WIPO has been busy staking out a brave new world of property rights, especially in the electronic domain. Now "intellectual property" includes computer programs, electronic images, and digital recordings, as well as pharmaceuticals and even biological processes and genetic codes.

The 1996 WIPO treaty outlaws the "circumvention" of electronic security measures. It makes it illegal, for example, to sidestep the security measures on a website (such as those requiring that users register or send payment in exchange for access). The treaty also prevents programmers from cracking open commercial software to view the underlying code. Similar restrictions had already gone into effect in the United States, thanks to the Digital Millennium Copyright Act (DMCA). These laws prevent programmers from crafting their own programs so that they are compatible with existing software, and prevent innovation in the form of "reengineering"—drawing on one design as the basis of another. Reengineering has been at the heart of many countries' economic development, including the United States'. In the 19th century, for example, Lowell, Massachusetts, textile manufacturers built their looms based on English designs.

In recent years, WIPO has faced a turf war over the intellectual property issue with none other than the World Trade Organization (WTO). Wealthy countries are attempting an end run around WIPO because it lacks enforcement power and because some poor countries have resisted its agenda. But the mass media, information technology, drug, and biotechnology industries in wealthy countries stand to lose a great deal from "piracy" and to gain a fortune in fees and royalties if given more extensive property rights. So they have introduced, under the name "Trade-Related Aspects of Intellectual Property Rights" (TRIPs), extensive provisions on intellectual property into recent WTO negotiations.

TRIPs would put the muscle of trade sanctions behind intellectual property rights. It would also stake out new intellectual property rights over plant, animal, and even human genetic codes. The governments of some developing countries have objected, warning that private companies based in rich countries will declare ownership over the genetic codes of plants long used for healing or crops within their countries—what activists have called "biopiracy." By manipulating just one gene of a living organism, a company can be declared the sole owner of an entire plant variety.

These proposals may seem like a new frontier of property rights, but except for the issue of ownership of life forms, TRIPs actually defend the old regime of property rights. It is because current electronic, chemical, and biological technology make virtually unlimited production and free distribution possible that the fight for private property has become so extreme.

THE WORLD TRADE ORGANIZATION (WTO)

Where did it come from?

Since the 1950s, government officials from around the world have met irregularly to hammer out the rules of a global trading system. Known as the General Agreements on Trade and Tariffs (GATT), these negotiations covered, in excruciating detail, such matters as what level of taxation Japan could impose on foreign rice, how many American automobiles Brazil could allow into its market, and how large a subsidy France could give its vineyards. Every clause was carefully crafted, with constant input from business representatives who hoped to profit from expanded international trade.

The GATT process however, was slow, cumbersome and difficult to monitor. As corporations expanded more rapidly into global markets they pushed governments to create a more powerful and permanent international body that could speed up trade negotiations as well as oversee and enforce provisions of the GATT. The result is the World Trade Organization, formed out of the ashes of GATT in 1995.

The WTO's ministerial meetings have been the target of massive anti-globalization protests. Over 50,000 people went to Seattle in 1999 to say no to the WTO's corporate agenda, successfully shutting down the first day of the ministerial meeting. African, Caribbean, and other least-developed country representatives walked out of the meeting. The WTO held its 2001 ministerial meeting in Doha, Qatar, safe from protest. The WTO initiated a new round of trade talks it promised would address thee need s of developing countries. The Doha Development round was in fact continued the WTO's pro-corporate agenda. Two years later "the Group of 20 developing countries" at the Cancún ministerial refused to lower trade barriers in their countries trade until the United States and EU cleaned up their unfair global agricultural systems. By the summer of 2006, five years after it began, the Doha round had collapsed and the WTO suspended trade negotiations.

What is it up to?

The WTO functions as a sort of international court for adjudicating trade disputes. Each of its 153 member countries has one representative, who participates in negotiations over trade rules. The heart of the WTO, however, is not its delegates, but its dispute resolution system. With the establishment of the WTO, corporations now have a place to complain to when they want trade barriers—or domestic regulations that limit their freedom to buy and sell—overturned.

Though corporations have no standing in the WTO—the organization is, officially, open only to its member countries—the numerous advisory bodies that provide technical expertise to delegates are overflowing with corporate representation. The delegates themselves are drawn from trade ministries and confer regularly with the corporate lobbyists and advisors who swarm the streets and offices of Geneva, where the organization is headquartered. As a result, the WTO has become, as an anonymous delegate told the *Financial Times,* "a place where governments can collude against their citizens."

Lori Wallach and Michelle Sforza, in their book *The WTO: Five Years of Reasons to Resist Corporate Globalization*, point out that large corporations are essentially "renting" governments to bring cases before the WTO, and in this way, to win in the WTO battles they have lost in the political arena at home. Large shrimping corporations, for example, got India to dispute the U.S. ban on shrimp catches that were not sea-turtle safe. Once such a case is raised, the resolution process violates most democratic notions of due process and openness. Cases are heard before a tribunal of "trade experts," generally lawyers, who, under WTO rules, are required to make their ruling with a presumption in favor of free trade. The WTO puts the burden squarely on governments to justify any restriction of what it considers the natural order of things. There are no amicus briefs (statements of legal opinion filed with a court by outside parties), no observers, and no public records of the deliberations.

The WTO's rule is not restricted to such matters as tariff barriers. When the organization was formed, environmental and labor groups warned that the WTO would soon be rendering decisions on essential matters of public policy. This has proven absolutely correct. The organization has already ruled against Europe for banning hormone-treated beef and against Japan for prohibiting pesticide-laden apples. Also WTO rules prohibit selective purchasing laws, even those targeted at human rights abuses. In 1998 the WTO court lodged a complaint against the Massachusetts state law that banned government purchases from Burma in an attempt to punish its brutal dictatorship. Had the WTO rules been in place at the time, the anti-Apartheid divestment movement would have violated them as well.

Why should you care?

At stake is a fundamental issue of popular sovereignty—the rights of the people to regulate economic life, whether at the level of the city, state, or nation. The U.S. does not allow businesses operating within its borders to produce goods with child labor, so why should we allow those same businesses—Disney, Gap, or Walmart—to produce their goods with child labor in Haiti and sell the goods here?

THE INTERNATIONAL LABOR ORGANIZATION (ILO)

Where did it come from?

The ILO was established in 1919 in the wake of World War I, the Bolshevik revolution in Russia, and the founding of the Third (Communist) International, a world federation of revolutionary socialist political parties. Idealistic motives mingled with the goal of business and political elites to offer workers an alternative to revolution, and the result was an international treaty organization (established by agreement between governments) whose main job was to promulgate codes of practice in work and employment.

After World War II the ILO was grafted onto the U.N. structure, and it now serves a wide range of purposes: drafting conventions on labor standards (182 so far), monitoring their implementation, publishing analyses of labor conditions around the world, and providing technical assistance to national governments.

Why should you care?

The ILO's conventions set high standards in such areas as health and safety, freedom to organize unions, social insurance, and ending abuses like workplace discrimination and child labor. It convenes panels to investigate whether countries are upholding their legal commitment to enforce these standards, and by general agreement their reports are accurate and fair. ILO publications, like its flagship journal, *The International Labour Review*, its *World Labor and Employment Reports*, and its special studies, are of very high quality. Its staff, which is headquartered in Geneva and numbers 1,900, has many talented and idealistic members. The ILO's technical assistance program is minuscule in comparison to the need, but it has changed the lives of many workers. (You can find out more about the ILO at its website: www.ilo.org.)

As a rule, international organizations are reflections of the policies of their member governments, particularly the ones with the most clout, such as the United States. Since governments are almost always biased toward business and against labor, we shouldn't expect to see much pro-labor activism in official circles. The ILO provides a partial exception to this rule, and it is worth considering why. There are probably four main reasons:

- The ILO's mission explicitly calls for improvements in the conditions of work, and the organization attracts people who believe in this cause. Compare this to the mission of the IMF (to promote the ability of countries to repay their international debts) or the WTO (to expand trade), for instance.
- Governments send their labor ministers (in the U.S., the Secretary of Labor) to represent them at the ILO. Labor ministers usually specialize in social protection issues and often serve as liaisons to labor unions. A roomful of labor ministers will generally be more progressive than a similar gaggle of finance (IMF) or trade (WTO) ministers.
- The ILO's governing body is based on tripartite principles: representatives from unions, employers, and government all have a seat at the table. By institutionalizing a role for non-governmental organizations, the ILO achieves a greater degree of openness and accountability.
- Cynics would add that the ILO can afford to be progressive because it is largely powerless. It has no enforcement mechanism for its conventions, and some of the countries that are quickest to ratify have the worst records of living up to them.

The ILO has significant shortcomings as an organization. Perhaps the most important is its cumbersome, bureaucratic nature: it can take forever for the apparatus to make a decision and carry it out. (Of course, that beats the IMF's approach: decisive, reactionary, and authoritarian.) The experience of the ILO tells us that creating a force capable of governing the global economy will be extremely difficult, and that there are hard tradeoffs between democracy, power, and administrative effectiveness. But it also demonstrates that reforming international organizations—changing their missions and governance systems—is worth the effort, especially if it brings non-governmental activists into the picture. ❏

Sources: David Mermelstein, ed., *The Economic Crisis Reader* (Vintage, 1975); Susan George and Fabrizio Sabelli, *Faith and Credit: The World Bank's Secular Empire* (Penguin Books, 1994); Hans-Albrecht Schraepler, *Directory of International Economic Organizations* (Georgetown University Press, 1997); Jayati Ghosh, Lectures on the history of the world economy, Tufts University, 1995; S.W. Black, "International Monetary Institutions," *The New Palgrave: A Dictionary of Economics*, John Eatwell, Murray Milgate, and Peter Newman, eds. (The Macmillan Press Limited, 1987).

ARTICLE 4.2

THE ABCs OF FREE-TRADE AGREEMENTS

BY THE *DOLLARS & SENSE* COLLECTIVE

January/February 2001; updated, December 2006

In the United States, the corporate media have framed the debate over "globalization" largely as a struggle between cosmopolitan advocates and their provincial opponents. The pro-globalization types are celebrated as champions not only of a "global market-place," but also of a worldwide community of peoples brought together by communications, transportation, and commerce, a "global village." Meanwhile, "anti-globalization" protesters face not only tear gas and truncheons, but also accusations of protectionism, isolationism, and disregard for those outside the United States.

International institutions—like the World Trade Organization (WTO), International Monetary Fund (IMF), and World Bank—as well as regional associations—such as the North American Free Trade Agreement (NAFTA), the European Union (EU), the Association of Southeast Asian Nations (ASEAN), and now the Central American Free Trade Agreement (CAFTA)—are primarily concerned with granting capital the freedom to move from country to country. It is true that many opponents of globalization have invoked national sovereignty as a first line of defense against this new wave of aggressive capitalist expansion. In some cases, this reaction has been accompanied by ugly nativist impulses, which join hostility towards international institutions and multinational corporations with hostility towards "foreign" workers. To its credit, however, much of the "global economic justice" movement has deftly avoided the nativist pitfall—avowing a solidarity that crosses all lines of nation and national origin, that stands up "for humanity and against neoliberalism."

Already, part of the movement is grappling with the problematic defense of national sovereignty, advocating instead a brand of grassroots democracy that does not exist very often in either international institutions or national states. Many activists even reject the "anti-globalization" label that has been hung on them, posing their own vision of "globalization from below" against a "globalization dominated by capital." Today, goods and capital pass freely across national frontiers while people run a gauntlet of border patrols and barbed wire. "Globalization from below" turns this status quo, which combines the worst of both worlds, on its head. Instead of the free movement of capital across national borders, "globalization from below" champions the free movement of people. Instead of equal treatment for all investors, no matter where they are investing, it demands equal human and civil rights for all people, no matter where they are living. Instead of greater worldwide integration of multinational corporations, it raises the banner of greater international solidarity among popular movements and organizations. Instead of the "race to the bottom," it calls for an "upward harmonization."

Instead of the rule of capital, the rule of the people. Instead of more inequality, less. Instead of less democracy, more.

That is an appealing vision for the future. At this point, however, "globalization dominated by capital" is still on the march—operating through both global institutions and regional associations. A decade of protests against the WTO and IMF (not only in the United States, but across the world) has shown that resistance is not futile. The immediate effect, however, may be to channel the globalization agenda back into regional "free-trade" agreements. Ultimately, the forces of resistance will need to be far greater to turn the tide. In the meantime, here's what we're up against.

THE NORTH AMERICAN FREE TRADE AGREEMENT (NAFTA)

The North American Free Trade Agreement (NAFTA) came into effect on January 1, 1994. The agreement eliminated most barriers to trade and investment among the United States, Canada and Mexico. For some categories of goods—certain agricultural goods, for example—NAFTA promised to phase out restrictions on trade over a few years, but most goods and services were to be freely bought and sold across the three countries' borders from the start. Likewise, virtually all investments—financial investments as well as investments in fixed assets such as factories, mines, or farms (foreign direct investment)—were freed from cross-border restrictions.

NAFTA, however, made no changes in the restrictions on the movement of labor. Mexican—and, for that matter, Canadian—workers who wish to come to the United States must enter under the limited immigration quotas or illegally. Thus NAFTA gave new options and direct benefits to those who obtain their income from selling goods and making investments, but the agreement included no parallel provision for those who make their incomes by working.

Supporters of NAFTA have argued that both firm owners and workers in all three countries can gain from the removal of trade and investment barriers. For example, the argument goes, U.S. firms that produce more efficiently than their Mexican counterparts will have larger markets, gain more profits, generate more jobs, and pay higher wages. The prime examples would include information technology firms, bio-tech firms, larger retailers, and other U.S. corporations that have an advantage because of skilled U.S. labor or because of experience in organization and marketing. On the other hand, Mexican firms that can produce at low cost because of low Mexican wages will be able to expand into the U.S. market. The main example would be assembly plants or *maquiladoras*.

Critics of the agreement have focused on problems resulting from extreme differences among the member countries in living standards, wages, unionization, environmental laws, and social legislation. The options that NAFTA creates for business firms put them at a great advantage in their dealings with workers and communities. For example, U.S. unions are weakened because firms can more easily shut down domestic operations and substitute operations in Mexico. With the government suppressing independent unions in Mexico, organization of workers in all three countries is undermined. (Actually, the formal Mexican labor laws are probably as good or better than those in the United States but they are usually not enforced.) While NAFTA may mean more jobs and better pay for computer software engineers in the United States, auto-assembly and parts workers in the United States, for example, see their wages stagnate or fall. Similarly, the greater freedom of international movement that NAFTA affords to firms gives them greater bargaining power over communities when it comes to environmental regulations. One highly visible result has been severe pollution problems in Mexican *maquiladora* zones along the U.S. border.

An additional and important aspect of NAFTA is that it creates legal mechanisms for firms based in one country to contest legislation in the other countries when it might interfere with their "right" to carry out their business. Thus, U.S. firms operating in Mexico have challenged stricter environmental regulations won by the Mexican environmental movement. In Canada, the government rescinded a public-health law restricting trade in toxic PCBs as the result of a challenge by a U.S. firm; Canada also paid $10 million to the complaining firm, in compensation for "losses" it suffered under the law. These examples illustrate the way in which NAFTA, by giving priority to the "rights" of business, has undermined the ability of governments to regulate the operation of their economies in an independent, democratic manner.

Finally, one of NAFTA's greatest gifts to business has been the removal of restrictions on the movement of financial capital. The immediate result for Mexico was the severe financial debacle of 1994. Investment funds moved rapidly into Mexico during the early 1990s, and especially after NAFTA went into effect. Without regulation, these investments were able to abandon Mexico just as rapidly when the speculative "bubble" burst, leading to severe drops in production and employment.

FTAA AND CAFTA: EXTENDING THE FREE TRADE AGENDA TO THE WESTERN HEMISPHERE

After the implementation of NAFTA, it looked like the Americas were on a fast track to a hemisphere-wide free-trade zone. In 1994, Clinton proposed to have the world's largest trading block in place by 2005. Instead, the Free Trade Area of the Americas (FTAA) stalled in its tracks when, in 1997, Congress denied Clinton "fast-track" negotiating authority. Bush revived the fast-track push in 2001 and succeeded in getting fast-track legislation through both the House of Representatives and the U.S. Senate in 2002.

What would a realized FTAA look like? There are two near-certainties. First, labor and environmental standards are unlikely to be on the agenda unless popular movements force the issue. Canadian Trade Minister Pierre Pettigrew, for example, told Parliament that labor and environmental side agreements like those in NAFTA would only impede negotiations (Canada chaired the FTAA negotiations process until late 1999 and remains an important booster of the pact). Second, the United States, which accounts for 70% of the hemispheric economy, would dominate any hemisphere-wide economic bloc. As a Brazilian businessman succinctly put it at a July 2000 meeting of the Common Market of the South (Mercado Comun del Sur, or Mercosur), Latin America's largest trading bloc, "Who rules in FTAA is the U.S."

While 2005 came and went without the FTAA, the U.S. Congress did approve by the narrowest of margins the Central American Free Trade Agreement (CAFTA). CAFTA is now in effect for trade between the United States and El Salvador, Honduras, Nicaragua, and Guatemala. The Dominican Republic has also ratified the agreement but Washington has held off on implementing the agreement in a bid to increase protections for large pharmaceutical companies from generic competition. Costa Rica signed the agreement but has yet to ratify it. Economic size alone assures that U.S. interests dominate the agreement. The combined economic output of the countries in Central America is smaller than the total income of just two U.S.-based agribusiness companies that will benefit from the accord: Cargill and Archer Daniels Midland.

CAFTA, modeled after the North American Free Trade Agreement, has all the shortcomings of NAFTA and will do more to promote sustainable development and no less to further human rights and labor abuses in Central America than NAFTA did in Mexico. A recent report from the "Stop CAFTA Coalition" documents the problems evident already just one year into the agreement. First, there are few signs that CAFTA is creating the promised regional textile complex to offset competition from China. Central American garment exports continue to lose market share to their Asian competitors. In addition, CAFTA is contributing to making difficult conditions in the Central American countryside yet worse. U.S. imports of fresh beef, poultry, and dairy products have increased dramatically, displacing local producers, and food prices have risen. Promised monies to contend with the disruption of rural life have not been forthcoming. Finally, CAFTA has done nothing to improve human rights or extend labor rights in Central America. In El Salvador government crackdowns on peaceful demonstrations have increased at the same time that exports have declined. And CAFTA poses yet another danger. Its rules, buried in the technical language of the investment chapter of the agreement, would make it more difficult for the six Central American nations to escape their heavy debt burdens or recover a debt crisis.

THE EUROPEAN UNION (EU)

The European Union (EU) forms the world's largest single market. From its beginnings in 1951 as the six-member European Coal and Steel Community, the association has grown both geographically (now including 15 countries in Central and Western Europe, with plans to expand into Eastern Europe) and especially in its degree of unity. Eleven of the EU's members now share a common currency (the euro), and all national border controls on goods, capital, and people were abolished between member countries in 1993.

Open trade within the EU poses less of a threat for wages and labor standards than NAFTA or the WTO. Even the poorer member countries, such as Spain, Portugal, and Greece, are fairly wealthy and have strong unions and decent labor protections. Moreover, most EU countries, including top economic powers like France, Germany, Italy, and the United Kingdom, are ruled by parties (whether "socialist," social democratic, or labor) with roots in the working-class movement. This relationship has grown increasingly distant in recent years; still, from the perspective of labor, the EU represents a kind of best-case scenario for freeing trade. The results are, nonetheless, cautionary.

The main thrust of the EU, like other trade organizations, has been trade. Labor standards were never fully integrated into the core agenda of the EU. In 1989, 11 of the then-12 EU countries signed the "Charter of the Fundamental Social Rights of Workers," more widely known as the "Social Charter." (Only the United Kingdom refused to sign.) Though the "Social Charter" did not have any binding mechanism—it is described in public communications as "a political instrument containing 'moral obligations'"—many hoped it would provide the basis for "upward harmonization," that is, pressure on European countries with weaker labor protections to lift their standards to match those of member nations with stronger regulations. The 11 years since the adoption of the "Social Charter" have seen countless meetings, official studies, and exhortations but few appreciable results.

Since trade openness was never directly linked to social and labor standards and the "Social Charter" never mandated concrete actions from corporations, European business leaders have kept "Social Europe" from gaining any momentum simply by ignoring it. Although European anti-discrimination rules have forced countries like Britain to adopt the same retirement age for men and women, and regional funds are dispersed each year to bring up the general living standards of the poorest nations, the social dimension of the EU has never been more than an appendage for buying off opposition. As a result, business moved production, investment, and employment in Europe toward countries with low standards, such as Ireland and Portugal.

The EU also exemplifies how regional trading blocs indirectly break down trade regulations with countries outside the bloc. Many Europeans may have hoped that the EU would insulate Europe from competition with countries that lacked social, labor, and environmental standards. While the EU has a common external tariff, each member can maintain its own non-tariff trade barriers. EU rules requiring openness between member countries, however, made it easy to circumvent any EU country's national trade restrictions. Up until 1993, member states used to be able to block indirect imports through health and safety codes or border controls, but with the harmonization of these rules across the EU, governments can no longer do so. Since then, companies have simply imported non-EU goods into the EU countries with the most lax trade rules, and then freely transported the goods into the countries with higher standards. (NAFTA similarly makes it possible to circumvent U.S. barriers against the importation of steel from China by sending it indirectly through Mexico.) EU members that wished to uphold trade barriers against countries with inadequate social, labor, and environmental protections ended up becoming less important trading hubs in the world economy. This has led EU countries to unilaterally abolish restrictions and trade monitoring against non-EU nations. The logic of trade openness seems to be against labor and the environment even when the governments of a trading bloc individually wish to be more protective.

THE ASSOCIATION OF SOUTH EAST ASIAN NATIONS (ASEAN) AND ASIA-PACIFIC ECONOMIC COOPERATION (APEC)

Founded in 1967 at the height of the Vietnam War, the Association of South East Asian Nations (ASEAN) sought to promote "regional security" for its five original members (Indonesia, Malaysia, Philippines, Singapore, and Thailand). After 1975, it focused on counteracting the spread of communism following the defeat of the U.S. military in Vietnam. Beginning in the 1980s, and especially since the collapse of the Soviet Union, the ASEAN agenda turned from fighting communism to "accelerating economic growth" through cooperation and trade liberalization. At the same time, the organization added the remaining countries of Southeast Asia (Brunei Darussalam, Cambodia, Laos, Myanmar, and even Vietnam) to its member list. Today ASEAN oversees a cohesive geographical region with a population of nearly 500 million (about twice that of the United States) and combined output of nearly $750 billion (about one-tenth that of the United States).

ASEAN has pushed for member countries to open up to international trade and capital. While Singapore grew rapidly beginning in the 1960s, and Indonesia, Malaysia, and Thailand grew quickly beginning in the 1970s, high levels of Japanese foreign direct investment pushed the growth rates of these Southeast Asian economies to near double-digit levels in the late 1980s. Still, in the 1990s, increased competition from other developing countries and regional trading partnerships (such as NAFTA and the EU) threatened the stability of these export economies. In 1992, ASEAN adopted its own "free trade" agreement. AFTA, the ASEAN Free Trade Area, lowered tariffs among member nations, and promoted intra-regional trade which now stands at about 25% of the exports of these nations, about twice the level in the early 1970s. In response to the Asian economic crisis, ASEAN member nations agreed at their 1998 summit to further open up their economies, especially their manufacturing sectors, to foreign investment. Ignoring the calls of grassroots movements for controls or taxes on international capital movements, the summit implemented plans allowing 100% foreign ownership of enterprises in member countries, duty-free imports of capital goods, and a minimum for corporate tax breaks of three years.

The ASEAN tradition of "non-intervention" in the internal political affairs of its member states meant that the organization turned a blind eye to the repression of pro-democracy movements in Myanmar, Indonesia, Cambodia, and other countries in the region. Nor has ASEAN insisted that member nations meet International Labor Organization (ILO) core labor conventions. Member states have failed to sign and even denounced conventions recognizing the freedom of workers to organize trade unions, abolishing child and forced labor, and outlawing discrimination in employment. At times, they have brutally attacked trade union movements. ASEAN has also failed to intervene in regional environmental problems, witnessed by its inability in 1999 to fashion an effective regional response to Indonesia's uncontrolled forest fires. The ASEAN reaction to the December 1999 WTO conference was no different. Leaders of ASEAN nations objected to U.S. calls to include core labor standards as part of trade agreements, insisting that they were an attempt to protect U.S. jobs. And Rodolfo Severino, secretary-general of ASEAN, complained that the United States and other rich countries had not lived up to the WTO textile agreement that would allow ASEAN garment exporters greater access to First World markets.

It is China's entry into the WTO, however, that has most threatened ASEAN interests. China had already replaced Southeast Asia as the favorite location of Japanese foreign direct investment, and Chinese exporters of toys, textiles, and other low-wage manufactured products have put ASEAN exporters under pressure. Unfortunately, the ASEAN response to Chinese competition has been to further liberalize its own rules on foreign direct investment.

Chinese competition for the ASEAN nations and the rest of the developing world intensified in January 2005, when the Multifiber Agreement (MFA), the 30-year-old the quota system for that guaranteed a share of the world's clothing market for dozens of poor countries, expired. Chinese-produced garments have flooded world markets undercutting garment producers across the globe. China increased it garments exports to the U.S. market by $6 billion in 2005, increasing its market share from 15% to nearly 27%. Cambodia and Indonesia maintained their market shares, but most Southeast garment producing nations lost market share to China in 2005. But hardest hit by the by the expiration of the MFA has been garment producers in former major quota holders, like Hong Kong, Taiwan, and South Korea, as well as garment producers in Mexico, and sub-Saharan African, despite those nations' trade preferences. The phasing out of the MFA has already cost Africa more than 250,000 jobs over the last few years, reports the International Textile, Garment and Leather Workers' Federation. Most jobs have been lost in Lesotho, South Africa, Swaziland, Nigeria, Ghana, Mauritius, Zambia, Madagascar, Tanzania, Malawi, Namibia and Kenya.

Long before this year's WTO conference, ASEAN member states recognized that their economic interests went well beyond the boundaries of Southeast Asia. In the late 1980s, Prime Minister Mahathir Mohammed of Malaysia called for the formation of a pan-Asian regional economic bloc to include, along with the ASEAN countries, Japan, China, Korea, Taiwan, and Hong Kong, the largest investors in Southeast Asia. Mahathir's proposal was met with stiff opposition from the West. At the United

States' insistence, the Asia-Pacific Economic Cooperation forum (including the United States, Canada, Australia, New Zealand, and Korea, along with ASEAN members Brunei Darussalam, Indonesia, Malaysia, and the Philippines) was formed. The Asia-Pacific Economic Cooperation (APEC) today consists of 21 members, having added Chile, China, Hong Kong, Taiwan, Mexico, Papua New Guinea, Peru, Russia, and Vietnam to its 12 founding members. Unlike ASEAN, APEC members do not form a cohesive region other than bordering on the Pacific. APEC has no formal criteria for membership, but actual or promised trade liberalization is a de facto condition for entry. While commitments made by APEC members are formally voluntary and non-binding, APEC pressures governments to remove trade and investment restrictions faster than they would following their own agenda.

APEC is heavily influenced by large corporations. In 1996 it even adopted "APEC means business" as its official slogan. While APEC is not an official trading bloc, APEC's push for lower tariffs has proceeded further and faster than the WTO's free-trade agenda. APEC is calling for free trade among APEC nations by 2010 for "developed nations" and 2020 for "developing nations." In addition, APEC pushes labor market policies guaranteed to impose hardships on workers. For instance, in response to the Asian economic crisis, APEC counseled member countries to "maintain flexibility in domestic labor markets," advice sure to mean lower wages and more layoffs for workers already suffering from the effects of the Asian economic crisis. And while pledging to promote "environmentally sustainable development," APEC has done little to combat the depletion of national resources and deforestation, especially in developing nations. APEC has also insisted that member economies harmonize food and product safety standards, which means high standards are likely to be replaced by the lowest common denominator. ❑

Sources: Brian Hanson, "What Happened to Fortress Europe?: External Trade Policy Liberalization in the European Union," International Organization, 52, no. 1 (Winter 1998), 55-86; Linda Lim, "ASEAN: New Modes of Economic Cooperation," in *Southeast Asia in the New World Order*, Wurfel and Burton; ASEAN Web, www.asean.or.id; APEC Secretariat, www.apecsec. org.sg,; SAY NO TO APEC <www.apec.gen.nz>.

Article 4.3

BEYOND THE WORLD CREDITORS' CARTEL

In Latin America and elsewhere, the IMF may be re-emerging—but in a changed landscape.

BY DARIUSH SOKOLOV
September/October 2009

One group of financiers seems to be doing nicely out of the global recession: the International Monetary Fund and other international financial institutions (IFIs) are enjoying a return to relevance and lining up for increased funding.

The London G20 Summit in April was the IMF's big comeback gig. In 2007 the fund's loan book was down to just $20 billion; now its capital is set to triple to $750 billion, plus permission to issue $250 billion in "special drawing rights" (the fund's quasi-currency which allows member countries to borrow from each others' reserves). Since September 2008 a range of East European and ex-Soviet states have taken out new loans. So too have Pakistan, El Salvador, and Iceland—the fund's first Western European client since Britain in 1976.

The World Bank and regional development banks are also getting in on the party. In Latin America, the World Bank's regional vice president Pamela Cox says she expects lending to triple in 2009 to $14 billion. The Inter-American Development Bank (IDB), the most active IFI in the region, expects to lend $18 billion—its typical loan portfolio is under $8 billion. And the development banks are queuing up behind the IMF with their caps out for capital increases: the Asian Development Bank wants to triple its capital to $165 billion; the IDB is asking for an extra $50 to $80 billion on top of its current $101 billion.

Why now? The IFIs, says Vince McElhinny of the Bank Information Center, a group that monitors them, are opportunists at heart. Just like any private bank or corporation they fight for market share, and as the world economy and global capital markets grow they need to increase their lending apace or lose relevance. The freezing of world capital markets, particularly severe in emerging markets, has created a need which they can seize as opportunity. The Institute of International Finance predicts private net capital flows to emerging markets of $141 billion in 2009, down from $392 billion in 2008, after a record $890 billion in 2007. The IFIs see themselves helping to fill this gap.

But the issues at stake here go beyond the IFIs' own agendas. On the one hand, their revival implies a reassertion of U.S. and global North dominance. They aren't called "Washington-based" just as a matter of real estate: the United States has a 17% voting share on the IMF and World Bank, enough to give it a veto on some major changes; Europe and the United States control the top management positions.

On the other hand, the story underscores how parts of the global South are gaining in economic power. In the crises of the 1990s, or so the neoliberal story went, the IMF stepped in to clean up the messes made when fragile Third World econo-mies exploded. This time around things are very different: the mess is in the North, and the likelihood is that the emerging economies of Asia and Latin America will emerge from it stronger and more independent. (It's important to note, though, that large areas in the South, notably Africa, are not part of this story—nor is Eastern Europe.) The so-called BRIC nations in particular (Brazil, Russia, India, China) are getting the bargaining power to back up their claims on the global financial system. Will these claims be met within the existing institutions, or by creating a new finan-cial architecture that bypasses Washington altogether? The future of the IFIs is a key arena in which global rebalancing of economic power is playing out.

New Financial Architecture?

In May 2007 finance ministers from Brazil, Argentina, Venezuela, Bolivia, and Ecuador signed the "Quito declaration" in the Ecuadorian capital. The plan includes a regional monetary fund and moves toward a South American single currency, but the first step is the creation of the Banco del Sur, a new regional development bank. While the bank's launch is behind schedule, this March its constitution was agreed to, with an initial capitalization of $7 billion. Besides the original five, Paraguay and Uruguay are also members. (Even Colombia had announced its support before its late-2007 row with Venezuela over hostages.)

The aim of Banco del Sur is to replace the Washington-based lenders altogether with institutions run by and for South America. Maria Jose Romero, who researches the IFIs at the Third World Institute in Montevideo, encapsulates this spirit. "In responding to the crisis Latin American countries have two options," she says. "We can return to the old institutions and the failed recipes of the 1990s, or we can move forward with alternatives."

For many Latin American countries a return to the IMF is politically out of the question. According to Mark Weisbrot, co-director of the Center for Economic and Policy Research in Washington, the decline of the IMF started with the Asian financial crisis over a decade ago. After the fund's failure to act as emergency lender of last resort to Asian banking systems in 1997, those states moved to build up size-able currency reserves, determined not to be dependent on the fund again; others followed suit.

This turning away has been more dramatic in Latin America, where IMF policies are blamed for precipitating the 1998 crisis in Argentina which led to the collapse of its banking system and eventually to its 2002 default. Argentina and Bolivia both paid off the last of their debts to the fund in 2006; in April 2007 Ecuador announced it had paid off its IMF loans and requested the fund withdraw its country manager; the same month Venezuela announced itself debt-free, and a few weeks later said it would withdraw from fund membership altogether. When Daniel Ortega won the Nicaraguan presidential election in May 2007 he promised the country would be "free from the fund" within five years.

How has this freedom-from-Washington line held in the current crisis? U.S.-friendly Mexico was the first to sign up for the new Flexible Credit Lines the IMF is granting without conditions to "pre-approved" governments, followed by Colombia—though neither has yet drawn on them. So far only El Salvador and Costa Rica have taken out new loans. In sharp contrast to Eastern Europe, most Latin American states had healthy reserve cushions coming into the crunch. And with commodity prices now rising again, it may be that the region's anti-IMF resolve is not going to face the test many had anticipated.

As for Banco del Sur, the arrival of crisis no doubt slowed the process: domestic firefighting comes before regional cooperation. But, according to Romero, in the medium term it will help push change:

"The crisis has focused attention to the failings of the existing financial system," she says. "It is helping build the impetus for Banco del Sur, as well as for moves to settle bilateral trade in local currencies [rather than dollars], which is the first step towards monetary union, and for broader South-South cooperation initiatives."

To be fair, Banco del Sur may not live up to proponents' hopes. With just $7 billion in capital, the bank won't be in the same league as the Washington-based IFIs. Nor is there any immediate plan to create an emergency monetary fund—an Ecuadorian proposal to that effect has been dropped. And the principle of one country one vote, perhaps the biggest rallying point of all, has been modified: equal votes will apply only on loans under $70m, above which approval is required from members with two-thirds of the capital contributions.

Finally, there is still no clarity on the focus of lending. Campaigners hope for a true emphasis on poverty reduction and projects to build regional cooperation, and have scored the provision of a socially focused "audit board." But some fear that more conservative members (read: Brazil) could push Banco del Sur toward being just one more development bank.

Across Asia, there are parallel developments. A proposal by Japan to set up an Asian Monetary Fund met the same fate as an earlier Malaysian-backed scheme called the East Asian Economic Caucus—both were dropped after expressions of disapproval from the IMF and U.S. officials. But now the Chiang Mai Initiative, a longstanding plan for a system of swap arrangements between the central banks of the southeast Asian countries plus China, Japan, and South Korea is expected to come on line this year, and the proposed size of the scheme was upped to $120 billion in February. Chiang Mai is linked to the IMF (members need IMF agreements in place to withdraw more than 20% of the total), but some see it leading towards an eventual independent regional fund. For now, though, at least officially, the talk is usually of "complementing," not supplanting, the IMF.

Rise of the BRICs

If the Quito project is the idealistic side of the regionalization movement, the BRIC bloc is global power shift as realpolitik. The BRICs together now account for 22% of world production (by purchasing power parity), up from 16% ten years ago and rising.

Even as they move ahead with building regional institutions independent of the IFIs, the BRICs are pushing for more power within the Washington-based institutions. Increased say at the IMF is one of the four governments' main demands. In March 2008 China's vote share was raised all the way up to 3.7%—putting the world's most populous country on a par with Belgium plus the Netherlands, combined population 27 million. The BRICs jointly muster a 9.82% quota.

According to Vince McElhinny, the BRICs' contributions to the fund's current capital boost are aimed at bolstering their demands for more say in IFI governance. When, a week before the BRIC summit, Brazil's President Lula announced a $10 billion contribution, he talked of thereby gaining "moral authority to keep pushing for changes needed at the IMF."

The IMF's desire to placate emerging powers such as the BRICs may explain the makeover it has displayed in its current comeback—dubbed "IMF 2.0" by *Time* magazine. Managing director Dominique Strauss-Kahn has called for the fund to spend against recession: less structural adjustment, more counter-cyclical stimulus. But the changes may be largely cosmetic. According to a study by the Third World Network, the actual conditions of recent IMF loans to Pakistan, Hungary, Ukraine, and other countries are familiar: the borrowers must reduce their fiscal deficits through public spending cuts, wage freezes, higher fuel tariffs, and interest rate hikes.

What real changes are the BRICs really likely to get? There's plenty of gossip flying around: some are touting Lula as the next World Bank president; perhaps China will get to pick Strauss-Kahn's successor.

Mark Weisbrot, however, does not see the U.S. government giving any ground on voting shares. "The U.S. would rather walk away from the IMF than give up control," he says.

Beyond the Cartel

Weisbrot describes the IMF as "the most important instrument of influence the U.S. government has in developing countries—beyond the military, beyond the CIA. Or, at least, that's the role it's played for most of the last 30 years. A good part of that influence has been lost recently; now they're trying to get it back."

The IMF's power has never really been about its own lending, however. Its influence over countries' economic policies is far greater than would be suggested by its share in overall capital flows. The real issue is the fund's role as "gatekeeper" of a global "creditors' cartel."

Multilateral loans from the World Bank and regional development banks and bilateral loans from the wealthy countries typically come with some form of "cross-conditionality" clause. You only get your loan if you first have an IMF agreement in place; installments only keep flowing so long as you stick to it. Similar conditions can also apply in private capital transactions. For instance,

Venezuela's 2007 threat to give up its IMF membership triggered a market sell-off because under covenants written into its sovereign bonds, a break with the fund would count as a "technical default."

Now, though, recent shifts in Latin America have dealt what Weisbrot says could be "a final blow to the IMF creditors' cartel in middle-income countries."

This is a continental tale, but Argentina is a good place to begin. The country cut itself off from international capital markets with its 2002 default, and is still being chased by "hold-out" bond investors in the New York courts. Yet Argentina grew at almost 9% a year from 2003 through 2007—the country's most rapid growth in 50 years, and some of the fastest growth rates on the continent. This expansion has been funded largely by selling bonds to another emerging regional power, Venezuela. These bond transfers are no subsidies—Argentina pays commercial interest rates—but they do come free of Washington conditions. For Weisbrot, "Venezuela's offers of credit, without policy conditions, to Argentina, Bolivia, Ecuador, Nicaragua, and other countries has changed the equation."

It's true that easy Venezuelan credit dried up early on in the crisis as oil prices plummeted. It's also true that Argentina is now allowing IMF staff in to monitor its economy and taking out new loans from the World Bank and the IDB. But it's telling that Argentina got these loans without any IMF agreement in place: the cartel, at least in its old form, appears to be broken. And then there's the other plank in Argentina's current crisis management strategy: a $10.2 billion swap line direct with China.

In short, the IMF and allied institutions have regained some lost ground in the crisis, but forms of "South-South cooperation" that stand to weaken the Washington-based creditors' cartel have kept on building too.

According to one very plausible interpretation, this crisis has been about the consequences of the rich countries' capital piling into the financial services sphere to compensate for the loss of manufacturing production to the Third World. Control of the world's financial capital flows was one last highly profitable channel where Northern capital still ruled unopposed. Increasingly, though, global-South states and corporations are cutting out the middle man to trade directly with each other. It's against the background of these new possibilities that the next chapter in the story of the IFIs will play out. ❑

Sources: "Special Drawing Rights (SDRs)," IMF fact sheet, Feb. 2009; "IMF 2.0," *Time*, April 20, 2009; Third World Network, "The IMF's Financial Crisis Loans: No change in conditionalities," March 2009; Institute of International Finance, "Capital Flows to Emerging Markets," June 10, 2009; "Latin America in the Midst of the Global Financial Meltdown: A Systemic Proposal," Latin American Shadow Financial Regulatory Committee Statement No. 19, December 2008; Felix Salmon's blog on Ecuador's default, blogs.reuters.com/felix-salmon/; Mark Weisbrot, "Ten Years After: The Lasting Impact of the Asian Financial Crisis," Center for Economic and Policy Research, August 2007; Tadahiro Asami, "Chiang Mai Initiative as the foundation of financial stability in East Asia," ASEAN, March 2005; DominicWilson and Roopa Purushothaman, "DreamingWith BRICs: The Path to 2050," Goldman Sachs Global Economics Paper No. 99, Oct. 2003; Eugenio Diaz-Bonilla, "Argentina's recent growth episode," RGE Monitor, Sept. 18, 2007; Graham Turner, *The Credit Crunch: Housing Bubbles, Globalisation and the Worldwide Economic Crisis,* Pluto Press, 2008.

Article 4.4

THE SOCIAL COSTS OF NEOLIBERALISM IN CHINA
An interview with economist Han Deqiang

July/August 2007

Han Deqiang is a prolific economist at the Economics and Management School, Beijing University of Aeronautics and Astronautics, and one of a growing number of Chinese scholars critical of the country's neoliberal development strategy. Han, however, did not just arrive at this stance. He has been critical of neoliberal ideology in China for almost two decades and has written many books and articles on the social crises that rural and urban workers have faced under China's new economic regime.

When I first met Han, in 2000, he was making his way around the country delivering sharp and eloquent lectures to university students refuting the then-dominant faith. At the time, I was conducting research on workers' protests against privatization in Zhengzhou, and most of the labor activists and workers' leaders I met were familiar with Han's devastating critiques of the privatization craze that swept China in the late 1990s and early 2000s. It would not be wrong to characterize him as a Chinese Noam Chomsky, albeit with his own oratorical flair!

In September 2005, I interviewed Han for about three hours. Our discussion focused on the impact of China's 2001 entry into the World Trade Organization and on the social costs, both in and outside of China, of the accelerated neoliberal development that followed that milestone. In January 2007, I followed up with a second interview. What follows is a translated and edited version of both interviews.

—Stephen Philion

STEPHEN PHILION: The last time I met with you was during the height of the East Asian financial crisis. At that time, we discussed the consequences you foresaw for China of entering the World Trade Organization (WTO). Five years later, which of those consequences have come about?

HAN DEQIANG: At the time, I argued the greatest damage would be to China's capacity to control its industrial and technological development autonomously. I think it's safe to say these last five years have more than proven that true. In China, any industry that wants to develop its own technology or markets has encountered increasingly great barriers.

Second, I predicted that unemployment would rise dramatically; this has also shown itself to be a reality. Of course, some say that there has been a shortage of migrant workers from the countryside recently, which allegedly proves that the WTO has not produced greater unemployment. But this requires a more careful analysis. In the late 1990s, agricultural commodity prices fell, and taxes became heavier. Hence the large mass of migrant workers and the ensuing rise in urban unemployment we saw then. However, starting around 2002-2003, the government implemented new tax cuts for farmers and increased education subsidies in poor rural districts. As a result of these new policies, the contradictions in the country-side were mollified some. Also, when the price of rice plummeted, large numbers of farmers stopped producing it. As a result, the price rebounded, improving the livelihood of farmers in 2003 and 2004. So rural dwellers now had less motivation to accept the kind of exploitation that exists in the for-export sector of urban industry, much less migrate to the cities in search of it! However, this doesn't nullify our argument that when foreign companies conquer national industries, greater unemployment results. The opposite actually. When Wal-Mart goes to Gweiyang or Beijing, say, they knock out, in an instant, four or five department stores.[1]

PHILION: And smaller shops?

HAN: Hah! Don't even go there! Medium-size department stores, neighborhood sellers, ones that were supposed to be able to dominate local markets by virtue of their size—they saw those advantages disappear.

Third, I have always acknowledged that WTO entry would provide China certain short-term gains. For example, increases in investment and exports undoubtedly occurred. But I argued that WTO entry was the equivalent of drinking moonshine to deal with thirst. This has two outcomes. One, of course, is the removal of thirst. After all, if there are no other liquids around, I have no choice but to turn to moonshine. But the other result, of course, is your death! So Chinese industry has resolved its investment problem, but that has been accompanied by its death knell.

From what I see, the social crisis facing China will continue to intensify, as will the neglect of China's economic autonomy, in addition to the eventual breakdown of the country's financial system. This is entirely foreseeable; it's only a matter of time before China faces something along the lines of the 1997 East Asian financial crisis. We cannot predict exactly when it will occur, but I suspect it isn't that far off in the future.

PHILION: How has the WTO affected large state-owned enterprises?

HAN: State-owned enterprises (SOEs) fall into two categories. The first are SOEs, like Shenyang Machine Factory or Luoyang Tractor Company, that are subject to competition with private companies. These quickly went bankrupt. Monopoly-sector SOEs, such as petroleum producers, are less directly affected by China's membership in the WTO.

PHILION: The Chinese leadership seems to be working under the assumption that as long as the SOEs that produce the greatest revenues remain vital, Chinese socialism can be sustained.

---

1 By 2006, there were already more than 50 Wal-Mart stores in China.

HAN: First of all, China's not socialist now.

PHILION: Yes, right. I mean in their sense of the phrase, so-called "socialism with Chinese characteristics."

HAN: Not likely either. It is true that in terms of tax contributions and profits, the small and medium-size SOEs are not great, but in the absolute numbers they employ, they are considerable. Their influence on local employment and finances is pretty substantial. So, in the aftermath of the near complete collapse of these small and medium-size SOEs, for the central state to rely on large enterprises alone for maintaining the subsistence of China's population of 1.3 billion becomes extremely difficult.

PHILION: It seems as though the leadership's hope is for local and foreign private capital to replace these small and medium-size companies as the source of investment and to resolve the unemployment problem in the process.

HAN: What I would contend is that for every one job saved by foreign capitalist investment, three to four will be lost unless the foreign investment produces for foreign export alone. This situation does exist, assuredly. Right now 60% of our export is fueled by foreign companies' investment. However, the potential for foreign investment to instigate future Chinese economic growth is weak. It can only largely resolve a segment of the unemployment problem. It can't do much in terms of advancing the upgrading or expansion of China's industrial system.

And its use to resolve the fiscal crisis facing China is even more problematic. From '49 on, we built our nation by using state enterprise to supplement or replace foreign enterprise's contribution to the economy. The idea of doing the opposite is a fantasy.

PHILION: China's leaders also seem to believe that as long as the monopoly-based state-owned enterprises are run well, their ability to determine the direction of the economic development will be strong.

HAN: This is a twofold issue. First, whether or not it's possible for the political leadership of a country with no state-owned enterprise to control the direction of the national economy. I think it might be possible. It's the European model, after all, and even in a certain way the American model. In these economies, by and large, control of enterprises is in the hands of private parties. But this doesn't have that much impact on the state's tax receipts and its role in regulating the economy. If the state is powerful, it can play a crucial role in the management of the economy even if it doesn't control much enterprise.

On the other hand, where the state controls a major portion of enterprises but is weak, it has a difficult time managing the economy. And if the collaboration between that weak state and private interests is deep, the result is distortion of policy by capitalists to the point that the state loses more and more capacity to control the economy and the direction of economic development. The key factor here is the strength of the government, not how many companies it controls.

PHILION: Then what is the likelihood of China going in the direction of Japan developmentally?

HAN: I don't think it's possible for China to go that route. The leadership doesn't even have that as a working concept. The Japanese experience is one that greatly emphasizes the role of state planning.

PHILION: Interesting, because the U.S. government complains that China still places too much emphasis on central planning in the economy.

HAN: America likewise is dissatisfied with Japan's level of state planning. America is also dissatisfied with France in this respect. [Laughs.] Is there any country that America is satisfied with? Seriously, today the role of the state and of monopoly SOEs is far greater in Japan than in China. Also, from what I understand of Japanese history, Japan has an elite that has a strong sense of responsibility for the nation's future. But I can't find any such elite in China today. If Japan's leaders lose a war, they feel great shame. They don't send their children off to America.

PHILION: What is your assessment of how different classes view the WTO and liberalization in China?

HAN: Chinese workers and farmers are in a pickle. But is it the damage caused by political power elites or that caused by markets that is greatest? Right now, in their view the pain caused by entry into the WTO is not as great as that caused by the power of government cadres. For example, state workers view layoffs as only indirectly caused by markets; the abuse of power by the Party is viewed as their direct cause.

PHILION: Of course they're interconnected.

HAN: That's right. Domestically it's a matter of a corrupt officialdom; internationally it's a matter of submitting to the will of international capital. The WTO represents international capital's control over China. But of course it is Chinese government policies that make this control possible. So what the masses experience is a problem created by their government, not by the WTO or global monopoly capital.

For example, state workers have to pay income tax once their wages exceed 800 yuan a month. But a worker in a foreign-owned enterprise does not have to pay the tax until after 2,000 or 3,000 yuan a month. This government tax policy results in a positive feeling toward foreign-owned companies on the part of the average Chinese worker. They don't see that the better wages and better profits in the private sector are a product of the government support that sector enjoys. Not to mention many other kinds of special benefits that foreign capitalists enjoy thanks to government policies that simultaneously disadvantage domestic state companies. The ironic result is that many state companies go to Hong Kong and falsely register as foreign companies in order to enjoy these advantageous policies—the so-called fake foreign devil problem.

PHILION: In the past few years, have these views changed at all?

HAN: There has been some change in attitude, yes—especially in terms of recognizing the threat that WTO entry poses to China's future. So the push for economic autonomy is a theme that you now see cropping up in every Chinese web discussion board, far more than five years ago.

PHILION: You've spoken about the kinds of losses that have befallen China upon entering the WTO. In the United States we hear the same concerns, only it's America that is considered to be the victim of China's entry into the WTO! This is so especially in terms of unemployment: it is frequently said that China should be held responsible for America's unemployment problems.

HAN: To be accurate, we should say that America's bosses need to take responsibility for America's unemployment problems. Why? Because since China entered the WTO, both China's workers and America's workers have been hurt. However, in fact, many bosses in China have also suffered losses due to the WTO. The operation of the WTO causes great losses to both workers *and* bosses in developing countries as well as to workers in developed countries. Broadly speaking, only one group doesn't suffer losses, namely, bosses in developed countries. So to get to the source of the United States' unemployment problem, Americans need to analyze the responsibility of the Bush administration, the bosses at GM and Microsoft, etc.

PHILION: Not to mention the Democratic Party!

HAN: Indeed. Whoever is promoting the WTO is promoting the interests of transnational corporations and doing harm to American and Chinese workers. It's not only developing countries' workers who are hurt by globalization; it's really the world. Globalization gives rise to global recession, not prosperity. Consider a number of indicators that demonstrate this. Globally, debt levels have increased since the 1980s, in terms of both national debt and average citizens' credit overload. Second, the whole world exists in a state of high unemployment. The U.S. unemployment rate is much higher than it was in the 1950s and 1960s. Ditto Europe, whose unemployment rate is even higher! Japan likewise. Third, growth rates have fallen globally compared to those in the 1950s and 1960s. This, of course, is hidden by large rates of credit-fuelled debt, without which growth rates would be even lower. All of this indicates global recession, not global prosperity.

PHILION: What about China's economy? Its promoters argue that liberalization has generated constant growth.

HAN: In the 1990s, China and the United States both grew. However, look at the overall global economic picture. Latin America has seen great declines in growth and serious crises; Africa even worse. The Middle East is in a state of chaos and misfortune, Russia's GDP is only half of what it was in the 1980s, and the East Asian "tigers" have been in a state of recession since the region's financial crisis. Japan's debt in proportion to GDP is the highest in the world, roughly 130%, and its rate of growth has been somewhere near zero. If the government hadn't invested so much in the economy, it's possible Japan's rate of growth would be negative, -4% or -5%! If this isn't depression, what is?

Thus, my definition of globalization is global depression. This departs, of course, from mainstream propaganda. Even many of the anti-globalization movements are fond of arguing that globalization still has its positive points, that it just needs to take into account and protect the interests of developing countries and of workers in developed countries. It's as though if we just removed some of the shortcomings of the process, all would be well. My view is that globalization is nothing short of a massive mistake.

PHILION: In the United States, especially but not solely in the Democratic Party, there's a common notion that the U.S. government must implement economic sanctions against China and pursue higher tariffs in order to protect American jobs. So, for example, Rep. Charles Schumer (D-N.Y.) recently asserted that the conditions China sets for foreign investors aren't as good as those the United States provides for Chinese importers.

HAN: That's quite the exaggeration, eh? Laughable! It's actually the exact opposite. American corporations have enjoyed such high profits in China. Which is in the better position to buy up a company abroad, China or the United States? The benefits China gives to U.S. investments in terms of tax breaks, reductions in land prices, and the like are the kinds of things a Chinese investor in the United States can only dream about. And in terms of volume, Chinese investment in the United States is small in comparison to what it's imagined to be by Schumer types. His words are typical politician rhetoric.

In any event, I welcome America protecting its own markets. Likewise, I can declare American commodities unwelcome in China, along with American investment. If the countries of the world stopped welcoming U.S. investment, watch and see how long America could stand it! Its empire would erode quickly! Its existence is dependent on foreign investment and foreign consumption of its exports in order to maintain a higher standard of living.

PHILION: How much influence will a recession or a worse crisis in the United States have on China? It seems as if China is more and more able to withstand the impact.

HAN: Well, I would say rather that if America catches a cold, China will catch a very serious cold or flu. The United States is still the main market for China's exports. An economic crisis in the United States would definitely result in large numbers of bankruptcies throughout China's coastal regions. And if a U.S. crisis caused the value of the dollar to drop, that would also have a huge impact on the Chinese economy because the real size of the U.S. debt would decrease, as would China's foreign exchange holdings. It would basically mean all our hard work in the service of American profits was a waste.

PHILION: How do you regard the possibility of revaluing the renminbi [the official name of China's currency, abbreviated RMB]?

HAN: To date we haven't seen a real revaluation, only a very small one. The pressure in China against revaluation is huge. Why? If we revalue the RMB upwards, China's exports will be less competitively priced, and the strategy of relying on foreign exports for development will fall apart. I suspect America's leadership wants us to devalue the currency by 20% or 30%. Or at the very least 10%. But even at 10%, the export companies in the coastal provinces would face a crisis of survival.

Of course, U.S. pressure on China to revalue is great. If the U.S. government is not willing to compromise on this issue, Chinese leaders will have a hard time dealing with the political discontent that would result. And if Chinese exports can't go to America, but American imports continue apace, the cycle of trade that makes China's development possible will not last. The United States simultaneously wants to reduce imports in order to protect its markets *and* open up more markets in China that it can export to. Short-term, that's possible; long-term, forget it.

PHILION: But in any case the reliance is mutual, no? The United States is quite reliant on cheap Chinese imports.

HAN: Yes, but American reliance on China is not as great as Chinese reliance on America's economy. Why is that? China's exports are low relative to overall U.S. imports, whereas China's exports to the United States are high in relation to total Chinese exports. Furthermore, American exports to China tend to be those that are less replicable. But what China produces can be produced in almost any country. Thus, when China negotiates, it's from a weaker position.

American politicians are shortsighted. Too much power is concentrated in U.S. hands now, and they don't wish to let other hands in on that control. They don't even take into consideration the needs of foreign leaders who collaborate on behalf of U.S. interests abroad. If American politicians continue like this, they won't have any collaborators left—they'll all be overthrown! What good is that in the eyes of the American ruling class, eh? [Laughs.] So if U.S. leaders really want to extend America's capacity to exploit the world's resources, they're going to have to learn to compromise more.

PHILION: Perhaps from their vantage point there is no alternative. Under this current stage of intensified global competition for profits, perhaps they have little choice but to enforce U.S. hegemony more forcefully and totally.

HAN: But if they really want to reorganize this world economy, they're going to have to increase demand for goods and services in developing countries. That would save the world economy, no? But U.S. politicians and elites won't do this.

PHILION: Has the pace of privatization since WTO entry been faster or slower than you anticipated?

HAN: Privatization has been the basic thrust of China's economic reform policies for the last 20 years. While privatization was already moving along quite rapidly, entering the WTO only added to that.

PHILION: What about privatization of large state-owned companies in China?

HAN: That's underway, but its form differs from other sectors of the state enterprise economy. Small enterprises are subjected to buy-outs or else bankruptcy. Larger companies typically don't need to declare bankruptcy—their profits are still guaranteed because of their monopoly position. And if they were sold off, too much "face" would be lost. However, there are still ways to move in that direction.

One way is to convert state enterprises into stock-holding companies and allow foreign purchase of the stock, thus handing part of the management power over to foreign investors. This mechanism presents an increased threat to the autonomy of the Chinese state—which wouldn't be the case if we were talking about Chinese investors buying up these shares, even though we'd still be talking about privatization. This kind, however, is not only a sell-off of companies, but in effect the sell-off of the country—a re-colonization! A foreign company doesn't even have to buy up an entire state enterprise; a proportion of shares that enables it to dominate production decisions and priorities will do the trick. It's a classic form of imperial control in the economic realm.

PHILION: In 2000, there was a widespread concern in the Chinese media, in academic and business circles, about the problem of insufficient domestic demand—consumers not buying goods, investors not investing, instead waiting to see if prices would go lower. The Chinese government made large investments in public projects to stimulate demand. Have the government's efforts to address the demand problem had any results?

HAN: There are two policies that could be used: expand national demand by reducing the income gap and getting more money into the hands of the masses; or create a bubble. What we're doing is the second one: creating a bubble to cover up the problems spawned by inadequate national demand. Primarily this is seen in real estate bubbles: real estate markets experienced great investment after portions of real estate were subjected to market reforms. Meanwhile, the first strategy has not been employed. In fact, the gap between the incomes of the rich and the poor has grown to a shocking degree, far faster than the growth in GDP.

PHILION: Can you talk about the economic policies of the current government?

HAN: In 2002, with the nomination of Hu Jintao as Party secretary, his apparent commitment to protecting China's national interests, unlike the previous leadership, gave those like myself some hope. He also expresses more concern about the gap between rich and poor, as well as the rights of urban and rural laborers. Our optimism has not been entirely mistaken. But we still feel that his responses to these problems have been inadequate.

The policy of eliminating rural taxes was well received; plainly, taxing the wealthy should come before taxing farmers! Also, the recent arrest of Go Cujun, who represents the pro-privatization wing of the Party, would not likely have taken place without Hu Jintao's support. These actions have contributed to a certain comfort level among critics of privatization in China, as have other developments. For example, recently the National Research Institute published a white paper on the failure of health care reform. This is the first time an official institution has publicly repudiated a particular aspect of economic reform. Also, the Technology Ministry recently took issue publicly with the view of China's head WTO negotiating representative Long Yuantu that China doesn't need its own technology, that we can purchase it all from foreign companies investing in China. This we consider an important event as well.

Naturally, the things that I see as positive, the neoliberal rightwingers in China see as a disaster.

PHILION: There is a neoliberal economist at Peking University who has come under considerable public criticism recently, and you've been a party to that. Five years ago, it would have been hard to imagine so many intellectuals and other comrades in such an open struggle with neoliberal economists in China.

HAN: You're right—now there are more academics who are critical of neoliberalism's price tag in China. Our numbers are better these days, as is our ability to coordinate with each other.

We are not critical of reform. There is obviously a need for reform and for attracting a certain amount of foreign investment in China. We don't at all advocate the closing off of China's market. Our opponents like to accuse us of being against reform. What we are opposed to is their neoliberalism that sees markets as the be-all and end-all. We support socialist reform that improves the social position of workers and farmers and that strengthens the position of China. We're not against that kind of reform at all!

PHILION: Wal-Mart's agreement to allow unions in its facilities in China has been in the news. Will this have any impact, or is it more appearance than substance?

HAN: As I see it, China's requirement that a union be established at Wal-Mart does not mean the situation of Wal-Mart's workers has improved. Nor does it mean that China's workers will be able to create independent unions, free from the official Party-controlled All China Federation of Trade Unions (ACFTU). Instead, we see Wal-Mart creating a union that will be under the control of the employer in order to erode the pressure from unofficial, underground union movements. This ends up making the ACFTU look good and seem able to accomplish something real. At the same time, it can put a pretty face on foreign investors' role in China as being no different from Chinese companies. Look at it this way: Wal-Mart has established a union, so it's become a Chinese company! This suits ACFTU leaders who are sympathetic with such employer-friendly unions as well as many intellectuals who stand by such unions and look at labor issues from the perspective of employers, whether we're talking about state-owned enterprises or domestic or foreign-owned capitalist companies.

PHILION: The government has recently placed some regulations on multinational corporations investing in China—which, tellingly, the corporations have been resisting. Do you think they are likely to be effective?

HAN: Regulations on foreign investors have existed forever, and when concern is expressed in civil society about investors, new regulations are devised. Nonetheless, whether it's central government ministries, or local governments, or state-owned enterprise administrators, none tend to take these regulations too seriously. Attracting business investment and allowing foreign investors access to China's national resources and control over critical industrial sectors remain the central policy directions—ones that are proceeding at a rapid pace.

PHILION: What are the present prospects for household income distribution in terms of developing a viable domestic consumer market for China's future growth?

HAN: In 2006, across sectors, salaries generally increased, especially among lower-level wage earners. The rate of unpaid back wages has also decreased. These are all favorable phenomena. However, consumer goods have seen rapid price inflation, which has hit low-wage workers especially hard, essentially eliminating what wage gains they've experienced. That's in part why income disparities continue to grow.

PHILION: Have there been any improvements in the conditions for workers in the SOEs? Is the SOE sector likely to continue to be a source of labor protests in the future, or do you see it becoming quieter? Why so?

HAN: The policy of mass layoffs that was so widespread in the state sector until recently has basically ended. Also, state workers who are presently employed have more wage security than private-sector workers, so they are less inclined toward conflict. However, those state workers who have been laid off or reassigned remain dissatisfied with the status quo. ❏

Article 4.5

FROM NAFTA TO THE SPP

Here comes the Security and Prosperity Partnership, but—what security? whose prosperity?

BY KATHERINE SCIACCHITANO
January/February 2008

Which is closer to your vision of North America?

Vision A: Three interdependent countries with vibrant social movements, respect for labor rights, and environmentally sustainable economies anchored in provision of social needs and respect for cultural autonomy?

Or Vision B: An unequal alliance dominated by the United States, complete with pumped up oil and gas production, increasing militarization, corporate transnational planning groups, and guest worker programs to ensure cheap, vulnerable labor?

If your answer is Vision A, there's good news and bad news. The good news is that this past August at a summit of the leaders of the United States, Canada, and Mexico in Montebello, Quebec, labor, environmental and globalization activists braved riot police and tear gas to demand democratic input into North American decision-making. The bad news is that the summit was about the Security and Prosperity Partnership of North America (SPP)—the real-world name of Vision B.

While left activists and researchers in Canada and Mexico have been spreading the word about the SPP for several years, so far in the United States the SPP, which was officially launched in March 2005, has mainly caught the attention of the right wing, which sees it as a stealth plan to impose a European Union-style government on the continent.

The SPP is *not* a North American version of the European Union. But it *is* a stealth plan—one aimed at bypassing the kind of international solidarity that halted the Free Trade Agreement of the Americas and the Multilateral Agreement on Investment. The European Union emerged after years of public debate and a treaty ratified by member states. By contrast, the SPP is not a treaty and will never be submitted to the U.S., Mexican, or Canadian legislatures. Instead it attempts to reshape the North American political economy by direct use of executive authority. And while the European Union maintains an explicit role for government in addressing inequality within and between countries, the SPP's foundation is an unequal alliance where the United States retains the political and economic trump cards.

Designed to shore up the United States' weakening position as a global hegemon, the SPP's primary goals are to link economic integration of the three countries to U.S. security needs; deepen U.S. access to oil, gas, electricity, and water resources throughout the continent; and to provide a privileged—and institutionalized—role for transnational corporations in continental deregulation. The stakes for labor, the environment, and civil liberties in all three countries couldn't be higher. Yet because of the SPP's reliance on executive authority to push the agenda, many of the SPP's initiatives remain virtually invisible, even to many activists.

SPP Basics

The North American Free Trade Agreement (NAFTA), which went into effect in 1994, was designed to enhance the access of transnational capital from the United States to cheap Mexican labor and Canadian natural resources. The SPP deepens these relations and harnesses the so-called war on terror to an expanded U.S.-Mexican-Canadian trade agenda and a lopsided energy grab to secure U.S. access to dwindling continental oil and gas reserves.

As its name implies, the SPP has two basic parts: the Security Agenda and the Prosperity Agenda. Both are rooted in the United States' deteriorating global position, particularly its increased competition for access to global oil and gas reserves and worsening trade balance with China.

With the explicit aim of securing North America from "internal" as well as external threats, the Security Agenda coordinates intelligence activities among the three countries and streamlines the movement of "low risk" goods and people (especially so-called "NAFTA professionals") across borders. It also involves extensive military coordination, much of it focused on protecting energy and transportation infrastructure. (Consolidating a North American military structure no doubt also serves as an offensive hedge against Venezuela's attempt to shape an independent South American energy policy.)

The Prosperity Agenda continues the Security Agenda's focus on energy. World demand is growing as traditional sources from the Middle East, Russia, and South America are becoming less secure; and the resulting price increases and realignment of power threaten a redistribution of wealth and power in favor of the oil and gas producers, many of them in the Global South. The Prosperity Agenda aims first and foremost at consolidating U.S. control over North American energy supplies, first by expanding production in Canada and Mexico, and second by increasing U.S. access to that production by deregulating energy markets. In addition to expanding energy production, Prosperity Agenda activities include a tri-national framework for "minimizing" regulatory "barriers"; special committees on the auto and steel industries; removal of constraints on movement of capital and financial services; and expanded and streamlined cross-border transportation networks—networks that will facilitate not only trade within the continent, but more outsourcing to Asia.

The official SPP website posts official documents, but ongoing discussions are shrouded within tightly controlled annual summits, ministerial level meetings, and working groups that exclude civil society participation. Corporations, however, have a privileged view of the road ahead and provide guidance and direction through a specially-created North American Competitiveness Council. U.S. members of the NACC include Wal-Mart, Merck, GE, UPS, FedEx, and Kansas City Southern.

The U.S. Chamber of Commerce and the Council of the Americas—whose website brags that its blue-chip members represent the majority of private U.S. investment in Latin America—serve as the U.S. secretariat.

NACC advice is taken seriously. In February 2007, the NACC issued detailed recommendations for energy integration, streamlining regulatory processes, and the speedy resumption of trade after emergencies. Six months later at their August 2007 summit, the countries announced an energy cooperation agreement, an avian flu preparedness plan with emergency border-management procedures, and a regulatory cooperation framework. The regulatory framework—complete with goals and action plan—specifically incorporates NACC recommendations to increase reliance on voluntary standards and to analyze regulations for their cost to trade. Although the framework doesn't say exactly how principles would be applied to different industries, the NACC's 2007 report gives several telling examples, including regulations harmonizing "hours of service" for truck drivers that would expand permissible weekly driving hours, which safety advocates are already challenging in court. Canadian plans to "harmonize" pesticide use to U.S. levels—an action that will raise exposure levels for most regulated pesticides—also provide a glimpse at the kinds of regulatory changes we can expect from the SPP.

"Community" from the Top

In the United States, the best-known proponent of the SPP is Robert Pastor, director of the Center for North American Studies at American University. NAFTA broke new ground by linking Mexico (a developing economy) with the United States and Canada (two major industrialized nations) in a pact to increase trade and investment. Predictably, NAFTA increased rather than decreased inequality. But for Pastor, NAFTA's real problem was its failure to build continent-wide institutions to push integration even further. He sees the SPP as a means of building those institutions, and envisions it as a new model for global governance—by and for elites—that could be used to link other developed and developing countries.

Building a North American Community, a 2005 independent task force report of the Council on Foreign Relations on which Pastor served, reveals the breadth of SPP's ambitions. The report called for a security perimeter around the three countries by 2010, so that goods and people would be checked once on entry and then move freely—while being tracked—within the continent, greatly diminishing the costs of trade. There would be a common tariff for goods from outside North America. Currently, NAFTA rules of origin require checking goods to ensure they contain sufficient North American content to qualify for duty-free treatment under NAFTA. A common external tariff would save money by eliminating the need to check for North American content. It would also facilitate expanded supply chains and outsourcing.

"Full labor mobility" would be preceded by greatly expanded guest worker programs tying immigration status to employment. "Development" funds for Mexico

would translate into transportation and energy infrastructure to help foreign investment push past the *maquila* zone on the border into central and southern Mexico
where poverty is greatest and wages lowest.

Intelligence sharing and joint military exercises would increase "interoper-
ability" and protect strategic energy and transportation infrastructure. Mexican
reticence to accept U.S. troops on its soil—the result of eight U.S. invasions since its
independence—would be overcome in small steps such as joint disaster coordination and plans for fighting organized crime.

Academic and political exchange programs and North American Studies
centers would help build a North American identity. Policy areas not touched by
NAFTA or never implemented would be revisited. As one SPP participant put it,
during NAFTA negotiations, the Canadians wouldn't talk about exporting water,
the Mexican's wouldn't talk about privatizing oil, and the United States wouldn't
talk about immigration. Barriers to maximizing energy production and cross border
trade in oil, gas, and electricity would be eliminated and pressure put on Mexico's
state-owned energy company, Pemex, to dramatically open itself to private investment. Air, rail, and trucking companies would be given unlimited access to all three
countries.

Meanwhile, a common regulatory scheme would make "harmonized" (read:
lower) North American standards the default approach to new regulations, and
countries would have to justify more stringent requirements. A seamless North
American market would create economies of scale for the largest corporations.
Delays and costs of checking goods for compliance at the borders would be mini-
mized. A rule of "tested once" would eliminate "duplicative" reviews of product
safety and—according to the council—substantially raise profits for biotechnology
and pharmaceutical firms.

The Perils of Being Close

U.S. corporations and elites that dominate continental production chains clearly
stand to gain the most from the SPP. But in fact, the SPP's earliest roots lie in proposals by Canadian businesses and think tanks for what Canadians call "deep integration." Essentially a strategy for bypassing U.S. protectionism, deep integration
seeks to leverage Canada's geographic proximity for greater access to U.S. markets.
The idea received a serious boost in the days after 9/11. The United States buys 80%
of Canada's exports, and so when the United States closed its borders following the
attacks, Canadian businesses lost millions of dollars every hour. Canadian elites
promptly concluded—correctly—that the price of continued access to U.S. markets
was deeper cooperation on security matters.

Canada, like Mexico, quickly signed a "smart-border" agreement and began
conforming its security practices to the needs of the Bush administration's war on
terror. In 2002 Canadian officials provided information that helped the United
States deport a Canadian citizen, Maher Arar, to Syria, where he was tortured. The

Canadian government has since apologized, and Arar, a software engineer whose wife stood as a candidate for the New Democratic Party in 2004, has signed on to a public demand that SPP provisions be submitted to Canadians for a vote.

But the SPP's dangers for Canadians go beyond threats to civil liberties. Like NAFTA and the Canadian U.S. Free Trade Agreement (CUFTA) before it, the SPP is a Trojan horse aimed at trapping Canadian workers into a downward spiral of global competition and neoliberal policies.

Both NAFTA and CUFTA were sold to Canadians on the grounds that increasing trade would boost employment and productivity; that would in turn solidify the economic base for Canadian social spending, including the deeply popular single-payer health insurance program. Instead, elites used the logic of competition to tighten first monetary and then fiscal policy—much as Reagan did in the United States in the 1980s. As in the United States, recession followed. Canadian exports, particularly of raw materials, increased, but overall competitiveness came largely from pushing up unemployment and driving down wages. Meanwhile, budget politics were used to squeeze rather than support social spending. The resulting deterioration in services became the pretext for experiments in private health care provision that could jeopardize the entire single-payer system. In many cases, it is Canadian divisions of U.S. transnationals that are profiting.

Not surprisingly, Canadian activists began arguing for abrogating NAFTA and reversing cutbacks in health care funding and other public services. With its security trump card and stratagem of rule by executive order, the SPP helps sidestep popular opposition to belt-tightening and the more expansive deep integration agenda.

Deep Integration and Natural Resources

Energy provides the strategic example of how SPP and deep integration would merge the interests of Canadian and U.S. elites at the expense of ordinary Canadians.

The United States is the world's largest energy consumer, and by 2025 it will be importing one third of its supply. Canada is the largest supplier of crude oil and natural gas to the United States, and has been deregulating its energy sector since the 1980s to increase access to U.S. markets. Now that rising oil prices have increased the financial feasibility of oil production from the vast Alberta oil sands, total Canadian oil reserves are second only to Saudi Arabia's. Canadian oil concerns are more eager than ever to increase sales to the United States.

In a fully integrated, privatized North American energy market, U.S. users would buy the lion's share of energy resources; at the same time, demand would increase for Canadian production, and so would prices. Not surprisingly, fully integrating North American energy markets figures prominently in the hopes of both U.S. and Canadian elites.

But the same mechanism would make energy more expensive for Canadian consumers, who will be in direct competition with U.S. buyers. In addition, easily-tapped Canadian conventional reserves are dwindling rapidly. Raising oil production accelerates their depletion and risks Canadian energy and environmental security. The huge quantities of gas and water needed for production from the oil sands increase environmental risks even more, and also make economic feasibility dependent on continued high oil prices.

Finally, Canada is home to a quarter of the earth's fresh water. Although it is not mentioned in official SPP documents, Canadian activists believe that SPP includes discussions of bulk water exports to the United States, threatening Canadian water security just as the world enters a period of anticipated severe water shortages.

From NAFTA to the SPP

If Canada's path to the SPP can be described as a voluntary regression from developed welfare state to exporter of natural resources, Mexico's reveals the combination of coercion and repression running through the SPP and NAFTA.

Mexico bought into NAFTA and neoliberalism as a result of the 1980s debt crisis. U.S. banks made huge low-interest loans to developing countries and then ratcheted up interest rates. When Mexico defaulted, the United States and the International Monetary Fund renegotiated Mexico's loans and saddled Mexico with free-market reforms that opened the country to foreign investment. Wages and living standards plummeted. Mexico abandoned what remained of its development plans and turned to neoliberalism, free trade, and the promise of increased foreign direct investment to pay its bills.

Foreign investment never materialized on the level expected. Meanwhile, Mexico enthusiastically reduced agricultural tariffs under NAFTA even as the United States flooded it with subsidized corn. Two million small farmers were driven from their land, increasing unemployment and driving down wages. Today half of all Mexicans live in poverty, with 15 million in extreme poverty. Half of new labor-market entrants can't find employment in Mexico, and remittances from migrants to the United States outstrip foreign direct investment. The situation will become even more dire when all remaining agricultural tariffs under NAFTA expire later in 2008.

Any economic plan actually centered on the needs of the Mexican people would include renegotiating NAFTA's agricultural provisions. Instead, agriculture is off the table, and immigration has taken center stage. Rebuffed by the anti-immigrant backlash in the U.S., Mexico is turning to Canada for an expanded guest-worker program, and the two countries have set up an SPP working group to discuss labor mobility.

Meanwhile, SPP negotiators are discussing funds to address "uneven development." In practice this means connecting Central and Southeastern Mexico—regions which have some of Mexico's highest poverty rates and lowest wages, but also some of its richest gas reserves—to U.S. markets. The region is also the target of former president Vicente Fox's 2001 Plan Puebla Panama, an $8 billion infrastructure program aimed at integrating southern Mexico with the CAFTA countries. The overall vision: stepped-up development of energy and gas reserves, an even lower-wage workforce for *maquila* production than on the U.S. border, and transportation and energy networks needed to produce and carry finished goods to U.S. consumers.

Of course, appropriating land for highways and other projects requires massive dispossession of farmers and indigenous peoples. Since many of the peasants NAFTA has displaced have already crossed the border to the United States, stepped-up immigration control and labor repression are both in the offing. So far, the two countries appear poised to limit migration from the CAFTA countries into southern Mexico, regulate the flow of Mexican immigrants to the United States in the north, and seal a captive, repressed workforce in between.

Mexico's participation in the SPP's security perimeter will greatly stiffen security along its southern border, where several hundred thousand migrants annually try to cross into Mexico from Central America to get to the United States. And the United States has already tightened security along Mexico's northern border, where 500,000 cross annually.

Bush's $1.4 billion request to the U.S. Congress for a "Plan Mexico," which he hopes eventually to extend to Central America, is linked to this plan. Billed as a "new paradigm" for security cooperation and fighting drug crime, in reality it's another step toward a U.S.-led continental military and security structure. It won't position U.S. soldiers on Mexican ground, but it will deepen coordination and provide intelligence, training, and equipment to Mexican military and police. The resources are certain to be used to against Mexico's growing social movements. Mexico's anti-terrorism law has already made it easier to criminalize protest. In 2002, the People's Front for Defense of the Land managed to halt construction of an airport that was part of Plan Pueblo Panama, and the Front also participated in the Zapatista campaign to boycott the last presidential election. In April 2006 the group came to the aid of flower growers and vendors in a confrontation with police in nearby San Salvador Atenco. Thirty five hundred police beat 200 of the town's 300 inhabitants; arrested 150; sexually assaulted 30 women; and killed two youths. For his part in the resistance, the movement's leader was sentenced to 67 years in prison—the first prosecution under Mexico's post-9/11 anti-terrorism law.

Mexico's Energy Matters Too

As with Canada, Mexican energy is where the largest stakes are being played. Mexico is currently the third largest supplier of oil to the United States, yet estimates are that Mexican oil and natural gas reserves could be exhausted in as little as ten years. The SPP's plan to step up Mexican oil production by completely privatizing gas production and increasing private investment in its oil sector will strip Mexico of crucial resources for development at a time when world oil prices make them most valuable.

The main barrier to the SPP's privatization strategy is the Mexican constitution, which guarantees the benefits of the energy sector to the Mexican people and places management of oil and gas in the hands of state-owned Pemex. Pemex is a symbol of national sovereignty, and Mexico refused to commit to privatizing Pemex during NAFTA negotiations. But legislation in the '90s chipped away at Pemex's jurisdiction while expanding the scope for private sector contracts. More importantly, Pemex was severely undermined during the 1980s debt crisis, when oil and gas revenues were chained to foreign debt repayment.

THE RIGHT AND THE SPP

So far in the United States, the most vocal opposition to the SPP has come from the right. *The New American*, a glossy magazine published by a subsidiary of the John Birch Society, recently dedicated an entire issue to the "North American Union," featuring shadowy images of a unified North America and of people pledging allegiance to a Photoshopped combination of the U.S., Canadian, and Mexican flags.

In that issue, Howard Phillips, chairman of the Coalition to Block the North American Union, predicts that under the SPP, "new transnational bodies would gain authority over our economy, our judiciary, and our lawmaking institutions." Other commentators complain that the SPP's working groups operate behind closed doors, "without any participation or authorization from Congress" to propose "continental 'integration' on a wide range of political, economic, and social issues," and point out that SPP will benefit elites: "NAFTA has greatly benefited the corporate and financial elites in all three countries"; "its contemplated successor the SPP, if allowed to go forward, will inflict more of the same."

On these points right-wing critiques appear to share some common ground with the left, but lack an alternative economic vision and analysis of deeper democratic deficits in the three countries. Instead, economic nationalism and extreme nativism are the hallmarks of critiques of SPP from the right, from the John Birch Society to Ron Paul to Lou Dobbs. Hence anti-immigration rhetoric and fear-mongering about a loss of U.S. sovereignty are staples of right-wing discussions of the SPP. One of the articles in *The New American*, entitled "The North American Union Invasion," warns: "Despite the great harm that Americans face from rampant illegal immigration—crime, terrorism, economic devastation—our political and business elitists push for more amnesties."

There is a danger that if the right dominates discussion of the SPP, legitimate left critiques will be drowned out. "As in the immigration debate, these people's framing and rhetoric make it almost impossible for the left to do anything but recoil in horror," Judy Ancel of Cross Border Network told *D&S*. Indeed, some on the left, including Christopher Hayes, in a *Nation* cover story, have dismissed concerns about the SPP, which Hayes calls "a relatively mundane formal bureaucratic dialogue." Hayes quotes a Commerce Department official who said the SPP is "Simple stuff like, for instance, in the US we sell baby food in several different sizes; in Canada, it's just two different sizes." Online comments in response to Hayes's article indicate that many on the left think otherwise.

In Canada and Mexico the opposition to SPP is better organized and hence less vulnerable to being thrown off balance by the right (or by government officials)—all the more reason for U.S. activists to make common cause with left activists to the north and south.

—*Alissa Thuotte & Ryan Lynch*

Sources: *The New American*, "North American Union edition," October 15th, 2007; Christopher Hayes, "The NAFTA Superhighway," *The Nation*, August 27th 2007; Richard D. Vogel, "The NAFTA Corridors: Offshoring U.S. Transportation Jobs to Mexico, *Monthly Review*, January 2006.

As a result, Pemex has been chronically starved for funds for exploration and development. The shortage is routinely used as an argument for privatization. The SPP has plans to release a report this year highlighting Pemex's purported inefficiencies and need for private capital. Sixty percent of Pemex's revenues go to supplying nearly 40% of Mexico's national budget; no private firm could survive under similar constraints. Ironically, the 1970s loans that led to the 1980s debt crisis were made so Mexico could develop newly discovered oil during a period of record prices. Those record prices were the result of the 1973 OPEC oil boycott. OPEC deposited the profits from those price hikes in U.S. banks, and those funds in turn became the capital U.S. banks used to lend to Mexico. Chaining Pemex's revenues to debt repayment in the 1980s meant Mexico was forced to increase output and add to what by then was a glut of world energy supplies—thereby contributing to lower world prices and weakening its own revenues. In effect, Mexico went into debt slavery to help undermine OPEC and cheapen the cost of energy for U.S. corporations. SPP's agenda brings the cycle full circle, with the United States willing to accelerate exhaustion of Mexico's remaining reserves to bolster its own increasingly precarious international energy position.

Upping the Ante

The SPP ups the ante for activists. Until now, labor and progressives—at least in the United States—have tended to focus on specific targets such as trade agreements or demands for debt relief. And when we analyzed NAFTA, we analyzed it in class terms, not in geopolitical terms. But the SPP's goals are broader and deeper even than NAFTA's goals. They aim at nothing short of remaking the political and economic governance structure of North America.

The wishes of Canadian and Mexican elites notwithstanding, the SPP's primary purpose is to buoy U.S. capitalism's flagging international position, from its trade deficit to its energy deficit. U.S. security, energy and transportation needs are the touchstones, and the draft agreement aligns the policies of Canada and Mexico—and appropriates natural resources—to meet those needs. Economic integration is conditioned on military integration, which in turn aims at consolidating the U.S. position in the hemisphere.

While the United States maintains most of the economic leverage in the triad, most hot-button issues are in Mexico and Canada. For U.S. activists in particular, bringing these issues alive will first require a much deeper understanding of our neighbors, and an ability to link their issues to domestic U.S. concerns.

Chief among the dangers for ordinary people in all three countries are the environmental consequences. Increasing rates of fossil fuel extraction in North America may feed the U.S. energy habit, but the solution is short term. The contributions to global warming for North America and the world, however, will not be.

The SPP's bundling of security with economic concerns also fuels Bush's war on terror, the accelerating militarization of U.S. foreign policy, and continued U.S.

leadership of neoliberal globalization. Canada's commitments of troops in Afghanistan, increased military spending, and willingness to find common ground with the United States on Latin America and the Caribbean are one product of the noxious mix. Another is Mexico's willingness to serve as a counter-weight to Venezuelan attempts to harness its oil wealth to alternative regional and global development strategies.

In terms of daily governance, the SPP privatizes the regulatory functions of government on an international scale not seen before in industrialized democracies. NAFTA and other WTO agreements limit the legislative and regulatory powers of member states by imposing global standards such as "market access" and "national treatment" on how countries treat foreign investors. These standards create "one way roads" to privatization once countries begin liberalizing a sector. Applied to Canadian experiments in private health care, they could end up forcing Canada first to open its doors to for-profit foreign providers and insurance companies, and then to pay them the same subsidies given to Canadian public and nonprofit operators. In the United States (where health insurance is already private), they could be used to prevent the United States from putting its own single-payer system in place.

By contrast, the SPP bypasses national authority to create formal, tri-national structures for corporate regulatory input *prior* to involvement by legislatures or citizens. Many SPP goals are thus hidden at their inception; even after they emerge, most will be buried in the daily workings of executive agencies who have been directed to give maximum attention to corporate needs and trade. In the United States, a short list of agencies already involved in the SPP includes the Department of Justice, the Department of State, the Federal Trade Commission, the Federal Communications Commission, the Departments of Agriculture and Energy, and the Department of Homeland Security.

Finally, the SPP is a frontal assault on labor and civil liberties. Plan Mexico should be seen as a threat to human rights throughout the continent. The North American labor movement desperately needs a democratic Mexico where independent organizing and labor rights can be exercised without threat of violence. Instead, the SPP will intensify exploitation of Mexican labor and deepen the low wage neoliberal model in both the United States and Canada, as well.

What It Will Take

Currently, Bush is politically weakened by the Iraq war, Mexico's president Felipe Calderón by his election scandal, and Canadian prime minister Stephen Harper by his lack of a parliamentary majority, raising the question of whether the SPP will survive the leaders' terms in office.

But even if it were stopped in its current form, much of the SPP would continue. A Framework for Regulatory Cooperation has been signed, complete with goals for action and annual work plans. The North American Energy Working Group—now integrated into the SPP—was actually established in 2001. Plan Mexico, once funded, will take on its own life, and the push to privatize Pemex will continue.

Opposition to Plan Pueblo Panama gives some indication of the depth and breadth of the activism that will be needed to be effective with the SPP's agenda. Calderón recently revived Plan Puebla Panama, with an added military component—no doubt inspired by the SPP. Yet it was stalled for many years by protests against displacement of farmers and destruction of the environment, and a vibrant cross-border network of activists has grown up around it. The breadth of the Plan Puebla Panama led activists to conclude that opposing environmentally destructive infrastructure projects wasn't sufficient: what is necessary is a deeper understanding of the economic and political vision behind Plan Pueblo Panama, and development of an alternative analysis.

An effective response to the SPP agenda will require the same kind of expanded cross-border contacts and focused study of the North American and global political economies. This is the very work the left needs to do to begin creating economic and political alternatives that reflect its values.

The challenge is particularly difficult for activists in the United States. Unlike the left in countries where domestic agendas have been affected by U.S. actions for many years, most in the United States think of domestic issues as controlled by domestic politics. But as rising oil prices combine with a falling dollar, and U.S. economic autonomy begins to be more constrained, more people in the United States may understand the need for different allies.

U.S. activists need a democratic Mexico with strong labor rights and a Canadian welfare state that survives the ravages of neoliberal globalization. We need to build an environmental agenda based on conservation and renewable resources and an economic agenda based on diversity and human rights. We need a progressive voice that can drown out right wing cries that the problem of globalization is the loss of U.S. dominance and power. Most of all, we need an international, powerful, and organized response from the left, and popular forces to challenge the more deeply coordinated and increasingly militarized forces of international capital. Reasoned opposition is no longer enough. ❑

Sources: Alejandro Álvarez Béjar,"Pemex: De La Reestructuracion á La Privatizacion," *Revista Venezolana de Economía y Ciencias Sociales*, Instituto de Investigaciones Económicas y Sociales, num. 4, octubre-diciembre de 1998; Alejandro Álvarez Béjar, "Predatory Oil Exploitation in the South East Region of Mexico and Alternatives to Neoliberal Structural Change" (2007), LASA conference paper; Laura Carlsen, "Deep Integration"—the Anti-Democratic Expansion of NAFTA, and October 4, 2007, "Plan Mexico and the Billion-Dollar Drug Deal," America's Program, Center for International Policy, May 2007; Council on Foreign Relations, *Building a North American Community*, Independent Task Force Report No. 53 (2005) (on the web at www.cfr.org); Robert A. Pastor, *Toward a North American Community*, Institute for International Economics (2001); Canadian Centre for Policy Alternatives, *Whose Canada? Continental Integration, Fortress North America, and the Corporate Agenda*, Ricardo Grinspun and Yasmine Shamsie, editors (McGill Queen's University Press, 2007).

Article 4.6

WOMEN OF NAFTA

BY MARTHA OJEDA, FELICITAS CONTRERAS, AND YOLANDA TREVIÑO
September/October 2007

The outstanding collection *NAFTA From Below: Maquiladora Workers, Farmers, and Indigenous Communities Speak Out on the Impact of Free Trade in Mexico*, combines worker testimony with analytical and historical essays to provide a devastating picture of the effects of neoliberal international trade policies—culminating in the North American Free Trade Agreement (NAFTA)—on workers throughout Mexico. The book, available in both English and Spanish, also offers inspiring accounts of resistance to those policies.

The book's early chapters focus on *maquiladora* workers in the north of the country, addressing key labor issues such as health and safety, environmental concerns, and freedom of association. Later chapters take up organizing by agricultural workers in the south, especially in the state of Chiapas, in response to neoliberal "reforms." That the Zapatista uprising in Chiapas began on January 1, 1994, the very day that NAFTA went into effect, was no accident.

One of the book's achievements is to show how the struggles of industrial workers in the north of Mexico are related to those of agricultural workers in the south. Knitting these struggles together is one of the central aims of the Coalition for Justice in the Maquiladoras, which produced *NAFTA From Below*. The coalition has helped bring *maquila* workers and organizers from the north together with members of grassroots *campesino* and indigenous groups in the south to help strengthen cooperative projects in both regions and to share information about the history of organized struggle in the workplace. Women's strong leadership roles in workplace struggles in the north have been of particular interest to organizers in the south, especially as former agricultural workers from the south migrate to work in *maquiladoras* near the northern border.

Women played a central role in the struggle of workers at a Sony plant in Nuevo Laredo for a democratic union, described in the selections that follow. The events at Sony vividly illustrate the frequent conflicts between Mexico's corrupt official unions and rival independent unions that Chris Tilly and Marie Kennedy describe. The Sony workers' struggle was also a key early test of NAFTA's labor side-agreement, the North American Agreement on Labor Cooperation, and the bodies it established, known as National Administrative Offices (NAOs), to investigate violations.

These excerpts include testimony from Martha Ojeda (co-editor of *NAFTA From Below*, with Rosemary Hennessy), a *maquila* worker from 1973 to 1994 who is now executive director of the Coalition for Justice in the Maquiladoras; from Felicitas (Fela) Contreras, an activist with CETRAC (Center for Workers and Communities) in Nuevo Laredo who worked at the Sony plant from 1985 through

1998; and from Yolanda Treviño, a former Sony worker who testified before the NAO as part of the Sony workers' NAFTA complaint.

MARTHA A. OJEDA: Official history is always written so that the reality people were living is hidden. If everyone told the part they lived or knew, the truth would be in their collective word.

In 1979 Sony arrived in my town [Nuevo Laredo].… Sony manually assembled audiocassettes and Beta videocassettes. In 1982, after the first devaluation of the peso, there were more than 1,000 workers working three shifts in five plants, and by then the workers were also producing the VHS videocassette and the 3.5 inch diskette.

They began to bring machines for semiautomatic and automatic assembly of the cassettes. The plastic molding injection plant was providing the plastic cases and the components for the audio and video plants. It was the boom of assembly line production.

In this era children with birth defects began to be born, but the company doctor said that this happened because the parents were alcoholics or because they had genetic problems. By 1993 there were 2,000 employees in seven plants in three shifts. There was a lot of overtime, but still it wasn't enough to meet production quotas.

The molding ingestion plants never stopped working; they were going three shifts seven days a week. For the first time the company proposed twelve-hour shifts for four and three days a week. This implied that Sony got their production, because the machines were running around the clock, but they avoided paying overtime. This twelve-hour shift was unknown to workers because it didn't exist in the Federal Labor Law.

It was in this labor and political context that in October 1993 we visited Fidel Velázquez, the CTM national leader, in Mexico City and solicited union elections within the framework of the CTM. All of the *maquilas* were affiliated with this union because it was the only one; if you didn't belong to it there was no other alternative for workers anywhere. But the leaders negotiated the contract with the company even before it was established in the locality.

Fidel told us that he agreed with the elections (but he never said when they would be). We trusted his word and began the process that the Federal Labor Law sets down for forming the union sections.

On January 1, 1994, we were informed of the Zapatista uprising, but equally surprising to us was to find out in the newspaper on January 4 that Chema Morales had declared that on the order of Fidel Velázquez he would be the new Secretary General of the *maquilas*—without sectionals—and, worst of all, he was already named to the Labor Board at the state level because of his position as Secretary General, not only of the Maquila Union but also of the Workers Federation of Nuevo Laredo.

Shocked, we tried to communicate with Fidel Velázquez, but our efforts were in vain. Then we learned that he was coming to Ciudad Victoria, the capital of Tamaulipas, on January 12. We traveled all night. But when we arrived it was obvious that they would not let us enter. We guessed that Fidel would come in by the side door and we waited there until he arrived with the media.

I demanded publicly that he retract his authorization of Chema Morales as Secretary General. Then I asked for a public debate with him and with Chema. I don't know if I was the only woman from the provinces who had publicly challenged him, but what I do know is that so much corruption repulsed me and gave me the courage to make sure that the two of them, both Chema and Fidel, would be exposed even to the President of the Labor Board of the state who was present. He had authorized naming Chema to be Secretary General even though he had never worked in the *maquilas*, and according to the union by-laws that was one of the requirements.

In the face of the media and all of the evidence, Fidel looked ridiculous and he had no alternative but to accept that there would be union elections. So he declared that he would send a national representative to hold them. When I went to say good-bye to him at the podium he told me, "You are going to eat fire." And I told him, "I'm ready." But I never imagined what he was referring to.

FELICITAS ("FELA") CONTRERAS: In 1993 they began to change the delegates in all of the *maquiladoras* who did not agree with the CTM. I heard that there were going to be elections in all the *maquilas*, not only in Sony, and we were asking when Sony's turn would be. But before the elections they were changing the delegates. They fired the ones we wanted and after work we had meetings to change the delegates so that they would really be for us. We met in one house and another with Martha because we wanted to change the delegates who were imposed by the CTM. I would get home at 4:00 or 5:00 in the morning. We always were hiding here and there, and that is how we put together a slate, even though they fired our candidates.

Those union delegates who were with Chema Morales (of the CTM) developed their slates with the old delegates from Sony… They preferred Chema instead of our democratic union. In April of 1994 the day arrived for the elections, and Chema's representative from the union and a representative of Fidel Velázquez were set up in the parking lot of Plant #7. We had our slate, but they didn't give us a chance to let our other co-workers know that the voting was taking place.

Representatives of Fidel Velázquez and of the company were there. They told the people to go to the parking lot and they arranged to meet the other shift and take them out to vote. They said on this side go all those in favor of the blue slate, on the other side those in favor of the CTM slate. Our slate won because everyone came to our side. But Fidel's representative said that the other delegates from the CTM won. And so we said, "How is that possible if we are all here, voting for our slate? We were the majority. What are we going to do?" We were really mad! Those who were working came out and we took to the streets to protest that they were doing this fraudulent election, and we made signs that said, "We want democratic elections!!"

YOLANDA TREVIÑO: On Saturday April 16, which was my day off, I went to plant #3 to see what resolution Mayor Horacio Garza had been able to make as to when we would have new elections. The *compañeras* who had spoken with him told us that he wasn't going to help us. That's when we started to hold our protest on the sidewalk in front of the plants, showing our frustration, but in a peaceful manner. We didn't stop anyone who wanted to from going into work and we didn't commit any act of violence.

We continued protesting in this way until Horacio Garza and Maricela López arrived. We had a meeting there with Horacio and he told us to stop the protest and that afterwards he would help us. We answered that the only thing we wanted was Señor Avila's word that they would hold new elections. But he said no. So Horacio Garza left and soon afterward the police and the firemen arrived. The girls were afraid when they saw the police and some of them asked if they were going to take us away, but we told them if we didn't act violently then they shouldn't either.

But that wasn't the case. Francisco Xavier Rios [Vice President of Human Resources at Sony] signaled to the police with a motion of his hand to enter through a side door, and they positioned themselves on the inside lot of the company. Then without any warning the police began to push us with their Plexiglas shields and their billy clubs. They beat us badly; they knocked a *compañera* unconscious, a woman named Alicia Soto, and they pushed the rest of us down with their shields, insulting us all the while, calling us names like "goddamn bitches."

I have been told that the company claims that the police didn't commit any acts of violence and that they only person who acted violently was Alicia who attacked the police with a magazine. I ask you: how is it possible that a 24 year old woman can harm a group of 35 well-armed police agents carrying Plexiglas shields and billy clubs? How is it possible to say they didn't commit acts of violence when my friend Alicia was knocked out by a blow to the head and has had problems ever since? I have here the newspaper *El Mañana*, dated 17 April, which shows very clearly a picture of Alicia unconscious. If they don't want to read the newspapers they should just look at their own videos because they were filming the entire attack.

FELICITAS ("FELA") CONTRERAS: They had pressed charges against us—Martha Ojeda and various others—because Sony had lost millions with the work stoppage. They issued a summons for us to appear at the police department and told us that our lives were not even worth enough to pay for the company's losses.

They wanted us to say that Martha was responsible, and they pitted us against each other. They told Lupe that I had confessed that Martha was doing it all, and they told me that Lupe confessed that Martha told us to stop working. But of the 40 they called to testify all of us said, "We are all responsible, and so you will have to arrest all of us not just Martha." All of our *compañeras* were outside the police department yelling that they would have to arrest everyone. But since there were more than a thousand and we didn't all fit in the cells, after hours of interrogations and threats they let us go.

On the fifth day, in the early morning, around 5:00 am the governor—Manuel Cavazos Lerma—ordered that the state police from Reynosa, Matamoros and Cd.

Victoria be brought in. The police arrived and the soldiers with machine guns and rifles. And they said to you, "Get out of here or I'll kill you." According to them they came to restore order, and with blows and kicks. They awakened us and ran after those who were sleeping on the sidewalk. You were waking up with a gun pointing in your face and they were yelling, "Get out or we will kill you."

We withdrew, and we were like this for five days and nights. In those days the trucks tried to mow us down because they wanted to take out the production, but we were all sleeping in the main gate so they couldn't cross and take it out.

Unfortunately, we didn't get it. We didn't get our union, and they fired a lot of people without giving them any severance payment because they said that they were leaders of the movement. We stayed there because we wanted an independent union.

In 1994 NAFTA was signed, and they said that the rights of workers would not be violated. But they beat us up and violated our rights. With the help of CJM and the lawyers from ANAD a demand was presented to the NAO. In 1995 we had a hearing and we all went to San Antonio to testify. Sony brought lawyers from New York and they said that our testimony was a lie, but we took the newspapers and the evidence, the videos. We won this trial, but we didn't really win anything because they didn't punish or fine Sony and we never had the elections or anything. They just put in these offices [the NAO] just to prop up NAFTA.

For me NAFTA was no good. The workers are still just as poor. The only difference is that now there are many settlements, *colonias*, many squatters, a lot of insecurity and a contaminated river. Before I used to drink water from the river and now you can't, and you can't go into it either. Our air is contaminated. There is a lot of sickness. There is a lot of illiteracy. The only one NAFTA helped were the businessmen because they are the ones that have gotten rich. And now they say, "I am going to China; I screwed the Mexicans so now I'm going to screw the Chinese." That is what stays with me about NAFTA. We are poor and screwed.

MARTHA A. OJEDA: Each one of my *compañeras* risked her life, her children, and her family. They kidnapped Yolanda and threatened her. They persecuted the others, calling them on the phone and intimidating them. Wherever any of them are, because there were many and I will never forget one, to each of them I render homage and a special tribute to their *"coraje"*—their courage and bravery—for trying to reclaim workers' right to freedom of association. For resisting and never giving up.

That is what NAFTA left me after 20 years in the *maquilas*: it gave me the opportunity to denounce at a global level the failure of this agreement and of the side agreements and to share the rebellion and resistance of my *compañeras*. It taught me that there is a world of solidarity. It clarified the horizon we are looking for, and above all the hope to reach it with a team like this team of women, united until the end. ❑

Chapter 5

LABOR IN THE INTERNATIONAL ECONOMY

Article 5.1

INTERNATIONAL LABOR STANDARDS

BY ARTHUR MacEWAN
September/October 2008

Dear Dr. Dollar:

U.S. activists have pushed to get foreign trade agreements to include higher labor standards. But then you hear that developing countries don't want that because cheaper labor without a lot of rules and regulations is what's helping them to bring industries in and build their economies. Is there a way to reconcile these views? Or are the activists just blind to the real needs of the countries they supposedly want to help?

—*Philip Bereaud, Swampscott, Mass.*

In 1971, General Emilio Medici, the then-military dictator of Brazil, commented on economic conditions in his country with the infamous line: "The economy is doing fine, but the people aren't."

Like General Medici, the government officials of many low-income countries today see the well-being of their economies in terms of overall output and the profits of firms—those profits that keep bringing in new investment, new industries that "build their economies." It is these officials who typically get to speak for their countries. When someone says that these countries "want" this or that—or "don't want" this or that—it is usually because the countries' officials have expressed this position.

Do we know what the people in these countries want? The people who work in the new, rapidly growing industries, in the mines and fields, and in the small shops and market stalls of low-income countries? Certainly they want better conditions—more to eat, better housing, security for their children, improved health and safety. The officials claim that to obtain these better conditions, they must "build their economies." But just because "the economy is doing fine" does not mean that the people are doing fine.

In fact, in many low-income countries, economic expansion comes along with severe inequality. The people who do the work are not getting a reasonable share of the rising national income (and are sometimes worse off even in absolute terms). Brazil in the early 1970s was a prime example and, in spite of major political change, remains a highly unequal country. Today, in both India and China, as in several other countries, economic growth is coming with increasingly severe inequality.

Workers in these countries struggle to improve their positions. They form—or try to form—independent unions. They demand higher wages and better working conditions. They struggle for political rights. It seems obvious that we should support those struggles, just as we support parallel struggles of workers in our own country. The first principle in supporting workers' struggles, here or anywhere else, is supporting their right to struggle—the right, in particular, to form independent unions without fear of reprisal. Indeed, in the ongoing controversy over the U.S.-Colombia Free Trade Agreement, the assassination of trade union leaders has rightly been a major issue.

Just how we offer our support—in particular, how we incorporate that support into trade agreements—is a complicated question. Pressure from abroad can help, but applying it is a complex process. A ban on goods produced with child labor, for example, could harm the most impoverished families that depend on children's earnings, or could force some children into worse forms of work (e.g., prostitution). On the other hand, using trade agreements to pressure governments to allow unhindered union organizing efforts by workers seems perfectly legitimate. When workers are denied the right to organize, their work is just one step up from slavery. Trade agreements can also be used to support a set of basic health and safety rights for workers. (Indeed, it might be useful if a few countries refused to enter into trade agreements with the United States until we improve workers' basic organizing rights and health and safety conditions in our own country!)

There is no doubt that the pressures that come through trade sanctions (restricting or banning commerce with another country) or simply from denying free access to the U.S. market can do immediate harm to workers and the general populace of low-income countries. Any struggle for change can generate short-run costs, but the long-run gains—even the hope of those gains—can make those costs acceptable. Consider, for example, the Apartheid-era trade sanctions against South Africa. To the extent that those sanctions were effective, some South African workers were deprived of employment. Nonetheless, the sanctions were widely supported by mass organizations in South Africa. Or note that when workers in this country strike or advocate a boycott of their company in an effort to obtain better conditions, they both lose income and run the risk that their employer will close up shop.

Efforts by people in this country to use trade agreements to raise labor standards in other countries should, whenever possible, take their lead from workers in those countries. It is up to them to decide what costs are acceptable. There are times, however, when popular forces are denied even basic rights to struggle. The best thing we can do, then, is to push for those rights—particularly the right to organize independent unions—that help create the opportunity for workers in poor countries to choose what to fight for. ❑

Article 5.2

THE GLOBALIZATION CLOCK

Why corporations are winning and workers are losing.

BY THOMAS PALLEY
May/June 2006

Political economy has historically been constructed around the divide between capital and labor, with firms and workers at odds over the division of the economic pie. Within this construct, labor is usually represented as a monolithic interest, yet the reality is that labor has always suffered from internal divisions—by race, by occupational status, and along many other fault lines. Neoliberal globalization has in many ways sharpened these divisions, which helps to explain why corporations have been winning and workers losing.

One of these fault lines divides workers from themselves: since workers are also consumers, they face a divide between the desire for higher wages and the desire for lower prices. Historically, this identity split has been exploited to divide union from nonunion workers, with anti-labor advocates accusing union workers of causing higher prices. Today, globalization is amplifying the divide between people's interests as workers and their interests as consumers through its promise of ever-lower prices.

Consider the debate over Wal-Mart's low-road labor policies. While Wal-Mart's low wages and skimpy benefits have recently faced scrutiny, even some liberal commentators argue that Wal-Mart is actually good for low-wage workers because they gain more as consumers from its "low, low prices" than they lose as workers from its low wages. But this static, snapshot analysis fails to capture the full impact of globalization, past and future.

Globalization affects the economy unevenly, hitting some sectors first and others later. The process can be understood in terms of the hands of a clock. At one o'clock is the apparel sector; at two o'clock the textile sector; at three the steel sector; at six the auto sector. Workers in the apparel sector are the first to have their jobs shifted to lower-wage venues; at the same time, though, all other workers get price reductions. Next, the process picks off textile sector workers at two o'clock. Meanwhile, workers from three o'clock onward get price cuts, as do the apparel workers at one o'clock. Each time the hands of the clock move, the workers taking the hit are isolated. In this fashion globalization moves around the clock, with labor perennially divided.

Manufacturing was first to experience this process, but technological innovations associated with the Internet are putting service and knowledge workers in the firing line as well. Online business models are making even retail workers vulnerable—consider Amazon.com, for example, which has opened a customer support center and two technology development centers in India. Public sector wages are also in play, at least indirectly, since falling wages mean falling tax revenues. The problem is that each time the hands on the globalization clock move forward, workers are divided: the majority is made slightly better off while the few are made much worse off.

Globalization also alters the historical divisions within capital, creating a new split between bigger internationalized firms and smaller firms that remain nationally centered. This division has been brought into sharp focus with the debate over the trade deficit and the overvalued dollar. In previous decades, manufacturing as a whole opposed running trade deficits and maintaining an overvalued dollar because of the adverse impact of increased imports. The one major business sector with a different view was retailing, which benefited from cheap imports.

However, the spread of multinational production and outsourcing has divided manufacturing in wealthy countries into two camps. In one camp are larger multinational corporations that have gone global and benefit from cheap imports; in the other are smaller businesses that remain nationally centered in terms of sales, production and input sourcing. Multinational corporations tend to support an overvalued dollar since this makes imports produced in their foreign factories cheaper. Conversely, domestic manufacturers are hurt by an overvalued dollar, which advantages import competition.

This division opens the possibility of a new alliance between labor and those manufacturers and businesses that remain nationally based—potentially a potent one, since there are approximately seven million enterprises with sales of less than $10 million in the United States, versus only 200,000 with sales greater than $10 million. However, such an alliance will always be unstable as the inherent labor-capital conflict over income distribution can always reassert itself. Indeed, this pattern is already evident in the internal politics of the National Association of Manufacturers, whose members have been significantly divided regarding the overvalued dollar. As one way to address this division, the group is promoting a domestic "competitiveness" agenda aimed at weakening regulation, reducing corporate legal liability, and lowering employee benefit costs—an agenda designed to appeal to both camps, but at the expense of workers.

Solidarity has always been key to political and economic advance by working families, and it is key to mastering the politics of globalization. Developing a coherent story about the economics of neoliberal globalization around which working families can coalesce is a key ingredient for solidarity. So too is understanding how globalization divides labor. These narratives and analyses can help counter deep cultural proclivities to individualism, as well as other historic divides such as racism. However, as if this were not difficult enough, globalization creates additional challenges. National political solutions that worked in the past are not adequate to the task of controlling international competition. That means the solidarity bar is further raised, calling for international solidarity that supports new forms of international economic regulation. ❑

Article 5.3

FREE MARKETS AND DEATH SQUADS IN HAITI

The U.S.-backed regime in Haiti is violently cracking down on worker organizing.

BY RICKY BALDWIN
September/October 2004

On February 29, a right-wing coup took control of the Haitian capital, Port-au-Prince, and sent President Jean-Bertrande Aristide into exile. Within two days, the same right-wing troops began attacking Haitian factory workers and sharecroppers at the behest of factory managers and large landowners, according to the grassroots labor federation Batay Ouvriye (Workers' Struggle).

The first assault came in the Codevi Free Trade Zone (FTZ) in the border community of Ouanaminthe. Thirty-four workers at the Dominican-owned sweatshop Grupo M, a subcontractor for Levi Strauss, had been fired for involvement with the union SOKOWA, an affiliate of Batay Ouvriye. The Codevi workers were demonstrating outside the plant on March 2 to demand that the 34 workers be rehired when management made a call, and in rolled troops fresh from overthrowing the elected government.

Armed men beat and handcuffed many of the demonstrators, then forced them—except for the original 34—back to work, sans union. With only about 100,000 permanent full-time jobs in a nation of almost 8 million inhabitants, according to Charles Arthur, director of the U.K.-based Haiti Support Group, being fired is no small matter.

Once the richest colony in the world, Haiti is now universally recognized as the poorest nation in the Western Hemisphere. The World Bank puts the poverty rate there at over 75%. The CIA's *World Fact Book* (2004) reports that "80% live in abject poverty" and three-fourths of the 3.6 million Haitian workforce have no formal jobs. Moreover, most of the formal jobs that do exist are seasonal or part-time, according to local observers.

Neoliberals, in the U.S. government and in Haiti, supported the coup (or the "liberation," as some Haitian business leaders have dubbed it) wholeheartedly. Their support quickly proved to have little to do with freedom, marketwise or otherwise, and everything to do with enforcing the domination of local and international elites.

Free Trade at Gunpoint

Armed attacks like the one at Grupo M were soon repeated elsewhere, says Yannick Etienne, lead organizer with Batay Ouvriye. Large landowners in the Northwest communities of Ma Wouj and Bombardopolis called in troops to battle sharecroppers campaigning for a larger share of their produce. "Rebels," as the forces who overthrew Aristide are commonly called, have also attacked members of the active peasant group Tet Kole, as well as wage-earning farm workers demanding the legal minimum wage.

The "rebel" troops had crossed into Haiti in the vicinity of the Codevi FTZ from the Dominican Republic, where several of their leaders had been in exile, facing charges of mass murder stemming from the first U.S.-backed coup against Aristide in 1991. Among them, Guy Philippe and Gilbert Dragon had been trained by the CIA in Ecuador, and Louis-Jodel Chamblain and Jean-Pierre Baptiste had been leaders in the CIA-organized Front for Haitian Advancement and Progress (FRAPH).

In the three bloody years following the 1991 coup, FRAPH functioned as an umbrella group for right-wing death squads that terrorized Haiti's democratic movement and drove its nascent labor unions underground. FRAPH itself was originally composed of army veterans from the brutal U.S.-supported Duvalier dictatorships that ruled Haiti from 1957 to 1986. Then as now, says Etienne, the motivation of U.S. and Haitian armed action has been the same: "cheap labor."

After this year's coup, Haitian business leaders immediately began meeting with coup leaders, calling them "liberators" even as U.S. Secretary of State Colin Powell admitted they were murderous "thugs." This collaboration between "thugs" and Haitian businessmen is hardly surprising, Arthur notes, because the Haitian elites owe their power to thuggery of another era: the 1915-1934 U.S. occupation. Then, U.S. Marines slaughtered 20,000 resisters, disbanded the Haitian parliament, and rewrote the country's constitution—effectively turning Haiti into a U.S. cheap-labor plantation.

U.S. Senator Mike Dewine (R-Ohio) continued this tradition when he proposed the Haiti Economic Recovery and Opportunity (HERO) Act, S. 489, this spring. The bill, supported by the Haitian business sector and opposed by Haitian labor unions, would essentially extend the existing free-trade zones to include the whole of Haiti. (A free-trade zone is a designated area where a government, typically in the global South, lifts normal trade barriers such as tariffs, gives tax breaks, suspends environmental, labor, and other regulations, and takes a range of steps to encourage investment by foreign corporations.) The bill, currently in the Senate Finance Committee, encourages foreign direct investment, for example, by awarding garments assembled in Haiti duty-free status for import into the United States.

"The HERO Act will ensure the multinationals' power to profit from the terrible misery of the Haitian people," says Etienne. "It will allow them to obtain cloth[ing] at preferential prices ... without the slightest concern for workers' rights. They are concerned, rather, with stifling these rights."

No Saviors

Yet, contrary to some expectations, Batay Ouvriye and other worker groups are not agitating to bring President Aristide back this time. When the Clinton administration reluctantly returned Aristide to power in 1994, under intense international pressure, there were strings attached. Aristide was forced to accept neoliberal austerity measures that reversed most of his government's populist reforms. Massive privatization, a suppressed minimum wage, and the establishment of new free-trade zones such as the Codevi FTZ were among these requirements.

When Aristide was re-elected in 2000, labor unions began to make a comeback, and in 2003 the government nearly doubled the legal minimum wage. The Haitian minimum wage in 1994 was 36 gourdes a day, or about $2.40. But by the time it was raised to 70 gourdes in 2003, over the strident objections of the U.S. Agency for International Development, the higher amount was equivalent to only around $1.70, about one-third of the cost of living in Haiti. Many workers had to fight for enforcement of even this abysmally low minimum wage, receiving little help from the Aristide government.

More disturbingly, the Aristide government also began cracking down on emerging workers' organizations. In 2003 riot police beat and shot at garment assembly workers demonstrating at a Port-au-Prince factory belonging to Wilbes & Co., a supplier of Wal-Mart, K-Mart, Target, Sears, and other discount outlets. When orange pickers unionized the year before at the major liqueur supplier Guacimal, they faced beatings, imprisonment, and death by dismemberment at the hands of Haitian police.

As a consequence, says Etienne, many Haitian workers now see Aristide as a collaborator and are looking elsewhere for salvation, even as their situation quickly worsens. "The forces lining up for power now represent the bosses' interests even more directly," she says. "But we, at Batay Ouvriye, are very clear that neither one has nor had workers' organization on its agenda. Of course, it is we, workers, who have to roll back our shirt sleeves to fight for our rights independently."

Shirt Sleeves Around the World

Batay Ouvriye has been fighting for workers' rights since the mid-1990s in the Port-au-Prince garment district, where workers assemble goods for export under Dickensian conditions. At HAACOSA, for example, a subcontractor for uniform giant Cintas, workers earn well below the minimum wage, have no access to clean water, and work behind locked gates in suffocating heat and filth. Attempts to unionize have been met with beatings or firings, but the workers persist.

A great deal of Batay Ouvriye's work consists of education, including basic literacy classes (adult literacy is about 53%, and much lower among workers) and legal rights training. The group ties into a network of local and international unions and solidarity groups which lend support by pressuring employers and government officials with letters, faxes, e-mails, and phone calls. But the system requires constant vigilance, as at Grupo M.

Grupo M's contract employer, Levi Strauss, has a Code of Conduct that requires respect for union rights among its subcontractors. Thanks to the anti-sweatshop movement of the 1990s, such codes are common in big corporations, including several in Haiti. Most are difficult to enforce. But the Grupo M plant in the Codevi FTZ had received a startup loan of $20 million from the World Bank, and with the help of international supporters Batay Ouvriye campaigned successfully to make the loan conditional on respect for workers' rights.

So when the troops attacked workers at Grupo M, Batay Ouvriye quickly mobilized an international call for the World Bank and Levi Strauss to intervene. They did, and Grupo M promised to rehire the 34 fired workers. Managers later balked at rehiring them all, although eventually all 34 did return to work.

At the same time, the plant forced workers to accept mysterious "vaccinations" which the workers feared were sterilizations. Their fears may have been justified: the Haitian Doctors' Union reports evidence that the injections contained contraceptives, including the fact that there were several miscarriages and numerous menstrual problems among workers who received the shots. And one worker says a doctor at the local hospital told her that Grupo M was running a "family planning program." When the workers went on strike in protest in June, plant managers brought in armed troops, this time from the Dominican Republic, to strip and question female workers at gunpoint. Workers say the soldiers also beat up a pregnant woman and threw her in a mud puddle.

Two days into the strike, management agreed to negotiate and the strikers agreed to return to work. However, when the workers arrived at the plant the next day, they discovered that management had locked them out. Now Grupo M is threatening to close the plant in the Codevi FTZ. But Haitian workers will not give up, says Yannick Etienne, at Grupo M or elsewhere. "The struggle," she says, "is just beginning." ❑

Sources: Paul Farmer, *The Uses of Haiti*, Common Courage Press, 1994; The International Centre for Trade Union Rights, *International Union Rights*, June 2003; *Haitian Times*, October 15, 2003. To help, contact www.batayouvriye.org or www.haitisupport.gn.apc.org.

Article 5.4

OAXACA'S DANGEROUS TEACHERS

BY DAVID BACON

September/October 2006

At 8:30 a.m. on October 21, 2002, Oaxaca state police arrested a dangerous schoolteacher.

Romauldo Juan Gutierrez Cortez was pulled over as he was driving to his school in the rural Mixteca region. Police took him to Oaxaca de Juárez, the state capital, where he was held for days on false charges. Gutierrez is the state coordinator for the Binational Front of Indigenous Organizations (the Frente), which had organized a loud, embarrassing protest during a visit to Oaxaca by Mexican President Vicente Fox not long before. Oaxaca Governor Jose Murat was out for revenge.

As Gutierrez languished in jail, Oaxacan migrant farm workers north of the border in California's central valley picketed the Mexican consulate, held press conferences, and clogged Murat's phone lines with calls and faxes. In Oaxaca itself, other Frente members organized similar protests. After a week, the governor succumbed to the pressure: Gutierrez was released.

Since then, the Frente has organized many other binational campaigns. Cooperation across the border is today one of the most important tools Oaxacans have for defending human rights in their home state.

Thousands of indigenous people migrate from Oaxaca's hillside villages to the United States every year—among Mexican states, Oaxaca has the second-highest concentration of indigenous residents. They leave in part because of a repressive political system that thwarts economic development in Mexico's poor rural areas. Lack of development in turn pushes people off the land. From there, they find their way to other parts of Mexico or the United States, where they often live in poverty even as they send money home. This economic reality was the central issue in this year's heated presidential election, which was marred by charges of vote fraud.

The people who have been driven from Oaxaca to the United States by economic crisis have carried a tradition of militant social movements with them. By organizing across the border, the Frente and other Oaxacan organizations increase their power. Binational pressure freed Gutierrez from Murat's jail, where local efforts alone might not have succeeded. Many other human rights violations in Oaxaca over the last decade have resulted in cross-border resistance, and the Frente was at the heart of many of these protests.

Winning political change in Mexico itself is central to the Frente's activity. For Oaxaca's indigenous residents, greater democracy and respect for human rights are the keys to eventually achieving a government committed to increasing rural family income. That in turn might make it possible for people to make a living at home, instead of heading to California for survival.

Migration: A Consequence of Economic Reforms

"Migration is a necessity, not a choice," Gutierrez explains. "There is no work here. You can't tell a child to study to be a doctor if there is no work for doctors in Mexico. It is a very daunting task for a Mexican teacher to convince students to get an education and stay in the country. It is disheartening to see a student go through many hardships to get an education here in Mexico and become a professional, and then later in the United States do manual labor. Sometimes those with an education are working side by side with others who do not even know how to read."

Lack of economic opportunity in Oaxaca's villages is a result of Mexican economic development policies. For more than two decades, under pressure from the World Bank, the International Monetary Fund, and conditions placed on U.S. bank loans and bailouts, the government has encouraged foreign investment, while cutting expenditures intended to raise rural incomes. Prices have risen dramatically since the government cut subsidies for necessities like gasoline, electricity, bus fares, tortillas, and milk.

The government also closed the CONASUPO stores, which bought corn at subsidized prices from farmers to help them stay on the land and sold tortillas, milk, and food to the urban poor. The North American Free Trade Agreement's subsidies to U.S. farmers have forced Mexican agricultural prices down. The end of the *ejido* land reform system has allowed the reconcentration of land ownership and rural wealth. The sale of government enterprises to private investors led to layoffs and the destruction of unions. Foreign investors may now own land and factories anywhere in Mexico, without Mexican partners.

The Mexican government estimates that 37.7%, or 40 million, of its 106 million citizens live in poverty, with 25 million, or 23.6%, living in extreme poverty. According to a representative of EDUCA, a Oaxacan education and development organization, 75% of the state's 3.4 million residents live in extreme poverty. It is the second-poorest state in Mexico, after Chiapas.

Meanwhile, President Fox boasts that Mexicans in the United States—often working for poverty wages—are sending home over $18 billion a year. "Migration helps pacify people," Gutierrez says. "Poverty is a ticking time bomb, but as long as there is money coming in from family in the United States, there is peace. To curb migration our country has to have a better employment plan. We must push our government to think about the working class."

The economic reforms of the last two decades are deeply unpopular, and people like Oaxaca's teachers would change them if they could. But those who have benefited from them have a big stake in suppressing any dissent or advocacy of political and economic alternatives. Governor Murat's campaign to stifle change by silencing Gutierrez is only a small part of Oaxaca's long history of human rights violations.

Teaching Resistance

Oaxaca has many dangerous teachers like Gutierrez. In the 1970s and 1980s, more than a hundred of Oaxaca's teachers were killed in the struggle for control of their union, Section 22 of the National Union of Education Workers. Today Section 22 is one of Mexico's most militant unions, and in many villages teachers are also community leaders and repositories of Mexico's most progressive traditions.

On one recent afternoon, Gutierrez stood at the back of a classroom in rural Santiago Juxtlahuaca, dapper in a pressed white shirt and chinos. Two boys and two girls, wearing new tennis shoes undoubtedly sent by family members working in the north, stood at the blackboard, giving a report and carefully gauging his reaction. As they recounted the history of Mexico's expropriation of oil in 1936, a smile curved beneath Gutierrez's pencil mustache. The expropriation was a high point in Mexican revolutionary nationalism. "Education is a very noble field, which I love," Gutierrez says. "But today it means confronting the government. You have to be ready to fight for the people and their children, and not just in the classroom."

Not just in the classroom, but throughout Oaxaca and also the United States. Today over 60,000 Oaxacans labor in California's San Joaquin Valley alone. Many times that number are dispersed in communities throughout the United States. In the countryside of the Mixteca, village after village has been emptied of working-age residents.

Gutierrez's role in the Binational Front of Indigenous Organizations illustrates his understanding of the need to challenge human rights violations on both sides of the border. If Mexico's indigenous migrants succeed, they may be able to help force a change in the political structure at home, and thereby influence the migration of Mexican citizens abroad.

Suppressing the News

Today, though, Oaxaca's political system is still controlled by Mexico's old ruling Party of the Institutionalized Revolution (PRI). The PRI lost its control over the national government to the National Action Party (PAN) in 2000. While the PAN has more direct ties to Mexico's growing corporate class, and received the bulk of that class's campaign money in the 2006 election, both parties pursue the same neoliberal economic policies that line party leaders' pockets and those of their corporate allies. Efforts to change this system bring down their wrath, as Gutierrez discovered.

"Before my arrest I thought we had a decent justice system," he says. "I knew it wasn't perfect, but I thought it worked." In prison, Gutierrez met members of a local union who had been there for months, along with other political prisoners. "There are over 2,000 complaints of political oppression in the state that have not been investigated," Gutierrez charges. His own case adds one more.

The news outlets that expose these abuses also find themselves in the government's crosshairs. *Noticias,* an independent newspaper founded in 1978, learned this the hard way. In 2004, the paper exposed public works fraud in the Murat administration. And in that fall's gubernatorial election, *Noticias* supported the left-wing candidate of the Party of the Democratic Revolution (PRD). The PRD lost amid charges of vote rigging. On December 1, the same day Murat's PRI successor, Ulises Ruiz, took office, hooligans broke into *Noticias's* building and threatened the reporters.

More provocations followed, and six months later state police and dozens of thugs belonging to the Revolutionary Confederation of Workers and Peasants (CROC) surrounded *Noticias's* offices. CROC is a labor federation founded by the PRI in the early 1950s. Though in some areas it functions as a normal union, the PRI often uses it to protect employers from labor unrest and to intimidate the party's opponents.

Amnesty International reports that 102 of *Noticias's* 130 employees belonged to CROC, but their relationship with the union had been strained, and CROC leadership called a strike "against the express wishes of the *Noticias* workforce." The Ruiz administration ordered it to stop publishing. Thirty-one workers decided to defend the office, where they were barricaded in for days and not permitted visitors, or even food and water.

CROC's secretary for labor and conflict, Ulises Bravo, told the *Miami Herald* that the strike was "completely labor-related and [had] nothing to do with a political agenda. *Noticias* ... tried to make this into a political issue because that gets them publicity and sells more papers."

Oaxaca's other newspapers stayed out of the fray. The *Miami Herald's* Jonathan Clark reports that "Privately, editors and reporters say they fear reprisals from the government for reporting on the issue. Editors reluctantly admit they need the government's publicity money to survive financially, and reporters say they fear that they will be harassed or fired for what they write."

Facing a news blockade in Oaxaca, the journalists hit the phones. From inside the besieged newsroom, reporter Cesar Morales got on the air in Fresno, California. He was interviewed by Rufino Dominguez, a Frente coordinator, and journalist Eduardo Stanley, cohosts of a bilingual program for Mixtec migrants on community radio station KFCF. Morales described "an assault by more than a hundred plain-clothes police, and thugs brought in to beat us." He called for help, and letters and faxes from California deluged Oaxaca.

In this case, binational pressure was not enough. The PRI eventually evicted the journalists and closed the paper's offices. *Noticias* is still distributed in Oaxaca, but it is written, edited, and printed elsewhere. Nevertheless, Oaxacans in California had developed a new ability to use media in their binational campaigns.

The Frente's Cross-Border Social Movement

Oaxacans abroad don't just protest conditions at home. The Frente defends worker rights in California fields, has convinced the state's courts to provide indigenous language interpreters, and helps keep alive the traditions that are the cultural glue binding together Mixtec, Zapotec, Triqui, and Chatino communities.

The Frente was, in fact, founded in California. Leaders like Dominguez have a long history organizing strikes and other movements in Mexico. When they arrived in California in 1987, they started the group with meetings in the San Joaquin Valley, Los Angeles, and San Diego. At first it was called the Mixtec/Zapotec Binational Front, because organizers wanted to unite Mixtec and Zapotec immigrants, two of the largest indigenous groups in Oaxaca.

Soon it had to change its name. Triquis and other indigenous Oaxacans wanted to participate, so the organization became the Indigenous Oaxacan Binational Front. Then Purepechas from Michoacan and indigenous people from other Mexican states also joined, and it became the Binational Front of Indigenous Organizations. Through all the changes, its binational character has only grown stronger.

Oaxacans have formed many other organizations during their long migration through Mexico and the United States. Most of these organizations are composed of members from a single town, and many of them are not as political as the Frente. The Frente is also different in that it unites people speaking different languages, from different indigenous groups, in order to promote community and workplace struggles for social justice.

Racism against indigenous people in Mexico has required them to develop a history of community resistance, and to fight for their own cultural identity. Centolia Maldonado, one of the Frente's leaders in Oaxaca, recalls her bitter experience as a migrant in northern Mexico. "They called us 'Oaxaquitas'—Indians," she remembers. "The people from the north were always valued more. There is terrible discrimination when people migrate."

In 1992, the Frente used the celebrations of the 500-year anniversary of the arrival of Christopher Columbus in the Americas as a platform to dramatize its call for indigenous rights. Dominguez says the protest countered "people who say that Christopher Columbus was welcomed when he came. They never talk about the massacres or the genocide that occurred in our villages, on the whole of the American continent. We wanted to tell the other side of the story."

The Frente's response to the Zapatista uprising on January 1, 1994, strengthened its commitment to cross-border action. The Frente pressured the Mexican government to refrain from using massive military force in Chiapas. From Fresno, California, across the border to Baja California and Oaxaca, Frente activists went on hunger strikes and demonstrated in front of consulates and government offices. That action, Dominguez says, "helped us realize that when there's movement in Oaxaca, there's got to be movement in the United States to make an impression on the Mexican government."

Participatory democracy is important in indigenous village life, and the Frente honors this tradition in its binational assemblies, where members discuss its political positions in detail. As a result, those political positions take into account the transnational nature of members' problems. The Frente opposes U.S. proposals for guest worker programs, arguing that they treat migrants only as temporary workers, not as people who belong to and are creating communities. Instead, the Frente calls for the legalization of undocumented migrants in the United States.

It also demands that the Mexican government fulfill the right of Mexican citizens living in the United States to vote in their country's elections. The Fox administration agreed to create a system to handle those votes in the 2006 election, but there were so many restrictions that only about 40,000 of the estimated 12 million Mexican citizens in the United States were able to cast ballots.

Attacks on Human Rights Escalate during an Election Year

In the late 1990s, the Frente in Oaxaca began an alliance with the PRD. Dominguez explains, "Mexican electoral laws don't permit a social organization to run independent candidates, so we have to make an alliance. Within the PRD there are divisions and internal problems, but it's all we have." Within this alliance, the Frente keeps its independence. "We should have a relationship with political parties without losing our identity and being dependent on politicians," Dominguez says.

In the recent presidential campaign, the Frente supported the PRD candidate, former Mexico City mayor Andres Manuel Lopez Obrador. Frente activist Leoncio Vasquez said the country faced a clear choice in political direction. "Lopez Obrador declared openly that he'd put poor people first," Vasquez explained. "He's against corruption and corporations who violate workers' and human rights." Raising rural income was the centerpiece of Lopez Obrador's proposals on migration. He was particularly critical of President Fox's support for the Bush guest worker proposal.

During the campaign, attacks on human rights in Oaxaca escalated. On May 19, Moises Cruz Sanchez, a PRD activist in the Mixtec town of San Juan Mixtepec, was gunned down in front of his wife and children as he left a local restaurant. The two gunmen fled, and police couldn't seem to find them.

That month in Fresno the Frente organized demonstrations against a planned visit by Governor Ruiz to California. Response to the protests revealed increasing cooperation between U.S. and Mexican authorities. After receiving a copy of a letter sent to the Mexican consulate to protest Ruiz's visit, Detective Dean Williamson of the Fresno Police paid a surprise visit to the Frente's office on Tulare Street. "It's an official procedure," said Williamson, "in which we're trying to clarify possible threats affecting public security."

Then violence escalated again in Oaxaca. In early May, the state's teachers struck for higher salaries and an end to human rights violations. Thousands of teachers occupied the main square in the state capital. Over 120,000 Oaxaca residents joined them in the largest rally in the state's history. On June 11, Ruiz promised business owners he would use a heavy hand to put down the protest. At four in the morning on June 14, helicopters began hovering over the tents of the sleeping teachers. As parents woke their children, billowing clouds of tear gas filled the cobblestone streets. Hundreds of police charged in. Within minutes, scores were beaten, and one pregnant woman miscarried. But Ruiz underestimated the teachers. They retook the square at the end of the day, and the following morning 300,000 people marched through Oaxaca demanding Ruiz's resignation.

In the following weeks, the protestors formed the Oaxaca Popular People's Assembly (APPO). Doctors and nurses joined, shutting down clinics. The government responded with increased violence. A state university student was killed in the street, and Jose Jimenez Colmanares, husband of a striking teacher, was gunned down during a protest march. Gunmen fired on the Channel 9 radio station after it had been occupied by demonstrators. Two reporters from *Noticias*, which recently opened another editorial office in the Oaxacan capital, were also shot at.

The APPO has many active indigenous members, some of whom also belong to the Frente. In the Mixteca, protestors occupied the Huahuapan de Leon city hall. Ruiz issued arrest orders for 50 leaders, including three Frente statewide officials.

On July 2, Mexicans went to the polls. The results gave a microscopic 200,000-vote majority to PAN candidate Felipe Calderon. Demands for a recount and accusations of fraud were immediate.

A million people rallied in Mexico City's main square on July 16, and two million on July 30, to demand a recount. The PRD and its candidate refuse to accept the results without one—a contrast to 1988, when leftist candidate Cuauhtemoc Cardenas conceded although it appeared that fraud robbed him of victory.

Whether the PRD will get the recount it demands is still unclear. Regardless, millions of Mexicans see a clear difference in political direction between the current political establishment and the PRD and the social forces that support it.

Pointing to attacks on striking steel workers in Michoacan and Sonora, the stationing of tanks outside the Mexican Congress, and the raging conflict in Oaxaca, Dominguez says that "A tiny group is trying to hold onto power by increasingly violent and illegal means."

But many Mexicans are challenging the lack of human rights that keeps that establishment in power. The Frente is an important part of that movement. "Indigenous people are always on the bottom in Oaxaca," Vasquez says. "The rich use their economic resources to maintain a government that puts them first. Big corporations control what's going on in Mexico, and those who criticize the government get harassed constantly, with arbitrary arrest and even assassination. That's one of the reasons why people from our communities have been forced to leave to find a means of survival elsewhere." ❏

Article 5.5

NIKE TO THE RESCUE?

Africa needs better jobs, not sweatshops.

BY JOHN MILLER
September/October 2006

"IN PRAISE OF THE MALIGNED SWEATSHOP"
WINDHOEK, Namibia—Africa desperately needs Western help in the form of schools, clinics and sweatshops.

On a street here in the capital of Namibia, in the southwestern corner of Africa, I spoke to a group of young men who were trying to get hired as day laborers on construction sites.

"I come here every day," said Naftal Shaanika, a 20-year-old. "I actually find work only about once a week."

Mr. Shaanika and the other young men noted that the construction jobs were dangerous and arduous, and that they would vastly prefer steady jobs in, yes, sweatshops. Sure, sweatshop work is tedious, grueling and sometimes dangerous. But over all, sewing clothes is considerably less dangerous or arduous—or sweaty—than most alternatives in poor countries.

Well-meaning American university students regularly campaign against sweatshops. But instead, anyone who cares about fighting poverty should campaign in favor of sweatshops, demanding that companies set up factories in Africa.

The problem is that it's still costly to manufacture in Africa. The headaches across much of the continent include red tape, corruption, political instability, unreliable electricity and ports, and an inexperienced labor force that leads to low productivity and quality. The anti-sweatshop movement isn't a prime obstacle, but it's one more reason not to manufacture in Africa.

Imagine that a Nike vice president proposed manufacturing cheap T-shirts in Ethiopia. The boss would reply: "You're crazy! We'd be boycotted on every campus in the country."

Some of those who campaign against sweatshops respond to my arguments by noting that they aren't against factories in Africa, but only demand a "living wage" in them. After all, if labor costs amount to only $1 per shirt, then doubling wages would barely make a difference in the final cost.

One problem … is that it already isn't profitable to pay respectable salaries, and so any pressure to raise them becomes one more reason to avoid Africa altogether.

One of the best U.S. initiatives in Africa has been the African Growth and Opportunity Act, which allows duty-free imports from Africa—and thus has stimulated manufacturing there.

—Op-ed by Nicholas Kristof, *New York Times*, June 6, 2006

Nicholas Kristof has been beating the pro-sweatshop drum for quite a while. Shortly after the East Asian financial crisis of the late 1990s, Kristof, the Pulitzer Prize-winning journalist and now columnist for the *New York Times*, reported the story of an Indonesian recycler who, picking through the metal scraps of a garbage dump, dreamed that her son would grow up to be a sweatshop worker. Then, in 2000, Kristof and his wife, *Times* reporter Sheryl WuDunn, published "Two Cheers for Sweatshops" in the *Times Magazine*. In 2002, Kristof's column advised G-8 leaders to "start an international campaign to promote imports from sweatshops, perhaps with bold labels depicting an unrecognizable flag and the words 'Proudly Made in a Third World Sweatshop.'"

Now Kristof laments that too few poor, young African men have the opportunity to enter the satanic mill of sweatshop employment. Like his earlier efforts, Kristof's latest pro-sweatshop ditty synthesizes plenty of half-truths. Let's take a closer look and see why there is still no reason to give it up for sweatshops.

A Better Alternative?

It is hardly surprising that young men on the streets of Namibia's capital might find sweatshop jobs more appealing than irregular work as day laborers on construction sites.

The alternative jobs available to sweatshop workers are often worse and, as Kristof loves to point out, usually involve more sweating than those in world export factories. Most poor people in the developing world eke out their livelihoods from subsistence agriculture or by plying petty trades. Others on the edge of urban centers work as street-hawkers or hold other jobs in the informal sector. As economist Arthur MacEwan wrote a few years back in *Dollars & Sense*, in a poor country like Indonesia, where women working in manufacturing earn five times as much as those in agriculture, sweatshops have no trouble finding workers.

But let's be clear about a few things. First, export factory jobs, especially in labor-intensive industries, often are just "a ticket to slightly less impoverishment," as even economist and sweatshop defender Jagdish Bhagwati allows.

Beyond that, these jobs seldom go to those without work or to the poorest of the poor. One study by sociologist Kurt Ver Beek showed that 60% of first-time Honduran *maquila* workers were previously employed. Typically they were not destitute, and they were better educated than most Hondurans.

Sweatshops don't just fail to rescue people from poverty. Setting up export factories where workers have few job alternatives has actually been a recipe for serious worker abuse. In *Beyond Sweatshops*, a book arguing for the benefits of direct foreign investment in the developing world, Brookings Institution economist Theodore Moran recounts the disastrous decision of the Philippine government to build the Bataan Export Processing Zone in an isolated mountainous area to lure foreign investors with the prospect of cheap labor. With few alternatives, Filipinos took jobs in the garment factories that sprung up in the zone. The manufacturers typically paid less than the minimum wage and forced employees to work overtime in factories filled with dust and fumes. Fed up, the workers eventually mounted a series of crippling strikes. Many factories shut down and occupancy rates in the zone plummeted, as did the value of exports, which declined by more than half between 1980 and 1986.

Kristof's argument is no excuse for sweatshop abuse: that conditions are worse elsewhere does nothing to alleviate the suffering of workers in export factories. They are often denied the right to organize, subjected to unsafe working conditions and to verbal, physical, and sexual abuse, forced to work overtime, coerced into pregnancy tests and even abortions, and paid less than a living wage. It remains useful and important to combat these conditions even if alternative jobs are worse yet.

The fact that young men in Namibia find sweatshop jobs appealing testifies to how harsh conditions are for workers in Africa, not the desirability of export factory employment.

Oddly, Kristof's desire to introduce new sweatshops to sub-Saharan Africa finds no support in the African Growth and Opportunity Act (AGOA) that he praises. The Act grants sub-Saharan apparel manufacturers preferential access to U.S. markets. But shortly after its passage, U.S. Trade Representative Robert Zoellick assured the press that the AGOA would not create sweatshops in Africa because it requires protective standards for workers consistent with those set by the International Labor Organization.

Antisweatshop Activism and Jobs

Kristof is convinced that the antisweatshop movement hurts the very workers it intends to help. His position has a certain seductive logic to it. As anyone who has suffered through introductory economics will tell you, holding everything else the same, a labor standard that forces multinational corporations and their subcontractors to boost wages should result in their hiring fewer workers.

But in practice does it? The only evidence Kristof produces is an imaginary conversation in which a boss incredulously refuses a Nike vice president's proposal to open a factory in Ethiopia paying wages of 25 cents a hour: "You're crazy! We'd be boycotted on every campus in the country."

While Kristof has an active imagination, there are some things wrong with this conversation.

First off, the antisweatshop movement seldom initiates boycotts. An organizer with United Students Against Sweatshops (USAS) responded on Kristof's blog: "We never call for apparel boycotts unless we are explicitly asked to by workers at a particular factory. This is, of course, exceedingly rare, because, as you so persuasively argued, people generally want to be employed." The National Labor Committee, the largest antisweatshop organization in the United States, takes the same position.

Moreover, when economists Ann Harrison and Jason Scorse conducted a systematic study of the effects of the antisweatshop movement on factory employment, they found no negative employment effect. Harrison and Scorse looked at Indonesia, where Nike was one of the targets of an energetic campaign calling for better wages and working conditions among the country's subcontractors. Their statistical analysis found that the antisweatshop campaign was responsible for 20% of the increase in the real wages of unskilled workers in factories exporting textiles, footwear, and apparel from 1991 to 1996. Harrison and Scorse also found that "antisweatshop activism did not have significant adverse effects on employment" in these sectors.

Campaigns for higher wages are unlikely to destroy jobs because, for multinationals and their subcontractors, wages make up a small portion of their overall costs. Even Kristof accepts this point, well documented by economists opposed to sweatshop labor. In Mexico's apparel industry, for instance, economists Robert Pollin, James Heintz, and Justine Burns from the Political Economy Research Institute found that doubling the pay of nonsupervisory workers would add just $1.80 to the production cost of a $100 men's sports jacket. A recent survey by the National Bureau of Economic Research found that U.S. consumers would be willing to pay $115 for the same jacket if they knew that it had not been made under sweatshop conditions.

Globalization in Sub-Saharan Africa

Kristof is right that Africa, especially sub-Saharan Africa, has lost out in the globalization process. Sub-Saharan Africa suffers from slower growth, less direct foreign investment, lower education levels, and higher poverty rates than most every other part of the world. A stunning 37 of the region's 47 countries are classified as "low-income" by the World Bank, each with a gross national income less than $825 per person. Many countries in the region bear the burdens of high external debt and a crippling HIV crisis that Kristof has made heroic efforts to bring to the world's attention.

But have multinational corporations avoided investing in sub-Saharan Africa because labor costs are too high? While labor costs in South Africa and Mauritius are high, those in the other countries of the region are modest by international standards, and quite low in some cases. Take Lesotho, the largest exporter of apparel from sub-Saharan Africa to the United States. In the country's factories that subcontract with Wal-Mart, the predominantly female workforce earns an average of just $54 a month. That's below the United Nations poverty line of $2 per day, and it includes regular forced overtime. In Madagascar, the region's third largest exporter of clothes to the United States, wages in the apparel industry are just 33 cents per hour, lower than those in China and among the lowest in the world. And at Ramatex Textile, the large Malaysian-owned textile factory in Namibia, workers only earn about $100 per month according to the Labour Resource and Research Institute in Windhoek. Most workers share their limited incomes with extended families and children, and they walk long distances to work because they can't afford better transportation.

On the other hand, recent experience shows that sub-Saharan countries with decent labor standards *can* develop strong manufacturing export sectors. In the late 1990s, Francis Teal of Oxford's Centre for the Study of African Economies compared Mauritius's successful export industries with Ghana's unsuccessful ones. Teal found that workers in Mauritius earned ten times as much as those in Ghana—$384 a month in Mauritius as opposed to $36 in Ghana. Mauritius's textile and garment industry remained competitive because its workforce was better educated and far more productive than Ghana's. Despite paying poverty wages, the Ghanaian factories floundered.

Kristof knows full well the real reason garment factories in the region are shutting down: the expiration of the Multifiber Agreement last January. The agreement, which set national export quotas for clothing and textiles, protected the garment industries in smaller countries around the world from direct competition with China. Now China and, to a lesser degree, India, are increasingly displacing other garment producers. In this new context, lower wages alone are unlikely to sustain the sub-Saharan garment industry. Industry sources report that sub-Saharan Africa suffers from several other drawbacks as an apparel producer, including relatively high utility and transportation costs and long shipping times to the United States. The region also has lower productivity and less skilled labor than Asia, and it has fewer sources of cotton yarn and higher-priced fabrics than China and India.

If Kristof is hell-bent on expanding the sub-Saharan apparel industry, he would do better to call for sub-Saharan economies to gain unrestricted access to the Quad markets—the United States, Canada, Japan, and Europe. Economists Stephen N. Karingi, Romain Perez, and Hakim Ben Hammouda estimate that the welfare gains associated with unrestricted market access could amount to $1.2 billion in sub-Saharan Africa, favoring primarily unskilled workers.

But why insist on apparel production in the first place? Namibia has sources of wealth besides a cheap labor pool for Nike's sewing machines. The *Economist* reports that Namibia is a world-class producer of two mineral products: diamonds (the country ranks seventh by value) and uranium (it ranks fifth by volume). The mining industry is the heart of Namibia's export economy and accounts for about 20% of the country's GDP. But turning the mining sector into a vehicle for national economic development would mean confronting the foreign corporations that control the diamond industry, such as the South African De Beers Corporation. That is a tougher assignment than scapegoating antisweatshop activists.

More and Better African Jobs

So why have multinational corporations avoided investing in sub-Saharan Africa? The answer, according to international trade economist Dani Rodrik, is "entirely due to the slow growth" of the sub-Saharan economies. Rodrik estimates that the region participates in international trade as much as can be expected given its economies' income levels, country size, and geography.

Rodrik's analysis suggests that the best thing to do for poor workers in Africa would be to lift the debt burdens on their governments and support their efforts to build functional economies. That means investing in human resources and physical infrastructure, and implementing credible macroeconomic policies that put job creation first. But these investments, as Rodrik points out, take time.

In the meantime, international policies establishing a floor for wages and safeguards for workers across the globe would do more for the young men on Windhoek's street corners than subjecting them to sweatshop abuse, because grinding poverty leaves people willing to enter into any number of desperate exchanges. And if Namibia is closing its garment factories because Chinese imports are cheaper, isn't that an argument for trying to improve labor standards in China, not lower them in sub-Saharan Africa? Abusive labor practices are rife in China's export factories, as the National Labor Committee and *BusinessWeek* have documented. Workers put in 13- to 16-hour days, seven days a week. They enjoy little to no health and safety enforcement, and their take-home pay falls below the minimum wage after the fines and deductions their employers sometimes withhold.

Spreading these abuses in sub-Saharan Africa will not empower workers there. Instead it will take advantage of the fact that they are among the most marginalized workers in the world. Debt relief, international labor standards, and public investments in education and infrastructure are surely better ways to fight African poverty than Kristof's sweatshop proposal. ❏

Sources: Arthur MacEwan, "Ask Dr. Dollar," *Dollars & Sense*, Sept–Oct 1998; John Miller, "Why Economists Are Wrong About Sweatshops and the Antisweatshop Movement," *Challenge*, Jan–Feb 2003; R. Pollin, J. Burns, and J. Heintz, "Global Apparel Production and Sweatshop Labor: Can Raising Retail Prices Finance Living Wages?" Political Economy Research Institute, Working Paper 19, DATE; N. Kristof, "In Praise of the Maligned Sweatshop,"*New York Times*, June 6, 2006; N. Kristof, "Let Them Sweat," *NYT* , June 25, 2002; N. Kristof, "Two Cheers for Sweatshops," *NYT* , Sept 24, 2000; N. Kristof, "Asia'[s Crisis Upsets Rising Effort to Confront Blight of Sweatshops," *NYT*, June 15, 1998; A. Harrison and J. Scorse, "Improving the Conditions of Workers? Minimum Wage Legislation and Anti-Sweatshop Activism," *Calif. Management Review*, Oct 2005; Herbert Jauch, "Africa's Clothing and Textile Industry: The Case of Ramatex in Namibia," in *The Future of the Textile and Clothing Industry in Sub-Saharan Africa*, ed. H. Jauch and R. Traub-Merz (Friedrich-Ebert-Stiftung, 2006); Kurt Alan Ver Beek, "Maquiladoras: Exploitation or Emancipation? An Overview of the Situation of Maquiladora Workers in Honduras," *World Development*, 29(9), 2001; Theodore Moran, *Beyond Sweatshops: Foreign Direct Investment and Globalization in Developing Countries* (Brookings Institution Press, 2002); "Comparative Assessment of the Competitiveness of the Textile and Apparel Sector in Selected Countries," in *Textiles and Apparel: Assessment of the Competitiveness of Certain Foreign Suppliers to the United States Market*, Vol. 1, U.S. International Trade Commission, Jan 2004; S. N. Karingi, R. Perez, and H. Ben Hammouda, "Could Extended Preferences Reward Sub-Saharan Africa's Participation in the Doha Round Negotiations?," *World Economy*, 2006; Francis Teal, "Why Can Mauritius Export Manufactures and Ghana Can Not?," *The World Economy*, 22 (7), 1999; Dani Rodrik, "Trade Policy and Economic Performance in Sub-Saharan Africa," Paper prepared for the Swedish Ministry for Foreign Affairs, Nov 1997.

Article 5.6

OUTSIZED OFFSHORE OUTSOURCING

The scope of offshore outsourcing gives some economists and the business press the heebie-jeebies.

BY JOHN MILLER
September/October 2007

At a press conference introducing the 2004 *Economic Report of the President*, N. Gregory Mankiw, then head of President Bush's Council of Economic Advisors, assured the press that "Outsourcing is probably a plus for the economy in the long run [and] just a new way of doing international trade."

Mankiw's comments were nothing other than mainstream economics, as even Democratic Party-linked economists confirmed. For instance Janet Yellen, President Clinton's chief economist, told the *Wall Street Journal*, "In the long run, outsourcing is another form of trade that benefits the U.S. economy by giving us cheaper ways to do things." Nonetheless, Mankiw's assurances were met with derision from those uninitiated in the economics profession's free-market ideology. Sen. John Edwards (D-N.C.) asked, "What planet do they live on?" Even Republican House Speaker Dennis Hastert (Ill.) said that Mankiw's theory "fails a basic test of real economics."

Mankiw now jokes that "if the American Economic Association were to give an award for the Most Politically Inept Paraphrasing of Adam Smith, I would be a leading candidate." But he quickly adds, "the recent furor about outsourcing, and my injudiciously worded comments about the benefits of international trade, should not eclipse the basic lessons that economists have understood for more than two centuries."

In fact Adam Smith never said any such thing about international trade. In response to the way Mankiw and other economists distort Smith's writings, economist Michael Meeropol took a close look at what Smith actually said; he found that Smith used his invisible hand argument to favor domestic investment over far-flung, hard-to-supervise foreign investments. Here are Smith's words in his 1776 masterpiece, *The Wealth of Nations*:

> By preferring the support of domestic to that of foreign industry, he [the investor] intends only his own security; and by directing that industry in such a manner as its produce may be of the greatest value, he intends only his own gain, and he is in this, as in many other cases, led by an invisible hand to promote an end, which was no part of his intention.

Outsized offshore outsourcing, the shipping of jobs overseas to take advantage of low wages, has forced some mainstream economists and some elements of the business press to have second thoughts about "free trade." Many are convinced that the painful transition costs that hit before outsourcing produces any ultimate benefits may be the biggest political issue in economics for a generation. And some recognize, as Smith did, that there is no guarantee unfettered international trade will leave the participants better off even in the long run.

Keynes's Revenge

Writing during the Great Depression of the 1930s, John Maynard Keynes, the pre-eminent economist of the twentieth century, prescribed government spending as a means of compensating for the instability of private investment. The notion of a mixed private/government economy, Keynes's prosthesis for the invisible hand of the market, guided U.S. economic policy from the 1940s through the 1970s.

It is only fitting that Paul Samuelson, the first Nobel Laureate in economics, and whose textbook introduced U.S. readers to Keynes, would be among the first mainstream economist to question whether unfettered international trade, in the context of massive outsourcing, would necessarily leave a developed economy such as that of the United States better off—even in the long run. In an influential 2004 article, Samuelson characterized the common economics wisdom about outsourcing and international trade this way:

> Yes, good jobs may be lost here in the short run. But …the gains of the winners from free trade, properly measured, work out to exceed the losses of the losers. … Never forget to tally the real gains of consumers alongside admitted possible losses of some producers. … The gains of the American winners are big enough to more than compensate the losers.

Samuelson took on this view, arguing that this common wisdom is "dead wrong about [the] *necessary* surplus of winning over losing" [emphasis in the original]. In a rather technical paper, he demonstrated that free trade globalization can sometimes

---

OFFSHORED? OUTSOURCED? CONFUSED?

The terms "offshoring" and "outsourcing" are often used interchangeably, but they refer to distinct processes:

Outsourcing – When a company hires another company to carry out a business function that it no longer wants to carry on in-house. The company that is hired may be in the same city or across the globe; it may be a historically independent firm or a spinoff of the first company created specifically to outsource a particular function.

Offshoring or *Offshore Outsourcing* – When a company shifts a portion of its business operation abroad. An offshore operation may be carried out by the same company or, more typically, outsourced to a different one.

ATTRIBUTES OF JOBS OUTSOURCED

- No Face-to-Face Customer Servicing Requirement
- High Information Content
- Work Process is Telecommutable and Internet Enabled
- High Wage Differential with Similar Occupation in Destination Country
- Low Setup Barriers
- Low Social Networking Requirement

give rise to a situation in which "a productivity gain in one country can benefit that country alone, while permanently hurting the other country by reducing the gains from trade that are possible between the two countries."

Many in the economics profession do admit that it is hard to gauge whether intensified offshoring of U.S. jobs in the context of free-trade globalization will give more in winnings to the winners than it takes in losses from the losers. "Nobody has a clue about what the numbers are," as Robert C. Feenstra, a prominent trade economist, told *BusinessWeek* at the time.

The empirical issues that will determine whether offshore outsourcing ultimately delivers, on balance, more benefits than costs, and to whom those benefits and costs will accrue, are myriad. First, how wide a swath of white-collar workers will see their wages reduced by competition from the cheap, highly skilled workers who are now becoming available around the world? Second, by how much will their wages drop? Third, will the U.S. workers thrown into the global labor pool end up losing more in lower wages than they gain in lower consumer prices? In that case, the benefits of increased trade would go overwhelmingly to employers. But even employers might lose out depending on the answer to a fourth question: Will cheap labor from abroad allow foreign employers to out-compete U.S. employers, driving down the prices of their products and lowering U.S. export earnings? In that case, not only workers, but the corporations that employ them as well, could end up worse off.

Bigger Than A Box

Another mainstream Keynesian economist, Alan Blinder, former Clinton economic advisor and vice-chair of the Federal Reserve Board, doubts that outsourcing will be "immiserating" in the long run and still calls himself "a free-trader down to his toes." But Blinder is convinced that the transition costs will be large, lengthy, and painful before the United States experiences a net gain from outsourcing. Here is why.

First, rapid improvements in information and communications technology have rendered obsolete the traditional notion that manufactured goods, which can generally be boxed and shipped, are tradable, while services, which cannot be boxed, are not. And the workers who perform the services that computers and satellites have now rendered tradable will increasingly be found offshore, especially when they are skilled and will work for lower wages.

Second, another 1.5 billion or so workers—many in China, India, and the former Soviet bloc—are now part of the world economy. While most are low-skilled workers, some are not; and as Blinder says, a small percentage of 1.5 billion is nonetheless "a lot of willing and able people available to do the jobs that technology will move offshore." And as China and India educate more workers, offshoring of high-skill work will accelerate.

Third, the transition will be particularly painful in the United States because the U.S. unemployment insurance program is stingy, at least by first-world standards, and because U.S. workers who lose their jobs often lose their health insurance and pension rights as well.

How large will the transition cost be? "Thirty million to 40 million U.S. jobs are potentially offshorable," according to Blinder's latest estimates. "These include scientists, mathematicians and editors on the high end and telephone operators, clerks and typists on the low end."

Blinder arrived at these figures by creating an index that identifies how easy or hard it will be for a job to be physically or electronically "offshored." He then used the index to assess the Bureau of Labor Statistics' 817 U.S. occupational categories. Not surprisingly, Blinder classifies almost all of the 14.3 million U.S. manufacturing jobs as offshorable. But he also classifies more than twice that many U.S. service sector jobs as offshorable, including most computer industry jobs as well as many others, for instance, the 12,470 U.S. economists and the 23,790 U.S. multimedia artists and animators. In total, Blinder's analysis suggests that 22% to 29% of the jobs held by U.S. workers in 2004 will be potentially offshorable within a decade or two, with nearly 8.2 million jobs in 59 occupations "highly offshorable." Table 1 provides a list of the broad occupational categories with 300,000 or more workers that Blinder considers potentially offshorable.

Mankiw dismissed Blinder's estimates of the number of jobs at risk to offshoring as "out of the mainstream." Indeed, Blinder's estimates are considerably larger than earlier ones. But these earlier studies either aim to measure the number of U.S. jobs that will be outsourced (as opposed to the number at risk of being outsourced), look at a shorter period of time, or have shortcomings that suggest they underestimate the number of U.S. jobs threatened by outsourcing. (See "Studying the Studies.")

Global Arbitrage

Low wages are the reason U.S. corporations outsource labor. Table 2 shows just how large the international wage differentials were for computer programmers in 2002. Programmers in the United States make wages nearly *ten times* those of their counterparts in India and the Philippines, for example.

Today, more and more white-collar workers in the United States are finding themselves in direct competition with the low-cost, well-trained, highly educated workers in Bangalore, Shanghai, and Eastern and Central Europe. These workers

TABLE 1: MAJOR OCCUPATIONS RANKED BY OFFSHORABILITY

Occupation	Category	Index Number	Number of Workers
Computer programmers	I	100	389,090
Telemarketers	I	95	400,860
Computer systems analysts	I	93	492,120
Billing and posting clerks and machine operators	I	90	513,020
Bookkeeping, accounting, and auditing clerks	I	84	1,815,340
Computer support specialists	I and II	92/68	499,860
Computer software engineers: Applications	II	74	455,980
Computer software engineers: Systems software	II	74	320,720
Accountants	II	72	591,311
Welders, cutters, solderers, and brazers	II	70	358,050
Helpers—production workers	II	70	528,610
First-line supervisors/managers of production and operating workers	II	68	679,930
Packaging and filling machine operators and tenders	II	68	396,270
Team assemblers	II	65	1,242,370
Bill and account collectors	II	65	431,280
Machinists	II	61	368,380
Inspectors, testers, sorters, samplers, and weighers	II	60	506,160
General and operations managers	III	55	1,663,810
Stock clerks and order fillers	III	34	1,625,430
Shipping, receiving, and traffic clerks	III	29	759,910
Sales managers	III	26	317,970
Business operations specialists, all other	IV	25	916,290

Source: Alan Blinder, "How Many U.S. Jobs Might Be Offshorable?" *CEPS Working Paper* #142, March 2007, figures from Bureau of Labor Statistics and author's judgments.

often use the same capital and technology and are no less productive than the U.S. workers they replace. They just get paid less.

This global labor arbitrage, as Morgan Stanley's chief economist Stephen Roach calls it, has narrowed international wage disparities in manufacturing, and now in services too, by unrelentingly pushing U.S. wages down toward international norms. ("Arbitrage" refers to transactions that yield a profit by taking advantage of a price differential for the same asset in different locations. Here, of course, the "asset" is wage labor of a certain skill level.) A sign of that pressure: about 70% of laid-off workers in the United States earn less three years later than they did at the time of the layoff; on average, those reemployed earn 10% less than they did before.

And it's not only laid-off workers who are hurt. A study conducted by Harvard labor economists Lawrence F. Katz, Richard B. Freeman, and George J. Borjas finds that every other worker with skills similar to those who were displaced also loses out. Every 1% drop in employment due to imports or factories gone abroad shaves 0.5% off the wages of the remaining workers in that occupation, they conclude.

Global labor arbitrage also goes a long way toward explaining the poor quality and low pay of the jobs the U.S. economy has created this decade, according to Roach. By dampening wage increases for an ever wider swath of the U.S. workforce, he argues, outsourcing has helped to drive a wedge between productivity gains and wage gains and to widen inequality in the United States. In the first four years of this decade, nonfarm productivity in the United States has recorded a cumulative increase of 13.3%—more than double the 5.9% rise in real compensation per hour over the same period. ("Compensation" includes wages, which have been stagnant for the average worker, plus employer spending on fringe benefits such as health

TABLE 2: AVERAGE SALARIES OF PROGRAMMERS

Country	Salary Range
Poland and Hungary	$4,800 to $8,000
India	$5,880 to $11,000
Philippines	$6,564
Malaysia	$7,200
Russian Federation	$5,000 to $7,500
China	$8,952
Canada	$28,174
Ireland	$23,000 to $34,000
Israel	$15,000 to $38,000
USA	$60,000 to $80,000

Source: *CIO* magazine, November 2002, from Merrill Lynch *Smart Access Survey*.

insurance, which has risen even as, in many instances, the actual benefits have been cut back.) Roach reports that the disconnect between pay and productivity growth during the current economic expansion has been much greater in services than in manufacturing, as that sector weathers the powerful forces of global labor arbitrage for the first time.

Doubts in the Business Press?!

Even in the business press, doubts that offshore outsourcing willy-nilly leads to economic improvement have become more acute. Earlier this summer, a *BusinessWeek* cover story, "The Real Cost of Offshoring," reported that government statistics have underestimated the damage to the U.S. economy from offshore outsourcing. The problem is that since offshoring took off, *import* growth, adjusted for inflation, has been faster than the official numbers show. That means improvements in living standards, as well as corporate profits, depend more on cheap imports, and less on improving domestic productivity, than analysts thought.

Growing angst about outsourcing's costs has also prompted the business press to report favorably on remedies for the dislocation brought on by offshoring that deviate substantially from the non-interventionist, free-market playbook. Even the most unfazed pro-globalization types want to beef up trade adjustment assistance for displaced workers and strengthen the U.S. educational system. But both proposals are inadequate.

More education, the usual U.S. prescription for any economic problem, is off the mark here. Cheaper labor is available abroad up and down the job-skill ladder, so even the most rigorous education is no inoculation against the threat of offshore outsourcing. As Blinder emphasizes, it is the need for face-to-face contact that stops jobs from being shipped overseas, not the level of education necessary to perform them. Twenty years from now, home health aide positions will no doubt be plentiful in the United States; jobs for highly trained IT professionals may be scarce.

Trade adjustment assistance has until now been narrowly targeted at workers hurt by imports. Most new proposals would replace traditional trade adjustment assistance and unemployment insurance with a program for displaced workers that offers wage insurance to ease the pain of taking a lower-paying job and provides for portable health insurance and retraining. The pro-globalization research group McKinsey Global Institute (MGI), for example, claims that for as little as 4% to 5% of the amount they've saved in lower wages, companies could cover the wage losses of all laid-off workers once they are reemployed, paying them 70% of the wage differential between their old and new jobs (in addition to health care subsidies) for up to two years.

While MGI confidently concludes that this proposal will "go a long way toward relieving the current anxieties," other globalization advocates are not so sure. They recognize that economic anxiety is pervasive and that millions of white-collar workers now fear losing their jobs. Moreover, even if fears of actual job loss are overblown, wage insurance schemes do little to compensate for the downward pressure offshoring is putting on the wages of workers who have not been laid off.

Other mainstream economists and business writers go even further, calling for not only wage insurance but also taxes on the winners from globalization. And globalization has produced big winners: on Wall Street, in the corporate boardroom, and among those workers in high demand in the global economy.

Economist Matthew Slaughter, who recently left President Bush's Council of Economic Advisers, told the *Wall Street Journal*, "Expanding the political support for open borders [for trade] requres making a radical change in fiscal policy." He proposes eliminating the Social Security-Medicare payroll tax on the bottom half of workers—roughly, those earning less than $33,000 a year—and making up the lost revenue by raising the payroll tax on higher earners.

The goal of these economists is to thwart a crippling political backlash against trade. As they see it, "using the tax code to slice the apple more evenly is far more palatable than trying to hold back globalization with policies that risk shrinking the economic apple."

Some even call for extending global labor arbitrage to CEOs. In a June 2006 *New York Times* op-ed, equity analyst Lawrence Orlowski and New York University

---

STUDYING THE STUDIES

When economist Alan Blinder raised alarm bells in 2006 about the potentially large-scale offshoring of U.S. jobs, his results were inevitably compared to earlier research on offshore outsourcing. Three studies have been especially influential. The 2002 study (revised in 2004) by Forrester Research, a private, for-profit market research firm, which estimated that 3.3 million U.S. service sector jobs would move offshore by 2015, caused perhaps the biggest media stir. It was picked up by *BusinessWeek* and the *Wall Street Journal*, and hyped by Lou Dobbs, the CNN business-news anchor and outspoken critic of offshoring.

Forrester researcher John McCarthy developed his estimate by poring over newspaper clippings and Labor Department statistics on 505 white-collar occupations and then making an educated guess about how many jobs would be shipped offshore by 2015.

The Forrester study projects actual offshoring, not the number of jobs at risk of offshoring, so its estimate is rightfully lower than Blinder's. But the ample possibilities for technological change between now and 2015 convince Blinder that the Forrester estimate is nonetheless too low.

A 2003 study by University of California economists Ashok Bardhan and Cynthia Kroll estimated that about 11% of all U.S. jobs in 2001 were vulnerable to offshoring. Bradhan and Kroll applied the "outsourceability attributes" listed in "Attributes of Jobs Outsourced" to occupations where at least some outsourcing either has already taken place or is being planned.

Blinder considers the Bardhan and Kroll estimate for 2001 to be comparable to his estimate that 20% to 30% of the employed labor force will be at risk of offshore outsourcing within the next ten to twenty years, especially considering that Bardhan and Kroll do not allow for outsourcing to spread beyond the occupations it is currently affecting. This is like "looking only slightly beyond the currently-visible tip of the iceberg," according to Blinder.

The McKinsey Global Institute (MGI), a research group known for its unabashedly favorable view of globalization, has done its best to put a positive spin on offshore

assistant research director Florian Lengyel argued that offshoring the jobs of U.S. chief executives would reduce costs and release value to shareholders by bringing the compensation of U.S. CEOs (on average 170 times greater than the compensation of average U.S. workers in 2004) in line with CEO compensation in Britain (22 times greater) and in Japan (11 times greater).

Yet others focus on the stunning lack of labor mobility that distinguishes the current era of globalization from earlier ones. Labor markets are becoming increasingly free and flexible under globalization, but labor enjoys no similar freedom of movement. In a completely free market, the foreign workers would come here to do the work that is currently being outsourced. Why aren't more of those workers coming to the United States? Traditional economists Gary Becker and Richard Posner argue the answer is clear: an excessively restrictive immigration policy.

Onshore and Offshore Solidarity

Offshoring is one of the last steps in capitalism's conversion of the "physician, the lawyer, the priest, the poet, the man of science, into its paid wage laborers," as

---

outsourcing. Its 2003 study, which relied on the Forrester offshoring estimates, concluded that offshoring is already benefiting the U.S. economy. For instance, MGI calculates that for every dollar spent on a business process outsourced to India, the U.S. economy gains at least $1.12. The largest chunk—58 cents—goes back to the original employer in the form of cost savings, almost exclusively in the form of lower wages. In addition, 30% of Indian offshoring is actually performed by U.S. companies, so the wage savings translate into higher earnings for those companies. The study also argues that offshore outsourcing frees up U.S. workers to do other tasks.

A second MGI study, in 2005, surveyed dozens of companies in eight sectors, from pharmaceutical companies to insurers. The study predicted that multinational companies in the entire developed world will have located only 4.1 million service jobs in low-wage countries by 2008—a figure equal to only 1% of the total number of service jobs in developed countries.

But the MGI outsourcing studies have serious limitations. For instance, Blinder points out that MGI's analysis looks at a very short time frame, and that the potential for outsourcing in English-speaking countries such as the United States is higher than elsewhere, a fact lost in the MGI studies' global averages.

In their 2005 book *Outsourcing America*, published by the American Management Association, public policy professors Ron Hira and Anil Hira argue that MGI's 2003 report "should be viewed as a self-interested lobbying document that presents an unrealistically optimistic estimate of the impact of offshore outsourcing." For instance, most of the data for the report came from case studies conducted by MGI that are unavailable to the public and unsupported by any model. Moreover, the MGI analysis assumes that the U.S. economy will follow its long-term trend and create 3.5 million jobs a year, enough to quickly reemploy U.S. workers displaced by offshoring. But current U.S. job creation falls far short of that trend. A recent White House fact sheet brags that the U.S. economy has created 8.3 million jobs since August 2003. Still, that is less than 2.1 million jobs a year, and only 1.8 million jobs over the last 12 months.

MGI's Farrell is right about one thing. "If the economy were stronger," she says, "there wouldn't be such a negative feeling" about work getting offshored. But merely assuming high job growth doesn't make it so.

Marx and Engels put it in the *Communist Manifesto* 160 years ago. It has already done much to increase economic insecurity in the workaday world and has become, Blinder suggests, the number one economic issue of our generation.

Offshoring has also underlined the interdependence of workers across the globe. To the extent that corporations now organize their business operations on a global scale, shifting work around the world in search of low wages, labor organizing must also be global in scope if it is to have any hope of building workers' negotiating strength.

Yet today's global labor arbitrage pits workers from different countries against each other as competitors, not allies. Writing about how to improve labor standards, economists Ajit Singh and Ann Zammit of the South Centre, an Indian non-governmental organization, ask the question, "On what could workers of the world unite" today? Their answer is that faster economic growth could indeed be a positive-sum game from which both the global North and the global South could gain. A pick-up in the long-term rate of growth of the world economy would generate higher employment, increasing wages and otherwise improving labor standards in both regions. It should also make offshoring less profitable and less painful.

The concerns of workers across the globe would also be served by curtailing the ability of multinational corporations to move their investment anywhere, which weakens the bargaining power of labor both in advanced countries and in the global South. Workers globally would also benefit if their own ability to move between countries was enhanced. The combination of a new set of rules to limit international capital movements and to expand labor mobility across borders, together with measures to ratchet up economic growth and thus increase worldwide demand for labor, would alter the current process of globalization and harness it to the needs of working people worldwide. ❑

Sources: Alan S. Blinder, "Fear of Offshoring," CEPS Working Paper #119, Dec. 2005; Alan S. Blinder, "How Many U.S. Jobs Might Be Offshorable?" CEPS Working Paper #142, March 2007; N. Gregory Mankiw and P. Swagel, "The Politics and Economics of Offshore Outsourcing," Am. Enterprise Inst. Working Paper #122, 12/7/05; "Offshoring: Is It a Win-Win Game?" McKinsey Global Institute, August 2003; Diane Farrell et al., "The Emerging Global Labor Market, Part 1: The Demand for Talent in Services," McKinsey Global Institute, June 2005; Ashok Bardhan and Cynthia Kroll, "The New Wave of Outsourcing," Research Report #113, Fisher Center for Real Estate and Urban Economics, Univ. of Calif., Berkeley, Fall 2003; Paul A. Samuelson, "Where Ricardo and Mill Rebut and Confirm Arguments of Mainstream Economists Supporting Globalization," *J Econ Perspectives* 18:3, Summer 2004; Alan S. Blinder, "Free Trade's Great, but Offshoring Rattles Me," *Wash. Post,* 5/6/07; Michael Mandel, "The Real Cost of Offshoring," *BusinessWeek,* 6/18/07; Aaron Bernstein, "Shaking Up Trade Theory," *BusinessWeek,* 12/6/04; David Wessel, "The Case for Taxing Globalization's Big Winners," *WSJ,* 6/14/07; Bob Davis, "Some Democratic Economists Echo Mankiw on Outsourcing," *WSJ;* N. Gregory Mankiw, "Outsourcing Redux," gregmankiw.blogspot.com/2006/05/outsourcing-redux; David Wessel and Bob Davis, "Pain From Free Trade Spurs Second Thoughts," *WSJ,* 3/30/07; Ajit Singh and Ann Zammit, "On What Could Workers of the World Unite? Economic Growth and a New Global Economic Order," from *The Global Labour Standards Controversy: Critical Issues For Developing Countries,* South Centre, 2000; Michael Meeropol, "Distorting Adam Smith on Trade," *Challenge,* July/Aug 2004.

Chapter 6

MIGRATION

THE RIGHT TO STAY HOME

Transnational communities are creating new ways of looking at citizenship and residence that correspond to the realities of migration.

BY DAVID BACON
September/October 2008

For almost half a century, migration has been the main fact of social life in hundreds of indigenous towns spread through the hills of Oaxaca, one of Mexico's poorest states. That's made migrants' rights, and the conditions they face, central concerns for communities like Santiago de Juxtlahuaca. Today the right to travel to seek work is a matter of survival. But this June in Juxtlahuaca, in the heart of Oaxaca's Mixteca region, dozens of farmers left their fields, and weavers their looms, to talk about another right—the right to stay home.

In the town's community center two hundred Mixtec, Zapotec, and Triqui farmers, and a handful of their relatives working in the United States, made impassioned speeches asserting this right at the triannual assembly of the Indigenous Front of Binational Organizations (FIOB). Hot debates ended in numerous votes. The voices of mothers and fathers arguing over the future of their children echoed from the cinderblock walls of the cavernous hall. In Spanish, Mixteco, and Triqui, people repeated one phrase over and over: *el derecho de no migrar*—the right to *not* migrate. Asserting this right challenges not just inequality and exploitation facing migrants, but the very reasons why people have to migrate to begin with. Indigenous communities are pointing to the need for social change.

About 500,000 indigenous people from Oaxaca live in the United States, including 300,000 in California alone, according to Rufino Dominguez, one of FIOB's founders. These men and women come from communities whose economies are totally dependent on migration. The ability to send a son or daughter across the border to the north, to work and send back money, makes the difference between eating chicken or eating salt and tortillas. Migration means not having to manhandle a wooden plough behind an ox, cutting furrows in dry soil for a corn crop that can't be sold for what it cost to plant it. It means that dollars arrive in the mail when kids need shoes to go to school, or when a grandparent needs a doctor.

Seventy-five percent of Oaxaca's 3.4 million residents live in extreme poverty, according to EDUCA, an education and development organization. For more than two decades, under pressure from international lenders, the Mexican government has cut spending intended to raise rural incomes. Prices have risen dramatically since price controls and subsidies were eliminated for necessities like gasoline, electricity, bus fares, tortillas, and milk.

CITIZENSHIP, POLITICAL RIGHTS, AND LABOR RIGHTS

Citizenship is a complex issue in a world in which transnational migrant communities span borders and exist in more than one place simultaneously. Residents of transnational communities don't see themselves simply as victims of an unfair system, but as actors capable of reproducing culture, of providing economic support to families in their towns of origin, and of seeking social justice in the countries to which they've migrated. A sensible immigration policy would recognize and support migrant communities. It would reinforce indigenous culture and language, rather than treating them as a threat. At the same time, it would seek to integrate immigrants into the broader community around them and give them a voice in it, rather than promoting social exclusion, isolation, and segregation. It would protect the rights of immigrants as part of protecting the rights of all working people.

Transnational communities in Mexico are creating new ways of looking at citizenship and residence that correspond more closely to the reality of migration. In 2005 Jesús Martínez, a professor at California State University in Fresno, was elected by residents of the state of Michoacán in Mexico to their state legislature. His mandate was to represent the interests of the state's citizens living in the United States. "In Michoacán, we're trying to carry out reforms that can do justice to the role migrants play in our lives," Martínez said. In 2006 Pepe Jacques Medina, director of the Comité Pro Uno in Los Angeles' San Fernando Valley, was elected to the Federal Chamber of Deputies on the ticket of the left-leaning Party of the Democratic Revolution (PRD) with the same charge. Transnational migrants insist that they have important political and social rights, both in their communities of origin and in their communities abroad.

The two parties that control the Mexican national congress, the Institutional Revolutionary Party (PRI) and the National Action Party (PAN), have taken steps to provide political rights for migrants. But while Mexico's congress voted over a decade ago to enfranchise Mexicans in the United States, it only set up a system to implement that decision in April 2005. They imposed so many obstacles that in the 2006 presidential elections only 40,000 were able to vote, out of a potential electorate of millions.

While it is difficult for Mexicans in the United States to vote in Mexico, they are barred from voting in the United States altogether. But U.S. electoral politics can't remain forever immune from expectations of representation, and they shouldn't. After all, the slogan of the Boston Tea Party was "No taxation without representation"; those who make economic contributions have political rights. That principle requires recognition of the legitimate social status of everyone living in the United States. Legalization isn't just important to migrants—it is a basic step in the preservation and extension of democratic rights for all people. With and without

Raquel Cruz Manzano, principal of the Formal Primary School in San Pablo Macuiltianguis, a town in the indigenous Zapotec region, says only 900,000 Oaxacans receive organized health care, and the illiteracy rate is 21.8%. "The educational level in Oaxaca is 5.8 years," Cruz notes, "against a national average of 7.3 years. The average monthly wage for non-governmental employees is less than 2,000 pesos [about $200] per family," the lowest in the nation. "Around 75,000 children have to work in order to survive or to help their families," says Jaime Medina, a reporter for Oaxaca's daily *Noticias*, "A typical teacher earns about 2200 pesos every two weeks [about $220]. From that they have to purchase chalk, pencils and other school supplies for the children." Towns like Juxtlahuaca don't even have waste water treatment. Rural communities rely on the same rivers for drinking water that are also used to carry away sewage.

---

visas, 34 million migrants living in the United States cannot vote to choose the political representatives who decide basic questions about wages and conditions at work, the education of their children, their health care or lack of it, and even whether they can walk the streets without fear of arrest and deportation.

Migrants' disenfranchisement affects U.S. citizens, especially working people. If all the farm workers and their families in California's San Joaquin Valley were able to vote, a wave of living wage ordinances would undoubtedly sweep the state. California's legislature would pass a single-payer health plan to ensure that every resident receives free and adequate health care. If it failed to pass, San Joaquin Valley legislators, currently among the most conservative, would be swept from office.

When those who most need social change and economic justice are excluded from the electorate, the range of possible reform is restricted, not only on issues of immigration, but on most economic issues that affect working people. Immigration policy, including political and social rights for immigrants, are integral parts of a broad agenda for change that includes better wages and housing, a national healthcare system, a national jobs program, and the right to organize without fear of being fired. Without expanding the electorate, it will be politically difficult to achieve any of it. By the same token, it's not possible to win major changes in immigration policy apart from a struggle for these other goals.

Anti-immigrant hysteria has always preached that the interests of immigrants and the native born are in conflict, that one group can only gain at the expense of the other. In fact, the opposite is true. To raise wages generally, the low price of immigrant labor has to rise, which means that immigrant workers have to be able to organize effectively. Given half a chance, they will fight for better jobs, wages, schools, and health care, just like anyone else. When they gain political power, the working class communities around them benefit too. Since it's easier for immigrants to organize if they have permanent legal status, a real legalization program would benefit a broad range of working people, far beyond immigrants themselves. On the other hand, when the government and employers use employer sanctions, enforcement, and raids to stop the push for better conditions, organizing is much more difficult, and unions and workers in general suffer the consequences.

The social exclusion and second-class status imposed by guestworker programs only increases migrants' vulnerability. De-linking immigration status and employment is a necessary step to achieving equal rights for migrant workers, who will never have significant power if they have to leave the country when they lose their jobs. Healthy immigrant communities need employed workers, but they also need students, old and young people, caregivers, artists, the disabled, and those who don't have traditional jobs.

"There are no jobs here, and NAFTA [the North American Free Trade Agreement] made the price of corn so low that it's not economically possible to plant a crop anymore," Dominguez asserts. "We come to the U.S. to work because we can't get a price for our product at home. There is no alternative." Without large-scale political change, most communities won't have the resources for productive projects and economic development that could provide a decent living.

Because of its indigenous membership, FIOB campaigns for the rights of migrants in the United States who come from those communities. It calls for immigration amnesty and legalization for undocumented migrants. FIOB has also condemned the proposals for guestworker programs. Migrants need the right to work, but "these workers don't have labor rights or benefits," Dominguez charges. "It's like slavery."

At the same time, "we need development that makes migration a choice rather than a necessity—the right to not migrate," explains Gaspar Rivera Salgado, a professor at UCLA. "Both rights are part of the same solution. We have to change the debate from one in which immigration is presented as a problem to a debate over rights. The real problem is exploitation." But the right to stay home, to not migrate, has to mean more than the right to be poor, the right to go hungry and be homeless. Choosing whether to stay home or leave only has meaning if each choice can provide a meaningful future.

In Juxtlahuaca, Rivera Salgado was elected as FIOB's new binational coordinator. His father and mother still live on a ranch half an hour up a dirt road from the main highway, in the tiny town of Santa Cruz Rancho Viejo. There his father Sidronio planted three hundred avocado trees a few years ago, in the hope that someday their fruit would take the place of the corn and beans that were once his staple crops. He's fortunate—his relatives have water, and a pipe from their spring has kept most of his trees, and those hopes, alive. Fernando, Gaspar's brother, has started growing mushrooms in a FIOB-sponsored project, and even put up a greenhouse for tomatoes. Those projects, they hope, will produce enough money that Fernando won't have to go back to Seattle, where he worked for seven years.

This family perhaps has come close to achieving the *derecho de no migrar*. For the millions of farmers throughout the indigenous countryside, not migrating means doing something like what Gaspar's family has done. But finding the necessary resources, even for a small number of families and communities, presents FIOB with its biggest challenge.

Rivera Salgado says, "we will find the answer to migration in our communities of origin. To make the right to not migrate concrete, we need to organize the forces in our communities, and combine them with the resources and experiences we've accumulated in 16 years of cross-border organizing." Over the years FIOB has organized women weavers in Juxtlahuaca, helping them sell their textiles and garments through its chapters in California. It set up a union for rural taxis, both to help farming families get from Juxtlahuaca to the tiny towns in the surrounding hills, and to provide jobs for drivers. Artisan co-ops make traditional products, helped by a cooperative loan fund.

The government does have some money for loans to start similar projects, but it usually goes to officials who often just pocket it, supporters of the ruling PRI, which has ruled Oaxaca since it was formed in the 1940s. "Part of our political culture is the use of *regalos*, or government favors, to buy votes," Rivera Salgado explains. "People want *regalos*, and think an organization is strong because of what it can give. It's critical that our members see organization as the answer to problems, not a gift from the government or a political party. FIOB members need political education."

But for the 16 years of its existence, FIOB has been a crucial part of the political opposition to Oaxaca's PRI government. Juan Romualdo Gutierrez Cortéz, a school teacher in Tecomaxtlahuaca, was FIOB's Oaxaca coordinator until he stepped down at the Juxtlahuaca assembly. He is also a leader of Oaxaca's teachers union, Section 22 of the National Education Workers Union, and of the Popular Association of the People of Oaxaca (APPO).

A June 2006 strike by Section 22 sparked a months-long uprising, led by APPO, which sought to remove the state's governor, Ulises Ruíz, and make a basic change in development and economic policy. The uprising was crushed by Federal armed intervention, and dozens of activists were arrested. According to Leoncio Vásquez, an FIOB activist in Fresno, "the lack of human rights itself is a factor contributing to migration from Oaxaca and Mexico, since it closes off our ability to call for any change." This spring teachers again occupied the central plaza, or *zócalo*, of the state capital, protesting the same conditions that sparked the uprising two years ago.

In the late 1990s Gutierrez was elected to the Oaxaca Chamber of Deputies, in an alliance between FIOB and Mexico's left-wing Democratic Revolutionary Party (PRD). Following his term in office, he was imprisoned by Ruíz' predecessor, José Murat, until a binational campaign won his release. His crime, and that of many others filling Oaxaca's jails, was insisting on a new path of economic development that would raise rural living standards and make migration just an option, rather than an indispensable means of survival.

Despite the fact that APPO wasn't successful in getting rid of Ruíz and the PRI, Rivera Salgado believes that "in Mexico we're very close to getting power in our communities on a local and state level." FIOB delegates agreed that the organization would continue its alliance with the PRD. "We know the PRD is caught up in an internal crisis, and there's no real alternative vision on the left," Rivera Salgado says. "But there are no other choices if we want to participate in electoral politics. Migration is part of globalization," he emphasizes, "an aspect of state policies that expel people. Creating an alternative to that requires political power. There's no way to avoid that." ❏

Article 6.2

"THEY WORK HERE, THEY LIVE HERE, THEY STAY HERE!"

French immigrants strike for the right to work—and win.

BY MARIE KENNEDY AND CHRIS TILLY

July/August 2007

France has an estimated half-million undocumented immigrants, including many from France's former colonies in Africa. The *sans-papiers* (literally, "without papers"), as the French call them, lead a shadowy existence, much like their U.S. counterparts. And as U.S. immigrants did in 2006 with rousing mass demonstrations, the French undocumented have recently taken a dramatic step out of the shadows. But the *sans-papiers* did it in a particularly French way: hundreds of them occupied their workplaces.

Snowballing Strikes

The snowflake that led to this snowball of sit-in strikes was a November immigration law, sponsored by the arch-conservative government of President Nicolas Sarkozy, that cracked down on family reunification and ramped up expulsions of unauthorized immigrants. The law also added a pro-business provision permitting migration, and even "regularization" of undocumented workers, in occupations facing labor shortages. The French government followed up with a January notice to businesses in labor-starved sectors, opening the door for employers to apply to local authorities for work permits for workers with false papers whom they had "in good faith" hired. However, for low-level jobs, this provision was limited to migrants from new European Union member countries. Africans could only qualify if they were working in highly skilled occupations such as science or engineering—but not surprisingly, most Africans in France are concentrated in low-wage service sector jobs.

At that point, African *sans-papiers* took matters into their own hands. On February 13, Fodie Konté of Mali and eight co-workers at the Grande Armée restaurant in Paris occupied their workplace to demand papers. All nine were members of the Confédération Générale du Travail (CGT), France's largest union federation, and the CGT backed them up. In less than a week, Parisian officials agreed to regularize seven of the nine, with Konté the first to get his papers.

The CGT and *Droits Devant!!* (Rights Ahead!!), an immigrant rights advocacy group, saw an opportunity and gave the snowball a push. They escorted Konté and his co-workers to meetings and rallies with other undocumented CGT workers, where they declared, "We've started it, it's up to you to follow." Small groups began to do just that. Then on April 15, fifteen new workplaces in Paris and the surrounding region sprouted red CGT flags as several hundred "irregular" workers held sit-ins. At France's Labor Day parade on May 1, a contingent of several thousand undocumented, most from West African countries such as Mali, Senegal, and Ivory Coast, were the stars.

But local governments were slow to move on their demands, so with only 70 workers regularized one month into the sit-ins, another 200 *sans-papiers* upped the ante on May 20 by taking over twenty more job sites. Still others have joined the strike since. As of early July, 400 former strikers have received papers (typically one-year permits), and the CGT estimates that 600 are still sitting tight at 41 workplaces.

Restaurants, with their visible locations on main boulevards, are the highest profile strike sites. But strikers are also camping out at businesses in construction, cleaning, security, personal services, and landscaping. Though the movement reportedly includes North Africans, Eastern Europeans, and even Filipinos, its public presence has consisted almost entirely of sub-Saharan Africans, a stunning indication of the degree of racial segregation in immigrant jobs. Strikers are overwhelmingly men, though the female employees of a contract cleaning business, Ma Net, made a splash when they joined the strike on May 26, and groups representing domestics and other women workers began to demonstrate around the same time.

"To Go Around Freely..."

The *sans-papiers* came to France by different means. Some overstayed student or tourist visas. Others paid as much as 7,500 euros ($12,000) to a trafficker to travel to the North African coast, clandestinely cross by boat to Spain, and then find their way to France. Strike leader Konté arrived in Paris, his target, two long years after leaving Mali. A set of false papers for 200 euros, and he was ready to look for work.

But opportunities for the undocumented are, for the most part, limited to jobs with the worst pay and working conditions. The French minimum wage is 8.71 euros an hour (almost $13), but strikers tell of working for 3 euros or even less. "With papers, I would get 1,000 euros a month," Issac, a Malian cleaner for the Quick restaurant chain who has been in France eleven years, told *Dollars & Sense*. "Without papers, I get 300." Even so, he and many others send half their pay home to families who depend on them. Through paycheck withholding, the *sans-papiers* pay taxes and contribute to the French health care and retirement funds. But "if I get sick, I don't have any right to reimbursement," said Camara, a dishwasher from Mali. He told *L'Humanité*, the French Communist Party newspaper, how much he wished "to go around freely." "In the evening I don't go out," he said. "When I leave home in the morning, I don't even know if I will get home that night. I avoid some subway stations" that are closely monitored by the police.

When asked how he would reply to the claim that the undocumented are taking jobs from French workers, Issac replied simply, "We are French workers—just without any rights. Yes, we're citizens, because France owned all of black Africa!"

Business Allies

The surprise allies in this guerrilla struggle for the right to work are many of the employers. When workers seized the Samsic contract cleaning agency in the Paris suburb of Massy, owner Mehdi Daïri first called the police. When they told him there was nothing they could do, he pragmatically decided to apply for permits for his 300-plus employees. "It's in everybody's best interest," he told *Le Monde*, the French daily newspaper. "Their action is legitimate. They've been here for years, working, contributing to the social security system, paying taxes, and we're satisfied with their work." He even has his office staff make coffee for the strikers every morning.

Though some businesses have taken a harder line against the strikers, the major business associations have called for massive regularization of their workforces. According to *L'Humanité*, André Dauguin, president of the hotel operators association, is demanding that 50,000 to 100,000 undocumented workers be given papers. Didier Chenet, president of another association of restaurant and hotel enterprises, declared that with 20,000 jobs going unfilled in these sectors, the *sans-papiers* "are not taking jobs away from other workers."

For the CGT, busy with defensive battles against labor "reforms" such as cutbacks in public employees' pensions, the strike wave represents a step in a new direction. The core of the CGT remains white, native-born French workers. As recently as the 1980s, the Communist Party, to which the CGT was then closely linked, took some controversial anti-immigrant stands. Raymond Chauveau, the general secretary of the CGT's Massy local, acknowledged to *Le Monde* that some union members still have trouble understanding why the organization has taken up this issue. But he added, "Today, these people are recognized for what they are: workers. They are developing class consciousness. Our role as a union is to show that these people are not outside the world of work." While some immigrant rights groups are critical of the CGT for suddenly stepping into the leadership of a fight other groups had been pursuing for years, it is hard to deny the importance of the labor organization's clout.

Half Empty or Half Full?

With only 400 of 1,400 applications for work permits granted four months into the struggle, the CGT is publicly voicing its impatience at the national government's insistence that local authorities make each decision on a case-by-case basis rather than offering broader guidelines. But Chauveau said he is proud that they have compelled the government to accept regularization of Africans in low-end jobs, broadening the opening beyond the intent of the 2007 law. And on its website, the CGT boasted that the *sans-papiers* "have compelled the government to take its first steps back, when that had seemed impossible since the [May 2007] election of Nicolas Sarkozy." Perhaps even more important for the long term is that class consciousness Chauveau mentioned. This is "a struggle that has changed my life," stated Mamadou Dembia Thiam of Senegal, a security guard who won his work authorization in June. "Before the struggle, I was really very timid. I've changed!" Changes like that seem likely to bring a new burst of energy to the struggling French labor movement. ❑

Resources: Confédération Générale du Travail, www.cgt.fr; Droits Devant!!, www.droitsdevant.org.

Article 6.3

MADE IN ARGENTINA
Bolivian Migrant Workers Fight Neoliberal Fashion

BY MARIE TRIGONA
January/February 2007

Dubbed "the Paris of the South," Buenos Aires is known for its European architecture, tango clubs, and *haute couture*. But few people are aware that Argentina's top fashion brands employ tens of thousands of undocumented Bolivian workers in slave-labor conditions. In residential neighborhoods across Buenos Aires, top clothing companies have turned small warehouses or gutted buildings into clandestine sweatshops. Locked in, workers are forced to live and work in cramped quarters with little ventilation and, often, limited access to water and gas. The *Unión de Trabajadores Costureros* (Union of Seamstress Workers—UTC), an assembly of undocumented textile workers, has reported more than 8,000 cases of labor abuses inside the city's nearly 400 clandestine shops in the past year. Around 100,000 undocumented immigrants work in these unsafe plants with an average wage—if they are paid at all—of $100 per month.

According to Olga Cruz, a 29-year-old textile worker, slave-labor conditions in textile factories are systematic. "During a normal workday in a shop you work from 7 a.m. until midnight or 1 a.m. Many times they don't pay the women and they owe them two or three years' pay. For not having our legal documents or not knowing what our rights are in Argentina, we've had to remain silent. You don't have rights to rent a room or to work legally."

Another Bolivian textile worker, Naomi Hernández, traveled to Argentina three years ago in hopes of a well-paying job. "I ended up working in a clandestine sweatshop without knowing the conditions I would have to endure. For two years I worked and slept in a three-square-meter room along with my two children and three sewing machines my boss provided. They would bring us two meals a day. For breakfast a cup of tea with a piece of bread and lunch consisting of a portion of rice, a potato, and an egg. We had to share our two meals with our children because according to my boss, my children didn't have the right to food rations because they aren't workers and don't yield production." She reported the subhuman conditions in her workplace and was subsequently fired.

Diseases like tuberculosis and lung complications are common due to the subhuman working conditions and constant exposure to dust and fibers. Many workers suffer from back injuries and tendonitis from sitting at a sewing machine 12 to 16 hours a day. And there are other hazards. A blaze that killed six people last year brought to light abusive working conditions inside a network of clandestine textile plants in Buenos Aires. The two women and four children who were killed had been locked inside the factory.

The situation of these workers shows that exploitation of migrant labor is not just a first-world/third-world phenomenon. The system of exploitative subcontracting of migrant workers that has arisen in U.S. cities as a result of neoliberal globalization also occurs in the countries of the global south—as does organized resistance to such exploitation.

Survival for Bolivian Workers

Buenos Aires is the number one destination for migrants from Bolivia, Paraguay, and Peru, whose numbers have grown in the past decade because of the declining economic conditions in those countries. More than one million Bolivians have migrated to Argentina since 1999; approximately one-third are undocumented.

Even when Argentina's economy took a nosedive in the 1990s, Bolivians were still driven to migrate there given their homeland's far more bleak economic conditions. Over two-thirds of Bolivians live in poverty, and nearly half subsist on less than a dollar a day. For decades, migration of rural workers (44% of the population) to urban areas kept many families afloat. Now, facing limited employment opportunities and low salaries in Bolivia's cities, many workers have opted to migrate to Argentina or Brazil.

Buenos Aires' clandestine network of sweatshops emerged in the late 1990s, following the influx of inexpensive Asian textile imports. Most of the textile factory owners are Argentine, Korean, or Bolivian. The workers manufacture garments for high-end brands like Lacár, Kosiuko, Adidas, and Montage in what has become a $700 million a year industry.

In many cases workers are lured by radio or newspaper ads in Bolivia promising transportation to Buenos Aires and decent wages plus room and board once they arrive. Truck drivers working for the trafficking rings transport workers in the back of trucks to cross into Argentina illegally.

For undocumented immigrants in Argentina, survival itself is a vicious cycle. The undocumented are especially susceptible to threats of losing their jobs. Workers can't afford to rent a room; even if they could, many residential hotel managers are unwilling to rent rooms to immigrants, especially when they have children.

Finding legal work is almost impossible without a national identity card. For years, Bolivian citizens had reported that Alvaro Gonzalez Quint, the head of Bolivia's consulate in Buenos Aires, would charge immigrants up to $100—equivalent to a textile worker's average monthly pay—to complete paperwork necessary for their documentation. The Argentine League for Human Rights has also brought charges against Gonzalez Quint in federal court, alleging he is tied to the network of smugglers who profit from bringing immigrants into Argentina to work in the sweatshops.

A New Chapter in Argentina's Labor Struggles

Argentina has a notable tradition of labor organizing among immigrants. Since the 19th century, working-class immigrants have fought for basic rights, including Sundays off, eight-hour workdays, and a minimum wage. The eight-hour workday became law in 1933, but employers have not always complied. Beginning with the 1976-1983 military dictatorship, and continuing through the neoliberal 1990s, many labor laws have been altered to allow flexible labor standards. University of Buenos Aires economist Eduardo Lucita, a member of UDI (Economists from the Left), says that although the law for an eight-hour workday stands, the average workday in Argentina is 10 to 12 hours. "Only half of workers have formal labor contracts; the rest are laboring as subcontracted workers in the unregulated, informal sector. For such workers there are no regulations for production rates and lengths of a workday—much less criteria for salaries." The average salary for Argentines is only around $200 a month, in contrast to the minimum of $600 required to meet the basic needs of a family of four.

Today, the extreme abuses in the new sweatshops have prompted a new generation of immigrant workers to organize.

"We have had to remain silent and accept abuse. I'm tired of taking the blows. We are starting to fight, *compañeros*; thank you for attending the assembly." These are the words of Ana Salazar at an assembly of textile workers that met in Buenos Aires on a Sunday evening last April. The UTC formed out of a neighborhood assembly in the working class neighborhood of Parque Avalleneda. Initially, the assembly was a weekly social event for families on Sundays, the only day textile workers can leave the shop. Families began to gather at the assembly location, situated at the corner of a park. Later, because Argentina's traditional unions refuse to accept undocumented affiliates, the workers expanded their informal assembly into a full-fledged union.

Since the factory fire that killed six on March 30, 2006, the UTC has stepped up actions against the brand-name clothing companies that subcontract with clandestine sweatshops. The group has held a number of *escraches*, or exposure protests, outside fashion makers' offices in Buenos Aires to push the city government to hold inspections inside the companies' textile workshops. Workers from the UTC also presented legal complaints against the top jean manufacturer Kosiuko.

At a recent surprise protest, young women held placards: "I kill myself for your jeans," signed, "a Bolivian textile worker." During the protest, outside Kosiuko's offices in the exclusive Barrio Norte neighborhood, UTC presented an in-depth research report into the brand's labor violations. "The Kosiuko company is concealing slave shops," said Gustavo Vera, member of the La Alemeda popular assembly. "They disclosed false addresses to inspectors and they have other workshops which they are not reporting to the city government." The UTC released a detailed list of the locations of alleged sweatshops. Most of the addresses that the Kosiuko company had provided turned out to be private residences or stores.

To further spotlight large brand names that exploit susceptible undocumented workers, the UTC held a unique fashion show in front of the Buenos Aires city legislature last September. "Welcome to the neoliberal fashion show—Spring Season 2006," announced the host, as spectators cheered—or jeered—the top brands that use slave labor. Models from a local theatre group paraded down a red carpet in brands like Kosiuko, Montagne, Porte Said, and Lacar, while the host shouted out the addresses of the brands' sweatshops and details of subhuman conditions inside shops.

"I repressed all of my rage about my working conditions and violations of my rights. Inside a clandestine workshop you don't have any rights. You don't have dignity," said Naomi Hernández, pedaling away at a sewing machine during the "fashion show."

After the show, Hernández stood up in front of the spectators and choked down tears while giving testimony of her experience as a slave laborer in a sweatshop: "I found out what it is to fight as a human being." She says her life has changed since joining the UTC.

Inspection-Free Garment Shops

To date, the union's campaign has had some successes. In April of 2006, the Buenos Aires city government initiated inspections of sweatshops employing Bolivians and Paraguayans; inspectors shut down at least 100. (Perhaps not surprisingly, Bolivian consul Gonzalez Quint has protested the city government's moves to regulate sweatshops, arguing that the measures discriminate against Bolivian employers who run some of the largest textile shops.) But since then, inspections have been suspended and many clothes manufacturers have simply moved their sweatshops to the suburban industrial belt or to new locations in the city. The UTC has reported that other manufacturers force workers to labor during the night to avoid daytime inspections.

Nestor Escudero, an Argentine who participates in the UTC, says that police, inspectors, and the courts are also responsible for the documented slave-labor conditions inside textile factories. "They bring in illegal immigrants to brutally exploit them. The textile worker is paid 75 cents for a garment that is later sold for $50. This profit is enough to pay bribes and keep this system going."

Since 2003, thousands of reports of slave-labor conditions have piled up in the courts without any resolution. In many cases when workers have presented reports to police of poor treatment, including threats, physical abuse, and forced labor, the police say they can't act because the victims do not have national identity cards.

Seeing their complaints go unheeded is sometimes the least of it. Escudero has confirmed that over a dozen textile workers have received death threats for reporting to media outlets on slave-labor conditions inside the textile plants. Shortly after the UTC went public last spring with hundreds of reports of abuses, over a dozen of the union's representatives were threatened. And in a particularly shocking episode, two men kidnapped the 9-year-old son of José Orellano and Monica Frías, textile workers who had reported slave-labor conditions in their shop. The attackers held the boy at knifepoint and told him to "tell your parents that they should stop messing around with the reports against the sweatshops." The UTC filed criminal charges of abandonment and abuse of power against Argentina's Interior Minister Aníbal Fernández in November for not providing the couple with witness protection.

The Road Ahead

Although the Buenos Aires city government has yet to make much headway in regulating the city's sweatshops, the UTC continues to press for an end to sweatshop slavery, along with mass legalization of immigrants and housing for immigrants living in poverty. Organizing efforts have not been in vain. In an important victory, the city government has opened a number of offices to process immigration documents free of charge for Bolivian and Paraguayan citizens, circumventing the Bolivian Consulate.

The UTC has also proposed that clandestine textile shops be shut down and handed over to the workers to manage them as co-ops and, ultimately, build a cooperative network that can bypass the middlemen and the entire piece-work system. Already, the Alameda assembly has joined with the UTC to form the Alameda Workers' Cooperative as an alternative to sweatshops. Nearly 30 former sweatshop workers work at the cooperative in the same space where the weekly assemblies are held.

Olga Cruz now works with the cooperative sewing garments. She says that although it's a struggle, she now has dignity that she didn't have when she worked in one of the piece-work shops. "We are working as a cooperative, we all make the same wage. In the clandestine shops you are paid per garment: they give you the fabric and you have to hand over the garment fully manufactured. Here we have a line system, which is more advanced and everyone works the same amount."

Fired for reporting on abusive conditions at her sweatshop, Naomi Hernández has also found work at the cooperative. "We are freeing ourselves, that's what I feel. Before I wasn't a free person and didn't have any rights," said Hernández to a crowd of spectators in front of the city legislature. She sent a special message and invitation: "Now we are fighting together with the Alameda cooperative and the UTC. I invite all workers who know their rights are being violated to join the movement against slave labor." ❑

Resources: To contact UTC activists at La Alameda assembly in Parque Avellaneda, email: asambleaparqueavellaneda@hotmail.com. To see videos of recent UTC actions, go to: www. revolutionvideo.org/agoratv/secciones/luchas_obreras/costureros_utc.html; www.revolutionvideo. org/agoratv/secciones/luchas_obreras/escrache_costureros.html.

Article 6.4

THE RISE OF MIGRANT WORKER MILITANCY

IMMANUEL NESS
September/October 2006

Testifying before the Senate immigration hearings in early July, Mayor Michael Bloomberg affirmed that undocumented immigrants have become indispensable to the economy of New York City: "Although they broke the law by illegally crossing our borders or overstaying their visas, and our businesses broke the law by employing them, our city's economy would be a shell of itself had they not, and it would collapse if they were deported. The same holds true for the nation." Bloomberg's comment outraged right-wing pundits, but how much more outraged would they be if they knew that immigrant workers, beyond being economically indispensable, are beginning to transform the U.S. labor movement with a bold new militancy?

After years of working in obscurity in the unregulated economy, migrant workers in New York City catapulted themselves to the forefront of labor activism beginning in late 1999 through three separate organizing drives among low-wage workers. Immigrants initiated all three drives: Mexican immigrants organized and struck for improved wages and working conditions at greengroceries; Francophone African delivery workers struck for unpaid wages and respect from labor contractors for leading supermarket chains; and South Asians organized for improved conditions and a union in the for-hire car service industry. (In New York, "car services" are taxis that cannot be hailed on the street, only arranged by phone.) These organizing efforts have persisted, and are part of a growing militancy among migrant workers in New York City and across the United States.

Why would seemingly invisible workers rise up to contest power in their workplaces? Why are vulnerable migrant workers currently more likely to organize than are U.S.-born workers? To answer these questions, we have to look at immigrants' distinct position in the political economy of a globalized New York City and at their specific economic and social niches, ones in which exploitation and isolation nurture class consciousness and militancy.

Labor Migration and Industrial Restructuring

New immigrant workers in the United States, many here illegally, stand at the crossroads of two overwhelming trends. On one hand, industrial restructuring and capital mobility have eroded traditional industries and remade the U.S. political economy in the last 30 years in ways that have led many companies to create millions of low-wage jobs and to seek vulnerable workers to fill them. On the other hand, at the behest of international financial institutions like the International Monetary Fund, and to meet the requirements of free-trade agreements such as NAFTA, governments throughout the global South have adopted neoliberal policies that have restructured their economies, resulting in the displacement of urban workers and rural farmers alike. Many have no choice but to migrate north.

A century ago the United States likewise experienced a large influx of immigrants, many of whom worked in factories for their entire lives. There they formed social networks across ethnic lines and developed a class consciousness that spurred the organizing of unions; they made up the generation of workers whose efforts began with the fight for the eight-hour day around the turn of the last century and culminated in the great organizing victories of the 1930s and 1940s across the entire spectrum of mining and manufacturing industries.

Today's immigrants face an entirely different political-economic landscape. Unlike most of their European counterparts a century ago, immigration restrictions mean that many newcomers to the United States are now here illegally. Workers from Latin America frequently migrate illegally without proper documentation; those from Africa, Asia, and Europe commonly arrive with business, worker, student, or tourist visas, then overstay them.

The urban areas where many immigrants arrive have undergone a 30-year decline in manufacturing jobs. The growing pool of service jobs which have come in their stead tend to be dispersed in small firms throughout the city. The proliferation of geographically dispersed subcontractors who compete on the basis of low wages encourages a process of informalization—a term referring to a redistribution of work from regulated sectors of the economy to new unregulated sectors of the underground or informal economy. As a result, wages and working conditions have fallen, often below government-established norms.

Although informal work is typically associated with the developing world—or Global South—observers are increasingly recognizing the link between the regulated and unregulated sectors in advanced industrial regions. More and more the regulated sector depends on unregulated economic activity through subcontracting and outsourcing of work to firms employing low-wage immigrant labor. Major corporations employ or subcontract to businesses employing migrant workers in what were once established sectors of the economy with decent wages and working conditions.

Informalization requires government regulatory agencies to look the other way. For decades federal and state regulatory bodies have ignored violations of laws governing wages, hours, and workplace safety, leading to illegally low wages and declining workplace health and safety practices. The process of informalization is furthered by the reduction or elimination of protections such as disability insurance, Social Security, health care coverage, unemployment insurance, and workers compensation.

By the 1990s, substandard jobs employing almost exclusively migrant workers had become crucial to key sectors of the national economy. Today, immigrants have gained a major presence as bricklayers, demolition workers, and hazardous waste workers on construction and building rehab sites; as cooks, dishwashers, and busboys in restaurants; and as taxi drivers, domestic workers, and delivery people.

Employers frequently treat these workers as self-employed. They typically have no union protection and little or no job security. With government enforcement shrinking, they lack the protection of minimum-wage laws and they have been excluded from Social Security and unemployment insurance.

These workers are increasingly victimized by employers who force them to accept 19th-century working conditions and sub-minimum wages. Today, New York City, Los Angeles, Miami, Houston, and Boston form a nexus of international labor migration, with constantly churning labor markets. As long as there is a demand for cheap labor, immigrants will continue to enter the United States in large numbers. Like water, capital always flows to the lowest level, a state of symmetry where wages are cheapest.

In turn, the availability of a reserve army of immigrant labor provides an enormous incentive for larger corporations to create and use subcontracting firms. Without this workforce, employers in the regulated economy would have more incentive to invest in labor-saving technology, increase the capital-labor ratio, and seek accommodation with unions.

New unauthorized immigrants residing and working in the United States are ideal workers in the new informalized sectors: Their undocumented legal status makes them more tractable since they constantly fear deportation. Undocumented immigrants are less likely to know about, or demand adherence to, established labor standards, and even low U.S. wages represent an improvement over earnings in their home countries.

Forging Migrant Labor Solidarity

The perception that new immigrants undermine U.S.-born workers by undercutting prevailing wage and work standards cannot be entirely dismissed. The entry of a large number of immigrants into the underground economy unquestionably reduces the labor market leverage of U.S.-born workers. But the story is more complicated. In spite of their vulnerability, migrant workers have demonstrated a willingness and a capacity to organize for improvements in their wages and working conditions; they arguably are responding to tough conditions on the job with greater militancy than U.S.-born workers.

New York City has been the site of a number of instances of immigrant worker organizing. In 1998, Mexicans working in greengroceries embarked on a citywide organizing campaign to improve their conditions of work. Most of the 20,000 greengrocery workers were paid below $3.00 an hour, working on average 72 hours a week. Some did not make enough to pay their living expenses, no less send remittances back home to Mexico. Following a relentless and coordinated four-year organizing campaign among the workers, employers agreed to raise wages above the minimum and improve working conditions. Moreover, the campaign led state Attorney General Eliot Spitzer to establish a Greengrocer Code of Conduct and to strengthen enforcement of labor regulations.

In another display of immigrant worker militancy, beginning in 1999 Francophone African supermarket delivery workers in New York City fought for and won equality with other workers in the same stores. The workers were responsible for bagging groceries and delivering them to affluent customers in Manhattan and throughout the city. As contractors, the delivery workers were paid no wage, instead relying on the goodwill of customers in affluent neighborhoods to pay tips for each delivery.

The workers were employed in supermarkets and drug stores where some others had a union. Without union support themselves, delivery workers staged a significant strike and insurrection that made consumers aware of their appalling conditions of work. In late October, workers went on strike and marched from supermarket to supermarket, demanding living wages and dignity on the job. At the start of their campaign, wages averaged less than $70 a week. In the months following the strike the workers all won recognition from the stores through the United Food and Commercial Workers that had earlier neglected to include them in negotiations with management. The National Employee Law Project, a national worker advocacy organization, filed landmark lawsuits against the supermarkets and delivery companies and won backwage settlements as the courts deemed them to be workers—not independent contractors in business for themselves.

Immigrant workers have organized countless other campaigns, in New York and across the country. How do new immigrants, with weak ties to organized labor and the state, manage to assert their interests? The explanation lies in the character of immigrant work and social life; the constraints immigrant workers face paradoxically encourage them to draw on shared experiences to create solidarity at work and in their communities.

The typical migrant worker can expect to work twelve-hour days, seven days a week. When arriving home, immigrant workers frequently share the same apartments, buildings, and neighborhoods. These employment ghettos typify immigrant communities across the nation. Workers cook for one another, share stories about their oppressively long and hard days, commiserate about their ill treatment at work, and then go to sleep only to start anew the next day.

Migrant women, surrounded by a world of exploitation, typically suffer even more abuse their male counterparts, suffering from low wages, long hours, and dangerous conditions. Patterns of gender stratification found in the general labor market are even more apparent among migrant women workers. Most jobs in the nonunion economy, such as construction and driving, are stereotypically considered "men's work." Women predominate in the garment industry, as domestic and child care workers, in laundries, hotels, restaurants, and ever more in sex work. A striking example of migrant women's perilous work environment is the massive recruitment of migrant women to clean up the hazardous materials in the rubble left by the collapse of the World Trade Center without proper safety training.

Isolated in their jobs and communities, immigrant workers have few social ties to unions, community groups, and public officials, and few resources to call upon to assist them in transforming their workplaces. Because new immigrants have few social networks outside the workplace, the ties they develop on the job are especially solid and meaningful—and are nurtured every day. The workers' very isolation and status as outsiders, and their concentration into industrial niches by employers who hire on the basis of ethnicity, tend to strengthen old social ties, build new ones, and deepen class solidarity.

Immigrant social networks contribute to workplace militancy. Conversely, activism at work can stimulate new social networks that can expand workers' power. It is through relationships developed on the job and in the community that shared social identities and mutual resentment of the boss evolves into class consciousness and class solidarity: migrant workers begin to form informal organizations, meet with coworkers to respond to poor working conditions, and take action on the shop floor in defiance of employer abuse.

Typically, few workplace hierarchies exist among immigrants, since few reach supervisory positions. As a result, immigrant workers suffer poor treatment equally at the hands of employers. A gathering sense of collective exploitation usually transforms individualistic activities into shared ones. In rare cases where there are immigrant foremen and crew leaders, they may recognize this solidarity and side with the workers rather than with management. One former manager employed for a fast-food sandwich chain in New York City said: "We are hired only to divide the workers but I was really trying to help the workers get better pay and shorter hours."

Migrant workers bring social identities from their home countries, and those identities are shaped through socialization and work in this country. In cities and towns across the United States, segmentation of migrant workers from specific countries reinforces ethnic, national, and religious identities and helps to form other identities that may stimulate solidarity. Before arriving in the United States, Mexican immigrant workers often see themselves as peasants but not initially as "people of color," while Francophone Africans see themselves as Malian or Senegalese ethnics but not necessarily "black." Life and work in New York can encourage them to adopt new identifications, including a new class consciousness that can spur organizing and militancy.

Once triggered, organizing can go from workplace to workplace like wildfire. When workers realize that they can fight and prevail, this creates a sense of invincibility that stimulates militant action that would otherwise be avoided at all costs. This demonstration effect is vitally important, as was the case in the strikes among garment workers and coal miners in the history of the U.S. labor movement.

"Solidarity Forever" vs. "Take This Job and Shove It"

The militancy of many migrant workers contrasts sharply with the passivity of many U.S.-born workers facing the same low wages and poor working conditions. Why do most workers at chain stores and restaurants like Wal-Mart and McDonalds—most of whom were born in the United States—appear so complacent, while new immigrants are often so militant?

Migrants are not inherently more militant or less passive. Instead, the real workplace conditions of migrant workers seem to produce greater militancy on the job. First, collective social isolation engenders strong ties among migrants in low-wage jobs where organizing is frequently the only way to improve conditions. Because migrants work in jobs that are more amenable to organizing, they are highly represented among newly unionized workers. Strong social ties in the workplace drive migrants to form their own embryonic organizations at work and in their communities that are ripe for union representation. Organizing among migrant workers gains the attention of labor unions, which then see a chance to recruit new members and may provide resources to help immigrant workers mobilize at work and join the union.

Employers also play a major role. Firms employing U.S. workers tend to be larger and are often much harder to organize than the small businesses where immigrants work. In 2003, the Merriam-Webster dictionary added the new word McJob, defined as "a low-paying job that requires little skill and provides little opportunity for advancement." The widely accepted coinage reflects the relentless 30-year economic restructuring creating low-end jobs in the retail sector.

Organizing against Home Depot, McDonalds, Taco Bell, or Wal-Mart is completely different from organizing against smaller employers. Wal-Mart uses many of the same tactics against workers that immigrants contend with: failure to pay overtime, stealing time (intentionally paying workers for fewer hours than actually worked), no health care, part-time work, high turnover, and gender division of labor. The difference is that Wal-Mart has far more resources to oppose unionization than do the smaller employers who are frequently subcontractors to larger firms. But Wal-Mart's opposition to labor unions is so forceful that workers choose to leave rather than stay and fight it out. Relentless labor turnover mitigates against the formation of working class consciousness and militancy.

The expanding non-immigrant low-end service sector tends to produce unskilled part-time jobs that do not train workers in skills that keep them in the same sector of the labor market. Because jobs at the low end of the economy require little training, workers frequently move from one industry to the next. One day a U.S.-born worker may work as a sales clerk for Target, the next day as a waiter at Olive Garden. Because they are not stuck in identity-defined niches, U.S. workers change their world by quitting and finding a job elsewhere, giving them less reason to organize and unionize.

The fact that U.S.-born workers have an exit strategy and migrant workers do not is a significant and important difference. Immigrant workers are more prone to take action to change their working conditions because they have far fewer options than U.S.-born workers. Workers employed by companies like Wal-Mart are unable to change their conditions, since they have little power and will be summarily fired for any form of dissent. If workers violate the terms of Wal-Mart's or McDonalds' employee manual by, say, arriving late, and then are summarily fired, no one is likely to fend for them, as is usually the case among many migrant workers. While migrant workers engage in direct action against their employers to obtain higher wages and respect on the job, U.S. workers do not develop the same dense connections in labor market niches that forge solidarity. Employers firing new immigrants may risk demonstrations, picket lines, or even strikes.

Immigrant workers are pushed into low-wage labor market niches as day laborers, food handlers, delivery workers, and nannies; these niches are difficult if not impossible to escape. Yet immigrant workers relegated to dead-end jobs in the lowest echelons of the labor market in food, delivery, and car service work show a greater eagerness to fight it out to improve their wages and conditions than do U.S. workers who can move on to another dead-end job.

The Role of Unions

Today's labor movement is in serious trouble; membership is spiraling downward as employers demand union-free workplaces. Unionized manufacturing and service workers are losing their jobs to low-wage operations abroad. Unions and, more importantly, the U.S. working class, are in dire straits and must find a means to triumph over the neoliberal dogma that dominates the capitalist system.

As organizing campaigns in New York City show, migrant workers are indispensable to the revitalization of the labor movement. As employers turn to migrant labor to fill low-wage jobs, unions must encourage and support organizing drives that emerge from the oppressive conditions of work. As the 1930s workers' movement demonstrates, if conditions improve for immigrants, all workers will prosper. To gain traction, unions must recognize that capital is pitting migrant workers against native-born laborers to lower wages and improve profitability. Although unions have had some success organizing immigrants, most are circling the wagons, disinterested in building a more inclusive mass labor movement. The first step is for unions to go beyond rhetoric and form a broad and inclusive coalition embracing migrant workers. ❑

Article 6.5

REMITTANCES TO THE RESCUE?

BY ALISSA THUOTTE
May/June 2008

Remittances—the money sent home to families by migrants living in foreign countries—have been gaining attention in the last few years from international institutions such as the World Bank, the Inter-American Development Bank (IDB), and the International Monetary Fund. These organizations and others have begun to study remittances with an eye to their potential for reducing poverty in the poor and near-poor countries to which most of these funds flow. It turns out that remittances are a mixed blessing. They offer a relatively stable source of incoming funds. At the same time, however, they can create an alarming dependence on behalf of their recipients, heightening their vulnerability to shifting political and economic winds in the host countries over which they have no control.

Remittances have been, until very recently, very much on the rise, with about 10% of the world's population now receiving some remittance income. In 2006, 150 million migrants across the globe sent $300 billion in 1.5 billion transactions. Remittances now represent nearly one-third of total financial flows to the developing world—more than official development assistance and, depending on the country, more even than foreign direct investment. Fifty-nine countries receive more than $1 billion annually in remittances, and 45 receive more than 10% of their GDP. Moreover, remittance flows have tended to be much more stable than foreign direct investment or portfolio (stocks and bonds) investment (see graph, "Remittances versus Other External Financing").

One third of the money sent originates in the United States; most of the rest is sent from Europe and the Middle East. A significant volume of remittance money circulates within the developing world as well, however: so-called "South-South" flows account for 30% to 45% of total remittances, according to the World Bank.

Latin America and the Caribbean is the region receiving the highest level of remittances per capita, averaging $102 annually, and the region's remittance flows have risen tenfold in real terms over the last 20 years. In 2006 the region received $62.3 billion from migrants abroad—five times the amount of "official development assistance" it received—with remittances to Mexico ($24.2 billion) accounting for over a third. After climbing at double-digit rates in the last decade, the flow now appears to be leveling off: a recent survey by an IDB fund estimated 2007 remittances to the region at $66.5 billion, only a 7% increase over the previous year.

Most of the money received in this region is used for everyday living expenses, everything from food and home repairs to school tuition. What interests economists most, though, is the potential for remittances to contribute to economic development—when, for example, recipients put the money toward new small business ventures that may over time provide employment to others and expand local economies. According to a 2007 World Bank report, the data suggest that remittances do tend to increase bank deposits, reflecting at least some potential for such investment.

Research has generally found that higher remittance flows are, to a modest degree, associated with lower poverty, better health, and higher levels of education in the developing world. In ten out of eleven Latin American and Caribbean countries examined in a 2006 World Bank study, children from families receiving remittances were more likely to remain in school than those whose parents were not supported by such funds.

Yet the increasing remittance flows have a downside: families and national economies that come to rely on the extra income become vulnerable to far-distant events and trends. Take the case of Mexico. One consequence of the current bust in the U.S. housing market is that construction, which employs many Mexican workers, has slowed—and along with it, the flow of money back home. Remittances to Mexico grew only 1% in 2007, and in January of this year *fell* 6% compared to the same period last year, according to the IDB.

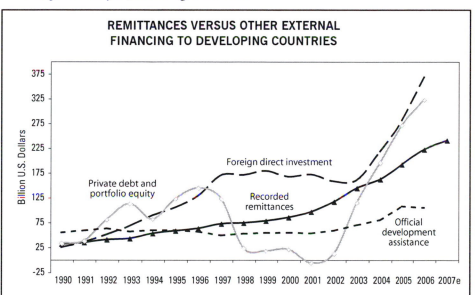

REMITTANCES VERSUS OTHER EXTERNAL FINANCING TO DEVELOPING COUNTRIES

Note: **Private debt and portfolio equity** refers to the net flow of stock and bond purchases by foreign investors plus commercial bank loans from foreign banks. **Foreign direct investment** refers to the net flow of funds invested directly by companies to establish or control business enterprises abroad. **Official development ment assistance** refers to loans, grants, and other aid given by the governments of developed countries. Remittance figure for 2007 is estimated.

Sources: World Bank: "Global Economic Prospects 2006: Economic Implications of Remittances and Migration," "World Development Indicators 2008," and "Global Development Finance 2008."

And the falloff in construction work is not the only factor depressing Mexican migrants' ability to send money home. Thanks to increasingly visible anti-immigrant sentiment in the United States, stricter border enforcement—including the threat of incarceration, as opposed to just deportation, for undocumented migrants caught crossing the border—and penalties for employers who hire undocumented workers, it has become harder for immigrants to enter the country and find decent jobs. As the dollar falls in value against foreign currencies, those who have been in the United States for some time may have to work longer hours and cut their expenses just to be able to send home the same amounts.

Migration and remittances have certainly transformed many Latin American towns, but not always for the better. So-called "migra-villages" have seen their working-age adult population shrink. Remittance money can help build new homes, but they often remain empty in their owners' absence; new schools get built, but enrollment does not necessarily increase. Family members left behind may stop working and wait month-to-month for money from overseas, weakening local economies—not a sustainable set-up in the long run.

And surprisingly, remittances do not necessarily flow most heavily toward the poorest families that need them the most. In fact, the World Bank's 2006 study found that in the 11 Latin American and Caribbean countries for which data were

WESTERN UNION CALLING

While it has undeniably become easier and more convenient to send money across the border in the last decade, activists charge transfer services, especially Western Union, with taking advantage of their most loyal customers. Remittances represent a nearly $1 billion a year industry for Western Union; global migration is so central to the company's profits that "forecasts of border movements drive the company's stock," according to the *New York Times*. Western Union's huge slice of the industry pie allows the company to charge fees from 4% to as high as 20% of the amount remitted.

The Oakland, Calif.-based Boycott Western Union campaign asserts that the company fails to invest an adequate portion of its earnings in the communities of the customers from which it profits. Its campaign aims to convince Western Union to sign a Transnational Community Benefits Agreement—like the Community Reinvestment Act for banks—that would "ensure community reinvestment of $1 per every transaction while also forcing the company to reduce its fees and establish fairer exchange rates."

In the meantime, experts at the IDB and elsewhere insist that this is a perfect opportunity for banks to get more involved, and are trying to encourage partnerships between U.S. and Latin American banks and to extend networks into Latin America's more rural areas, where access to banking is notoriously scarce. More competition, they argue, would help push transfer fees down and improve customer service.

available, remittance income was actually distributed slightly more unequally than total household income: the top 20% took in 51% of total income, but 54% of remittances. Who receives remittances varies sharply from country to country. Contrast Mexico, for instance, where 61% of the households receiving remittances in 2004 were in the bottom 20% by (non-remittance) income, with Peru, where fewer than 6% were, while 40% were in the top income quintile.

Today, remittance checks are helping millions of households across the global South to keep food on the table and a roof overhead. Although the evidence hardly hails them as a long-term solution to global poverty, as long as remittance flows continue, they should be both facilitated *and* rigorously regulated. ❏

Sources: Jason DeParle, "Migrant Money Flow: A $300 Billion Current," *New York Times*, 11/18/07; Pablo Fajnzylber and J. Humberto Lopez, "Close to Home: The DevelopmentaImpact of Remittances in Latin America," (World Bank, 2007); "Sending Money Home: Worldwide Remittance Flows to Developing Countries," (IFAD/IDB, 2007); Manuel Orozco, "The Remittance Marketplace: Prices, Policy, and Financial Institutions," (Pew Hispanic Center, 6/7/04); Elisabeth Malkin, "Mexicans Barely Increased Remittances in '07," *New York Times*, 2/26/08; Jason DeParle, "World Banker and His Cash Return Home," *New York Times*, 3/17/08; Donald Greenlees, "As the Dollar Slides, Two Continents Feel the Side Effects in Divergent Ways," *New York Times*, 3/27/08; Jason DeParle, "Western Union Empire Moves Migrant Cash Home," *New York Times*, 11/22/07; Eduardo Porter, "Struggling to Draw Workers Sending Money Back Home," *New York Times*, 6/7/04; Devesh Kapur, "Remittances: the New Development Mantra?" (U.N. Conf. on Trade and Dev't, April 2004); Kevin Plumberg, "Weak Dollar Makes Immigrant Life Tougher," Reuters, 2/11/08; Ami Bonilla, "Mexicans Send Less Cash Home, Bad News for All," New America Media, 8/9/07; Maria Sacchetti, "Beating the Bank," *Boston Globe*, 4/15/08.

Chapter 7

ECONOMIC DEVELOPMENT

Article 7.1

WORLD HISTORY AND ECONOMIC DEVELOPMENT
Lessons from New Comparisons of Europe and East Asia

BY RAVI BHANDARI AND KENNETH POMERANZ
August 2009

Development prescriptions that assume that the rest of the world can (or should) mimic a stylized North Atlantic path to the modern world dominated the 1950s to 1970s, with limited success. The neo-liberal prescriptions of the last 30 years were no better at creating long-term dynamism, and often imposed horrific social costs.

Most of the success stories of post-1945 development are clustered in East Asia: Taiwan, South Korea, Hong Kong, Singapore, and (with more caveats), coastal China. Among other things, almost the entire *net* reduction in global poverty numbers during the last 30 years has occurred in China, which largely ignored the "Washington Consensus" on development strategy. This geographic clumping has encouraged discussion of an "East Asian development path." Sometimes this is said to derive from 20th century corporatist institutions, sometimes from supposedly timeless "Asian values" of discipline and respect for education; but none of these are sufficiently "East Asian" to explain very much.

A new comparative history of economic development yields different lessons. It highlights differences in political-economic relations between cores and peripheries and differential access to fossil fuels in explaining why the most dynamic regions in the West out-distanced their East Asian counterparts in the 19th century, casting particular doubt on arguments that focus on allegedly more perfect markets in the West. A second theme is the role of labor-intensive industries, often based in the countryside and employing people from households still connected to agriculture (creating relatively low rates of both urbanization and proletarianization). This period of catch-up growth unfolds with less growth of landlessness and less inequality than in most of the industrializing West. However, in China (by far the biggest East Asian country) we also see problems related to trade-dependence, resource shortages, and environmental degradation. These problems have made the indefinite extension of this path highly unlikely, and have engendered familiar strategies—socially and environmentally disquieting—for China's interior.

Comparative-Historical Theories of Development

Recent scholarship suggests a rough comparability in living standards between advanced areas in 18th century China and those in Europe. This allows us to use China to raise questions about Europe, and its 19th century breakthrough to sustained per capita growth. If the divergence in economic performance was quite late, it makes untenable any simple contrast between Western growth and non-Western stagnation. It also means that any explanation resting on cultural or institutional differences (which preceded the divergence by centuries) face a new burden of proof. We must either explain why some difference that was not particularly advantageous earlier became so later, or find offsetting disadvantages that fell away at a particular point, rather than looking only for "advantages" within Europe.

By contrast, most social science in both the Marxist and Weberian traditions was born from contemplation of a West that (briefly) held the world's only industrial societies, and took Western Europe as the standard of "real" historical change; other places were examples of failed, absent, or deviant development. The "new world history," or "California School," of which the work discussed here forms a part, does not deny that this approach yielded many insights, but suggests that reciprocal comparisons may be more valuable today: comparisons in which we also ask, "Why wasn't England the Yangzi Delta or the Kinai—wealthy agro-commercial areas with lots of handicrafts that did not initiate large-scale energy-intensive manufacturing?" Such comparisons are useful for separating the necessary and the contingent in North Atlantic growth; many structures happened to be in place as the West industrialized, and were adapted to serve that process—e.g. financial markets originally designed mostly to finance war were also useful for financing new technologies like railways that required lots of patient capital—but it does not follow that they were necessary to the process. Reciprocal comparisons allow us to take more seriously the possibilities that other societies had advantages as well as disadvantages, and to see the possibilities for transformative change that draws upon, rather than simply overcoming, indigenous institutions and expectations.

Others have taken these elements and combined them in other ways. André Gunder Frank, for instance, shared the emphasis here on the relative prosperity of early modern East Asia—indeed, he went much further, suggesting that Europe did not become more prosperous until the middle of the 19th century—and also used it to raise doubts about whether Western institutions were more conducive to growth. He also questioned the significance of any differences in local institutions, favoring an exclusive significance on the dynamics of a world system. Others, such as R. Bin Wong and Jack Goldstone, have differed from the analysis here in the opposite direction, focusing more or less exclusively on reciprocal comparisons while minimizing (at least for the pre-1850 period) the significance of trans-continental connections (including violent ones) and questions of resource endowments and extraction that will figure prominently in later parts of this essay.

But all of us have concluded that the evidence is inconsistent with any assertion that early modern European culture or economic institutions led directly to superior economic performance, much less that they were both necessary and sufficient for the creation of modernity.

Early Modern Economies and the Origins of the Great Divergence

An emerging consensus among European economic historians has moved away from seeing industrialization as a British-centered "Big Bang." Instead, they put industrialization back into its historical context: in long processes of slowly-growing markets, division of labor, many small innovations, and gradual accumulation. The gradual market-driven growth thus highlighted was crucial, but it didn't differentiate Europe from East Asia. Smithian dynamics worked just as well in much of China and Japan, but didn't transform basic possibilities—eventually, highly developed areas everywhere came up against serious resource constraints, in part because commercialization and proto-industrialization accelerated population growth. Britain ultimately needed not only technology and institutions, but also the Americas, coal, and various favorable conjunctures. In Flanders and even Holland, proto-industrialization and productive commercial agriculture led to results more like China's Yangzi Delta or Japan's Kinai region than like England.

Some readers may object to comparing regions within China and Japan to European countries, but China more closely resembles all of Europe than any one European country in its range of environments, living standards and so on. The Yangzi Delta (with about 31.5 million people in 1770, exceeding France plus the Low Countries), the empire's most developed region, can be compared to Britain (or Britain plus the Netherlands) in terms of its prosperity and its position within a larger system. The rice-exporting, cloth-importing Middle Yangzi might be better compared to Poland. Such comparisons illuminate parallels and differences in the structuring of inter-regional relationships within world areas, and relate economic development to larger contexts, rather than searching within each region for its "key to success" or "fatal flaw."

In an influential version of the gradualist story, Jan DeVries has placed the Industrial Revolution within a larger "*industrious* revolution"—a concept which helps resolve a paradox. The grain-buying power of European day wages fell sharply between 1430 and 1550, and took centuries to regain 1430 levels. Yet death inventories from 1550 on show ordinary people slowly gaining more possessions. These trends can be reconciled because people worked more hours per year for money, allowing them to buy both more non-food goods and stable amounts of increasingly expensive bread. Leisure probably decreased—though this is hard to pin down—and people certainly spent less time making goods for their own households. Instead, they specialized more and bought more, including many goods (baked bread, manufactured candles, etc.) which "saved time" on domestic chores.

Chinese trends were similar. The rice-buying power of day wages generally fell in late imperial times, but nutritional standards do not seem to have fallen, or to have been inferior to Europe's. Average Chinese caloric intake in the late 1700s appears to compare well with Europe (and that of the Yangzi Delta with England); China probably led in vitamin intake; and most surprisingly, protein consumption in the Delta and England seems to have been comparable, at least for the vast majority of both societies. Rough nutritional parity is also suggested by Chinese life expectancies, which were comparable to England's (and thus above Continental Europe's) until at least 1750. Moreover, while Chinese birth rates (contrary to mythology) appear to have been no higher than European ones between 1550 and 1850, the rate of population growth was the same or slightly higher, suggesting that Chinese death rates were the same or lower.

There is abundant anecdotal evidence that the consumption of "non-essentials" by ordinary Chinese was rising modestly between about 1500 and 1750, much as it was in Western Europe. Quantitative estimates for various commodities suggest that in most cases China circa 1750 stacked up well against Europe, and the Yangzi Delta fairly well against England. Yangzi Delta labor productivity in the largest sector of all 18th century economies—agriculture—was 90% of England's as late as 1820, leaving both far ahead of almost all of Continental Europe. Total factor productivity was much higher in the Yangzi Delta, because of greatly superior land productivity. In the second largest sector, textiles, the earnings per day of Yangzi Delta producers exceeded those of their English counterparts even in the late 18th century, though the beginnings of mechanization must have caused their productivity to fall behind by then.

The Yangzi Delta may not have stacked up quite as well overall against England as it did sector by sector, because the mix of sectors was different. Lacking much in the way of ores, forest, fossil fuels, or even waterpower (being essentially flat), the Delta had less of its labor force in energy-intensive industry. For example, using one 1704 data set, charcoal was 20 times as costly relative to labor in Canton as it was in London, though real wages were roughly equal. And while the Delta's long-distance trade was very large, it was, as we shall see, leveling off by the late 1700s.

Generally speaking, though, the economic performance of these two regions was surprisingly similar. Europe-China comparisons are more difficult to do than those for England and the Yangzi Delta, because conditions varied much more and statistics are less reliable; but the data we have also suggest fairly close comparability in 1750 and perhaps 1800.

But another feature of East Asian cores was strikingly different from the early modern West (and probably South Asia). From the 16th century on, a growing percentage of rural European workers (whether in agriculture or other occupations) were proletarians—people who owned no means of production and worked for wages. In the most advanced parts of 18th century Europe they became a majority. In China, however (and, for different reasons, also Japan), proletarians were under 10% of the 18th century rural population; almost every household either owned some land or had secure tenancy. On the positive side, this reflected both hard-won customary rights and the state's desire for a peasantry sufficiently independent to be ruled without going through local magnates. More negatively, it reflected very low reproduction rates among those who were proletarianized. Since sex-selective infanticide and neglect skewed male/female ratios, and a few elite males had concubines as well as wives, the poorest men rarely married. (This was perhaps their most intense social grievance; it disappeared for a while after the Revolution, but has reappeared due to sex-selective abortion.)

Given secure tenure, even full-time tenants earned more than twice as much as rural wage laborers. Since urban unskilled wages were very close to rural ones, the poor had little incentive to head for the cities. They were much better off heading for the frontier, where gaining access to land was relatively easy: average incomes were lower, but the chance for a newcomer to reach that average was much better. Consequently, the large non-agricultural labor force in areas like the Lower Yangzi remained embedded in farm households, which produced both agricultural commodities and light manufactures for sale. The resulting economy produced relatively high average incomes, some cushion against market fluctuations, and probably less inequality than in the early modern West, but it needed a continued frontier (both to trade with and to send migrants to), and it produced fewer of the urban agglomeration effects that *may* have been important to early industrial innovation.

Parity did not last. In the 19th century, output and specialization soared in Europe, while in China, per capita non-grain consumption probably declined: 1900 figures for cloth, sugar, and tobacco, for instance, are below even conservative estimates for 1750.

Much of the difference was ecological, but not because "population pressure" was necessarily producing more serious problems within Chinese core areas than in cores of Europe. Dry-farming areas in North China seem to have been maintaining the soil as well as those in England circa 1800; nutrient balances in South China's paddy rice regions (where periodic inundation provided nutrients that supplemented impressive applications of recycled human and animal wastes) would compare very favorably to anything in Europe. Even for wood supply and deforestation there was no clear Western European advantage circa 1750, despite its much sparser population. China used fuel very efficiently, and was actually better off in certain ways than Western Europe, where deforestation, sandstorms, and other signs of environmental stress were all increasing in the 18th century. Still, high fuel prices mattered, since they made people in China unlikely to try substituting heat energy for labor.

One can find some signs of serious problems and of relatively stable conditions in cores at both ends of Eurasia, and the research available leaves many gaps; however, the current state of our understanding no longer supports older, taken-for-granted notions that because they were more densely populated, East Asian cores must have been worse off than European ones in the 18th century. On the whole, the current research seems to suggest rough comparability. What is clear, however, is that in the early 19th century—when both population and per capita consumption were growing as never before in Western Europe—some ecological variables, such as forested area, underwent a surprising stabilization, after declining considerably amidst the much slower growth of the early modern period. In China, by contrast, ecological problems accelerated despite a slowdown in population growth and a probable stagnation or even decline of per capita consumption.

The basic explanation of this ecological divergence appears to be twofold. One is the English transition to fossil fuels. This required new technology, but also luck. Before railways, most of China's coal deposits were far too many land-locked miles away from its core regions to be economical, regardless of any breakthroughs in extraction and use. In England, by contrast, early deforestation and abundant coal outcroppings in places accessible to London caused widespread early use of this less-preferred fuel, but production would have stalled at early 18th century levels without steam engines to pump water from deeper mines. Early steam engines, meanwhile, were so inefficient that for roughly a century their only use was at the pithead, where fuel was virtually free (fuel prices throughout the early modern world were largely driven by transport costs). But once the engines had *some* use, they were worth tinkering with, eventually reaching a point where they revolutionized trans-port and opened a new world of cheap, energy-intensive production.

Secondly, Western Europe benefited from a surge in imports of various land-intensive products from less developed areas, especially in the Americas. As demand for food, fiber, building materials, and fuel (Malthus' "four necessities") mounted, cores everywhere had to acquire some of these land-intensive products by trading with peripheries that wanted the manufactures, especially textiles, that cores produced.

But that trade tended to run into one of two problems. Where families in the peripheral areas were largely free to allocate their own labor, export booms stimulated population growth through natural increase and/or immigration. Over time, some labor switched into handicrafts, reducing exportable surpluses of raw materials and demand for imported manufactures. The Middle and Upper Yangzi, North China, and other Chinese hinterlands followed this path around 1750-1850, and what had been by far the world's largest long-distance staple trades declined. Moreover, the terms of trade shifted against manufactures: a bolt of medium-quality cloth bought roughly half as much rice in 1850 as in 1750. Core regions felt the pinch: the Yangzi Delta population stagnated while that of China overall was doubling.

In peripheries with less flexible institutions, such as Eastern Europe, these trade-dampening dynamics were weaker. Few people migrated in, people could not switch into handicrafts on any great scale, and since cash crop producers were often coerced, export booms did not necessarily increase their birth or survival rates. But such regions also responded less to external demand for their primary products in the first place. Thus, the Baltic trade had reached a plateau by 1650 at a fraction the size of China's long distance staple trades.

The Americas, however, were different. Smallpox and other disasters depopulated the region, and most of the new labor force were either slaves, purchased from abroad, or indentured whites transported by land-owners in order to generate exports to Europe. Moreover, plantations in particular often became highly specialized; thus slaves, despite their poverty, were a significant market for coarse cloth and other low-end manufactures. Consequently, the circum-Caribbean slave region (from Brazil to what became the U.S. South) was in some important ways the first "modern" periphery, with large bills to pay for imported capital goods (in this case human ones) and a market for some mass consumer goods. Combined with its ecological bounty, this meant that, unlike most Eurasian peripheries, the Americas kept expanding as a source of land-intensive exports.

Thus, contrary to conventional wisdom, Western Europe broke through resource constraints partly because markets in its peripheries *weren't* unencumbered. They were actually freer in East Asia, which led to a more equal dispersion of proto-industry and an ecological cul-de-sac. One reason for China's declining per capita consumption after about 1750 was a shift in population distribution: as the still relatively prosperous Yangzi Delta went from being about 16% of China to being 9% (and 6% by 1950), hinterlands had much more weight in Chinese aggregates. And while living standards in some hinterlands may have kept creeping upwards, others, as we shall see, declined drastically.

Europe in a Chinese Mirror

Once we stop explaining the bottlenecks China hit as due to peculiar pathologies, we can see more clearly the importance of an unexpected relaxing of land constraints—both through coal and through the Americas—in enabling parts of Northwestern Europe to gain population, specialize more in manufacturing, and consume more per capita without raw material prices soaring. Even in 1830—before the great mid-century boom in North American grain, meat, and timber exports, and when its sugar consumption per capita was just 20% of what it would be by 1900—replacing Britain's New World imports with local products would have required about 23 million acres (mostly to substitute for cotton). This exceeds even E.A. Wrigley's estimate of the additional forest acres that would have been needed to replace the coal boom—and either number roughly matches Britain's total arable land plus pastureland. Thus, positive resource shocks, only partly due to technology, allowed England to stretch ecological constraints that might otherwise have slowed its growth, much as the filling up of China's interior hobbled the Yangzi Delta.

In China, ecological problems mounted in the 19th century—not primarily in cores, but in areas like the over-logged Northwest and Southwest, the North China plain, and alongside rivers whose beds rose as highland forest clearance increased erosion. These problems were exacerbated, as we will see, by a decline in transfer payments from richer regions that had been used in large part for environmental management. In short, though European and Chinese cores had much in common, they were hitched to very different peripheries: filling up, turning to handicrafts, hitting ecological constraints, and exporting fewer primary products in China; and vastly expanded, ecologically rich, and outward-oriented in the Americas.

So colonies (and former colonies) mattered a lot—not necessarily because they yielded especially high profits, as dependency models have claimed, but because they were a special *kind* of trading partner—one which allowed European cores to change labor and capital into land-saving imports in a way that expanded trade closer to home couldn't.

East Asia from the Great Divergence to a (Partial) New Convergence

After recovering from mid-19th century shocks, Japan's economy began to grow faster than ever, benefiting both from new technologies (which were adapted to internal conditions) and from new trading partners with different factor endowments. China had a much rougher late 19th and early 20th century. But it is also true that, after suffering huge mid-century disasters—in part because its state was much weaker than Japan's—China's wealthiest regions also resumed economic growth, benefiting from some technological changes and from new trading opportunities that to some extent replaced the primary products, markets for light manufactures, and outlets for emigration once provided by internal hinterlands. Rice from Southeast Asia, for instance, helped to feed much of the Yangzi Delta and rapidly growing Shanghai, replacing lost shipments from the interior; Guangdong and Fujian soon imported rice, too. Timber and other land-intensive products were imported to coastal areas, while old and new light manufactures—cloth, straw mats, cane chairs, cigarettes, and patent medicines—were exported, along with people. It was some of China's hinterlands that had a hundred-year crisis.

Some internal regions, like the Middle Yangzi, gradually recovered to pre-1850 levels after the mid-19th century rebellions and then reached a plateau. Others, such as North China, declined dramatically, with ecological and political problems reinforcing each other. The Chinese state was battered both by rebellion and by foreign incursions. As it began to recover, its priorities shifted to reflect a more dangerous environment. Defending and developing relatively prosperous and now contested coastal regions became a top priority. Conversely, less attention was devoted to an older "reproductive" statecraft: using revenues from rich regions to underwrite flood control, emergency granaries, irrigation, and other efforts to stabilize family farming and Confucian society in poorer, more ecologically fragile areas. For instance, the state sharply reduced its massive subsidies (between 10% and 20% of all government spending from 1820-1850) for flood control and water transport on the Yellow River and Grand Canal (the canal having been superseded by railways and coastal steamships). The savings were largely diverted to paying indemnities for lost wars and attempts at military modernization. Subsidies for deep wells in semi-arid regions disappeared, even though the water table was falling as population grew. Thus, certain interior regions suffered simultaneously from being pushed into near-autarchy as long-distance internal trade declined, from population growth, and from a loss of state assistance with worsening environmental problems. Floods, droughts and violence all increased dramatically. (That the late 19th century had especially severe El Niños didn't help.) By contrast, new imports and increased government attention helped stabilize at least some ecological challenges closer to the coast, and levels of violence were much lower there.

Thus, this period provided a strong foretaste of a phenomenon much noted in recent decades: an economic decoupling of coastal and interior China, as the coast became more oriented toward external trading partners and once-crucial inter-regional transfer payments declined. Under these circumstances, coastal China—both the parts seized by imperialists (Taiwan, Hong Kong, the treaty ports, and more briefly Manchuria) and the rest—achieved substantial per capita growth in the early 20th century, despite huge problems. Enough of this growth reached ordinary people for some social indicators to improve: for instance, the average height of railway labor recruits from the Lower Yangzi increased at almost Japanese rates from around 1890-1937. Much of this was powered by growth in rural industry, which adapted new technologies but built in many other ways on historical precedents. In Jiangsu province (which included Shanghai), almost half of manufacturing output still occurred in villages on the eve of World War II. However, interior regions experienced little or even negative growth, much greater social unrest, and a shredding of what had been, by pre-modern standards, a relatively effective safety net. Xia Mingfang has estimated that roughly 1.2 million Chinese died in famines between 1644 and 1796, while 38 million died from 1875-1937—almost all of them in the North and Northwest.

It is therefore not surprising that Maoist political economy, while undoubtedly revolutionary in many ways, in other ways recalled certain tasks and even solutions from the high Qing era. In some sense collectivization made everyone a proletarian, but in another, every rural household was guaranteed access to farm work where, like smallholders or secure tenants, they earned incomes based on their average, not their marginal, product. Subsequent de-collectivization made the comparison to Qing tenures even stronger, though it is now being undermined as farmland as seized for various development projects. (More modest land reforms also preceded industrial booms in Japan, Taiwan, and South Korea.) Massive (if sometimes counterproductive) efforts were made to industrialize the countryside, rather than assuming that higher living standards would have to come from moving people out of the countryside. Migration to cities essentially stopped by 1960. Funds were again directed from wealthier to poorer regions, and (despite the disasters of the Great Leap) emphasis was placed on subsistence security for poor people and fragile regions. The per capita growth rates are unimpressive next to post-1978 achievements, but the social gains were dramatic: literacy soared and life expectancy nearly doubled between 1950 and 1976. So was the creation of infrastructure, including a crucial tripling of China's irrigated area, almost all of it in the North and Northwest.

An enormous amount changed after 1978, but it's also important to notice what did not. Rural industry, which added 130 million jobs before its job creation leveled off (as it became more capital-intensive) in the mid-1990s, was in many ways a more important engine of growth than the more glamorous reorganization of urban economies. Despite rapid urban growth, China remains more rural than other comparably industrial countries (just barely more urban than England in 1840). The diversification of rural economic activities means that by 2000 more than two-thirds of rural income came from non-agricultural activities, about the same level Taiwan reached circa 1980. (In India, by contrast, the figure is about 45%, and in South Korea 20%.) In the more successful parts of the countryside, families with local land-leasing rights also provide much of the industrial work force; indeed, villages often insure that as many native households as possible have some stake in the more lucrative parts of the local economy before any migrants are employed in good jobs. Though this model is now fraying in many ways, it is worth reiterating some of its achievements: enormous poverty reduction and labor-absorption, vastly fewer semi-legal urban slums than in most of the developing world, and so on.

If we look at things regionally, we again see familiar patterns. This rural industrialization is again very concentrated in coastal areas (though it takes in a bit more of the coast than before); as of a few years ago, over half of rural industrial value added came from three provinces. And, as the export boom suggests, those areas are again more oriented towards a wider world than towards the rest of China. China's ratio of foreign trade to GDP now far exceeds the highest levels reached in Japanese history. Both exports and imports play a role here, as coastal China is importing hugely increased amounts of oil, metals, raw cotton, lumber, and so on— just as Japan, Taiwan, and Korea have come to do. Despite those imports, however, coastal China's economy is still far less resource-intensive than that of the interior: for instance, energy use per dollar of GDP in Jiangsu, Zhejiang, and Guangdong is about 40% of what it is in Gansu and Xinjiang.

And there's the rub—or rather, rubs. Being six times the population of Japan, Korea, and Taiwan, China can't ever import the quantities of primary products per capita that the other countries do. Internally, the rapid growth of inland/coastal and urban/rural inequalities is both a problem in itself and a threat to the basic development model. Incomes in rural areas that remain heavily agricultural now lag so far behind those in other areas that guaranteed access to land is no longer enough to keep people in the countryside (the rural population stopped growing in absolute terms in 1996, just about when rural industry stopped adding significant numbers of jobs). Despite still-significant barriers, net rural-urban migration is now approaching 20 million per year. Here China seems to be following Japanese trends, with a 50-year lag; after remaining relatively rural for its level of industrialization until the 1950s, Japan then began two decades of extremely rapid urbanization at the same time that it moved strongly into higher value-added industries. But when Japan began this push, its unemployment rate was 2%, so that even as the cities bulged, everyone found jobs. China's situation is very different, and its success at avoiding massive peri-urban slums will be hard to sustain. And the prospects for the West absorbing a further surge in manufactured imports from Asia are much murkier than in the 1950s.

One result has been the "Go West" initiative: a massive, government-led campaign to jumpstart economic development through mining, hydropower construction, and other capital-intensive, resource-oriented projects in Western China, to generate primary products for the East. Han Chinese migration to these areas (long restricted to avoid provoking ethnic resentment) is now being subsidized to fill skilled jobs. Lakes, mines, and so on—previously off-limits for various reasons—are now being opened, often over local (and sometimes international) opposition. In general, a long-standing paternalism towards minorities here (which, granted, has been slowly weakening for some time) is now being decisively pushed aside. And this initiative also carries huge ecological risks: removing trees at high elevations where re-growth is slow, quick and dirty mining, diversion of water from the Himalayan glaciers and annual snow melt (some of which currently goes to South and Southeast Asia), and so on. Perhaps half the hydroelectric dams built in West China since 1949 are now silted up, and some new ones are expected to provide power for only 20 years.

In one sense, "Go West" is an effort to stitch the country together, increasing interdependence and reducing economic (and perhaps ethnic) differences. In other ways, it may exacerbate differences. The coastal economy is increasingly semi-private—only 20% of industry remains truly state-owned in many coastal provinces—and the new rich are playing an increasing role in providing local services, as elites in rich areas traditionally did. The West, meanwhile, is seeing a revival of state (often military)-led development, with 60-80% of industry state-owned and far fewer high status jobs outside the state sector. Thus, it is not hard to imagine growing regional differences in social and political orientation as well as in living standards. Rather than a projection of the "East Asian" development seen on the coast across more of the Chinese landscape, developments in the interior (especially the far west) seem to have more in common with colonial or "internal colonial" styles of development.

Conclusion

A comparative history of development casts further doubt on the unique advantages of North Atlantic paths to the modern world; it reminds us that more labor-intensive (and less resource-intensive) "East Asian" paths accounted for much of the world's economic growth during both the period before 1800 and the period since 1945, and may sometimes offer a less socially-disruptive transition to modernity. They should be taken as seriously as models drawn from North Atlantic experiences, not pigeonholed as a regionally specific curiosity. But the East Asian path is no panacea, either—when projected onto the gigantic scale represented by China, it eventually runs up against massive social and environmental problems of its own. We still do not know how to have cores without hinterlands. ❑

Sources: For reasons of both length and style, the footnotes have been removed from this paper. Sources (and a more fully developed version of the argument) can be found in a series of publications by Kenneth Pomeranz, including: *The Great Divergence: China, Europe and the Making of the Modern World Economy*, Princeton University Press, 2000; "Beyond the East-West Binary: Resituating Development Paths in the Eighteenth Century World," *Journal of Asian Studies*, May, 2002; "Is There an East Asian Development Path? Long-Term Comparisons, Constraints, and Continuities," *Journal of the Economic and Social History of the Orient*, 2001; "Standards of Living in 18th Century China: Regional Differences, Temporal Trends, and Incomplete Evidence," in Robert Allen, Tommy Bengtsson, and Martin Dribe, eds., *Standards of Living and Mortality in Pre-Industrial Times*, Oxford University Press, 2005; "Chinese Development in Long-run Perspective," *Proceedings of the American Philosophical Society*, March, 2008.

Article 7.2

IS DECREASING INFANT MORTALITY
DUE TO NEOLIBERAL POLICIES?
BY ARTHUR MacEWAN
July/August 2000

Dear Dr. Dollar,

Defenders of the International Monetary Fund (IMF) and the World Bank,
including U.S. Treasury Secretary Lawrence Summers, claim that during the
past two decades there have been dramatic improvements in lowering infant-
mortality rates and increasing longevity in Third World countries due to the
IMF, World Bank, and neoliberal economic policies generally. What validity is
there to this position?

— *Larry Siegel, Bedford Hills, N.Y.*

There is not much validity to the claim.

In spite of the persistence of great inequality and poverty in the world,
throughout the last 50 years infant-mortality rates have fallen and life expectancy
has risen in almost all countries. The gains in many low-income countries are especially impressive. Yet these improvements were no greater in the 1980s and 1990s,
when neoliberalism gained dominance, than in earlier periods, and they cannot be
tied to the neoliberalism of the IMF and World Bank.

Public-health programs, such as inoculation against smallpox and improvements in sanitation, are responsible for most of these improvements. Yet these
types of social programs are, to say the least, not central elements in the neoliberal
agenda, which encourages government cutbacks and privatization. Of course, the
neoliberals justify their approach by arguing that their policies lead to economic
growth, which then leads to the expansion of social programs. Neoliberal policies,
however, have not greatly improved economic growth, nor is there any automatic
connection between economic growth and improvements in infant-mortality rates
and longevity.

Chile is one case that might lend support to the claims made by supporters of
the IMF and World Bank. In that country, where neoliberal policies were imposed
by the military dictatorship in the mid-1970s, the infant-mortality rate fell from 77
per 1,000 live births in 1970 to 32 in 1980, to 16 in 1990, and to 11 in 1997. (Life
expectancy data tell a similar tale, rising from 62.4 years in 1970 to 75.2 in 1997.)
The substantial success of the 1970s, however, can hardly be attributed to the neoliberal model, since free-market policies were not instituted until the latter part of
the decade and it takes time for economic policies to produce health results. Also,
the improvements occurred at least in part because the dictatorship departed from

its neoliberal policies, establishing government prenatal and neonatal programs.

Nowhere else in Latin America can advocates of neo-liberalism find support for their claims, even though the governments in the region have adopted neoliberal policies. For example, in Mexico, Brazil, Argentina, and Peru, infant-mortality rates and longevity figures have improved continuously, but no more than when "statist" policies were in force. Indeed, in Mexico improvements in the infant-mortality rate have slowed dramatically since 1990—precisely the years when neoliberal policies began having their impact on the country.

Also, to date, no other country in Latin America has matched the experience of Cuba. In 1997, the life expectancy in Cuba was 76 years and the infant-mortality rate was 7 per 1,000—the same as in the United States. Whatever one thinks of Cuban economic policies, they can hardly be classified as neoliberal!

Outside of Latin America, it is hard to find evidence that would support the IMF and World Bank on the basis of these social indicators. On the one hand, there is the case of South Korea, where a military dictatorship achieved great success with capitalist development under a regime of strong state control of the economy. The infant-mortality rate fell from 46 in 1970 to 12 in 1990, and life expectancy rose from 60 to 70. On the other hand, in sub-Saharan Africa, where the IMF and World Bank have had major roles in recent years, social indicators remain dismal and the era of increased neoliberal influence has not been better than earlier decades. Life expectancy rose from 44 years in 1970, to 48 in 1980, inched up to 50 in 1990 and then to 51 in 1997; the infant-mortality rates for those years have been 137, 115, 100, and 91. (Neoliberalism, it seems, has done little to counter the AIDS epidemic.)

Shifting attention to the wealthy capitalist countries, it is interesting to compare the United States and Japan. In spite of Japan's relative economic stagnation since the end of the 1980s, in 1997 life expectancy was 80 and the infant-mortality rate was a remarkable 3.7 per 1,000. In the U.S., where we talk about the great economic expansion of the 1990s, the figures for 1997 were 76 for life expectancy and 7.1 for infant mortality. There are many differences between the two countries that could explain Japan's better social indicators. Still, one economic fact is probably most relevant here, as in other parts of the world: the distribution of income in Japan is much less unequal than in the United States. ❏

All data used here are from World Bank sources.

Article 7.3

MEASURES OF GLOBAL POVERTY

BY ARTHUR MacEWAN
January/February 2008

Dear Dr. Dollar:

I hear all kinds of views about poverty in the developing world from different corners of the media. One minute you can get the impression that a huge swell is lifting everyone up and that millions of people in Asia are no longer in poverty. Then from a different source you get the impression that poverty is deepening and getting worse—the pictures of the kids with swollen bellies, etc. What's the reality?

            —*William Chin, Randolph, Mass.*

The reality of poverty, like many other "realities," is elusive! There are disputes over how to define poverty, and, even when we can agree on a definition, there are disputes over how to measure poverty. However, one aspect of the poverty reality is fairly clear: there are still a great many very poor people in the world.

One widely used standard used to measure poverty is $2 per day—that is, people whose income is less than $2 per day are considered "in poverty." And people are viewed as in "extreme poverty" if their income is less than $1 per day. By these standards, in 2004 about 2.5 billion people, 39% of the world's 6.4 billion people, were in poverty, and 969 million were in extreme poverty.

This standard, however, requires a bit of explanation. The $2/day and the $1/day are based on what people could buy in 1990. Translated into today's prices, these figures would be about $3.20/day and $1.60/day. Also, these amounts are defined in terms of real purchasing power, not in terms of actual exchange rates. Thus $1.60 per day represents what a person could buy with that amount in the United States, not what could be bought in a low-income country if the $1.60 were exchanged for the local currency. Generally the latter would be substantially more than the former.

The World Bank makes annual attempts to update the figures on how many people are in poverty and how many are in extreme poverty by these standards. According to the Bank, there has been some substantial progress in the last fifteen years. By the Bank's count, the number of people in extreme poverty dropped from 1.25 billion in 1990 to below a billion in 2004—or from 24% of the world's people to its 2004 figure of 15%. The absolute number below $2/day fell only slightly in this period, from 2.6 billion to 2.5 billion, but this was a drop from 49% to 39% of the population (because the population increased).

The World Bank's appraisal of the situation, however, is open to dispute. To begin with, there are always problems in measuring what happens to people's incomes over time, because prices change. While the Bank adjusts for price changes, it does not do so adequately. To measure what happens in a country, the bank uses price changes for that country as a whole. It seems, however, that the prices of the goods that the poor buy have generally risen more rapidly than prices for the society as a whole. Thus the Bank's estimates of poverty reduction are probably overstated.

Furthermore, as the Bank recognizes, its picture of overall progress for the world obscures some very great differences between countries. By the $2/day and $1/day standard, the last fifteen years have seen great progress in China and India, two countries that together account for more than one-third of the world's population and which have grown quite rapidly. Other parts of the world, especially much of sub-Saharan Africa and parts of Latin America, have not done so well.

But there is a bigger difficulty. The $2/day and $1/day definitions of extreme poverty and poverty are, at best, a questionable way to frame the problem. It is misleading to define the poverty line simply in absolute terms, as the value of a certain quantity of goods and services that people must purchase to meet their basic needs (as represented by the $2/day and $1/day cutoffs). Raising people's absolute incomes is important and leads to improvements in nutrition, shelter, longevity, and general well-being. But there is more to poverty than an absolute level of income.

Poverty is a social status, a relation among people, and our standard of what it means to be in poverty varies across societies and over time. As a society's economy grows, its standard of "need" changes, and thus the meaning of poverty changes. For example, as an economy grows, more work takes place away from the home, and thus people's need for transportation increases. Also, as incomes rise, people's standards of what they need in terms of food, clothing, shelter, and everything else change.

Roughly speaking, we can think of a society's standard of needs as determined by what the people in the middle have. If so, people are in poverty when their level of income is far below what the people in the middle have. This means that poverty is greatly affected by the distribution of income. In two societies where the absolute income of the bottom segment (say the bottom 20%) is the same, poverty will be greater in the society where income distribution is more unequal because in that society the bottom segment will be further from the norm and thus more lacking in that society's socially determined needs.

In China and India, in particular, the countries responsible for large reductions in poverty by the $2/day measure, income inequality has increased dramatically in recent decades. Thus, if we define poverty as a certain distance (in income terms) form the middle, it is possible that there are more people in poverty in China and India than there were twenty years ago, in spite of rapid economic expansion. And China and India are not unusual. Over the last few decades, many countries have seen rising inequality.

Even if one accepts the absolute poverty definition—the $2/day and $1/day standards—rising inequality makes the reduction of poverty with economic growth much less than it would be if, along with growth, income distribution were improving. The problem is that the World Bank and much of the U.N. effort to "make poverty history" largely ignore the issue of income distribution. For example, land redistribution is not on the table in World Bank and U.N. programs, yet unequal land holdings are at the foundation of the lack of income and political power experienced by the poor in many parts of the world. Or another example: the Bank and the United Nations tout education as a cure-all for poverty, but they give no consideration to the ways inequalities of income and political power restrict the emergence of effective school programs.

Whether one emphasizes the absolute or relative concept of poverty—or takes both into account—it is doubtful that much progress can be attained while ignoring the underlying issues of power and social structure that create and maintain poverty. ❑

MICROCREDIT AND WOMEN'S POVERTY

Granting this year's Nobel Peace Prize to microcredit guru Muhammad Yunus affirms neoliberalism.

BY SUSAN F. FEINER AND DRUCILLA K. BARKER
November/December 2006

The key to understanding why Grameen Bank founder and CEO Muhammad Yunus won the Nobel Peace Prize lies in the current fascination with individualistic myths of wealth and poverty. Many policy-makers believe that poverty is "simply" a problem of individual behavior. By rejecting the notion that poverty has structural causes, they deny the need for collective responses. In fact, according to this tough-love view, broad-based civic commitments to increase employment or provide income supports only make matters worse: helping the poor is pernicious because such aid undermines the incentive for hard work. This ideology is part and parcel of neoliberalism.

For neoliberals the solution to poverty is getting the poor to work harder, get educated, have fewer children, and act more responsibly. Markets reward those who help themselves, and women, who comprise the vast majority of microcredit borrowers, are no exception. Neoliberals champion the Grameen Bank and similar efforts precisely because microcredit programs do not change the structural conditions of globalization—such as loss of land rights, privatization of essential public services, or cutbacks in health and education spending—that reproduce poverty among women in developing nations.

What exactly is microcredit? Yunus, a Bangladeshi banker and economist, pioneered the idea of setting up a bank to make loans to the "poorest of the poor." The term "microcredit" reflects the very small size of the loans, often less than $100. Recognizing that the lack of collateral was often a barrier to borrowing by the poor, Yunus founded the Grameen Bank in the 1970s to make loans in areas of severe rural poverty where there were often no alternatives to what we would call loan sharks.

His solution to these problems was twofold. First, Grameen Bank would hire agents to travel the countryside on a regular schedule, making loans and collecting loan repayments. Second, only women belonging to Grameen's "loan circles" would be eligible for loans. If one woman in a loan circle did not meet her obligations, the others in the circle would either be ineligible for future loans or be held responsible for repayment of her loan. In this way the collective liability of the group served as collateral.

The Grameen Bank toasts its successes: not only do loan repayment rates approach 95%, the poor, empowered by their investments, are not dependent on "handouts." Microcredit advocates see these programs as a solution to poverty because poor women can generate income by using the borrowed funds to start small-scale enterprises, often home-based handicraft production. But these enterprises are almost all in the informal sector, which is fiercely competitive and typically unregulated, in other words, outside the range of any laws that protect workers or ensure their rights. Not surprisingly, women comprise the majority of workers in the informal economy and are heavily represented at the bottom of its already-low income scale.

Women and men have different experiences with work and entrepreneurship because a gender division of labor in most cultures assigns men to paid work outside the home and women to unpaid labor in the home. Consequently, women's paid work is constrained by domestic responsibilities. They either work part time, or they combine paid and unpaid work by working at home. Microcredit encourages women to work at home doing piecework: sewing garments, weaving rugs, assembling toys and electronic components. Home workers—mostly women and children—often work long hours for very poor pay in hazardous conditions, with no legal protections. As progressive journalist Gina Neff has noted, encouraging the growth of the informal sector sounds like advice from one of Dickens' more objectionable characters.

Why then do national governments and international organizations promote microcredit, thereby encouraging women's work in the informal sector? As an antipoverty program, microcredit fits nicely with the prevailing ideology that defines poverty as an individual problem and that shifts responsibility for addressing it away from government policy-makers and multilateral bank managers onto the backs of poor women.

Microcredit programs do nothing to change the structural conditions that create poverty. But microcredit *has* been a success for the many banks that have adopted it. Of course, lending to the poor has long been a lucrative enterprise. Pawnshops, finance companies, payday loan operations, and loan sharks charge high interest rates precisely because poor people are often desperate for cash and lack access to formal credit networks. According to Sheryl Nance-Nash, a correspondent for Women's eNews, "the interest rates on microfinance vary between 25% to 50%." She notes that these rates "are much lower than informal money lenders, where rates may exceed 10% per month." It is important for the poor to have access to credit on relatively reasonable terms. Still, microcredit lenders are reaping the rewards of extraordinarily high repayment rates on loans that are still at somewhat above-market interest rates.

Anecdotal accounts can easily overstate the concrete gains to borrowers from microcredit. For example, widely cited research by the Canadian International Development Agency (CIDA) reports that "Women in particular face significant barriers to achieving sustained increases in income and improving their status, and require complementary support in other areas, such as training, marketing, literacy, social mobilization, and other financial services (e.g., consumption loans, savings)." The report goes on to conclude that most borrowers realize only very small gains, and that the poorest borrowers benefit the least. CIDA also found little relationship between loan repayment and business success.

However large or small their income gains, poor women are widely believed to find empowerment in access to microcredit loans. According to the World Bank, for instance, microcredit empowers women by giving them more control over household assets and resources, more autonomy and decision-making power, and greater access to participation in public life. This defense of microcredit stands or falls with individual success stories featuring women using their loans to start some sort of small-scale enterprise, perhaps renting a stall in the local market or buying a sewing machine to assemble piece goods. There is no doubt that when they succeed, women and their families are better off than they were before they became micro-debtors.

But the evidence on microcredit and women's empowerment is ambiguous. Access to credit is not the sole determinant of women's power and autonomy. Credit may, for example, increase women's dual burden of market and household labor. It may also increase conflict within the household if men, rather than women, control how loan moneys are used. Moreover, the group pressure over repayment in Grameen's loan circles can just as easily create conflict among women as build solidarity.

Grameen Bank founder Muhammad Yunus won the Nobel Peace Prize because his approach to banking reinforces the neoliberal view that individual behavior is the source of poverty and the neoliberal agenda of restricting state aid to the most vulnerable when and where the need for government assistance is most acute. Progressives working in poor communities around the world disagree. They argue that poverty is structural, so the solutions to poverty must focus not on adjusting the conditions of individuals but on building structures of inclusion. Expanding the state sector to provide the rudiments of a working social infrastructure is, therefore, a far more effective way to help women escape or avoid poverty.

Do the activities of the Grameen Bank and other micro-lenders romanticize individual struggles to escape poverty? Yes. Do these programs help some women "pull themselves up by the bootstraps"? Yes. Will micro-enterprises in the informal sector contribute to ending world poverty? Not a chance. ❑

Sources: Grameen Bank, grameen-info.org; "Informal Economy: Formalizing the Hidden Potential and Raising Standards," ILO Global Employment Forum (Nov. 2001), www-ilo-mirror. cornell.edu/public/english/employment/geforum/informal.htm; Jean L. Pyle, "Sex, Maids, and Export Processing," World Bank, *Engendering Development; Engendering Development Through Gender Equality in Rights, Resources, and Voice* (Oxford University Press, 2001); Naila Kabeer, "Conflicts Over Credit: Re-Evaluating the Empowerment Potential of Loans to Women in Rural Bangladesh," *World Development* 29 (2001); Norman MacIsaac, "The Role of Microcredit in Poverty Reduction and Promoting Gender Equity," South Asia Partnership Canada, Strategic Policy and Planning Division, Asia Branch Canada International Development Agency (June, 1997), www.acdi-cida.gc.ca/index-e.htm.

Article 7.5

FAIR TRADE AND FARM SUBSIDIES
How Big a Deal? Two Views

November/December 2003

In September of 2003, the global free-trade express was derailed—at least temporarily—when the World Trade Organization talks in Cancún, Mexico, collapsed. At the time, the inconsistency of the United States and other rich countries—pressing poor countries to adopt free trade while continuing to subsidize and protect selected domestic sectors, especially agriculture—received wide attention for the first time. Where does ending agricultural subsidies and trade barriers in the rich countries rank as a strategy for achieving global economic justice? Dollars & Sense *asked progressive researchers on different sides of this question to make their case.*

MAKE TRADE FAIR

BY GAWAIN KRIPKE

Trade can be a powerful engine for economic growth in developing countries and can help pull millions of people out of poverty. Trade also offers an avenue of growth that relies less than other development strategies on the fickle charity of wealthy countries or the self-interest of multinational corporations. However, current trade rules create enormous obstacles that prevent people in developing countries from realizing the benefits of trade. A growing number of advocacy organizations are now tackling this fundamental problem, hoping to open a route out of poverty for tens of millions of people who have few other prospects.

Why Trade? Poor countries have few options for improving the welfare of their people and generating economic growth. Large debt burdens limit the ability of governments in the developing world to make investments and provide education, clean water, and other critical services. Despite some recent progress on the crushing problem of debt, only about 15% of the global South's $300 billion in unpayable debt has been eliminated.

Poor countries have traditionally looked to foreign aid and private investment to drive economic development. Both of these are proving inadequate. To reach the goals of the United Nations' current Millenium Development campaign, including reducing hunger and providing universal primary education, wealthy countries would have to increase their foreign aid from a paltry 0.23% of GDP to 0.7%. Instead, foreign aid flows are stagnant and are losing value against inflation and population growth. In 2001, the United States spent just 0.11% of GDP on foreign aid.

Likewise, although global foreign direct investment soared to unprecedented levels in the late 1990s, most developing countries are not attractive to foreign investors. The bulk of foreign private investment in the developing world, more than 76%, goes to ten large countries including China, Brazil, and Mexico. For the majority of developing countries, particularly the poorest, foreign investment remains a modest contributor to economic growth, on a par with official foreign aid. Sub-Saharan Africa, with the highest concentration of the world's poor, attracted only $14 billion in 2001.

In this environment, trade offers an important potential source of economic growth for developing countries. Relatively modest gains in their share of global trade could yield large benefits for developing countries. Gaining an additional 1% share of the $8 trillion global export market, for example, would generate more revenue than all current foreign aid spending.

But today, poor countries are bit players in the global trade game. More than 40% of the world's population lives in low-income countries, but these countries generate only 3% of global exports. Despite exhortations from the United States and other wealthy countries to export, many of the poorest countries are actually losing share in export markets. Africa generated a mere 2.4% of world exports of goods in 2001, down from 3.1% in 1990.

Many factors contribute to the poorest countries' inability to gain a foothold in export trade, but the core problem is that the playing field is heavily tilted against them. This is particularly true in the farm sector. The majority of the global South population lives in rural areas and depends on agriculture for survival. Moreover, poverty is concentrated in the countryside: more than three-quarters of the world's poorest people, the 1.1 billion who live on less than one dollar a day, live in rural areas. This means that agriculture must be at the center of trade, development, and poverty-reduction strategies throughout the developing world.

Two examples demonstrate the unfair rules of the global trading system in agriculture: cotton and corn.

"It's Not White Gold Anymore". Cotton is an important crop in Central and West Africa. More than two million households depend directly on the crop for their livelihoods, with millions more indirectly involved. Despite serious social and environmental problems that have accompanied the expansion of cotton cultivation, cotton provides families with desperately needed cash for health care, education, and even food. The cotton crop can make a big difference in reducing poverty. For example, a 2002 World Bank study found a strong link between cotton prices and rural welfare in Benin, a poor West African country.

Cotton is important at a macroeconomic level as well; in 11 African countries, it accounts for more than one-quarter of export revenue. But since the mid-1990s, the cotton market has experienced chronic price depression. Though prices have rebounded in recent months, they remain below the long-term average of $0.72 a pound. Lower prices mean less export revenue for African countries and lower incomes for African cotton farmers.

But not for U.S. cotton farmers. Thanks to farm subsidies, U.S. cotton producers are insulated from the market and have produced bumper crops that depress prices worldwide. The global price of cotton is 20% lower than it would be without U.S. subsidies, according to an analysis by the International Cotton Advisory Committee. Oxfam estimates that in 2001, as a result of U.S. cotton subsidies, eight countries in Africa lost approximately $300 million—about one-quarter of the total amount the U.S. Agency for International Development will spend in Africa next year.

Dumping on Our Neighbor. Mexico has been growing corn (or maize) for 10,000 years. Today, nearly three million Mexican farmers grow corn, but they are facing a crisis due to sharply declining prices. Real prices for corn have fallen 70% since 1994. Poverty is widespread in corn-growing areas like Chiapas, Oaxaca, and Guerrero. Every year, large numbers of rural Mexicans leave the land and migrate to the cities or to the United States to try to earn a living.

The price drops are due to increased U.S. corn exports to Mexico, which have more than tripled since 1994. These exports result in large part from U.S. government policies that encourage overproduction. While Mexican farmers struggle to keep their farms and support their families, the United States pours up to $10 billion annually into subsidies for U.S. corn producers. By comparison, the entire Mexican government budget for agriculture is $1 billion. Between 2000 and 2002, a metric ton of American corn sold on export markets for $20 less than the average cost to produce it. The United States controls nearly 70% of the global corn market, so this dumping has a huge impact on prices and on small-scale corn farmers in Mexico.

To be fair, the Mexican government shares some of the responsibility for the crisis facing corn farmers. Although the North American Free Trade Agreement (NAFTA) opened trade between the United States and Mexico, the Mexican government voluntarily lowered tariffs on corn beyond what was required by NAFTA. As NAFTA is fully phased in, though, Mexico will lose the option of raising tariffs to safeguard poor farmers from a flood of subsidized corn.

What do Poor Countries Want? Cotton and corn illustrate the problems that current trade regimes pose for developing countries and particularly for the world's poorest people. African countries want to engage in global trade but are crowded out by subsidized cotton from the United States. The livelihood of Mexican corn farmers is undermined by dumped U.S. corn. In both of these cases, and many more, it's all perfectly legal. WTO and NAFTA rules provide near impunity to rich countries that subsidize agriculture, and increasingly restrict developing countries' ability to safeguard their farmers and promote development.

How much do subsidies and trade barriers in the rich countries really cost the developing world? One study estimates that developing countries lose $24 billion annually in agricultural income—not a trivial amount. In today's political climate, it's hard to see where else these countries are going to find $24 billion to promote their economic development.

The benefits of higher prices for farmers in the developing world have to be balanced against the potential cost to consumers, both North and South. However, it's important to remember that many Northern consumers actually pay more for food *because of* subsidies. In fact, they often pay twice: first in higher food costs, and then in taxes to pay for the subsidies. Consumers in poor countries will pay more for food if farm commodity prices rise, but the majority of people who work in agriculture will benefit. Since poverty is concentrated in rural areas, the gains to agricultural producers are particularly important.

However, some low-income countries are net food importers and could face difficulties if prices rise. Assuring affordable food is critical, but this goal can be achieved much more cheaply and efficiently than by spending $100 billion on farm subsidies in the rich countries. The World Bank says that low-income countries that depend on food imports faced a net agricultural trade deficit of $2.8 billion in 2000-2001. The savings realized from reducing agricultural subsidies could easily cover this shortfall.

Each country faces different challenges. Developing countries, in particular, need flexibility to develop appropriate solutions to address their economic, humanitarian, and development situations. Broad-stroke solutions inevitably fail to address specific circumstances. But the complexity of the issues must not be used as an excuse for inaction by policy-makers. Failure to act to lift trade barriers and agricultural subsidies will only mean growing inequity, continuing poverty, and endless injustice.

Sources: Xinshen Diao, Eugenio Diaz-Bonilla, and Sherman Robinson, "How Much Does It Hurt? The Impact of Agricultural Trade Policies on Developing Countries," International Food Policy Research Institute, Washington, D.C., 2003; "Global Development Finance: Striving for Stability in Development Finance," World Bank, 2003; Lyuba Zarksy and Kevin Gallagher, "Searching for the Holy Grail? Making FDI Work for Sustainable Development," Tufts Global Development and Environment Institute/WWF, March 2003; Oxfam's website on trade issues, www.maketradefair.com.

FALSE PROMISES ON TRADE

BY DEAN BAKER AND MARK WEISBROT

Farmers throughout the Third World are suffering not from too much free trade, but from not enough. That's the impression you get from most media coverage of the recent World Trade Organization (WTO) meetings in Cancún. The *New York Times, Washington Post,* and other major news outlets devoted huge amounts of space to news pieces and editorials arguing that agricultural subsidies in rich countries are a major cause of poverty in the developing world. If only these subsidies were eliminated, and the doors to imports from developing countries opened, the argument goes, then the playing field would be level and genuinely free trade would work its magic on poverty in the Third World. The media decided that agricultural subsidies were the major theme of the trade talks even if evidence indicated that other issues—for example, patent and copyright protection, rules on investment, or developing countries' right to regulate imports—would have more impact on the well-being of people in those countries.

There is certainly some element of truth in the argument that agricultural subsidies and barriers to imports can hurt farmers in developing countries. There are unquestionably farmers in a number of developing countries who have been undersold and even put out of business by imports whose prices are artificially low thanks to subsidies the rich countries pay their farmers. It is also true that many of these subsidy programs are poorly targeted, benefiting primarily large farmers and often encouraging environmentally harmful farming practices.

However, the media have massively overstated the potential gains that poor countries might get from the elimination of farm subsidies and import barriers. The risk of this exaggeration is that it encourages policy-makers and concerned non-governmental organizations (NGOs) to focus their energies on an issue that is largely peripheral to economic development and to ignore much more important matters.

To put the issue in perspective: the World Bank, one of the most powerful advocates of removing most trade barriers, has estimated the gains from removing all the rich countries' remaining barriers to trade in manufactured and farm products *and* ending agricultural subsidies. The total estimated gain to low- and middle-income countries, when the changes are phased in by 2015, is an extra 0.6% of GDP. In other words, an African country with an annual income of $500 per person would see that figure rise to $503 as a result of removing these barriers and subsidies.

Simplistic Talk on Subsidies. The media often claim that the rich countries give $300 billion annually in agricultural subsidies to their farmers. In fact, this is not the amount of money paid by governments to farmers, which is actually less than $100 billion. The $300 billion figure is an estimate of the excess cost to consumers in rich nations that results from all market barriers in agriculture. Most of this cost is attributable to higher food prices that result from planting restrictions, import tariffs, and quotas.

The distinction is important, because not all of the $300 billion ends up in the pockets of farmers in rich nations. Some of it goes to exporters in developing nations, as when sugar producers in Brazil or Nicaragua are able to sell their sugar in the United States for an amount that is close to three times the world price. The higher price that U.S. consumers pay for this sugar is part of the $300 billion that many accounts mistakenly describe as subsidies to farmers in rich countries.

Another significant misrepresentation is the idea that cheap imports from the rich nations are always bad for developing countries. When subsides from rich countries lower the price of agricultural imports to developing countries, consumers in those countries benefit. This is one reason why a recent World Bank study found that the removal of *all* trade barriers and subsidies in the United States would have no net effect on growth in sub-Saharan Africa.

In addition, removing the rich countries' subsidies or barriers will not level the playing field—since there will still often be large differences in productivity—and thus will not save developing countries from the economic and social upheavals that such "free trade" agreements as the WTO have in store for them. These agreements envision a massive displacement of people employed in agriculture, as farmers in developing countries are pushed out by international competition. It took the United States 100 years, from 1870 to 1970, to reduce agricultural employment from 53% to under 5% of the labor force, and the transition nonetheless caused considerable social unrest. To compress such a process into a period of a few years or even a decade, by removing remaining agricultural trade barriers in poor countries, is a recipe for social explosion.

It is important to realize that in terms of the effect on developing countries, low agricultural prices due to subsidies for rich-country farmers have the exact same impact as low agricultural prices that stem from productivity gains. If the opponents of agricultural subsidies consider the former to be harmful to the developing countries, then they should be equally concerned about the impact of productivity gains in the agricultural sectors of rich countries.

Insofar as cheap food imports might have a negative impact on a developing country's economy, the problem can be easily remedied by an import tariff. In this situation, the developing world would gain the most if those countries that benefit from cheap imported food have access to it, while those that are better served by protecting their domestic agricultural sector are allowed to impose tariffs without fear of retaliation from rich nations. This would make much more sense, and cause much less harm, than simply removing all trade barriers and subsidies on both sides of the North-South economic divide. The concept of a "level playing field" is a false one. Mexican corn farmers, for example, are not going to be able to compete with U.S. agribusiness, subsidies or no subsidies, nor should they have to.

It is of course good that such institutions as the *New York Times* are pointing out the hypocrisy of governments in the United States, Europe, and Japan in insisting that developing countries remove trade barriers and subsidies while keeping some of their own. And the subsidy issue was exploited very skillfully by developing-country governments and NGOs at the recent Cancún talks. The end result—the collapse of the talks—was a great thing for the developing world. So were the ties that were forged among countries such as those in the group of 22, enabling them to stand up to the rich countries. But the WTO remedy of eliminating subsidies and trade barriers across the board will not save developing countries from most of the harm caused by current policies. Just the opposite: the removal of import restrictions in the developing world could wipe out tens of millions of farmers and cause enormous economic damage.

Avoiding the Key Issues. While reducing agricultural protection and subsidies just in the rich countries might in general be a good thing for developing countries, the gross exaggeration of its importance has real consequences, because it can divert attention from issues of far more pressing concern. One such issue is the role that the IMF continues to play as enforcer of a creditors' cartel in the developing world, threatening any country that defies its edicts with a cutoff of access to international credit. One of the most devastated recent victims of the IMF's measures has been Argentina, which saw its economy thrown into a depression after the failure of a decade of neoliberal economic policies. The IMF's harsh treatment of Argentina last year, while it was suffering from the worst depression in its history, is widely viewed in the developing world as a warning to other countries that might deviate from the IMF's recommendations. One result is that Brazil's new president, elected with an overwhelming mandate for change, must struggle to promote growth in the face of 22% interest rates demanded by the IMF's monetary experts.

Similarly, most of sub-Saharan Africa is suffering from an unpayable debt burden. While there has been some limited relief offered in recent years, the remaining debt service burden is still more than the debtor countries in that region spend on health care or education. The list of problems that the current world economic order imposes on developing countries is long: bans on the industrial policies that led to successful development in the West, the imposition of patents on drugs and copyrights on computer software and recorded material, inappropriate macroeconomic policies imposed by the IMF and the World Bank. All of these factors are likely to have far more severe consequences for the development prospects of poor countries than the agricultural policies of rich countries. ❑

Sources: Elena Ianchovichina, Aaditya Mattoo, and Marcelo Olareaga, "Unrestricted Market Access for Sub-Saharan Africa: How much is it worth and who pays," (World Bank, April 2001); Mark Weisbrot and Dean Baker, "The Relative Impact of Trade Liberalization on Developing Countries," (Center for Economic and Policy Research, June 2002).

Update: As of July 2008, the WTO negotiations have failed to reach an agreement, particularly on the issue of farm subsidies. Developing countries, especially India and China, demanded a deeper cut in the farm subsidies provided to U.S. and EU farmers and a much lower threshold for special safeguard mechanism for farmers in the developing countries. Meanwhile, developed countries, especially the United States, were not ready to budge from their position of reducing annual farm subsidies from $18 billion to $14.5 billion. The EU countries spend a total of $280 billion to support domestic farmers, while the official development assistance by the OECD countries to the developing world was $80 billion in 2004).

The IMF and the World Bank pushed the agenda of the structural adjustment program in more than 70 countries. The resulting decline in government spending has forced the farmers of the developing countries to deal with the mounting costs of cultivation. This, coupled with the vagaries of world farm-products prices (thanks to the Northern protectionism) has been driving the farmers in the South to much despair and hopelessness, and in the case of some 190,753 Indian farmers, suicide.

—Arpita Banerjee

Article 7.6

INEQUALITY WORSENS ACROSS ASIA, *WALL STREET JOURNAL* CHEERS

BY JOHN MILLER
November/December 2007

> A report from the Asian Development Bank, comparing more than a decade's worth of data from 22 developing countries, found significant increases in inequality across the region [Asia].
>
> But, as the ADB notes, this doesn't mean the rich are taking food from the mouths of the poor. Rather, the rich are getting richer faster than the poor are. In all but one developing country, per capita incomes for the bottom fifth of the work force increased at least slightly; Pakistan was the only exception.
> Poverty remains a serious problem throughout Asia—the ADB estimates 600 million people still live below the $1-a-day line, to use one popular measure. But "fixing" inequality won't fix poverty. As even the ADB recognizes, inequality can be a symptom of economic growth.
>
> While inequality of outcome can be a good thing, inequality of opportunity is another matter.
>
> The ADB worries that too much of the good inequality can lead to the bad variety by entrenching a new set of self-interested elites.
>
> The danger is that all this talk of "inequality" will lead to policies that, in the name of redistributing income, reduce economic growth and thus make it harder for Asia's poor to join the middle class. The Asian "pie" is growing for everyone. The challenge is to keep it that way, instead of quarreling over the relative size of the pieces.
>
> —*Wall Street Journal* editorial, 8/21/07

When ideologues of global capitalism step out of line, who better to let them know about it than the editors of the *Wall Street Journal*, the keepers of the free-market flame?

Just ask the economists and policy wonks at the Asian Development Bank (ADB), financial capital's Manila-based outpost in East Asia, who had the temerity to report in August that increasing inequality was a serious problem for Asia's economies. The *Journal*'s editors let them hear about it. "The danger," scolded the editors, "is that all this talk of 'inequality' will lead to policies that, in the name of redistributing income, reduce economic growth and thus make it harder for Asia's poor to join the middle class."

But the warning issued by the *Journal* editors is not just misleading, it is wrong. The evidence shows that countries that enjoy rapid economic growth are not more unequal than countries that grow slowly. In fact, a more equal distribution of income is not merely compatible with rapid growth; there are a number of avenues by which greater equality can actually promote growth. Finally, and most important for millions of people across Asia: poverty reduction depends on both raising a nation's income and reducing its inequality.

It is not that the ADB's bean counters got the numbers wrong. Of the 22 developing Asian economies in the ADB study, 15 saw inequality worsen since the early 1990s. That includes economic powerhouse China, where inequality worsened more rapidly and to higher levels than in any other country in the study other than Nepal. Even South Korea and Taiwan, once paragons of rapid and equitable growth, have seen inequality rise since 1993 .

Economists at the ADB tracked changes in the levels of inequality using Gini coefficients, economists' standard measure of economic inequality, in the 22 developing Asian countries for which there are sufficient data. The Gini coefficient ranges from zero to one: zero corresponds to perfect equality (every household has the same income), and one corresponds to maximal inequality (one household gets the entire national income). In the real world, Gini coefficients range from around 0.25 (Sweden, Denmark, Hungary) to nearly 0.60 (South Africa, Brazil, Haiti).

The ADB report found Gini coefficients rising across Asia. China's, for instance, rose from 0.41 in 1993 to 0.47 in 2004; it is now higher than that of the United States, 0.46 in 2004. (See Figure 1, which shows inequality levels by country, and Figure 2, which reports on changes in inequality levels.)

The trend toward a widening gap between the rich and poor in Asia is actually more alarming than even the ADB tables suggest. For one thing, the Asian financial crisis of the late 1990s sucked millions of dollars out of the caches of the continent's economic elites. Had it not been for this hit, Malaysia, Indonesia, and probably Thailand as well would have joined the worsening inequality column of the ADB report. Plus, the ADB tables rely on household expenditure data as opposed to the more difficult-to-obtain income data used in some countries to measure inequality. Inequality levels calculated from expenditure data are normally lower than those calculated from income data for the same population. In the Philippines, for example, where inequality data are available on both measures, the expenditure-based Gini coefficient is 0.40 for 2003, while the income-based figure is about 20% higher at 0.48.

The East Asian Miracle Under the Gun

While inequality can be a symptom of economic growth in capitalist economies, as the editors argue, what is remarkable about many East Asian economies is that prior to the 1990s they grew rapidly with far lower levels of inequality than elsewhere in the developing world. In some cases they saw inequality decline rather than worsen. For instance, in South Korea inequality declined from 1976 to 1993 even as the country's economy grew rapidly, posting average growth rates of 7.5% a year. Compared to Brazil, Latin America's fastest growing economy of the period, South Korea grew twice as quickly—with about half of Brazil's level of inequality.

The World Bank's famous 1993 "East Asian Miracle" study celebrated East Asia's "remarkable record of high growth and declining inequality." (Emphasis in the original.) From 1965 to 1990 the 23 economies of East Asia grew faster than all other regions of the world, three times as fast as the economies of Latin America and the Caribbean. Rapid growth in the region was spearheaded by the miraculous growth of eight high-performance economies—Japan; the "Four Tigers," Hong Kong, South Korea, Singapore, and Taiwan; and the three newly industrializing economies of southeast Asia, Indonesia, Malaysia, and Thailand—in which inequality remained low or improved over the same period. Because they were "unusually successful at sharing the fruits of growth," as the World Bank report put it, poverty declined rapidly and living conditions, from life expectancy to access to clean water and adequate shelter, improved dramatically in these high performance economies. A 1997 World Bank report went so far as to call rapid growth in East Asia "Everyone's Miracle."

"Everyone's" was surely an exaggeration even then. The editors of the

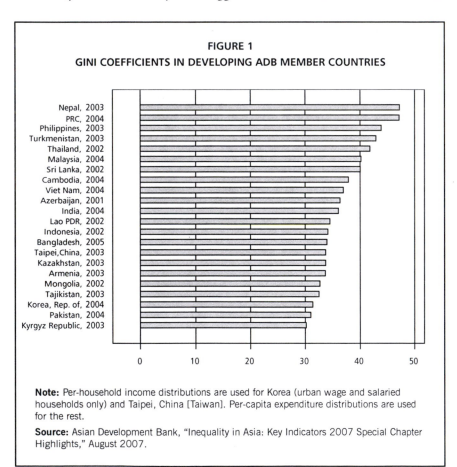

FIGURE 1

GINI COEFFICIENTS IN DEVELOPING ADB MEMBER COUNTRIES

Note: Per-household income distributions are used for Korea (urban wage and salaried households only) and Taipei, China [Taiwan]. Per-capita expenditure distributions are used for the rest.

Source: Asian Development Bank, "Inequality in Asia: Key Indicators 2007 Special Chapter Highlights," August 2007.

Wall Street Journal nonetheless contend that today's much more unequal economic growth in Asia should still be considered everyone's miracle. As they read the ADB report, despite widening inequality, at least some of the benefits of the economic growth have trickled down to the poorest 20% of households in these economies. Since 1993 the expenditures of the bottom quintile increased in all of these 22 Asian economies with the exception of Pakistan, albeit by far less than the expenditures of the richest 20%. (See Figure 3.) "These increases in inequality are not a story of the 'rich getting richer and the poor getting poorer'," confirms the ADB report. "Rather it is the rich getting richer faster than the poor."

That is enough to qualify as "pro-poor growth," according to the editors' absolute definition of the term: economic growth that does anything at all to alleviate poverty, no matter now lopsidedly it benefits the well-to-do.

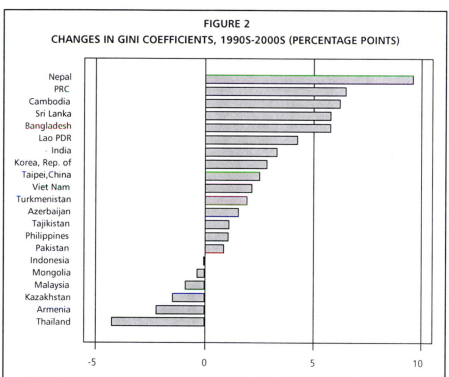

FIGURE 2

CHANGES IN GINI COEFFICIENTS, 1990S-2000S (PERCENTAGE POINTS)

Note: Years over which changes are computed are as follows: Armenia (1998-2003); Azerbaijan (1995-2001); Bangladesh (1991-2005); Cambodia (1993-2004); People's Republic of China (1993-2004); India (1993-2004); Indonesia (1993-2002); Kazakhstan (1996-2003); Republic of Korea (1993-2004); Lao PDR (1992-2002); Malaysia (1993-2004); Mongolia (1995-2002); Nepal (1995-2003); Pakistan (1992-2004); Philippines (1994-2003); Sri Lanka (1995-2002); Taipei,China (1993-2003); Tajikistan (1999-2003); Thailand (1992-2002); Turkmenistan (1998-2003); and Viet Nam (1993-2004). Gini calculated on income distribution for Republic of Korea and Taipei,China; expenditure distribution for all other countries.

Source: Asian Development Bank, "Inequality in Asia: Key Indicators 2007 Special Chapter Highlights," August 2007.

What Is Pro-Poor Growth?

It is true that rapid economic growth usually does more to alleviate poverty than slower economic growth. But if inequality grows at the same time, then much of the poverty-fighting potential of rapid economic growth is being lost. In some sense it may be accurate to say that the rich are not taking food from the mouths of the poor—but it's just as accurate to say that the benefits of economic growth that might otherwise have ended up on the tables of the poor have instead gone to the rich.

The evidence is clear. Had levels of inequality only remained unchanged over the last decade in the 15 countries that suffered worsening inequality, they would have seen a dramatic difference in the numbers of their citizens lifted from poverty.

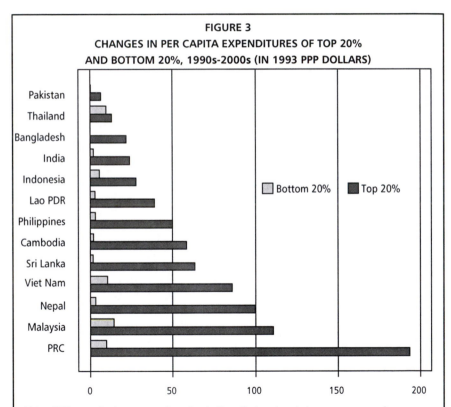

FIGURE 3

CHANGES IN PER CAPITA EXPENDITURES OF TOP 20% AND BOTTOM 20%, 1990s-2000s (IN 1993 PPP DOLLARS)

Notes: PPP, or purchasing power parity, refers to the adjustment made to currency comparisons across countries according to the price of a "basket" of goods in each country; in other words, PPP values control for the different prices of goods in different countries.

Years over which changes are computed are as follows: Bangladesh (1991-2005); Cambodia (1993-2004); People's Republic of China (1993-2004); India (1993-2004); Indonesia (1993-2002); Lao PDR (1992-2002); Malaysia (1993-2004); Nepal (1995-2003); Pakistan (1992-2004); Philippines (1994-2003); Sri Lanka (1995-2002); Thailand (1992-2002); and Viet Nam (1993-2004).

Source: Asian Development Bank, "Inequality in Asia: Key Indicators 2007 Special Chapter Highlights," August 2007.

The ADB report documents the large reductions in the percentage of the population living on less than $1 a day (a standard U.N. measure of poverty) that would have occurred had economic inequality not worsened. In China, the number would have been just about halved. (See Figure 4.)

By that standard, economic growth in most of these countries can hardly be considered pro-poor. Each percentage point of economic growth now does less to alleviate poverty than in the past. For instance, economists Hafiz Pasha and T. Palanivel found that national poverty in China fell 9.8% during both the 1980s and 1990s. But the economy needed a 9.0% per capita growth rate in the later decade, as opposed to a 7.8% rate in the earlier one, to effect the same reduction in poverty rates.

And contrary to the claims of the *Journal* editors, a widening difference between rich and poor can be, and at times has been, so great as to bring poverty alleviation to a halt altogether. In Thailand, for instance, the same 1993 World Bank study found that despite growth rates averaging 6.4% a year from 1975 to 1986, poverty rates increased over the same period. Rural Thais were hard hit by the falling prices of farm products, and economic differences between urban and rural dwellers widened. Similarly, between 1984 and 1991, rural Chinese suffered worsening poverty

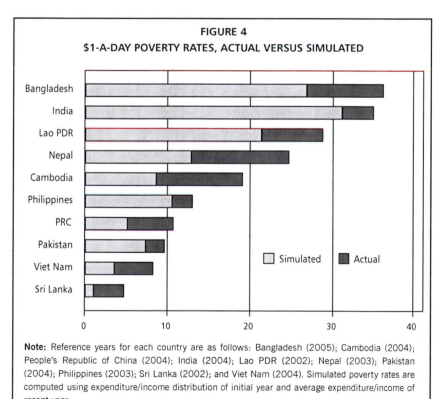

FIGURE 4
$1-A-DAY POVERTY RATES, ACTUAL VERSUS SIMULATED

Note: Reference years for each country are as follows: Bangladesh (2005); Cambodia (2004); People's Republic of China (2004); India (2004); Lao PDR (2002); Nepal (2003); Pakistan (2004); Philippines (2003); Sri Lanka (2002); and Viet Nam (2004). Simulated poverty rates are computed using expenditure/income distribution of initial year and average expenditure/income of recent year.

Source: Asian Development Bank, "Inequality in Asia: Key Indicators 2007 Special Chapter Highlights," August 2007.

as prices for farm products fell and rural output stagnated—even as the national economy was growing at double-digit rates.

While China's agricultural output subsequently picked up and poverty alleviation resumed, the widening gap between the economic standing of rural and urban Chinese continues to sap Chinese growth of its potential to ease poverty. Neglect of agriculture and of rural areas is a common feature that has contributed to rising inequality in many Asian economies; to improve the lot of the poor, the ADB recommends switching some public expenditures from urban to rural areas and from post-secondary education, which favors urban dwellers, to basic education, which is still not available to all, particularly in rural areas.

Tackling Poverty and Inequality

Neglecting to address inequality surely can compromise even the most dynamic economy's ability to fix poverty. That is not to say that fixing inequality alone will fix poverty. But there is now plenty of reason to believe that fixing inequality can enhance economic growth at the same time that it fights poverty. And contrary to the editors' admonishment, the ADB's talk about inequality might help lift the 600 million Asians who still live on less than a dollar a day out of poverty.

Today, even some mainstream economists are moving beyond the notion that rising inequality is necessary during developing countries' initial periods of rapid growth to establish the incentives to work, save, and invest. The record of the East Asian miracle economies provided an important exemplar of simultaneous rapid growth and low or declining inequality.

In recent years, economists and other social scientists have developed several explanations of how greater equality can in fact promote economic growth. More equal economies have more political stability, grant greater access to credit, spend more on education, and have more widespread land ownership than economies racked by inequality—each a factor that contributes to economic growth. Relative equality eases the social discontents and political conflicts that would otherwise discourage foreign investment and hamper economic growth. A more equal distribution of income allows the poor, who pay much higher interest rates than the rich in many developing countries, greater access to credit, adding to their personal investments and promoting economic growth. In relatively equal societies, more families have the savings necessary to send their children to school—obviously a spur to growth. And land reform, a key policy for reducing inequality in South Korea and Taiwan, raises agricultural productivity because small farmers cultivate their land more intensively than large landholders.

The ADB acknowledges several of these arguments. For instance, in the Beijing news conference launching the report, Ifzal Ali, the ADB's chief economist, called the rise in inequality in Asia today "a clear and present danger to the sustained growth," and warned that growing inequality could in some countries lead to "greater social conflict, from street demonstrations to violent civil wars."

Nonetheless, the ADB was not about to embrace massive redistribution policies that would dull market incentives. They do, however, endorse redistributive policies targeted at promoting "equality of opportunity" and "funded through mechanisms that do not detract from economic growth." Chief among their recommended polices are putting more public moneys into rural infrastructure including irrigation, electricity, transportation, and agricultural extension services, as well as expanding access to basic health care and primary education.

These measures are generally uncontroversial—although that does not mean they will be adopted any time soon. They would surely help. But they would be unlikely to arrest the widening inequality of the current period. To do that, public policy must also address the big picture: the decline in labor's share of the economic pie that corporate-led globalization has brought about.

Greater openness to trade, as economist Dani Rodrik has argued, erodes the bargaining power of labor by exposing workers, especially unskilled workers, to the competition of having their services replaced by imports from abroad.

Beyond that, export-led growth in many developing economies has failed to bring on the expected boom in manufacturing employment. As manufacturing exports from these countries increased with greater openness, so too did the quantity of manufactured goods imported into their domestic markets. So while export expansion was adding jobs, other jobs were being lost because of import penetration. Moreover, the new export industries are typically less labor-intensive than the older industries they replace. In China, for instance, relatively labor-saving joint ventures and foreign-owned firms in the country's new export zones have taken the place of relatively more labor-intensive state-owned manufacturing firms.

As a result, export promotion has done little to tighten labor markets and thereby improve labor's bargaining power. In the most detailed study to date, economists J. Felipe and G. Sipin found that in the Philippines, labor's share of national income fell by six percentage points from 1980 to 2002 as its economy globalized.

The case of China is also instructive, as economic sociologists Peter Evans and Sarah Staveteig point out. According to official statistics, manufacturing employment in China, the world's workshop, increased steadily from 1978 to 1995, nearly doubling from 53 million to 98 million jobs. But since then Chinese employment in manufacturing has fallen off. Manufacturing's share of Chinese employment has actually declined for nearly two decades now, even as China's share of world manufactured exports has increased more than fivefold.

With the manufacturing share of Chinese employment stagnant, hundreds of millions of people currently dependent on agricultural production for their incomes must either stay in that sector or move to the service sector. Both options suggest increased inequality and a more precarious quality of life for the vast majority of the Chinese population, argue Evans and Staveteig. If they stay in agriculture, the Chinese peasantry are likely to face stagnating incomes. A move into the service sector would allow a few new entrants to gain access to the more lucrative service jobs, but the vast majority will find poorly remunerated, insecure jobs offering personal services as the nannies, maids, drivers, and gardeners that their luckier compatriots will be able to hire.

While this widening inequality in the very countries that not long ago served as exemplars of growth with equality might not present a problem to the editors of the *Wall Street Journal*, it surely is a serious problem, as even the ADB acknowledges. But genuinely pro-poor economic growth will only come about when public policy confronts the current rules of the global economy—rules that the editors are so dedicated to defending, and that the ADB itself is reluctant to challenge. ❑

Sources: Asian Development Bank, Key Indicators 2007, Part 1: Inequality in Asia, August 2007; "Inequality Check," *Wall Street Journal* editorial, August 21, 2007; Richard McGregor, "ADB warns on rising inequality in China," *Financial Times*, August 8, 2007; Alan Wheatley, "Rising inequality danger for Asia, says ADB," Reuters, August 8, 2007; "For whosoever hath, to him shall be given, and he shall have more: Income inequality in emerging Asia is heading towards Latin American levels," *The Economist*, August 9, 2007; World Bank, "The East Asian Miracle: Economic Growth and Public Policy," 1993; Vinod Ahuja et al., "Everyone's Miracle," World Bank, 1997; Peter Evans and Sarah Staveteig, "Late 20th Century Industrialization and Changing Employment Structures in the Global South," Univ. of Calif. Berkeley, August 22, 2007; Hafiz A. Pasha and T. Palanivel, "Pro-Poor Growth and Policies: The Asian Experience," U.N. Development Programme, 2004; Judith Banister, "Manufacturing Employment in China," *Monthly Labor Review*, July 2005.

Article 7.7

HOW TO MAKE MUD COOKIES

A traditional Haitian remedy for hunger pangs could be a path to riches.

BY MAURICE DUFOUR
July/August 2008

Mud cookies are all the rage in Haiti today—a rage sparked by soaring food prices. The cookies, a traditional remedy for hunger pangs and a source of calcium for pregnant women, have become a staple because food is simply unaffordable for impoverished Haitians. With food prices showing no signs of leveling off, more and more Haitians are likely to rely on the biscuits for their nutritional needs—and the rage is likely to grow.

The cookies are easy to make. The main ingredient, an edible clay from Haiti's Central Plateau, is abundant, and salt and vegetable shortening are added in quantities that vary according to affordability. The cookies are then left out in the sun to bake. Besides being filling, they are dirt-cheap.

At least they have been up until now. The clay that is used to make the cookies is rapidly going up in price due to increasing demand. It now costs about five dollars to make 100 cookies, so even the "cookie jar" is out of reach of many Haitians, who make an average of about two dollars a day.

While it may seem that Haitians have reached rock bottom, they may, in fact, be sitting on a gold mine. Through the alchemy of comparative advantage, their sludge-filled biscuits could become their most valuable commodity, propel the country into the ranks of rich nations, and even provide a lasting solution to world hunger. After all, the logic of shifting more resources into the production of these biscuits is as "impeccable" as Lawrence Summers' argument for moving dirty industries from rich to poor countries.

Think of it. Clever marketers could label the exported cookies "organic" and "low-cal." Publicity campaigns could make favorable comparisons with Twinkies in terms of nutritive value without violating any truth-in-advertising regulations. Bakeries could diversify their offerings: mud pastries, mud quiches, mud rolls, mud scones, and so on. Franchising could be hugely lucrative. Soon, door-to-door deliveries of no-dough donuts could displace Dunkin' Donuts' delicacies. To steal market share from the famous franchise, marketers could mimic the name of the chain: how about "Muck-in-Donuts"? Sales experts from McDonald's could be brought in to coach vendors on the correct way of saying, "Would you like flies with that?"

It's a win-win situation, really. Haiti could climb out of poverty through increased export revenues, and businesses could even boost revenue by selling their carbon credits, since the baking process relies exclusively on solar energy. Production costs would subsequently come down, making the cookies more affordable.

If the IMF could then coax other Third World countries into producing their own varieties of mud cookies for export, the global supply of cookies would expand, and the price would drop even further. A cheap global supply of mud cookies would help to alleviate hunger throughout the global South. The United States would then be able to pare down its food aid to poor countries, freeing up money to spend on worthier pursuits, like bringing peace to Iraq. And, instead of handing out candies to Iraqi children, American soldiers could be distributing Haitian-made cookies, at a fraction of the cost.

Copyrighting the recipe would be unnecessary. Step-by-step instructions can easily be found in cookbooks such as Milton Friedman's *Capitalism and Freedom* or Freidrich von Hayek's *The Road to Serfdom*. An abridged version follows:

Start by pouring dollops of any cheap American grain—say, rice—into any poor country—say, Haiti. The imported grain should be heavily seasoned with subsidies from the U.S. government. While pocketing millions in subsidies, be sure to sing the praises of "free" trade, peppering your verses with denunciations of government interference in markets. If the intended importing country resists, turn up the heat, withholding crucial loans until its leader agrees to cut tariffs on American grain imports. The flood of cheap imports will undercut domestic grain production, push local farmers deeper into poverty, and make a formerly self-sufficient country dependent on grain imports. Check to make sure that enough bags of imported U.S. rice are labeled "foreign aid." Reassure impoverished Haitian farmers with the old saying that expresses the great virtue of open markets: "A rising tide lifts all goats."

To ensure Haitians get a balanced diet, you can add some "greens" in the form of grain-based biofuels, like ethanol. The biofuels should also be generously seasoned with subsidies from the U.S. government (this could also be followed by condemnations of the market distortions caused by government interference). Ramping up biofuel production will drive global food prices up even more. Fortunately, the mud cookie industry has been well established by now.

Sit back and watch as the Haitians simmer with rage. Don't let the crisis boil over, though. If food riots erupt, toss in some troops with orders to crack open a few heads. After all, you can't make an omelette without breaking eggs! To prevent the American public from getting squeamish at the sight of blood-filled streets in Haiti, get CNN to focus its attention on the Dalai Lama. Before long, a collective feeling of detachment will set in; images of a corpulent laughing Buddha will draw public attention away from the skeletons walking the streets of Cité Soleil. Eventually, the Caribbean pressure cooker will move to the back burner all by itself. Mud cookies will continue to sell like hotcakes.

Critics may start linking your recipe to rising food prices, so it is now time to blame out-of-control "Asian demand," another way of saying the Chinese should not be eating as many hamburgers as North Americans. Then claim that bad weather and bad harvests have left the global food pantry practically empty. Ignore the fact that per capita consumption of beef in the United States is about seven times greater than China's. Disregard the fact that half the rise in corn demand in the past three years has been due to ethanol production. Also overlook the Canadian government's recent decision to pay hog farmers $50 million to kill 150,000 pigs in order to raise the price of pork. Trust us—there's a real food shortage out there.

Don't remove your apron just yet. Flip through the cookbook of the Michael Milken Culinary Institute, where you'll find other "quick 'n easy dough" recipes. (The now-defunct institute, better known for cooking the books than for publishing cookbooks, remains an inspiration for many pinstriped pastry pros on Wall Street.)

The main ingredient for fast dough—grain futures—can be purchased at any commodity futures exchange. You'll need to buy huge quantities if you want to make lots of dough. But through leveraging, this shouldn't be a problem—you'll be using other people's money. Leaven with the nostrums of laissez-faire and watch your mix turn into a soufflé. This is market efficiency working its magic.

As the soufflé inflates, global grain prices will swell, along with the bellies of Haitian children. But at least unemployment on the island will come down as bakeries add more shifts to meet the demand for their cookies. Ignore the accusations of speculation and price manipulation; what you are doing is greasing the markets, otherwise known as "hedging." (You may want to use short(en)ing for grease, but only if you are sure the soufflé will deflate fairly soon.) To absolve yourself of any responsibility for escalating food costs, invoke "Asian demand" anew.

You can now pass the apron on to the head chef—U.S. agribusiness. The chef will assure the starving masses that only he can feed the world. Already bloated from subsidies, he will take advantage of government-granted monopolies—patent-protected genetically modified crops—to further tighten his grip over global food production. This he will do while delivering encomiums to unfettered markets.

Pay no attention to the epidemic of farmer suicides in India; they have nothing to do with the debt-inducing purchases of fertilizers and pesticides that must be used along with the costly patent-protected genetically modified seeds. Remind yourself that the subcontinent could become a huge market for Haiti's cookies. If the price of the mud cookies subsequently begins to soar, you can blame "Asian demand" once again. ❑

Article 7.8

REFORMING LAND REFORM

Land reform is back in the international spotlight.

BY RAVI BHANDARI AND ALEX LINGHORN

July/August 2009

Land lies at the heart of many of the world's most compelling contemporary issues: from climate change to armed conflict, from food security to social justice. Since the turn of the millennium, land issues have reclaimed center stage in national and international development debates, which increasingly focus on access to land in promoting economic growth and alleviating poverty.

The distribution of agricultural land in many poor countries is profoundly inequitable, giving rise to social tension, impaired development and extreme poverty. These exploitative imbalances are legacies of colonialism and institutionalized feudalism, posing serious threats to future prosperity and sustainable peace in many poor agrarian societies. Donor-driven development projects focusing on land governance have sought to impose market-led capitalist ideals, further polarizing power and marginalizing the poor. Exacerbating this dire situation are new commercial pressures on land, rapidly transforming it into a commodity to be traded between international banks, multinational companies, governments and speculators. Looming large is the paradigm-shifting presence of globalization, reinforced by international financial institutions seeking to unilaterally impose their macro-economic policies. This toxic blend of national feudalism and international hegemony has placed the world's poor agrarian societies in a perilous predicament. For one sixth of the world's population, nearly a billion farmers, without security of land ownership, the situation is grave. Confronted with this menacing dystopia, it has become increasingly urgent to assess the ways in which land is owned, accessed and regulated.

What is Land Reform?

Land reform is the process of transforming prevailing policies and laws that govern land ownership and access with the aim of instituting a more equal distribution of agricultural land while improving productivity. It can take the form of relatively benign tinkering with land tenure and administration systems or escalate to wholesale redistribution of land from rich to poor. Land reform, also known as agrarian reform, rarely occurs in isolation and is generally accompanied by structural changes to the agricultural sector to assist economic transformation.

The concept of land reform is far from new; since the time of the Roman Empire, nation states have been unable to resist tampering with land ownership and agricultural labor relations. In the last century, no less than 55 countries initiated programs of redistributive land reform, with many more altering their rural land ownership systems. Since the 1950s, powerful international institutions, such as the United Nations and the World Bank, have promoted western forms of private tenure in many developing countries, through the introduction of individualization, titling and registration programs. Their goal was to hasten capitalist transformation by securing land for progressive farmers while hoping that the disenfranchised landless would gain employment in urban industries. Capitalism's litigious obsession with private property rights has proved incongruous in the context of many developing countries which operate customary land ownership systems, where indigenous groups have traditional rights over land they have occupied for centuries.

Despite international interference, the early period of land reform (1950s–1970s) was characterized by nation states seeking to equitably reallocate resources from those who own the land to those who work the land, in a bid to redress historical imbalances and enhance development. These "land to the tiller" programs were particularly prevalent in post-colonial South America, where high levels of landlessness and gross inequity in land holdings exist. Reformation led to state-owned collectivized farming in China, the USSR and Cuba, while locally owned collectives prevailed in Mexico, Honduras and El Salvador. Overall these reforms failed, with a few notable successes clustered in East Asia. In many cases, land became concentrated in the hands of the state and, in feudal countries, real reform failed to materialize from the rhetoric. China's land reform was directly responsible for a famine that killed over 40 million people.

Land reform entered a new phase in the 1980s and 1990s, with widespread de-collectivization and a new approach, so-called "market-assisted land reform." This neo-liberal orthodoxy, set forth and funded by the World Bank, aims to redistribute land by facilitating a land market of "willing buyers" and "willing sellers." The World Bank provides the buyers with loans, who are then required to pay full market price and display the clear intention of maximizing productivity. These land markets generously rewarded the rich, who often took the opportunity to offload marginal land, and created an enormous debt burden on the poor. Aided by the World Bank's coercive advocacy, marked-assisted land reform supplanted state-led redistributive land reform as the dominant paradigm.

Since its inception almost 30 years ago, market-led land reform has largely been a failure. In the process of dehumanizing and commoditizing land, it contributed to a rise in landlessness and exacerbated and entrenched the gap between rich and poor. Its fundamental flaws lie in its failure to address existing inequalities or appreciate the gamut of issues associated with land in developing countries—issues such as poverty, conflict, minority and gender discrimination, and environmental degradation. Land, too, is the foundation for enjoying basic human rights. Farmers excluded from land ownership in poor agrarian societies are condemned to a life of extreme poverty and exploitation. In some countries, basic livelihood needs such as access to potable water and firewood, or education and even citizenship, are denied to those without land ownership certificates.

The rise in landlessness and inequality, both corollaries of failed land reform, has fuelled tensions across rural societies and contributed to conflict. In Nepal's case, failed land reform led to a decade-long civil war. In response, landless farmers' organizations have begun to establish themselves into powerful social movements to challenge the status quo and demand their rights to land. Governments and international institutions have finally begun to realize that authentic land reform is a prerequisite to alleviating poverty and achieving sustainable peace and economic prosperity.

All Eyes on Nepal

Nepal is one of the most relevant countries today for contemporary debate on land reform. Nepal made global headlines in 2001 when the crown prince embarked on a murderous rampage through the palace in Kathmandu, slaughtering the king and queen and most of the royal family before killing himself. However, it is the deeper question of land ownership in relation to political and economic power that is actually shaping developments in Nepal, as in so many other poor, agrarian countries around the globe.

This small, mountainous nation, landlocked and sandwiched between the giants of China and India, is home to 30 million people. It is one of the world's poorest countries, with half the population living below the poverty line. The dramatic topography renders 80% of the land uncultivable, yet three-quarters of the population depend on agriculture for their livelihood, one-third of whom are marginal tenants and landless farmers.

Nepal's pattern of land ownership is the corollary of over 200 years of autocratic monarchy, with successive kings treating the land as their personal property, distributing large tracts to military leaders, officials and family members, in lieu of salaries or as gifts. This feudal system deliberately precluded ordinary people from owning land and ensured their continued position as agricultural servants. Non-farmer elites began to accumulate considerable land holdings as a form of security and status, precipitating the now well-established class structure of landlordism: a dismal system whereby those who work the land have little ownership of it.

Landlessness affords no status in communities and disenfranchises millions from their basic human rights. Without a land certificate, people are denied access to many government services such as banking, electricity, telephone service, and potable water. The landless are further victimized by non-government services, preventing them from keeping livestock and prohibiting them from accessing community forestland.

Nepal's land governance was subject to capricious rulers until the first land act was introduced in 1964. In response to a fledgling land rights movement initiated by tenant farmers, the monarchy introduced the act with the aim of "showing a human face." It imposed land ceilings with redistribution of the surplus to needy farmers and pledged to end the ritual of offering vast land grants to royal favorites.

In practice, ceilings were not enforced, little land was redistributed, and landlords, rather than tenants, often benefited. No further significant land reform measures occurred for the next 30 years; the 1964 Land Act remains at the center of Nepal's land reform legislation even today.

The People's Movement of 1990 reintroduced multi-party democracy to the Kingdom of Nepal, bringing new hope. In 1996, amendments to the original land act stipulated that any tenant farmer who had cultivated a piece of land continuously for three or more years would be given the right of tenancy and the right to receive half the land they farmed. As the majority of tenants were unregistered, landlords reacted predictably by evicting them from their land and refusing to grant secure tenancy contracts. In a country as poorly developed as Nepal, where it can

A COMMUNITY-LED APPROACH TO LAND REFORM

An innovative model for land reform is rising from the ashes of market-led agendas and centralized state bureaucracies, one loosely termed "community-based land reform." Borrowing from success stories over the past half century and incorporating new insights into sustainable rural development, the model offers a democratized, devolved approach that involves communities in the planning, implementation, and ongoing management of land reform.

In this model, each rural community is authorized to control its own land relations, including redistribution, working within a clear set of parameters laid out by the state. Governments typically fear relinquishing power, but it is precisely through this process of devolution that the majority poor can be included, empowered, and mobilized to ensure the effectiveness and sustainability of the reform. This bottom-up approach is often more cost-effective than top-down methods because of its potential to harness the administrative powers of existing local institutions (in Nepal's case, Village Development Committees). Plus, accurate data on land ownership, tenancy, and other factors such as idle land—an important starting point for any reform program—is more likely to emerge from community-level institutions. Devolved reform offers more room for flexibility across varying ecological zones and social contexts, while locally tested pilot schemes can provide valuable feedback.

Community-led reform is not simply a development buzzword or the latest fad. It has proven success, notably, the elected Land Committees that facilitated Japan's successful reform. Landless populations are pressing for greater inclusion, rightly asserting that they hold the knowledge required to design the most viable model for land reform. Even the World Bank has admitted that "greater community involvement" may be required; the bank now describes market-assisted land reform as only one "option."

take many days to walk to the nearest road, and many more to reach a centralized bureaucracy, these amendments served to formally terminate tenancy rights for over half a million families.

The World Bank's mission to proselytize market-assisted land reform had by now reached Nepal. The bank proposed establishing a Land Bank to assist the poor in buying land from the rich. Matching willing buyers with willing sellers is an expensive and difficult process and leaves the door wide open to multi-level corruption. The concept of landless farmers borrowing huge sums of money to purchase land from feudal elites who had not acquired their lands through fair means did little to imbue a sense of justice.

It is clear from experiences in many other countries that international financial institutions (IFIs) such as the World Bank are not interested in pursuing an equitable and sustainable system of land access and ownership, nor are they concerned with enabling landless farmers to lead respectable lives and contribute fully to the socioeconomic and political life of their country. They persistently overlook the long-term benefits of providing secure access to land for the rural poor despite documentary evidence of poverty reduction, increased agricultural productivity, stimulation of the rural economy, and conflict prevention.

Land ceilings also came under attack from the World Bank, which criticized the Philippines, for instance, for implementing "land ownership ceilings [which] restrict the functioning of land markets." Of course, this is the intention of land ceilings. Instead of helping an impoverished farmer to invest in the land, create a livelihood, and improve production, World Bank policies opt to facilitate that farmer in selling it to someone in a better position. In Nepal, so far, the Land Bank has remained on the table, postponed by years of conflict and civil society resistance.

Land reform policies in Nepal have failed to significantly redistribute land,

---

LAND GRAB IN MADAGASCAR

In 2008, Daewoo Logistics of South Korea reached a now-infamous deal with the Madagascan government to lease 1.3 million hectares of land (over half the island's cultivable land) on which to grow food for the South Korean domestic market. Madagascar is part of the World Food Program, from which it receives food for the 600,000 people who live at subsistence level. Not a single grain from the Daewoo deal was to remain on the island. Farmers and opposition leaders rose up and took to the streets to demonstrate their disapproval, claiming that the people were losing control of their land, which would also be destroyed by Daewoo's mass deforestation plans. The land minister eventually rejected the deal; nonetheless, it was the last straw for a population increasingly betrayed by its government. The country has now plunged into crisis, with security forces killing over 100 antigovernment protesters and the situation likely to end only by coup or referendum.

improve agricultural productivity, or realign socioeconomic power imbalances. The main reason for this lies in the conflicts of interest of decision makers. Government leaders are closely tied to landlords, if they are not landlords themselves. This corrupt nexus of power has ensured the continued failure of land reform and the perpetuation of a feudal society. The primary result of imposing land ceilings was concealment of ownership; the primary result of land records reform was authenticating elite ownership; the primary result of tenancy registration was eviction; and the primary result of modernization was abuse of customary rights.

The increasing dispossession of the majority poor and the escalating autocracy of the king led Nepal into a decade of civil war with the opposition Maoists, from 1996 to 2006. Land reform was the rallying cry of the Maoists, who declared themselves the saviors of the poor and enemies of feudalism, colonialism, and foreign imperialism.

Over the next decade, the Maoists came to control over half the country's rural areas and, with public and political opinion turning against the monarchy, the war ended with the signing of the Comprehensive Peace Accord in 2006, paving the way for multi-party elections. The Maoists swept to victory in the 2008 election, confounding the international community but not Nepalese voters. Under intense popular pressure, the king was forced to abdicate and a new Federal Republic of Nepal was declared on May 28, 2008. The People's Movement played a significant role in the Maoist victory and that same civil society is clamoring for the Maoist-led government to deliver on its promises of land reform.

The land rights movement in Nepal has built a significant democratic power base in the form of the National Land Rights Forum, which has over 1.6 million landless members. The organization has developed a major groundswell of momentum to bolster its lobbying and policy advocacy. The movement is united, democratic, people-led, inclusive and peaceful, and should serve as a role model for land rights movements across the world. Nepal's land rights movement pursues a rights-based approach, advocating the intrinsic link between land rights and the fundamental human rights of subsistence, protection, participation and identity. This leverages existing international conventions, laws and constitutions that protect fundamental rights and is an effective way to ensure a framework for land reform which will address the structural causes of poverty. They claim it is the duty of nation states to devise inclusive policies which allow citizens to participate fully in society and not to abandon them to inequitable power structures and a free market system which will ride roughshod over their economic, social and cultural rights.

India also offers examples of successful people-centered movements that are peaceful and community-led. Sustained democratic pressure from India's civil society succeeded in putting land reform on the official agenda. The Janadesh rally in October 2007 witnessed 25,000 people marching 340 kilometers from Madhya Pradesh to Delhi to pressure the government into forming a national land reforms commission, which it duly did.

While it is vital to keep land reform firmly under the political spotlight, it is also essential not to politicize land rights movements. Farmers' organizations in

Indonesia became polarized between political parties, each pursuing separate or competing interests, which proved to be a major obstacle to implementing success-ful land reform. It is critical that land rights movements remain firmly in the hands of the landless farmers, where they are most effective. A sustainable and successful land rights movement needs to be led by those whose future security depends upon its success. The role of civil-society organizations and non-governmental organiza-tions is to support landless farmers in creating a solid institutional base and strong dynamic leadership while facilitating access to government policy-making forums, at local and national levels.

Civil society pressure has led Nepal's Maoist government to embark upon a "revolutionary" program of scientific land reform. Exactly how revolutionary or scientific it will be remains open to conjecture. Following two weeks of mass dem-onstrations by the land rights movement, the government recently established a Scientific Land Reform Commission to investigate available options and provide concrete recommendations. They have pledged to adopt an inclusive approach closely involving landless people in the process and to end feudal control over land once and for all.

Land Reform in Context

The redistribution of land, either through awarding new land to the landless or granting ownership rights to existing occupants, must not be seen as the final stage in the process but rather the initial stage in creating a viable and sustainable model to ensure livelihood stability and enhanced productivity. In many developing coun-tries there is a trend towards abandoning, selling, or mortgaging awarded lands, often to raise money for medical expenses or because of a lack of credit to finance production. The combined pressures of increasing land prices and a dearth of gov-ernment-support services has been the main catalyst for selling awarded lands. Without the necessary support systems, deprived farmers will understandably focus on solving their immediate food and economic security problems, reversing the land reform process and undermining the whole basis of a sustainable livelihood model.

In Indonesia, the government places certain obligations upon land reform beneficiaries to ensure a positive outcome: the land must be owner-cultivated and production must increase within two years. Negligent beneficiaries have their land expropriated without compensation. Such conditions are only reasonable if the newly entitled farmers are provided with the support they need, including improved infrastructure and access to markets, accompanied by financial, technical, and social services. Few governments or non-governmental organizations are committed to, or even capable of, providing the necessary support during this critical post-claim period.

The Philippines leads the way in rural support services, having established post-harvest facilities and continuous agricultural and enterprise development which focuses on community capacity building and rural infrastructure and finance.

Studies show that when agrarian reform is implemented properly and integrated support services are provided, farmers have higher incomes and invest in their farms more intensively. The examples of Japan, Korea, and Taiwan demonstrate that land reform is not only a social justice measure, but also the foundation for mobilizing agrarian societies towards rural, and, ultimately, urban industrialization.

In the case of Nepal, where broader macroeconomic policies do not support agriculture in general or small-scale producers in particular, land reform alone will not bring substantial income gains to the poor or a reduction in poverty and inequality. Indeed, if the macroeconomic context is adverse to agriculture—if, for example, exchange rate overvaluation and trade policies make agricultural imports too cheap for local growers to compete—then to encourage the poor to seek a living in farming is to lure them into debt and penury. A holistic approach to land reform must therefore be adopted to ensure viable and sustainable benefits.

Nepal is in the process of integrating into regional and global trading platforms that require a series of profound economic policy commitments. As a member of the World Trade Organization (WTO), Nepal has a legal obligation to align its economic policy with global requirements. The landless, near landless, and small-holders face an uncertain future in this era of globalization; Nepal must learn from the experiences of other developing countries that have courted the global players, adopted their policies, and paid the price. Succumbing blindly to globalization's holy trinity of privatization, liberalization, and deregulation is tantamount to self-sacrifice at its altar.

Land reform, and protective measures against unfair trade practices, must be in place before Nepal ventures into any international commitments to open its markets and resource wealth to international speculators. Indeed, the revenues of many transnational companies now far exceed those of the countries in which they operate. Such a concentration of lightly regulated power in international profit-seeking hands is ominous for small producers and even more so for the most marginalized members of agrarian societies. While genuine community-based agricultural investment is to be welcomed, the neocolonial pacts favored by foreign investors pose a serious threat to tenure security and to marginal farmers, many of whom could be pushed out of food production and forced to join the ranks of the rural hungry or city slum dwellers.

In 1995, Indonesia signed the Agreement on Agriculture with the WTO and agreed to open its markets. Liberalization of the domestic market for agricultural commodities spelled calamity for peasant farmers. International free trade agreements are not made with the intention of strengthening poor farmers' land rights. Furthermore, small-scale agricultural production simply cannot compete in a global market controlled by multinational corporations. Developed countries continue to bolster their agricultural export products with significant state subsidies while protecting their domestic market with prohibitive tariffs. Indonesia has since become the largest recipient of food in the world and is experiencing a startling rate of natural resource exploitation; deforestation currently occurs at the equivalent of 300 football fields every hour.

The WTO believes it is better for countries to buy food at the international market with money obtained from exports rather than attempting self-sufficiency; this paves the way for monoculture and contract farming while creating a precarious reliance on imports for basic food commodities. International trade is a natural phenomenon, but a significant degree of autonomy must be maintained; dependence on imports for basic needs such as food is dangerous. Strengthening agricultural self-sufficiency is especially important to developing countries that do not have the resources to sustain expensive food imports long-term.

Monoculture of cash crops in Indonesia has caused landlessness and has made small-scale farmers dependent on expensive agricultural inputs such as high-yield seed varieties, chemical fertilizers, and pesticides, which are often imported. Furthermore, these farming methods compromise ecological integrity and, as has been witnessed in Bangladesh and Indonesia, can lead to large-scale environmental degradation.

The repercussions of IFI interventions in developing countries, namely greater exploitation and inequality, illustrate the danger of imposing a capitalist model upon semi-feudal systems. International trade policies and programs in Indonesia, which were aimed at strengthening the position of agricultural exporters, proved to be overly discriminatory and served to weaken the bargaining position of local farmers. Large corporations were expected to develop farmers' institutions, but instead they exploited them by creating crop-buying monopsonies while forming cartels to raise the prices of their own products.

To accompany market liberalization, IFIs seek to impose the use of modern technology on agrarian societies. If this is not implemented diligently and judiciously, it leads to growth in rural unemployment. In Indonesia, the imposition of modern technology achieved just this, most notably among women, who were evicted from the land and became a pool of cheap labor for multi-national corporations—the same corporations that benefited most from the technology.

The deregulation that IFIs press for must not be carried out too hastily. Without a prior improvement in infrastructure to accompany the dismantling of para-state apparatuses, marginal areas will be alienated. This was seen in sub-Saharan Africa, where only those farmers close to urban centers benefited from the influx of private trade.

Commercialization of Land and the Last Great Global Land Grab

In addition to the globalization of trade, there are new, powerful commercial pressures for landless and marginalized farmers to contend with. Catalyzed by soaring food prices in 2008 and compounded by worldwide financial uncertainty, import-reliant, often oil-rich countries have begun scrambling to secure food sources for their domestic markets, in what has been called "the last great global land grab." Concurrent with this is the rampant growth of subsidized biofuel production to meet ambitious renewable fuel targets in the West, and the inception of carbon trading, which places a commercial value on standing forests and rangelands. Extractive mining and "ecotourism" add to the perilous predicament for vulnerable landless and marginal farmers.

The scramble for land often occurs in countries with a weak legal framework where farmers are not protected by secure land tenure systems. This results in the fertile land of the world's poorest countries becoming privatized and concentrated, creating a direct threat to food sovereignty, local production, and rural livelihoods. The increase in biofuel production is certain to intensify competition for land between indigenous forest users, land-poor farmers, agribusinesses, and financial speculators.

It is clear that potential foreign investment should be carefully analyzed to assess the full impact on the community as compared with the investors' financial interests before any deals are made. Sound investment should be accompanied by skills and knowledge sharing with local communities to establish foundations for long-term cooperation. The exploitation of natural resources for the sole purpose of shareholder gain is unsustainable.

The new REDD (Reduced Emissions from Deforestation and Degradation) scheme, which will offer developing countries financial incentives for preserving biomass stocks in standing forests, is an opportunity for states to define forest tenure and create community-based benefit-sharing mechanisms. Similarly, sustainable tourism can be used to reinforce community governance over biodiversity as a conservation strategy.

Land reform is a pressing issue shared by many developing countries that are shackled by entrenched inequities in land access and ownership. Highly unequal land ownership breeds social tension and political unrest and inhibits economic growth. While each developing country faces its own particular land related issues, some common themes prevail: the lack of political will to formulate and implement effective land reform, entrenched inequitable power structures, exclusive legal systems, poor dissemination of information, and the age-old millstones of corruption and excessive bureaucracy. Across the board, authorities are seen to be rich in rhetoric and poor in deed.

The rising discontent among landless and small-holder farmers has forced open an ideological debate between neo-liberalism, centralized elite domination, and pro-people policy making. The majority rural poor have begun to find their voice, and Nepal's civil war will act as a warning that their land grievances can quickly turn to violence.

Today, the worldwide financial crisis is threatening aid from the West and causing the demand for exports to shrink. Both factors render the billions of dollars of potential investment from multinational corporations and food-hungry, oil-rich nations enormously tempting to impoverished states. Governments must not be lured into exclusive market mechanisms that generate ever greater inequalities and create a profoundly negative effect upon community governance, food sovereignty, and peace building. Effective redistributive land reform, ensuring secure tenancy and ownership systems for marginal farmers, must occur in poor agrarian societies before opening their doors to global trade. The primary responsibility of all governments is to protect the basic human rights of their citizens, paying special attention to the poorest and most vulnerable.

Land reform is beginning to emerge from the vortex of market-led ideology to find itself at the epicenter of topical discourses on poverty alleviation, sustainable rural development, conflict transformation, food security, and fundamental human rights. IFIs continue to push reforms that consolidate and authenticate inequity, but land rights organizations are now enjoying a higher profile with increasing solidarity from a wide variety of state and non-state actors.

It is abundantly clear that the best approaches to land reform are those that integrate security, livelihood, resource management, and community empowerment. Land reform must redistribute land widely enough to preclude any dominant land-owning class and be accompanied by a support structure to sustain productivity. The expansion of rural markets that will follow will generate growth and this will lead to stable peace and national development. All eyes are on Nepal to see if the Maoist government seizes the unique chance to institute such an innovative, rational, and scientific process of land reform.

Acknowledgement: We wish to thank our research assistant, Nabaraj Subedi, for his invaluable help in contributing to this article and the editors of Dollars & Sense *for recognizing the importance of the current global debates on land reform and tenure security as a key policy issue for the 21st century.*

Sources: Ravi Bhandari, "The Peasant Betrayed: Towards a Human Ecology of Land Reform in Nepal," in Roy Allen (ed.) *Human Ecology Economics: A New Framework for Global Sustainability*; Ravi Bhandari, "The Significance of Social Distance in Sharecropping Efficiency: The Case of Rural Nepal," *Journal of Economic Studies*, September, 2007; Ravi Bhandari, "Searching for a Weapon of Mass Production in Nepal: Can Market-Assisted Land Reform Live Up to its Promise?" *Journal of Developing Societies*, June 2006; Community Self-Reliance Centre Nepal, *Land and Tenurial Security Nepal*, 2008; Elizabeth Fortin, "Reforming Land Rights: The World Bank and the Globalization of Agriculture," *Social and Legal Studies*, 2005; Lorenzo Cotula, *Fuelling Exclusion? The Biofuels Boom and Poor People's Access to Land*, International Institute for Environment and Development, 2008; International Land Coalition, *Land and Vulnerable People in a World of Change*, Global Bioenergy Partnership, 2008; International Land Coalition, *Secure Access to Land for Food Security*, UNDP-OGC, November 24, 2008; Alex Linghorn, "Land Reform: An International Perspective," *Land First*, July 2008; Alex Linghorn, "Commercial Pressures on Land," *Land First*, April 2009; Oxfam International, *Another Inconvenient Truth: How Biofuel Policies are Deepening Poverty and Accelerating Climate Change*, 2008; Rights and Resources Initiative, *Seeing People Through Trees: Scaling Up Efforts to Advance Rights and Address Poverty, Conflict, and Climate Change*, 2008.

Article 7.9

LAND REFORM UNDER LULA: ONE STEP FORWARD, ONE STEP BACK

BY CHRIS TILLY, MARIE KENNEDY, AND TARSO LUÍS RAMOS
August 2009

The Landless Workers' Movement (MST) of Brazil, which has mobilized more than a million Brazilians to occupy and farm large landholdings, was cautiously optimistic when Luiz Inácio "Lula" da Silva of the Workers Party won the presidency in 2002. "We campaign for Lula," remarked MST organizer Jonas da Silva (no relation) during the campaign, "even though we are critical of him for shaping his discourse for the middle class." In the country with perhaps the most unequal land distribution in the world, electing a pro-worker, pro-poor president marked a potential turning point.

But as Lula finishes up his second term (new presidential elections take place in October 2010), the MST's assessment is grim. Land redistribution has stagnated, the government continues to bet on agribusiness as a development strategy and, most threateningly, powerful regional politicians are moving to criminalize the land seizure movement as "terrorist." The MST is doing its best to fight back, but controversial recent MST strategies and antagonistic mass media have diminished the popularity of a movement that once enjoyed widespread national support.

Land Reform, "Não!" Agribusiness, "Sim!"

Lula followed on the two presidential terms of Fernando Henrique Cardoso, who had implemented an unapologetic neoliberal program of free trade, privatization, and containing the demands of workers and the urban and rural poor. There was good reason for hope, since the Workers Party had formed close alliances with the MST and a variety of other social movements. The post-dictatorship constitution of 1988 affirms that land is for socially productive uses, a requirement past governments have at times invoked under pressure to confiscate and redistribute property. But to the dismay of landless families hoping for a plot to cultivate, land redistribution actually moved slightly more *slowly* in Lula's first term than under Cardoso. As the end of his second term approaches, it seems unlikely that Lula will manage to settle more families through agrarian reform than his neoliberal predecessor. What's more, three-quarters of the land redistributed by Lula has been in the remote (and in many cases ecologically fragile) Amazonia region, far from the concentrations of people petitioning for land, such as in the impoverished Northeast. Nearly half of Cardoso's land grants were in Amazonia.

Despite the slow pace of land reform, there are some signs of progress. João Paulo Rodrigues, a MST National Directorate member based in São Paulo, noted,

"Lula has provided better supports for small farmers in the form of credit, technical assistance, education, electrification, and roads" – though still not enough. He added that the Lula administration has dropped the Cardoso government's campaign to criminalize the MST (though, as we will explain further below, various state governments have revived that effort). While the number of killings of landless activists surged the first year Lula was in power as the movement shifted land occupations into high gear, violence has now abated to a lower level than under Cardoso. "There is a change in the form of persecution," explained Maria Luisa Mendonça of Social Network for Justice and Human Rights (*Rede Social*), a human rights group that works closely with the MST. "Instead of killing activists, now they [state governments, which are chiefly responsible for law enforcement] arrest them. It's better than killing them, but it doesn't mean that the persecution has ended."

Lula's government has also undertaken other progressive reforms, most notably the "Bolsa Familia" (literally, family pocketbook) program that provides a basic income to the very poorest families. Though the aid does not confront the structural causes of poverty, it provides a crucial margin of survival and offers incentives for families to keep their children in school. Responding to criticism that Bolsa Familia is a form of clientelism, the MST's Rodrigues reasoned, "Yes, it's clientelism. But given the extreme poverty in Brazil and the large numbers of people going hungry, these clientelist policies are necessary." He quickly added, "Necessary, but insufficient." The MST's support (if grudging) is notable, because arguably the stipend reduces the incentive for families to take the risk of occupying land, potentially weakening the landless movement's social base.

The MST's biggest disappointment with Lula has been the former militant union leader's enthusiastic embrace of agribusiness. The Brazilian economy rode high on the commodities boom of the 2000s, with huge expansions in soy, sugar cane, and eucalyptus plantations (the last primarily for paper production). Factory farming is expanding at a ferocious clip: according to MST leader Rodrigues, in three years in the southern state of Rio Grande do Sul alone, 300,000 new hectares of eucalyptus have been planted (a hectare is about 2.5 acres), dwarfing the 100,000 hectares the MST has put into cultivation in its entire 25 years of activity. The environmental consequences have been predictably negative: monocropping, heavy use of chemical inputs and genetically modified strains, voracious water consumption (eucalyptus plantations have been dubbed "green deserts"), toxic by-products, and expansion into wetlands in the Amazon and other areas — especially in the case of sugar cane. Ironically, much of the sugar cane goes into Brazil's massive "eco-friendly" ethanol fuel industry. Unlike the U.S.'s corn-based ethanol industry, Brazil's cane-based system makes money without subsidies — but this accounting overlooks the unmeasured costs of environmental devastation and labor exploitation (or the fossil fuel used in its production and, in the case of export, transportation). The Brazilian government was to announce regional zoning barring sugar cane from Amazonia in February 2009, but that declaration has not yet materialized and human rights advocate Mendonça states flatly, "I don't think it's going to happen."

But if the environmental consequences of agribusiness have been dire, the social consequences are at least as ominous. Far from displacing Brazil's traditional landed oligarchy, the agribusiness boom has forged a new alliance between giant landowners, chemical-agricultural transnationals such as Monsanto and Syngenta, and the national government. The plantations generate exports, but few jobs: the MST estimates that eucalyptus monocropping creates one job per 185 hectares, as compared to one job per hectare for small-scale farming. Those jobs created are often poor, sometimes to the point of being subhuman. Social Network found that in 2007-8, half the reported cases of slave labor in Brazil (3,000 of 6,000 cases) were found in the sugar cane industry. Despite such concerns, the scale of government support has been nothing short of astounding. According to American University political scientist Miguel Carter, "from 2003 to 2007, state support for the rural elite was seven times larger than that offered to the nation's family farmers, even though the latter represent 87 percent of Brazil's rural labor force and produce the bulk of food consumed by its inhabitants." The reason for this asymmetry is not just economic pragmatism, but also political arithmetic: despite a nominally democratic system, the tiny minority of large landowners controls the majority of seats in Congress. As the MST's Rodrigues wryly observed, "Lula has a majority in the House of Representatives and only falls a little short in the Senate. But he gets that majority by proposing policies that serve agribusiness."

From Escalation to Criminalization

Sizing up the agribusiness menace and the opportunity posed by Lula's victory, the MST made two fateful decisions in 2003. One was to accelerate land occupations to force the land question with Lula's government. The second move was to depart from its historic policy of only taking lands that were fallow or where major violations of labor rights were taking place, and adding to its targets productive agribusiness plantations, which the movement sees as the principal threat to the survival and expansion of small farms in Brazil. In some cases, activists have adopted disruption, as when close to 2,000 women affiliated with the Peasant Women's Movement (MMC) — which, like the MST, is a member of the global peasant coalition La Vía Campesina — entered a facility of the Aracruz Cellulose corporation and speedily destroyed greenhouses and nearly eight million eucalyptus saplings on International Women's Day in April 2006. The protest was particularly embarrassing to Lula's government, taking place as it did just outside the city of Porto Alegre where the president was busy hosting the United Nations' International Conference on Agrarian Reform and Development (ICARRD) and positioning his government and Brazil as a world leader on land reform. The major Brazilian media, as tightly tied to the big landowners as is Brazil's Congress and always quick to find fault with the MST, cried foul. They were joined by a number of prominent intellectuals, such as José de Souza Martins, the country's best-known rural sociologist, who, even before the action, had branded the MST as Luddites.

Tactical escalation combined with media condemnation turned Brazilian public opinion, quite favorable in the late 1990s, against the MST. This even extends to likely supporters: in a mid-2009 interview, a youth organizer in a São Paulo *favela* (slum), whose philosophy and organizing approach mesh closely with the MST's, decried the organization's alleged violence and confrontational attitude; he conceded that his source for the information was the same media he didn't trust as a source on urban issues. A Social Network review of 300 articles about the MST in Brazil's four largest-circulation dailies found only eight that were neutral or partly positive. Complicating matters, being the largest and best-known agrarian reform movement in Brazil, the MST is saddled with the negative press coverage given to other radical groups working for land redistribution. Even as public opinion turned against the Landless Workers' Movement, former close MST allies such as the left-leaning Unified Federation of Workers (CUT) union closed ranks with the Lula administration against threats from the right, distancing themselves from the MST.

The worst was yet to come. In 2006, conservative Yeda Crusius won the governorship in Rio Grande do Sul, a state with strong MST organization and a high pitch of militant land struggles (including the Aracruz action). Crusius set out to target the MST. She attempted to eliminate the so-called "itinerant schools" that provide funding for teachers to travel to rural areas — a keystone of the infrastructure of the temporary encampments where MST families live while fighting to obtain land. The MST has developed its own curriculum and teacher training (based on Freirean pedagogy), oriented to the realities of rural life and a participatory vision of citizenship, and closing the itinerant schools would have wiped out this curriculum and compelled children to travel to the cities for their education. Crusius' administration spoke of "saving children from aggressive indoctrination." The governor finally backed off in mid-2009 as international criticism mounted, and the mayors of the state made it clear that they did not want farm children flooding their schools.

But even more significantly, once she was elected, Crusius swiftly mobilized the Office of the Federal Prosecutor to criminalize the MST, dusting off the dictatorship-era National Security Law to charge eight movement leaders with belonging to an organization that uses violent means to undermine democracy (charges were later dropped against two of the eight). The case includes far-fetched allegations, for example that the MST is allied with Colombia's rebel Revolutionary Armed Forces (FARC), but the prosecutions are bolstered by what lawyer/advocate Aton Fon Filho of Social Network calls "the most conservative judiciary in the country." Fon, who is defending the MST activists, said, "We think we'll win the case. But meanwhile, it has a huge propaganda impact — all those headlines saying 'MST leaders charged with terrorism!'"

The MST is not the only land rights organization suffering from a government crackdown. "There is more organized persecution of social movements in general," said Fon, though other prosecutions involve individual charges rather than an attempt to criminalize an entire organization. For example, in the state of

Tocantins in the north, the government has arrested 16 activists of the Movement of Dam Affected Peoples (MAB). And the killings of land reform leaders have not ended. Two activists from the Pastoral Land Commissions (the Catholic Church-based organizations that spawned the MST) in Mato Grosso do Sul were killed in June 2009. And in the Amazon state of Pará, trials are continuing of the accused in the 2005 murder of American nun Sister Dorothy Stang, who challenged deforestation and supported redistribution of lands the military dictatorship had awarded to local elites. According to Fon, "The person convicted of ordering the murder is free pending a fourth trial in the case while the rancher suspected of actually orchestrating the plot has yet to be tried."

A Cloudy Future

One could criticize the MST for ramping up its tactics at a delicate moment, but that would be missing the point: through its entire history, the MST has only been able to chip away at the disproportionate power of the landholding minority via high-profile tactics of civil disobedience and disruption. Others might argue that the MST is holding Lula's feet to the fire in terms of accountability and promises made on agrarian reform. But that said, what are the prospects for near-term success? "Agrarian reform depends on two things," the MST's Rodrigues explained. "The organization of the people, and a progressive government willing to work with us. In 25 years of work, we have made much progress in organizing, but we have not encountered a people's government truly committed to agrarian reform."

The 2010 presidential elections do not hold out much hope in this regard. The two likely leading candidates are Lula's chief of staff, Dilma Rousseff of the Workers' Party, and José Serra of the Brazilian Social Democratic Party (the party of Cardoso and Crusius). "Both are to the right of Lula," commented Rodrigues. Given the political context, the MST is doing its best to fend off legal challenges, build new alliances, and continue organizing. International support can be tremendously important, as in the case of the itinerant schools in Rio Grande do Sul. And the underlying social issues are not going away. At bottom, as long as the distribution of land in Brazil remains so lopsided, there will be a mission and a social base for organizing the landless. ❑

Chapter 8

NATURAL RESOURCES, HEALTH, AND THE ENVIRONMENT

Article 8.1

GENETIC ENGINEERING AND THE PRIVATIZATION OF SEEDS
BY ANURADHA MITTAL AND PETER ROSSET
March/April 2001

In 1998, angry farmers burned Monsanto-owned fields in Karnataka, India, starting a nationwide "Cremate Monsanto" campaign. The campaign demanded that biotech corporations like Monsanto, Novartis, and Pioneer leave the country. Farmers particularly targeted Monsanto because its field trials of the "terminator gene"—designed to prevent plants from producing seeds and so to make farmers buy new seed each year—created the danger of "genetic pollution" that would sterilize other crops in the area. That year, Indian citizens chose Quit India Day (August 9), the anniversary of Mahatma Gandhi's demand that British colonial rulers leave the country, to launch a "Monsanto Quit India" campaign. Ten thousand citizens from across the country sent the Quit India message to Monsanto's Indian headquarters, accusing the company of colonizing the food system.

In recent years, farmers across the world have echoed the Indian farmers' resistance to the biotech giants. In Brazil, the Landless Workers' Movement (MST) has set out to stop Monsanto soybeans. The MST has vowed to destroy any genetically engineered crops planted in the state of Rio Grande do Sul, where the state government has banned such crops. Meanwhile, in September 2000, more than 1,000 local farmers joined a "Long March for Biodiversity" across Thailand. "Rice, corn, and other staple crops, food crops, medicinal plants and all other life forms are significant genetic resources that shape our culture and lifestyle," the farmers declared. "We oppose any plan to transform these into genetically modified organisms."

Industrial Agriculture I: The Green Revolution

For thousands of years, small farmers everywhere have grown food for their local communities—planting diverse crops in healthy soil, recycling organic matter, and following nature's rainfall patterns. Good farming relied upon the farmer's accumulated knowledge of the local environment. Until the 1950s, most Third World agriculture was done this way.

The "Green Revolution" of the 1960s gradually replaced this kind of farming with monocultures (single-crop production) heavily dependent on chemical fertilizers, pesticides, and herbicides. The industrialization of agriculture made Third World countries increase exports to First World markets, in order to earn the foreign exchange they needed to pay for agrochemicals and farm machinery manufactured in the global North. Today, as much as 70% of basic grain production in the global South is the product of industrial farming.

The Green Revolution was an attempt by northern countries to export chemical- and machine-intensive U.S.-style agriculture to the Third World. After the Cuban revolution, northern policymakers worried that rampant hunger created the basis for "communist" revolution. Since the First World had no intention of redistributing the world's wealth, its answer was for First World science to "help" the Third World by giving it the means to produce more food. The Green Revolution was to substitute for the "red."

During the peak Green Revolution years, from 1970 to 1990, world food production per capita rose by 11%. Yet the number of people living in hunger (averaging less than the minimum daily caloric intake) continued to rise. In the Third World—excluding China—the hungry population increased by more than 11%, from 536 to 597 million. While hunger declined somewhat relative to total Third World population, the Green Revolution was certainly not the solution for world hunger that its proponents made it out to be.

Not only did the Green Revolution fail to remedy unequal access to food and food-producing resources, it actually contributed to inequality. The costs of improved seeds and fertilizers hit cash-poor small farmers the hardest. Unable to afford the new technology, many farmers lost their land. Over time, the industrialization of agriculture contributed to the replacement of farms with corporations, farmers with machines, mixed crops with monocultures, and local food security with global commerce.

Industrial Agriculture II: The New Biorevolution

The same companies that promoted chemical-based agriculture are now bringing the world genetically engineered food and agriculture. Some of the leading pesticide companies of yesterday have become what today are euphemistically called "life sciences companies"—Aventis, Novartis, Syngenta, Monsanto, Dupont, and others. Through genetic engineering, these companies are now converting seeds into product-delivery systems. The crops produced by Monsanto's Roundup-Ready brand seeds, for example, tolerate only the company's Roundup brand herbicide.

The "life sciences" companies claim that they can solve the environmental problems of agriculture. For example, they promise to create a world free of pesticides by equipping each crop with its own "insecticidal genes." Many distinguished agriculture scientists, corporate bigwigs, and economists are jumping on the "biotechnology" bandwagon. They argue that, in a world where more than 830 million people go to bed hungry, biotechnology provides the only hope of feeding our burgeoning population, especially in the Third World.

In fact, since genetic engineering is based on the same old principles of industrial agriculture—monoculture, technology, and corporate control—it is likely to exacerbate the problems of ecological and social devastation:

- As long as chemical companies dominate the "life sciences" industry, the biotechnology they develop will only reinforce intensive chemical use. Corporations are currently developing plants whose genetic traits can be turned "on" or "off" by applying an external chemical, as well as crops that die if the correct chemical—made by the same company—is not applied.
- The biotechnology industry is releasing hundreds of thousands of genetically engineered organisms into the environment every year. These organisms can reproduce, cross-pollinate, mutate, and migrate. Each release of a genetically engineered organism is a round of ecological Russian roulette. Recently, Aventis' genetically engineered StarLink corn, a variety approved by the U.S. Department of Agriculture only for livestock consumption, entered the food supply by mixing in grain elevators and cross-pollination in the field.
- With the advent of genetic engineering, corporations are using new "intellectual property" rights to stake far-reaching claims of ownership over a vast array of biological resources. By controlling the ownership of seeds, the corporate giants force farmers to pay yearly for seeds they once saved from each harvest to the next planting. By making seed exchanges between farmers illegal, they also limit farmers' capacity to contribute to agricultural biodiversity.

The False Promise of "Golden Rice"

The biotech industry is taking great pains to advertise the humanitarian applications of genetic engineering. "[M]illions of people—many of them children—have lost their sight to vitamin A deficiency," says the Council for Biotechnology Information, an industry-funded public relations group. "But suppose rice consumers could obtain enough vitamin A and iron simply by eating dietary staples that are locally grown?

... Biotechnology is already producing some of these innovations." More than $10 million was spent over ten years to engineer vitamin A rice—hailed as the "Golden Rice"—at the Institute of Plant Sciences of the Swiss Federal Institute of Technology in Zurich. It will take millions more and another decade of research and development to produce vitamin A rice varieties that can actually be grown in farmers' fields.

In reality, the selling of vitamin A rice as a miracle cure for blindness depends on blindness to lower-cost and safer alternatives. Meat, liver, chicken, eggs, milk, butter, carrots, pumpkins, mangoes, spinach and other leafy green vegetables, and many other foods contain vitamin A. Women farmers in Bengal, an eastern Indian state, plant more than 100 varieties of green leafy vegetables. The promotion of monoculture and rising herbicide use, however, are destroying such sources of vitamin A. For example, bathua, a very popular leafy vegetable in northern India, has been pushed to extinction in areas of intensive herbicide use.

The long-run solutions to vitamin A deficiency—and other nutritional problems—are increased biodiversity in agriculture and increased food security for poor people. In the meantime, there are better, safer, and more economical short-run measures than genetically engineered foods. UNICEF, for example, gives high-dose vitamin A capsules to poor children twice a year. The cost? Just two cents per pill.

Intellectual Property Rights and Genetic Engineering

In 1998, Monsanto surprised Saskatchewan farmer Percy Schmeiser by suing him for doing what he has always done and, indeed, what farmers have done for millennia—save seeds for the next planting. Schmeiser is one of hundreds of Canadian and U.S. farmers the company has sued for re-using genetically engineered seeds. Monsanto has patented those seeds, and forbids farmers from saving them.

In recent years, Monsanto has spent over $8.5 billion acquiring seed and biotech companies, and DuPont spent over $9.4 billion to acquire Pioneer Hi-Bred, the world's largest seed company. Seed is the most important link in the food chain. Over 1.4 billion people—primarily poor farmers—depend on farm-saved seed for their livelihoods. While the "gene police" have not yet gone after farmers in the Third World, it is probably only a matter of time.

If corporations like Monsanto have their way, genetic technology—like the so-called "terminator" seeds—will soon render the "gene police" redundant. Far from being designed to increase agricultural production, "terminator" technology is meant to prevent unauthorized production—and increase seed-industry profits. Fortunately, worldwide protests, like the "Monsanto Quit India" campaign, forced the company to put this technology on hold. Unfortunately, Monsanto did not pledge to abandon "terminator" seeds permanently, and other companies continue to develop similar systems.

Future Possible

From the United States to India, small-scale ecological agriculture is proving itself a viable alternative to chemical-intensive and bioengineered agriculture. In the United States, the National Research Council found that "alternative farmers often produce high per acre yields with significant reductions in costs per unit of crop harvested," despite the fact that "many federal policies discourage adoption of alternative practices." The Council concluded that "federal commodity programs must be restructured to help farmers realize the full benefits of the productivity gains possible through alternative practices."

Another study, published in the *American Journal of Alternative Agriculture,* found that ecological farms in India were just as productive and profitable as chemical ones. The author concluded that, if adopted on a national scale, ecological farming would have "no negative impact on food security," and would reduce soil erosion and the depletion of soil fertility while greatly lessening dependence on external inputs.

The country where alternative agriculture has been put to its greatest test, however, is Cuba. Before 1989, Cuba had a model Green Revolution-style agricultural economy (an approach the Soviet Union had promoted as much as the United States). Cuban agriculture featured enormous production units, using vast quantities of imported chemicals and machinery to produce export crops, while the country imported over half its food.

Although the Cuban government's commitment to equity and favorable terms of trade offered by Eastern Europe protected Cubans from undernourishment, the collapse of the East bloc in 1989 exposed the vulnerability of this approach. Cuba plunged into its worst food crisis since the revolution. Consumption of calories and protein dropped by perhaps as much as 30%. Nevertheless, today Cubans are eating almost as well as they did before 1989, with much lower imports of food and agrochemicals. What happened?

Cut off from imports of food and agrochemicals, Cuba turned inward to create a more self-reliant agriculture based on higher crop prices to farmers, smaller production units, urban agriculture, and ecological principles. As a result of the trade embargo, food shortages, and the opening of farmers' markets, farmers began to receive much better prices for their products. Given this incentive to produce, they did so, even without Green Revolution-style inputs. The farmers received a huge boost from the reorientation of government education, research, and assistance toward alternative methods, as well as the rediscovery of traditional farming techniques.

While small farmers and cooperatives increased production, large-scale state farms stagnated. In response, the Cuban government parceled out the state farms to their former employees as smaller-scale production units. Finally, the government mobilized support for a growing urban agriculture movement—small-scale organic farming on vacant lots—which, together with the other changes, transformed Cuban cities and urban diets in just a few years.

Will Biotechnology Feed the World?

The biotech industry pretends concern for hungry people in the Third World, holding up greater food production through genetic engineering as the solution to world hunger. If the Green Revolution has taught us one thing, however, it is that increased food production can—and often does—go hand in hand with more hunger, not less. Hunger in the modern world is not caused by a shortage of food, and cannot be eliminated by producing more. Enough food is already available to provide at least 4.3 pounds of food per person a day worldwide. The root of the hunger problem is not inadequate production but unequal access and distribution. This is why the second Green Revolution promised by the "life sciences" companies is no more likely to end hunger than the first.

The United States is the world's largest producer of surplus food. According to the U.S. Department of Agriculture, however, some 36 million of the country's people (including 14 million children) do not have adequate access to food. That's an increase of six million hungry people since the 1996 welfare reform, with its massive cuts in food stamp programs.

Even the world's "hungry countries" have enough food for all their people right now. In fact, about three quarters of the world's malnourished children live in countries with net food surpluses, much of which are being exported. India, for example, ranks among the top Third World agricultural exporters, and yet more than a third of the world's 830 million hungry people live there. Year after year, Indian governments have managed a sizeable food surplus by depriving the poor of their basic human right to food.

The poorest of the poor in the Third World are landless peasants, many of whom became landless because of policies that favor large, wealthy farmers. The high costs of genetically engineered seeds, "technology-use payments," and other inputs that small farmers will have to use under the new biotech agriculture will tighten the squeeze on already poor farmers, deepening rural poverty. If agriculture can play any role in alleviating hunger, it will only be to the extent that we reverse the existing bias toward wealthier and larger farmers, embrace land reform and sustainable agriculture, reduce inequality, and make small farmers the center of an economically vibrant rural economy. ❑

Article 8.2

ABCs OF AIDS PREVENTION

Uganda has been widely recognized for its successes in stemming the AIDS crisis, but its policies fail to address the inequalities that make women vulnerable to the disease.

BY JESSICA WEISBERG
January/Februay 2005

Uganda is one of a handful of countries to have dramatically reduced its overall HIV infection rate in the past 10 years. It's widely viewed as a global leader in AIDS policy and is seen as a model for other countries in Africa and the global South. Its approach, known as "ABC," stands for "Abstinence, Be faithful, and Condoms"—but critics refer to it as "A-B-and sometimes-C" because of policymakers' emphasis on the first two over the third.

Despite Uganda's notable successes in stemming the AIDS epidemic, ABC has serious limitations. The policy primarily targets male behavior and fails to protect a particularly vulnerable population: married women. It offers little to girls forced by poverty to exchange one of their only assets—their bodies—for basic necessities or school fees. And by focusing on prevention, the policy fails to expand affordable and available treatments to those who've already contracted the disease—or address the core economic and social inequalities that make women susceptible to infection.

Nevertheless, President Bush has routinely cited Uganda's emphasis on abstinence and fidelity in defending its own abstinence-oriented global initiatives. In fact, the United States has adopted the ABC model as the centerpiece of its international AIDS policy.

In his 2004 State of the Union address, Bush declared optimistically, "AIDS can be prevented." Prevented? AIDS can be *treated*; with anti-retroviral therapies, widely available since early 1996, the otherwise fatal illness takes on a chronic character. By prevention, the president was referring not to a vaccine but to abstinence. He's been known to say it "works every time."

A few months after the address, in May 2004, Congress passed the President's Emergency Plan for AIDS Relief (PEPFAR). It allocated $15 billion dollars for AIDS programs worldwide over five years, with a focus on 15 "target countries" which are home to more than 50% of all people with HIV: Botswana, Côte d'Ivoire, Ethiopia, Kenya, Mozambique, Namibia, Nigeria, Rwanda, South Africa, Tanzania, Uganda, Zambia, Vietnam, Guyana, and Haiti.

Twenty percent of PEPFAR funding will go to prevention programs. (The balance goes to support services and treatment.) By law, at least one-third of those prevention funds must be used to promote abstinence. The first allocation of $100 million in PEPFAR grants for abstinence programs was announced in October. Nine of the 11 organizations that won the grants were faith-based organizations. Under PEPFAR, such groups are allowed to exclude information about contraception from their educational programs. Ambassador Randall Tobias, head of the State Department's Office of Global AIDS, has cited Uganda's accomplishments when PEPFAR's abstinence program has faced questions.

Uganda's Way

Since Ugandan President Yoweri Museveni initiated the ABC program in the mid-1990s, the country has undergone enormous reductions in HIV prevalence (the percentage of individuals living with HIV/AIDS). The percent of infected individuals in Uganda has declined from around 30% in the early 1990s to 6% in 2004, according to the United Nations and the Ugandan government. Although some scientists question the validity of those specific figures, arguing that survey methodology is flawed and that the reduction in prevalence rates may in part reflect the deaths of those who had HIV in the 1990s, most agree that Uganda has secured the most dramatic turnaround in AIDS of any country to date. Museveni brought this about by aggressively raising AIDS awareness, by using radio and other modes of mass communication, involving churches and non-governmental organizations, and by crafting messages that resonated with Ugandan culture; for example, he introduced the slogan "zero grazing" to encourage monogamy in the cattle-oriented society.

The effectiveness of Uganda's AIDS prevention and treatment policies has varied, though, with respect to gender. Far more women than men have become infected with HIV since ABC was implemented. According to the Uganda AIDS Commission, there were 99,031 new HIV cases in the country in 2001. Of these, females were three to six times more likely to become infected by HIV than males in the 15 to 19 age bracket, according to the Uganda Women's Network. In the 20 to 24 age bracket, the HIV infection rate among women remains twice as high as that of men.

There are several reasons for this disparity. Most importantly, research indicates that marriage actually *increases* the chance of HIV infection. In fact, the most dramatic increase in prevalence rates in recent years has occurred among monogamous married women; even as the overall percentage of people with HIV has fallen, the percentage of married women with HIV has increased. One study found that in rural Uganda, 88% of HIV-infected women age 15 to 19 are married.

For the majority of married couples in Uganda, the woman is at least six years younger than her husband. Paul Zeitz of the advocacy group Global AIDS Alliance points out that abstinence programs could "in effect be encouraging women to marry earlier," placing them at risk of infection by older husbands. "What use is abstinence, what use is fidelity if he is already infected and brings it into the marriage?" Stephen Lewis asked the *Agence France Presse*. Zeitz goes so far as to argue: "Abstinence [promotion] could be leading to a public health crisis."

Take Suzan, a 17-year-old mother from Ndeeba, a Kampala suburb, whose 62-year-old husband recently died of AIDS. She was infected by her late husband, and is unable to afford treatment.

With such large age differences between wives and husbands, Ugandan women like Suzan often outlive their husbands. When a man dies, his family typically repossesses his assets, robbing the woman of all her property and making her remaining years all the more difficult. In Suzan's case, her husband's family has taken away both their land and her child.

Another Ugandan woman, Juliet, is a 27-year-old widow with four children. Her in-laws also took away her home and land upon her husband's death. She is now hospitalized with an advanced case of AIDS, and her children are struggling to support themselves.

Women like Suzan and Juliet are overlooked by the ABC program's emphasis on abstinence and fidelity. Both women were abstinent before marriage and then faithful, but neither their own behavior nor the ABC program did anything to protect them from contracting the disease or to treat them once they were infected.

Condoms too are of little use to married women in a culture where extramarital polygamy is common but wives are unaware of their husbands' affairs. Even if women have suspicions, many adhere to patriarchal mores against vocally questioning their husbands' behavior. Those same mores also deter women from telling their husbands to wear condoms.

Harriet Abwoli, interviewed in 2003 for the Human Rights Watch report "Just Die Quietly," described her experience: "He used to force me to have sex with him. He would beat me and slap me when I refused. I never used a condom with him. ... When I got pregnant I went for a medical check-up. When I gave birth, and the child had passed away, they told me I was HIV-positive. I cried. The doctor told me, 'Wipe your tears, the whole world is sick.'"

"Women do not have negotiation power," says researcher Sarah Kalloch, who has done considerable fieldwork in Uganda. "Women do not have control over their own bodies." Kalloch describes instances of wife-swapping, wife inheritance, and widespread marital rape. Rape and domestic violence are "virtually impossible to prosecute" due to legal discrimination. "ABC is not enough for women in Uganda. They need legal rights that give them control over their bodies, their relationships, and who they marry," Kalloch says.

They also need basic economic security. Uganda's abstinence program has attempted to reach "high risk" populations such as soldiers and truck drivers, but has sent mixed messages by disparaging female HIV victims for indulgent or "promiscuous" behavior. So long as extreme economic deprivation continues to force young girls to barter for food and basic economic needs with sex, this sort of message will do little to save those who lack access to income and resources.

In the poverty-stricken northern region of Uganda, it's common for parents to force their teen and pre-teen daughters into sex work. "The mother will simply say to her daughters, 'come back with food,'" said Paul Zeitz of Global AIDS Alliance. Zeitz refers to this practice as "survival sex," since selling sex is not a profession for most of these girls, but a measure driven by dire economic necessity. Most customers are truck drivers and traveling soldiers, who prefer young girls, believing that they are free of HIV. Truck drivers synchronize their routes with school tuition deadlines (which vary by region), when girls are most likely to be waiting at truck stops for customers, according to a study conducted by the group.

When asked if abstinence programs fail women, Randall Tobias said, "One of the best ways to protect vulnerable women from HIV is to instill the 'ABC' message in men...." To Tobias, "the ABC model is a simple conceptualization of the major tenets of what happened in Uganda and can be implemented elsewhere with some local adaptation."

But as Lynn Amowitz, a Harvard medical school professor who has researched women's health and human rights in Afghanistan, observes: "The forms discrimination and stigma take differ from country to country. In some places, it's widow inheritance, in others it's that women are considered minors." Extending abstinence programs to these countries, with their distinct social dynamics, is unlikely to slow the feminization of HIV and AIDS. Without specific prevention programs that take such practices into account, the burden of HIV/AIDS will continue to disproportionately affect women.

Already, 58% of the 25 million people living with AIDS in sub-Saharan Africa are women. Adult women are up to 1.3 times more likely to be infected with HIV than their male counterparts, and women and girls now make up three-quarters of the 6.2 million young people (age 15 to 24) with AIDS. Because women serve as the primary caregivers for their own children and work in disproportionate numbers in schools, as nurses, and in social services, the feminization of AIDS ravages the socioeconomic fabric of their communities. Furthermore, the epidemic will be passed on to future generations, as the likelihood of mother-to-child transmission is estimated at 30%.

Treatment Possibilities

The situation is not hopeless. Life-extending drugs such as nevaripine and anti-retroviral therapies do exist. The World Health Organization (WHO) has engineered generic anti-retrovirals that will reduce the cost of therapy to $148 dollars a year, compared to an average $548 a year for name-brand drugs.

But the Bush administration has put the breaks on treatment. Under PEPFAR, all drugs sold abroad must be approved by the FDA. Even generic drugs that have already undergone the WHO's meticulous prequalification standards must be reexamined by the FDA before they are distributed abroad through the program. This rule will indefinitely delay the availability of affordable medication.

What's more, PEPFAR allocates no funds for distributing nevaripine, which at a cost of $4 per person can reduce the likelihood of mother-to-child transmission by almost 90%. Likewise, it does not fund the development of microbicides, topical products that women could use, undetected, to prevent sexual transmission of HIV. Protesters at the International AIDS Conference in Bangkok last July condemned Ambassador Tobias and President Bush for prioritizing pharmaceutical patent rights over public health needs and ideology over efficacy.

Women's economic marginalization is a global problem, and severe in the 15 countries that PEPFAR will target. President Bush's vague declaration that "AIDS can be prevented" is, in fact, correct. Prevention programs can provide a cost-effective means of gradually reducing HIV prevalence, but only if such programs address specific economic inequities that underlie patterns of transmission, dismantle barriers to economic independence for women, empower married women, and deliver messages in a culturally accessible manner. Just as important, they cannot ignore the necessity of investing in treatment for women and their daughters, who are already infected. Otherwise, women's social and economic powerlessness will continue to render them disproportionately vulnerable to the HIV epidemic. For women, the solution to the AIDS crisis is a lot more complicated than A-B-C. ❏

Sources: "The ABC Debate Heats Up," *Africa News*, July 13, 2004; Garbus, Lisa and Elliot Marseille, *Country AIDS Analysis Project: HIV/AIDS in Uganda,* San Francisco: AIDS Policy Research Center, University of California San Francisco, 2003; "Health: Women Demand Stepped-Up AIDS Treatment, Prevention," Inter Press Service, 2002; Ingham, Richard, "U.N. Envoy Blasts U.S. for "Ideological Agenda" on Abstinence to Combat AIDS," Agence France Presse, Bangkok, July 15, 2004; "Just Die Quietly," Human Rights Watch, 2003; Klein, Alonso Luiza, "Women's Social Representation of Sex, Sexuality, and AIDS in Brazil," *Women's Experiences with HIV/AIDS: An International Perspective.* New York: Columbia University Press, 1996; Ntabade, Catherine, "Abolish Polygamy," The Uganda Women's Network; Otterman, Sharon, "AIDS: The U.S. Anti-AIDS Program," Council of Foreign Relations, November 28, 2003; <www.siecus.org/policy/PUpdates/pdate0073.html>; "Uganda Puts Morality Before Condoms," Global News Wire, July 15, 2004.

Article 8.3

FISHERFOLK OUT, TOURISTS IN

Sri Lanka's tsunami reconstruction plans displace devastated coastal residents to make way for tourism industry expansion.

BY VASUKI NESIAH AND DEVINDER SHARMA
July/August 2005

Two days after the south Asian tsunami struck last December, as thousands around him were grappling with its devastating impact, former German chancellor Helmut Kohl was airlifted from the roof of his holiday resort in southern Sri Lanka by the country's air force. Kohl is, of course, among the most elite of tourists, and his privileges are not representative of all tourists. Nonetheless, that aerial exit is symptomatic of the tourist industry's alienation from the local community. His easy flight away from the devastation, at a time when official relief supplies were still to reach the majority of victims, was an early indicator of the interplay between tsunami relief and the tourism industry. Kohl was barely airborne, and the waves barely receding, when plans were already afoot to ensure that the beaches of Sri Lanka were cleared of fisherfolk and rendered pristine for a new wave of tourists.

"Natural" Disasters?

Right from the start, global attention to the tsunami was no doubt heightened by the fact that tourists were among the victims. Reporters conducted their share of riveting tsunami escape interviews in airport departure lounges: first-rate, first-person accounts with first-world tourists. This is not the first time viewers in the rich countries have been plied with images of "natives" being overwhelmed by natural disasters, passively awaiting international humanitarian relief and rescue. Some parts of the globe are just scripted into tragedy and chaos; first-world television screens are accustomed to their loss, their displacement, their overwhelming misery. Against this backdrop, the tales of tourists offered a more newsworthy break from stories that simply echo yesterday's news reports about locals caught up in floods in Bangladesh or mudslides in Haiti.

But while being located in the trajectory of tsunami waves or monsoons is a given, the acute vulnerability of countries like Sri Lanka, Haiti, or Bangladesh to natural disasters only appears spontaneous. It is the socio-political landscape that determines the extent of exposure to adverse impact from such natural disasters. The political economy of exposure to natural disaster is disastrous for those made vulnerable—but not natural. For example, coastal mangrove forests would have contained the fury of the tsunami waves, except that they've been rapidly destroyed in recent years to make way for resorts and industrial shrimp farms. (See sidebar, "The Tsunami and the Mangroves.")

Defining that vulnerability as natural is, however, important to the tourism industry, whose job it is to produce exotic destinations through comparison and contrast. The devastation of repeated natural disasters is simply the "native predicament" in places like Sri Lanka, and one of the principle drives behind western tourism to the global South hinges on that predicament. Tourism often is, after all, a quest for a departure from the everyday of western suburbia—but in a neatly packaged module that insulates the visitor from the actual risks of the locale. Trafficking in that balance of otherness and insulation is the task of the tour masters.

The tsunami penetrated that insulation to some degree. However, even through the bloodletting of the last two decades, tourists visiting Sri Lanka have been remarkably insulated from it all: both from the civil war and from the country's impoverished social and economic circumstances. In fact, on the tourism industry's map, Sri Lanka is an adventure zone whose attraction lies at least partly in those circumstances, which make it a cheap vacation spot, a low-cost listing in a travel catalog of exotic but consumer-friendly destinations.

What Does Tourism Do?

Does the tourist industry simply feed off a pre-existing socio-economic predicament and perhaps even mitigate it, or does the industry exacerbate that predicament and entrench a country like Sri Lanka in an itinerary of peripheral economies served up for tourist consumption?

The argument is not that tourism per se is bad for Sri Lanka. Clearly the broader tradition of tourism and international travel has had a mixed, complex history. For the many who came, surfed, littered, took photographs, bought sex, batik shirts, or barefoot sarongs and left, there are others who ended up engaged by newly discovered solidarities. Even the interface with colonial exploration was double-edged. As political scientist Kumari Jayewardene and others have shown us, we have always had a line of itinerant travelers who washed onto our shore as tourists of one sort or another, only to develop more fundamental commitments to local communities—commitments that then fed into, or even helped catalyze, traditions of dissent and struggles for justice that have had enormous reach in our collective histories.

Such solidarity aside, tourism can be a significant source of revenue, employment, and infrastructure development. It also has a range of indirect effects since tourism generates demand in many sectors; every job created in the tourism industry is said to result in almost ten jobs in other industries, with enhanced demand in areas like agriculture and small industries, a whole spectrum of service-sector employment, and so on—the kind of thing that excites Central Bank policymakers, not to mention the middlemen who profit from those batik shirts and barefoot sarongs, from the increased demand for sex work and other informal sector labor. At a micro level, the jobs generated by the industry have enabled some financial autonomy for some sections of the working poor. Even when pay and working conditions are exploitative, this is an autonomy that may have particular significance for women and other groups who yield less financial decisionmaking power in the "old" economy.

Yet this baby came with a lot of muddy bath water even before the tsunamis washed in. The growth it has generated has often been of an unbalanced kind that worsened the country's financial vulnerability with little accountability to local communities. As they discovered through the shifting fortunes of the ceasefire, the post-9/11 drop in international travel, and recessions in distant lands, communities that work in the tourism industry have a heightened dependence on a fickle, fluctuating transnational market. The majority of the jobs tourism creates in the formal sector are service-sector jobs that are exploitative, badly paid, seasonal, and insecure; these problems are replicated many times over in the industry's large informal sector,

THE TSUNAMI AND THE MANGROVES

Since the 1980s, Asia has been plundered by large industrialized shrimp farms that have brought environmentally unfriendly aquaculture to its shores. Nearly 72% of global shrimp farming takes place in Asia, where the World Bank has been its largest funder. Even before the tsunami struck last December, shrimp cultivation, once termed a "rape-and-run" industry by the U.N. Food and Agricultural Organization, had already caused havoc in the region. Shrimp farms are only productive for two to five years. The ponds are then abandoned, leaving behind toxic waste, destroyed ecosystems, and displaced communities that have lost their traditional livelihoods. The whole cycle is then repeated in another pristine coastal area.

Now the shrimp farms—along with rapid tourism development—are also responsible for a share of the death and destruction the tsunami brought. Shrimp farming was expanded at the cost of tropical mangrove forests, which are among the world's most important ecosystems. Mangrove swamps have long been nature's protection for coastal regions, holding back large waves, weathering the impact of cyclones, and serving as a nursery for the three-fourths of commercial fish species that spend part of their life cycle there.

Ecologists tell us that mangroves provide double protection against storms and tsunamis. The first layer of red mangroves with their flexible branches and tangled roots hanging in the coastal waters absorb the first shock waves. The second layer of tall black mangroves then acts like a wall, withstanding much of the sea's fury.

But shrimp farming has continued its destructive spree, eating away more than half of the world's mangroves. Since the 1960s, for instance, aquaculture and industrial development in Thailand have resulted in a loss of over 65,000 hectares of mangroves. In Indonesia, Java has lost 70% of its mangroves, Sulawesi 49%, and Sumatra 36%. At the time the tsunami struck in all its fury, logging companies were busy axing mangroves in the Aceh province of Indonesia to export to Malaysia and Singapore.

In India, mangrove cover has been reduced by over two-thirds in the past three decades. In Andhra Pradesh, more than 50,000 people have been forcibly removed to make way for shrimp farms; throughout the country, millions have been displaced.

Whatever remained of the mangroves in India was cut down by the hotel industry, aided and abetted by the Ministry of Environment and Forests and the Ministry of Industries. Five-star hotels, golf courses, industries, and mansions ranging from prostitution to handicrafts. Its untrammeled exploitation of the coast has created unsustainable demands on the local environment that have had particularly bad impacts on coastal ecology. Equally pernicious, it has transformed more and more public land such as beaches into private goods, fencing out local residents.

Reconstruction for Whom?

The tragedy is that many of tourism's downsides may be exacerbated by the tsunami reconstruction plans. From Thailand to Sri Lanka, the tourist industry saw the tsunami through dollar signs. The governments concerned were on board from the outset, quickly planning massive subsidies for the tourism industry in ways that

> sprung up all along the coast, warnings from environmentalists notwithstanding. These two ministries worked overtime to dilute the Coastal Regulation Zone rules, allowing the hotels to take over even the 500-meter buffer zone that was supposed to be maintained along the beach.
>
> The recent tourism boom throughout the Asia-Pacific region coincided with the destructive fallout from industrial shrimp farms. In the past two decades, the entire coastline along the Bay of Bengal, the Arabian Sea, and the Strait of Malacca in the Indian Ocean, as well as all along the South Pacific Ocean, has witnessed massive investment in hotels and tourism facilities. By 2010, the region is projected to surpass the Americas to become the world's number two tourist destination, with 229 million arrivals.
>
> If only the mangroves were intact, the damage from the tsunami would have been greatly minimized. That's what happened in Bangladesh in 1960, when a tsunami wave hit the coast in an area where mangroves were intact. Not a single person died. These mangroves were subsequently cut down and replaced with shrimp farms. In 1991, thousands of people were killed when a tsunami of the same magnitude hit the same region.
>
> In Tamil Nadu, in south India, Pichavaram and Muthupet, with dense mangroves, suffered low human casualties and less economic damage from the recent tsunami than other areas. Likewise, Myanmar and the Maldives suffered much less from the killing spree of the tsunami because the tourism industry had so far not spread its tentacles to the virgin mangroves and coral reefs surrounding their coastlines. The large coral reef surrounding the Maldives islands absorbed much of the tidal fury, limiting the human loss to a little over 100 dead. Like mangrove swamps, coral reefs absorb the sea's fury by breaking the waves.
>
> Let's weigh the costs and benefits of destroying the mangroves. Having grown tenfold in the last 15 years, shrimp farming is now a $9 billion industry. It is estimated that shrimp consumption in North America, Japan, and Western Europe has increased by 300% within the last 10 years. But one massive wave of destruction caused by this tsunami in 11 Asian countries has exacted a cost immeasurably greater than the economic gain that the shrimp industry claims to have created.
>
> World governments have so far pledged $4 billion in aid, and private relief agencies are spending additional billions. The World Bank gave $175 million right away, and then-World Bank president James Wolfensohn said, "We can go up to even $1 billion to $1.5 billion depending on the needs...." But if only successive presidents of the World Bank had refrained from aggressively promoting ecologically unsound but market friendly economic policies, a lot of human lives and dollars could have been saved.   —Devinder Sharma

suggest the most adverse distributive impact. Infrastructure development will be even further skewed to cater to the industry rather than to the needs of local communities. Within weeks of the tsunami, the Alliance for the Protection of National Resources and Human Rights, a Sri Lankan advocacy group, expressed concern that "the developing situation is disastrous, more disastrous than the tsunami itself, if it is possible for anything to be worse than that."

The tsunami arrived at a critical moment in the recent history of Sri Lanka's political economy. Beginning in the late 1970s, Sri Lankan governments of both major parties followed the neoliberal prescriptions to cut tariffs and quotas, privatize, and deregulate more slavishly than many other Asian states. In 2002, the then-ruling center-right UNP issued a major blueprint for continued liberalization, "Regaining Sri Lanka," under the rubric of the "Poverty Reduction Strategy Plans" (PRSPs) that the World Bank and the IMF now require. But public opposition to these policies has intensified over time. In 2004 a center-left coalition won election on an anti-liberalization platform. Once in office, however, the chief party in the coalition appeared unwilling to truly change direction, and the "Regaining Sri Lanka" plan is still very much on the table.

Now, activists are warning that many of the plan's liberalization proposals will be revived and pushed through with little public dialogue and debate, given the emergency powers the government has given itself under cover of tsunami relief and reconstruction. In January, for example, the government revived a plan for water privatization that had earlier been tabled after public opposition. Official reconstruction plans are being prepared by a newly created agency, TAFREN, which a recent statement by a coalition of over 170 civil-society organizations describes as "composed entirely of big business leaders with vested interests in the tourist and construction industries, who are completely unable to represent the interests of the affected communities."

Proposals announced by TAFREN and by various government officials call for the building of multi-lane highways and the wholesale displacement of entire villages from the coast. Coastal lands are to be sliced up into designated buffer zones and tourism zones. The government is preventing those fishing families who wish to do so from rebuilding their homes on the coast, ostensibly because of the risk of future natural disasters; at the same time, it's encouraging the opening of both new and rebuilt beachfront tourist hotels.

The plans are essentially roadmaps for multinational hotel chains, telecom companies, and the like to cater to the tourism industry. Small-scale fishing operations by individual proprietors will become more difficult to sustain as access to the beach becomes increasingly privatized and fishing conglomerates move in. The environmental deregulation proposed in the PRSP will open the door to even more untrammeled exploitation of natural resources. None of the reconstruction planning is being channeled through decision-making processes that are accountable or participatory. Ultimately, it looks like reconstruction will be determined by the deadly combination of a rapacious private sector and government graft: human tragedy becomes a commercial opportunity, tsunami aid a business venture.

Not unpredictably, even the subsidies planned for the tourism industry in the wake of the tsunami are going to the hotel owners and big tour operators, not to the porters and cleaning women who were casual employees in hotels. Many of the local residents who were proprietors or workers in smaller tourism-related businesses, now unemployed, are not classified as tsunami-affected, so they are denied even the meager compensation they should be entitled to. The situation is much worse for the vast informal sector of sex workers, souvenir sellers, and others whose livelihood depended on the tourism industry. If the tsunami highlighted the acute vulnerability that accompanies financial dependence on the industry, the tsunami reconstruction plans look set to exacerbate this vulnerability even further.

A needs assessment study conducted by the World Bank in collaboration with the Asian Development Bank and Japan's official aid agency pegged the loss borne by the tourism industry at $300 million, versus only $90 million for the fishing industry. The ideological assumptions embedded in an assessment methodology that rates a hotel bed bringing in $200 a night as a greater loss than a fisherman bringing in $50 a month have far-reaching consequences. With reconstruction measures predicated on this kind of accounting, we are on a trajectory that empowers the tourism industry to be an even more dominant player than it was in the past, and, concomitantly, one that disempowers and further marginalizes the coastal poor.

Travel and Displacement

Much has been made of the unsightly fishing shanties that will not be rebuilt. Instead, fishing communities are going to be transformed into even more unsightly urban squalor, their residents crowded into "modern" apartment complexes like the sardines they may fish. However, this will be further inland. As they sit on the beach watching the ocean loll onto Lanka's shore, tourists will enjoy the coast in a sanitized, "consumer friendly" environment. Ironically, they may even be sitting in *cadjan* cabanas, a nostalgic nod to the *cadjan* homes of fishing communities of the past—a neatly consumable experience of the exotic without the interference of a more messy everyday.

But perhaps this *is* the new everyday that is proposed: the teeming hordes in designated settlements, a playground for tourists elsewhere. It's a product of the mercantile imagination—the imagination of tourist industry fat cats who will be raking in the tsunami windfall. With the building of planned superhighways, tourists will be able to zoom from airport to beach, shopping mall to spa, while the people who lived in these regions will become less mobile as they are shut out from entire stretches of coastal land. If tourism is about carefully planned displacement from the ordinary for a privileged few, the crossing of boundaries for recreation and adventure, here it is tied to the forced displacement of fishing communities and the instituting of new boundaries that exclude and dispossess. ❑

Article 8.3

MINDING THE TIMOR GAP

Billions of dollars in oil and gas revenues are at stake as Australia continues to bully East Timor out of its undersea energy resources.

BY FAISAL CHAUDHRY
July/August 2006

The outbreak of violent clashes between government forces and disgruntled former military personnel put East Timor, one of the world's newest nations, into the headlines this spring. East Timor achieved full independence in 2002 after nearly three decades of profoundly destructive occupation at the hands of an American-backed Indonesian military. The events of late May, widely attributed to the firing of about a third of the Timorese army following an unlawful strike by soldiers, and to "communal" strife, have roots in Timor's disastrous recent history and tenuous current circumstances. With even the sparse economic infrastructure that had been built up during Indonesia's occupation largely destroyed by the departing occupation and paramilitary forces in 1999, the country has faced great challenges in its efforts to rebuild and develop. Vast undersea oil and gas fields off Timor's coast could supply critically needed funds for development, but in the last several years Timor has been involved in a bitter fight to get neighboring Australia to recognize its rights to this valuable resource.

There are four main oil and gas fields in or near production in the Timor Gap area that are currently at issue; all of them would rightfully belong to Timor under prevailing principles of international maritime law. Nonetheless, Australia, 240 nautical miles across the Timor Sea, continues to try to legitimize its own claim to these resources. By pushing to extend a bilateral treaty framework forged with Indonesia in the 1970s and 1980s onto East Timor, Australia has been able to defer settlement of the most pressing issue—defining a permanent maritime boundary between the two countries—long into a designated future, at which point the oil and gas in the Timor Gap are expected to be exhausted.

Vast sums are at stake. Since 1999, for example, Australia has reaped all of the approximately $1 billion in revenues the now nearly exhausted Laminaria-Corallina field has generated; East Timor has received none. Given the weakness of Australia's position, which openly contravenes the global consensus on undersea resources as embodied in the U.N. Convention on the Law of the Sea (UNCLOS), it will be able to prolong the "interim" arrangements of the outdated bilateral treaty framework only as long as Australia continues to reject East Timor's rightful claim to these critical resources.

Development and Reconstruction in the Wake of Disaster

In December 1975 Indonesia invaded and occupied East Timor, nine days after the nation of 600,000 had declared its independence from Portugal. Indonesia's brutal occupation lasted for 24 years and took the lives of an estimated one-third of Timor's population. Following an August 1999 referendum in which the Timorese voted overwhelmingly for independence, Indonesian and Indonesia-backed militias rampaged across the country, killing more than 1,000, displacing 75% of the population, and destroying Timor's entire electrical grid, three-fourths of its buildings, and most of its other infrastructure. Beginning in late 1999, a United Nations-led international peacekeeping force brought calm, and Timor achieved full independence in May 2002.

But the new nation has struggled to rebuild and develop. Timor's 2004 GDP amounted to about $370 million, or $400 per capita. Overall, the country ranked 140 out of 177 on the U.N. Development Program's human development index in 2005, placing it just above Sudan, the Congo, and Zimbabwe. Timor is highly dependent on international aid: as of 2003 the country had received the largest quantity of overseas aid per capita of any post-conflict society. Moreover, this does not include the budgets of the several U.N. missions that have operated in Timor since 1999. Overall, these total aid inflows nearly equal the average annual GDP from the non-petroleum sector of the economy.

At the same time, Timor has become highly import dependent. In 2004, for example, its exports were just $7 million, almost all coffee. The same year, the country imported $113 million worth of goods. Ironically, nearly a third of the imports were fossil fuels. The government originally projected a budget shortfall of $126 million for 2005 to 2007, bringing with it the prospect of falling into debt to international financial institutions. The fiscal outlook has recently brightened, but it remains worrying.

Given these difficulties, control over Timor's gas and oil resources is crucial to its prospects for forging an independent path of development. The Timor Gap lies well inside the line halfway across the Timor Sea separating the two countries—the line that, under the terms of the UNCLOS, would likely mark the proper permanent maritime boundary between the two countries.

However, Australia is clinging to a series of treaties, initially negotiated with Indonesia from 1971 to 1973, which defined certain seabed boundaries that were far north of the median line. Though such boundary treaties are usually permanent, they apply only to the countries negotiating them—in this case, Australia and Indonesia. Portugal refused to take part in the negotiations, so the treaties did not apply to East Timor as a Portuguese colony, and certainly not today as an independent nation. (The name "Timor Gap" is not a physical reference, but rather refers to the discontinuity in the boundaries set under the early-1970s treaties resulting from Portugal's absence from the negotiations.)

The only western country to recognize Indonesia's 1975 annexation of East Timor, Australia began further negotiations with Indonesia in the late 1970s to try to "close" the "gap." These talks failed; eventually, the two countries agreed to drop the boundary issue and instead simply negotiate a plan for petroleum development. In 1989 they signed the Timor Gap Treaty, which rechristened the area a "Zone of Cooperation" (ZOC): the two countries agreed to split revenues from joint petroleum exploration operations in the gap equally. The 1989 treaty ignored not only the median line principle for determining maritime boundaries, but Timor's status as an illegally annexed and occupied territory as well.

Greater Sunrise, the largest of the four fields at the center of the current dispute, was discovered in 1974. Only 20% of its geographical area falls inside of the ZOC. The remaining three fields were all discovered in the mid- to late-1990's. Bayu-Undan, the next largest, and Elang-Kakatua are both located entirely within the ZOC. Laminaria-Corallina is located closer to East Timor's shoreline but falls just outside of the ZOC (though some geologists believe its reservoir extends into the ZOC). For this reason, if Australia manages to continue imposing the terms of its bilateral treaties with Indonesia on East Timor, Timor will receive none of the field's revenues. Revenue distribution for the other three main fields is somewhat

---

THE LAW OF THE SEA: A MINI-PRIMER

In 1945, President Harry Truman unilaterally declared that the United States would henceforth be entitled to all natural resources within its continental shelves—the shallow areas just off the coasts, extending out to where the sea floor drops down sharply. In so doing, Truman began a movement away from the older "cannon shot" principle of maritime law, under which a nation's rights extended only six kilometers from its shores. But exactly where continental shelves end and the ocean floor begins is often a matter of dispute, and by the early 1970s the new continental-shelf principle was already giving rise to conflicts. In response, a U.N.-mediated process of rewriting maritime law accelerated until, in 1982, the U.N. Convention on the Law of the Sea (UNCLOS) was completed. The new convention came into full force in November 1994. Both Indonesia and Australia are signatories; East Timor has yet to sign.

Under the convention, nations have full political and economic rights over the first 12 nautical miles from their shores, their "territorial waters," and partial rights over the next 12 nautical miles. The first 200 nautical miles are a so-called exclusive economic zone within which a nation has full rights to exploit marine and undersea resources.

What if, as in the case of East Timor and Australia, two nations are less than 400 nautical miles apart? In such cases, UNCLOS mandates negotiations as the first step for sorting out overlapping claims to common sea areas and endorses the median line principle as the guiding norm for resolving such claims. Australia itself has recognized the median line principle, for instance, in an unratified 1997 treaty with Indonesia concerning the water column boundary (for fisheries rather than undersea resources) in the exact area of the Timor Sea now at issue. And in July 2004, Australia accepted the median line principle to settle its maritime boundary with New Zealand—although in this case the seabed area in question is not believed to have significant oil or gas reserves.

more equitable but still extremely problematic. And Australia has tended to cast any shift in revenue arrangements as a "concession" on its part.

For example, as a consequence of sustained international pressure, under the January 2006 Certain Maritime Arrangements in the Timor Sea (or CMATS) agreement, one that's been hailed as something of a breakthrough, revenues from Greater Sunrise are to be divided equally once production begins in a few years (under a license that has already been assigned to an Australian company, Woodside Petroleum). Prior to this "breakthrough," the Australian government had long insisted that it would concede only 18% of the revenue from the field to Timor, in proportion with the portion of Greater Sunrise lying within the ZOC. But even though the new agreement reflects a significant victory for East Timor—as well as a testament to the force of ongoing pressure campaigns on Australia—the 50-50 split remains a far cry from the full 100% of the Sunrise revenues that Timor would be assigned under a median line principle for settling a permanent maritime boundary with Australia. (The January agreement covers only upstream revenues, in other words, resource extraction and transfer into a pipeline or sea vessel. The distribution of downstream revenues from Sunrise, i.e., processing activities such as refining, remains a major outstanding issue.) Under CMATS, revenue flows from the other two fields at issue, Elang-Kakatua and Bayu-Undan, are subject to a distribution scheme in which Australia will retain all earnings from downstream processing activities (for the gas) and 10% of revenues from upstream extraction (for oil and gas), with the other 90% of upstream earnings going to East Timor.

The $1 billion Australia has received in revenues from just the Laminaria-Corallina fields since 1999 is several times the amount of development aid Australia has provided to East Timor in the same period, and on account of which it has received and given itself great acclaim. In 2003 alone, revenue from Laminaria-Corallina came to $172 million, nearly twice as much as the Timorese government's budget for that year. Once the Greater Sunrise field comes into production, it is projected to yield as much as $40 billion in revenue over its lifetime; under CMATS Timor is due to receive only half of this amount.

Dodging International Law

Under the terms of UNCLOS, the median line between two nations should be their presumed boundary (see sidebar, "The Law of the Sea: A Mini-Primer"). In the case of the Timor Sea, however, Australia claims that its maritime boundaries with Timor are to be settled according to the geomorphology of the seabed—the outdated continental shelf principle. And, naturally, Australia maintains that its own continental shelf is especially elongated, extending all the way up to the so-called Timor Trough, approximately 40 nautical miles from Timor's shores. (The point is one on which geologists have disagreed.) Indonesia's 1971 seabed boundary treaties with Australia reflect this view, placing the boundary line just south of the Timor Trough, about 80 nautical miles north of the median line.

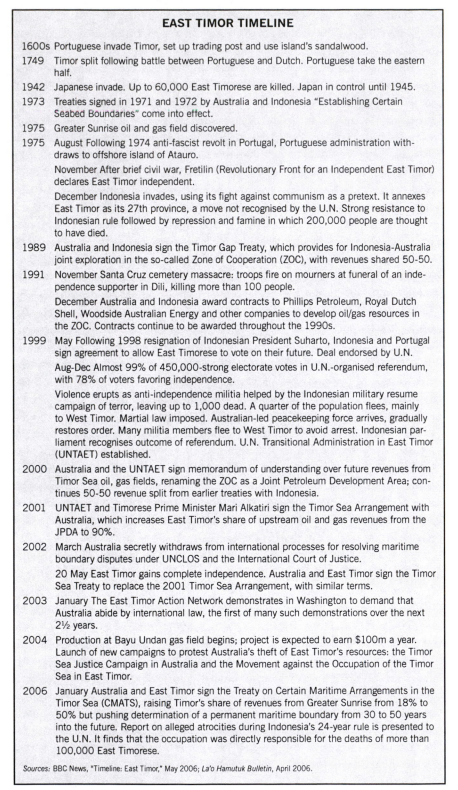

EAST TIMOR TIMELINE

1600s Portuguese invade Timor, set up trading post and use island's sandalwood.

1749 Timor split following battle between Portuguese and Dutch. Portuguese take the eastern half.

1942 Japanese invade. Up to 60,000 East Timorese are killed. Japan in control until 1945.

1973 Treaties signed in 1971 and 1972 by Australia and Indonesia "Establishing Certain Seabed Boundaries" come into effect.

1975 Greater Sunrise oil and gas field discovered.

1975 August Following 1974 anti-fascist revolt in Portugal, Portuguese administration withdraws to offshore island of Atauro.

November After brief civil war, Fretilin (Revolutionary Front for an Independent East Timor) declares East Timor independent.

December Indonesia invades, using its fight against communism as a pretext. It annexes East Timor as its 27th province, a move not recognised by the U.N. Strong resistance to Indonesian rule followed by repression and famine in which 200,000 people are thought to have died.

1989 Australia and Indonesia sign the Timor Gap Treaty, which provides for Indonesia-Australia joint exploration in the so-called Zone of Cooperation (ZOC), with revenues shared 50-50.

1991 November Santa Cruz cemetery massacre: troops fire on mourners at funeral of an independence supporter in Dili, killing more than 100 people.

December Australia and Indonesia award contracts to Phillips Petroleum, Royal Dutch Shell, Woodside Australian Energy and other companies to develop oil/gas resources in the ZOC. Contracts continue to be awarded throughout the 1990s.

1999 May Following 1998 resignation of Indonesian President Suharto, Indonesia and Portugal sign agreement to allow East Timorese to vote on their future. Deal endorsed by U.N.

Aug-Dec Almost 99% of 450,000-strong electorate votes in U.N.-organised referendum, with 78% of voters favoring independence.

Violence erupts as anti-independence militia helped by the Indonesian military resume campaign of terror, leaving up to 1,000 dead. A quarter of the population flees, mainly to West Timor. Martial law imposed. Australian-led peacekeeping force arrives, gradually restores order. Many militia members flee to West Timor to avoid arrest. Indonesian parliament recognises outcome of referendum. U.N. Transitional Administration in East Timor (UNTAET) established.

2000 Australia and the UNTAET sign memorandum of understanding over future revenues from Timor Sea oil, gas fields, renaming the ZOC as a Joint Petroleum Development Area; continues 50-50 revenue split from earlier treaties with Indonesia.

2001 UNTAET and Timorese Prime Minister Mari Alkatiri sign the Timor Sea Arrangement with Australia, which increases East Timor's share of upstream oil and gas revenues from the JPDA to 90%.

2002 March Australia secretly withdraws from international processes for resolving maritime boundary disputes under UNCLOS and the International Court of Justice.

20 May East Timor gains complete independence. Australia and East Timor sign the Timor Sea Treaty to replace the 2001 Timor Sea Arrangement, with similar terms.

2003 January The East Timor Action Network demonstrates in Washington to demand that Australia abide by international law, the first of many such demonstrations over the next 2½ years.

2004 Production at Bayu Undan gas field begins; project is expected to earn $100m a year. Launch of new campaigns to protest Australia's theft of East Timor's resources: the Timor Sea Justice Campaign in Australia and the Movement against the Occupation of the Timor Sea in East Timor.

2006 January Australia and East Timor sign the Treaty on Certain Maritime Arrangements in the Timor Sea (CMATS), raising Timor's share of revenues from Greater Sunrise from 18% to 50% but pushing determination of a permanent maritime boundary from 30 to 50 years into the future. Report on alleged atrocities during Indonesia's 24-year rule is presented to the U.N. It finds that the occupation was directly responsible for the deaths of more than 100,000 East Timorese.

Sources: BBC News, "Timeline: East Timor," May 2006; *La'o Hamutuk Bulletin*, April 2006.

Given the legal framework of UNCLOS, Australia's position is remarkable: its demand is for nothing less than to be allowed to claim nearly all of the 238-nautical-mile span between it and Timor as its own.

It is not surprising, then, that Australia has sought to avoid serious scrutiny of its claim under international law. In March 2002, the country announced that it would be exercising its option to withdraw from the jurisdiction of the International Court of Justice over disputes concerning resource exploitation in disputed areas and from the jurisdiction of UNCLOS' International Tribunal for the Law of the Sea over disputes concerning maritime boundaries. This decision came only two months before the end of East Timor's supervision by the U.N. Transitional Administration; at that point, as a fully independent and sovereign state, it would have been much closer to achieving standing to bring such maritime disputes in both venues.

A Perpetual "Interim"

Since 1999, Australia has been able to defer the issue of settling a permanent maritime boundary by instead focusing on "interim agreements" that seek to transfer the machinery of the previous bilateral treaty framework with Indonesia onto independent East Timor. The July 2001 Timor Sea Arrangement, negotiated while the United Nations was still overseeing Timor's transition to independence, began the process of re-legitimating the 1989 Timor Gap Treaty—a tainted pact, after all, negotiated with an occupying power whose sovereignty over the territory at issue had been recognized by almost no one other than Australia itself. In the 2001 arrangement, Australia sought to wash away this sullied history, primarily by re-christening the ZOC as a "Joint Petroleum Development Area" (JPDA) and by setting out a new, ostensibly more generous revenue split giving Timor 90% of upstream oil and gas revenues from activities in the JPDA.

In 2002, only 12 hours after achieving full sovereignty, the Timorese government agreed to a new Timor Sea Treaty essentially identical to the 2001 arrangement (and effectively negotiated by the U.N. transitional administration). The 2002 treaty again put off the matter of a permanent maritime boundary; at the same time, it set up a 30-year development authority for projects in the JPDA.

The Timorese government faced significant domestic criticism for signing the 2002 treaty. However, this criticism had more to do with strategy than with underlying goals, according to Charles Scheiner, a researcher with La'o Hamutuk/The Institute for Reconstruction Monitoring and Analysis, a civil society group that promotes transparency and public participation in the country's development. "It was made clear to the Timorese government that if it were not to sign the treaty, the much-needed revenues it would soon begin receiving from the Bayu-Undan field could be delayed indefinitely," he notes. Civil society and development groups wanted to keep up the fight for full independence, including fair and permanent maritime boundaries, but the government, under then-Prime Minister Mari

Alkatiri, was more worried about meeting its day-to-day need for revenue. Scheiner also views the recent opposition to Alkatiri, which led to his resignation this June, as largely unrelated to the domestic divisions over the country's maritime negotiations with Australia.

In 2004, Timorese Foreign Minister Jose Ramos-Horta offered to give up Timor's rightful claim to a permanent maritime boundary until all petroleum reserves in the Timor Gap area were exhausted. In exchange, he sought Australia's agreement to provide a larger share of revenue from the disputed petroleum and gas fields. At the time the offer was met with little enthusiasm by Australian Foreign Minister Alexander Downer, though it now seems to underlie Australia's willingness to reapportion upstream revenues from Greater Sunrise gas as part of this year's CMATS agreement.

While the greater share of Greater Sunrise revenues that CMATS gives Timor is welcome, in other respects the new agreement moves farther away from a just resolution. CMATS allows the settlement of a permanent boundary to be postponed for as long as 50 years, a significant jump over the Timor Sea Treaty's period of 30 years. As La'o Hamutuk notes, "[t]he 50 year duration appears to be based on commercial grounds, providing certainty for oil companies to explore and exploit petroleum resources without any changes of ownership until the oil and gas is used up."

In fact, CMATS mandates that the parties cannot even so much as raise "in any international organization matters that are, directly or indirectly, relevant to maritime boundaries or delimitation in the Timor Sea" and that neither party is under any "obligation to negotiate permanent maritime boundaries for the period" of the treaty. The agreement prohibits the parties from seeking relevant legal remedies and stipulates that nearly all disputes are to be settled through "negotiation" and "consultation." Australia's superior bargaining power will likely allow it to prevail in any such negotiations or consultations.

Given Australia's success at the negotiating table, by 2001 Timorese civil society groups began pressing to have Australia's revenues from resources falling on East Timor's side of the median line placed in trust until the boundary dispute is fully resolved. These calls have only continued in the wake of the CMATS, as has Australia's failure to respond to them in any way.

The Challenges Ahead

Today, both the Timorese government and civil society and development groups find themselves at a crucial juncture. First, they must assess any possibility that remains for working toward a permanent maritime boundary in accord with UNCLOS principles and decide whether strategies should instead focus solely on achieving greater equity, within the "interim" framework, where outstanding issues remain (downstream revenues from Sunrise, for example).

Second, this summer's civil strife has once again brought foreign troops— mainly Australian—into Timor. But Australia's assistance may have a price tag.

Some observers fear that Australia might, for example, demand that Timor repay its peacekeeping expenditures or even renegotiate CMATS so as to roll back the partial gains that treaty offered Timor.

Finally, even under the current treaty framework, within five years Timor will derive some 89% of its GDP and 94% of government revenues from oil and gas sales from Bayu-Undan alone, according to La'o Hamutuk's estimates. So even if Timor will not receive its fair share of oil and gas revenues, its dependence on the revenues it *will* receive will pose a complex series of challenges similar to those any petroleum-rich developing nation must face. There are good reasons that majorities in many poor but oil-rich countries have come to regard their oil as a curse. In many instances, these countries end up with worse corruption, more serious environmental hazards, slower economic development, and less investment in education and infrastructure than their resource-poor counterparts. Ensnared in the highly militarized geopolitics of the international oil business, they face the near-impossible challenge of managing their Big Oil corporate partners and the constant risk of oil-related intervention.

In 2005, the Timorese government established a Petroleum Fund to hold oil and gas revenues for future investment; the fund has some $600 million in deposits to date. In addition, the legislature has passed the Petroleum Act, Petroleum Fund Act, and a model Production Sharing Contract (a template for the individual contracts to be signed with oil companies) to establish a regulatory framework for managing petroleum resources from Timor's mainland and exclusive waters as well as from the JPDA.

The establishment of a regulatory framework for the petroleum industry is a welcome development, reducing the likelihood of unaccountable and arbitrary decisions that could squander the precious oil and gas revenues. Still, critics worry that it remains inadequate in several areas, including overall transparency, its provisions on corporate accountability, the level of power it places in the hands of the Prime Minister, and the level of community involvement it allows in ongoing decisions regarding the application of expected revenues to local development efforts. Moreover, the current framework does not adequately specify the exact relationship Timor will have with the multinational oil and gas companies it will have to rely on. (One item of NGO input the government did accept in drafting the Petroleum Act: a provision allowing for a government petroleum company that could own up to 20% of any oil and gas projects on land or in Timor's national waters.)

The recent violence and political turmoil in Timor only heightens the import of all of these questions. Typically, the western press has framed the story as one of a power-hungry leader (former Prime Minister Alkatiri) losing his grip over a failed-state-in-the-making—a narrative that does not begin to capture the complexities of Timor's history and current circumstances. Labeled a "Marxist" and an "extremist" by some of his critics, Alkatiri appeared at times to follow an economic-nationalist path that met with disapproval from Australia and other powers. He expressed reluctance to completely accept the dominant neoliberal development paradigm, although precisely how much his policies reflected this reluctance is a matter of debate. Under Alkatiri, notes La'o Hamutuk's Scheiner, "the government modified its public approach to Australia to become closer to the popular movement's call for an end to the occupation of the Timor Sea." As the full story behind his recent ouster comes to light, these factors may well turn out to be a part of it.

In any case, the connections between the recent upheaval and the general backdrop of unemployment and poverty that Timor Sea energy resources might be used to address are clear. If governments and activists continue to put pressure on Australia, whose ongoing appropriation of Timor's resources has been a principle cause of its current problems, the promise of the country's oil and gas wealth for beginning to meet people's needs and prevent further violence will only grow. But these resources need to be used properly to achieve genuine, equitable, and sustainable development. To these ends, the ongoing concern and understanding of Timor's situation by those outside its borders will be as important for its people as it has been throughout their country's recent and needlessly tragic history. ❑

Sources: *The La'o Hamutuk Bulletin*, Vol. 6, No. 4 (11/05) and Vol. 7, No. 1 (4/06), www.laohamutuk. org; East Timor and Indonesia Action Network, www.etan.org; Movement Against the Occupation of Timor, "Statement," April 2004, available at www.etan.org/news/2004/04move.htm; text of CMATS treaty, available at www.laohamutuk.org/Oil/Boundary/CMATStext.htm.

Article 8.5

THE GLOBAL OIL MARKET
How it operates, why it doesn't work, and who wants to keep it that way.

PAUL CUMMINGS
July/August 2008

Since the United States-led coalition invaded Iraq in March 2003, the price of a barrel of oil has just about quadrupled to around $135. With U.S. oil imports currently totaling 4.5 billion barrels a year, this translates into a staggering $600 billion annual oil bill. Many energy economists predict that oil prices could top $200 a barrel in the near future, particularly if U.S. opposition to Iran's nuclear enrichment program leads to a confrontation, either directly or through surrogate states.

Why are oil prices skyrocketing? Many economists and business analysts like to talk about "the fundamentals": supply (constrained) and demand (strong). They point to rapid economic growth in China and India driving demand. On the supply side, it's the OPEC cartel limiting production while tree-huggers in the United States block the development of new offshore and Alaskan oil supplies.

But other analysts claim the so-called fundamentals tell us little about why oil prices are rising rapidly. Recently the London *Times*'s economy and finance commentator, Anatole Kaletsky, noted that over the past nine months, as the price of oil has doubled, none of the basic determinants of supply or demand has changed much. China's demand growth is in fact slowing, as is the world's demand growth overall. Iraqi oil production is back up to prewar levels. Kaletsky views the current price spikes as symptoms of a classic financial bubble during which, typically, "prices end up bearing almost no relation to the balance of underlying supply and demand."

For now, the experts are displaying a remarkable lack of consensus on whether it's the actions of commodities traders and other financial-market movements or real supply and demand factors that explain the current oil price spike. In any case, the terms "supply" and "demand" are supposed to conjure up images of a free market. But the global oil market is anything but. Even leaving aside the role of financial markets in setting the price of oil, the supply of and demand for oil are heavily shaped by the actions of mammoth multinational oil companies and of governments in both the consuming and producing countries. And while the price of oil is rising fast, causing real pain to consumers, those extra dollars are going straight to the governments of the oil-rich countries and to the major oil companies—*not* to offset the tremendous costs that oil imposes, chiefly on the environment but in multiple other arenas as well.

Supply Management

From the very beginning of the modern oil industry, the supply of oil has been managed by powerful oil companies and the magnates who run them. The first was none other than John D. Rockefeller, who founded Standard Oil in 1870. By 1878 he had gained control of 90% of U.S. oil refining. In the 1880s Rockefeller used his strategic control of refining to build the first vertically integrated oil company, with oil fields, tankers, pipelines, refineries, and retail sales facilities under one corporate roof. By mercilessly undercutting competitors until they were near bankruptcy, and then buying them on the cheap, Standard Oil gained control of over half of the world's then-known oil supply. By the turn of the century Rockefeller had become the richest man in the world, with a fortune valued at around a billion dollars. Then, in 1911, the Supreme Court ruled that Standard Oil was a monopoly and, to create competition, split it into 34 companies, including Esso and Socony, which eventually became Exxon and Mobil, respectively.

Instead of competing, over the next 50 years Exxon, Mobil, and five other giant oil companies (the "majors") essentially formed a cartel. Leveraging their superior technology, production experience, and control of the retail market, the majors engaged in oil colonialism: they pumped and sold oil from a number of developing countries under highly favorable terms, earning vast profits.

In the 1950s, oil-rich countries began nationalizing their oil and training domestic oil technocracies to run the business. The advantages of collusion were no secret to them. In the 1960s Venezuela and Saudi Arabia organized OPEC (the Organization of Petroleum Exporting Countries), a cartel whose explicit purpose was to control the price of oil by regulating supply. By acting together, the oil-rich nations leveled the playing field with the majors and gained a larger share of oil profits.

With this context in mind, let's consider how oil gets to market today. Currently, around 75% of the world's oil is nationalized, managed by state-run oil companies that are monopolies in their own country. These state companies are often their country's largest employer, largest exporter, largest source of hard currency, and largest contributor to state revenue. State oil executives report to political authorities instead of a corporate board, and local political considerations can trump economic factors in their business decisions. For example, state oil companies may site new facilities in poorer communities to spur local economic development. More importantly, nationalized oil earns the money to pay for hospitals, schools, sanitation systems, and roads, projects rarely funded by Western oil corporations. The downside is that oil money all too frequently has been stolen by corrupt rulers or siphoned away to buy expensive weapons—Zaire's Mobutu Sese Seko and Iraq's Saddam Hussein were just two in a long line of oil-funded despots.

State oil ministers set oil production targets taking into consideration both economic and political factors, including current global economic performance, OPEC member production quotas, long-term contracts with oil corporations, International Monetary Fund debt repayment schedules, domestic revenue requirements, the desires of greedy and corrupt rulers, and the cost of oil extraction compared to oil's market price.

Of course, most of the state-owned oil across the globe lies within OPEC, whose policies fundamentally shape supply. The eleven member states of OPEC control over 50% of the world's oil. After both the 1973 Israeli-Arab war and the 1979 Islamic revolution in Iran, OPEC cut oil production, oil prices skyrocketed, cartel members earned hundreds of billions of dollars in windfall profits, and the world economy slid into recession.

Then, in the 1980s, a weak economy and more efficient cars cut oil demand, while newly discovered non-OPEC oil increased supply. OPEC tried to prop up plunging prices by cutting production. In particular, Saudi Arabia cut its output by nearly 8 million barrels per day. When other OPEC members began to cheat on their lower production quotas, the Saudis enforced market discipline by flooding the market with cheap oil, driving many suppliers out of business. With oil supply back under control, prices rose to around $20 a barrel, OPEC's market share was restored, and OPEC production quotas were honored. John D. Rockefeller would have applauded.

In 1990, the first "oil war" was launched when Iraq invaded Kuwait and seized its oil fields. With Iraqi troops poised to attack Saudi Arabia, a U.S.-led coalition drove the Iraqi army out of Kuwait. The Saudis once again demonstrated their market power by pumping enough additional oil to offset the loss of Kuwaiti and Iraqi oil production.

The cartel aims to keep the price of oil high, but it also seeks reasonable stability in the oil market. After all, the lion's share of the petrodollars that OPEC members earn are plowed back into the United States and the other wealthy consuming countries in the form of investments. If oil price volatility begins to damage the U.S. and other industrialized economies, those investments will likely suffer as well. But OPEC's ability to manage supply for the twin goals of profitability and stability is limited. In recent years conflicts in the Middle East, rapidly growing oil demand in China and India, and OPEC's own tendency to overshoot or undershoot planned production levels have all contributed to a more volatile oil market than OPEC perhaps intended.

The remaining 25% of global oil supply comes from fields owned by the majors or by Russia's ostensibly private energy giant Gazprom. This production is more responsive to market signals, but is still influenced by non-price factors such as government tax and environmental policies and Wall Street pressure to report high quarterly earnings.

Perhaps the clearest indicator that the supply of oil is managed and not a simple response to market signals is the curious fact that much of the oil that is brought to market is relatively expensive to produce because of high extraction costs (for instance, deep sea oil), transport costs (Alaskan oil), or refining costs (some of Africa's oil). At the same time, oil that could be brought to market far more cheaply—much of the oil in the Arabian Peninsula, for example—is left in the ground. Saudi oil costs just $1.50 per barrel to produce, while the average production cost of oil outside of the Middle East is $22 per barrel. In a free market, competition would cause the lowest-cost oil to be sold first, since cheap oil can undercut expensive oil. However, in the case of managed supply, producers of cheap oil can hold back their oil, allowing the market price to rise until it exceeds the production price of expensive oil. This means very high profits for the producers of cheap oil, while many energy analysts stimate that consumers are paying twice as much as they would if oil markets were free, Paul Roberts writes in *The End of Oil*.

Retail supplies are influenced by vertically integrated global oil delivery systems—pipelines, supertankers, refineries, delivery tanker trucks, assorted retail sales facilities—which are controlled by the Saudis, Venezuela, and the super-majors (the six largest private oil companies: ExxonMobil, Shell, BP, Chevron, ConocoPhillips, and Total S.A.). Every day 85 million barrels of oil flow to consumers around the world. The massive oil delivery systems are worth a combined $5 trillion dollars and create a large barrier to entry for alternative energy suppliers. Supply can be constrained for other reasons as well, for instance, environmental or other regulations that block expansion or construction of oil pipelines or refineries.

Occasionally a geopolitical or extreme weather event breaks the oil supply system and retail oil prices go through the roof, creating outrageous profits. For example, in the aftermath of Hurricane Katrina, U.S. gasoline prices doubled overnight. The oil industry denied using Katrina to fleece customers, but a 2006 investigation by the Federal Trade Commission found multiple examples of price gouging at the refining, wholesale, and retail levels. Coincidentally, in the last quarter of 2005, the accounting quarter following Katrina, ExxonMobil earned $9.9 billion, the largest quarterly profits ever reported by a U.S. company.

In 2007 oil prices were exploding along with much of Iraq. That year ExxonMobil earned $40.6 billion in profits on $400 billion in revenue, the highest yearly profit ever earned by a public corporation. Amazingly, even this record profit pales in comparison to the 2007 Saudi net oil revenue of $194 billion.

Captive Consumers

The demand for oil is no more a simple result of free-market forces than is the supply. To begin with, energy demand is not created directly by consumers: we do not desire gasoline the way we might desire a new house or a new pair of shoes. Instead, demand is "pulled" by the economy, whose mix of technologies and rate of growth determine how much energy, from oil and other sources, is required to power it. Oil heats tens of millions of homes, offices, and factories and powers 30% of the world's electric generation. Oil is also used as an input in the manufacture of petrochemicals such as plastics.

And, of course, oil moves mountains of raw materials, tons of finished goods, and billions of people every day. The world's armada of oil-fueled vehicles consists of nearly a billion cars, trucks, buses, tractors, bulldozers, ships and airplanes. The troubling reality is that this armada runs only on oil; there is no viable alternative fuel today, and oil companies intend to keep it that way.

Every year the armada grows, moving more people and more stuff over greater distances. Globalization has spread out the production and sales processes over ever-longer international supply chains. U.S. and Canadian commuters drive more and more miles as suburbanization moves home and work farther apart. And the average fuel efficiency of U.S. passenger vehicles *fell* by 5% during the past 20 years, due to aggressive marketing of SUVs and trucks.

Oil companies use their political clout to stop government efforts to increase fuel efficiency. Over the last 20 years, the oil industry has given $200 million to U.S. politicians, mostly Republicans, who believe in free markets but regularly give an invisible helping hand to the oil companies. During those same 20 years, oil lobbyists have rolled back gas mileage standards and created tax subsidies for buying eight-ton Hummers that inhale gas. Oil lobbyists have redirected funding from alternative energy technology to road and bridge repair.

Oil companies have also used their wealth and political power to crush electric powered transportation systems. In the 1920s city-dwellers commuted on electric trolleys, but oil and auto companies wanted to sell them buses and cars. Standard Oil, General Motors, Mack Truck, and Firestone Tire funded a dummy corporation, National City Lines (NCL), to replace trolleys with buses. It didn't matter if NCL lost money; its goal was to create demand for buses, cars, tires, and oil. If it could do so, its parent companies would make a fortune. By 1929 NCL had established its business model and when the Great Depression deepened, over 100 electric utility companies, located in most major cities, were forced to sell their trolley lines at a sharply discounted price to NCL, the only buyer with cash. Once NCL had control, the trolley systems were sold for scrap and within days a new fleet of buses arrived, followed by a tidal wave of cars. In the late 1940s, NCL had served its purpose and was failing. Government lawyers had been investigating NCL, and in 1949 they successfully prosecuted its parent companies for collusion to destroy the nation's trolley system. Each parent company paid a $5,000 fine, which wasn't too bad considering they had made on the order of $100 million in profits from NCL's illegal actions.

By 1990 the Los Angeles basin faced a serious public health problem due to smog from car exhaust. The state of California issued a mandate requiring car companies to develop a zero emission vehicle, or ZEV. Oil and automobile companies launched a full-fledged political campaign to overturn the ZEV mandate, including TV and magazine ads, direct mail, and thousands of calls from phone banks. The ZEV mandate was never enforced and, in 2003, was replaced with a minimal requirement that car companies sell a few gas-electric hybrid cars by 2008. That same year, in a remarkable episode chronicled in the 2006 documentary "Who Killed the Electric Car?," GM was taking back the hundreds of EV1 electric vehicles it had leased to U.S. drivers beginning in 1996. The carmaker assembled most of the EV1s at a site in Arizona where it proceeded to crush them—despite very positive feedback from EV1 lessees, many of whom wanted to purchase and keep the cars. Explanations for GM's decision to halt the EV1 program and destroy the cars vary.

GM says it determined the venture could never be profitable, in part because hoped-for breakthroughs in battery technology did not occur. One thing is certain: the car did become less marketable once California gave in to pressure from the oil and auto industries (including GM) and lifted the ZEV mandate.

In 1994 oil companies attacked Ballard Power Systems for developing a hydrogen fuel cell to power cars. With a game plan similar to the one they'd used to undermine the ZEV mandate, they took out ads decrying the fuel cell, challenged the company's veracity at trade conferences, and questioned its ability to actually bring a viable product to market. Oil companies pointed out that useable hydrogen was in short supply and an entirely new hydrogen refining, delivery, and fueling infrastructure would need to be built at the cost of many billions of dollars. As a result of these attacks Ballard backed off, and further development of its fuel cell was hidden in an internal R&D program for over a decade.

So the demand for oil is driven by economic and social trends far beyond the control of individual consumers, who are stuck, at least in the short term, paying whatever price the oil companies set if they want to fill their tanks and heat their homes.

Finally, it's impossible to get the whole picture of demand for oil without recognizing one very special oil consumer: the U.S. military. Every tank, armored vehicles, truck, humvee, jet, and missile runs on refined oil, as do most ships. In 2007, the U.S. military consumed about 250 million barrels of oil and 2.6 billion gallons of jet fuel, making it the world's single largest fuel-burning entity. Without oil the Army and Marines could not maneuver, the Air Force could not fly, and most of the Navy could not sail. The United States would be a paralyzed superpower, unable to project power throughout the world. Since all the other military forces in the world also run on oil, the ability to cut their oil lifelines is a tremendous strategic advantage in any conflict. These factors make oil more than just another commodity. Oil is a weapon, a strategic commodity, a national security resource; it is not just like wheat or widgets. By the same token, any shift in U.S. foreign policy that reduces the country's military engagements can also represent a sizeable drop in U.S. oil demand.

Multiple Market Failures

Today's global oil market is working well for the major oil companies, their managers, and their shareholders. It is also working well for the oil-producing countries, at least to the extent that they are garnering vast revenues. (Of course, the extent to which these revenues are benefiting ordinary people in the oil-rich countries varies dramatically.)

But the oil market is characterized by many kinds of market failure: the workings of the market are producing less-than-optimal results on multiple levels. For instance, oil price spikes can lead to "demand shocks" that suck money rapidly out of the economies of the oil-importing nations. If the global financial system cannot get this money re-invested and generating demand quickly, the result can be a drop in global demand followed by an economic downturn. According to energy econo-mist Philip Verleger, over the last 50 years there have been six major oil price spikes, each causing economic losses that have totaled more than $1 trillion. Verleger posits that a 20% increase in the price of a barrel of oil results in a 0.5% decline in global economic growth. Based on that formula, the current $100 spike in the price of oil, if sustained, could wind up causing a reversal in the global economy from a baseline of 2% growth to a 1% contraction.

By and large, Americans have benefited from the fact that the price of oil world-wide is denominated in dollars rather than another currency. Right now, though, the falling value of the dollar against other major currencies is one factor pushing up the price of oil in the United States. Moreover, not only can fluctuations in the value of the dollar affect oil prices; oil market shifts can affect the value of the dollar. Hence, a second type of market failure in the global oil market is the increased "risk premium" that attaches to a whole range of financial transactions when a build-up of petrodollars makes the financial markets worry about an increased risk of either a devaluation of the dollar or a run on the dollar. In both cases the U.S. Federal Reserve may not be able to successfully intervene because trillions of petrodollars are outside of the Fed's control. In general, increased risk is bad for the economy and leads to higher interest rates and slower economic growth.

A third group of oil market failures are environmental. Oil is a dirty business that pollutes the air, water, and earth, often in health-threatening ways. Take oil spills for example. In Ecuador a pipeline runs over the Andes, connecting Ecuador's eastern jungle oil fields to its Pacific coast refinery. When earthquakes or landslides break the pipeline, all the oil between the break and the shut-off valve simply pours out, contaminating a broad swath of the mountain below.

Six thousand miles to the north, Exxon's supertanker, the Valdez, struck Bligh Reef on March 24, 1989, spilling 11 million gallons of oil into Prince William Sound. The oil contaminated 1,500 miles of Alaskan shoreline; nearly 20 years later, local economies dependent on fishing and tourism have still not entirely recovered. There are thousands of similar cases all over the planet.

The mother of all oil market failures is climate change. When oil is con-verted to energy, it gives off CO_2 which traps heat in the atmosphere and, in large quantity, can alter the climate. The result is a global, cumulative, and intergen-erational problem that an increasing number of climate scientists fear may become a crisis of biblical proportions: higher sea levels flooding coastal cities around the globe; droughts, heat waves, pests, and more frequent extreme weather events affecting food supplies and human health.

No matter where CO_2 originates, it spreads quickly through-out the entire atmo-sphere, and so makes the problem a global one. The longevity of atmospheric CO_2 creates a cumulative problem. Since 1850, our species has dumped so much carbon into the sky that atmospheric CO_2 levels are at their highest point in a million years. That is 500,000,000,000,000 pounds of carbon stuck in the sky, as if the atmo-sphere were an open sewer! And that longevity makes the problem intergenerational:

it will take the earth 16 generations (400 years) to reabsorb 80% of the CO_2 we emit today, and the remaining 20% will stay in the sky for thousands of years.

Solving climate change begins by realizing that the oil market doesn't have to be managed for the benefit of a small number of extremely rich people. We must also put to rest the canard that oil resources are best allocated by the free market's "invisible hand." Columbia University economist Joseph Stiglitz points out, "the reason that the hand may be invisible is that it is simply not there—or at least that if is there, it is palsied." The public needs to fight to remove the control of oil pricing from the oil corporations and establish an oil market that is more fair and sustainable.

In a sustainable energy market, the price of gasoline and other fossil fuel products should reflect the real costs these energy sources impose—above all, on the environment. That means prices that are higher than what Americans are accustomed to. But a progressive oil agenda would include recapturing that additional revenue and using it to compensate low-income consumers and, especially, to move the economy toward one based on renewable energy. Paying that extra dollar or more a gallon at the pump would feel very different if U.S. consumers knew the money was being spent not to line the pockets of dictators and oil executives, but instead to offset the extra cost for low-income families and, especially, to generously fund myriad projects to put the economy on a green-energy path. ❑

Sources: Sohbet Karbuz, "US military energy consumption: facts and figures," *Energy Bulletin*, May 20, 2007; Chalmers Johnson, "The Arithmetic of America's Military Bases Abroad: What Does It All Add Up To?" www.tomdispatch.com, 2004; OPEC, "World Oil Outlook 2007"; Paul Roberts, *The End of Oil* (Houghton Mifflin, 2005); U.S. Federal Trade Comm., "Investigation of Gasoline Price Manipulation and Post-Katrina Gasoline Price Increases: Report to Congress" (Spring 2006); Eric Noe, "For Oil Giants, Pricey Gas Means Big Profits," ABC News, Jan. 25, 2006; Steven Mufson, "ExxonMobil's Profit in 2007 Tops $40 Billion," *Washington Post*, Feb. 2, 2008; U.S. Energy Information Admin., "OPEC Oil Export Revenues 2007"; Michael Renner, "Five Hundred Million Cars, One Planet—Who's Going to Give?" (Worldwatch Institute, August 2003); Daniel Engber, "How Gasoline Becomes CO2: A gallon turns into 19 pounds?" Slate.com, Nov. 1, 2006; Matthew Kahn, "The Environmental Impact of Suburbanization," *Jrnl of Policy Analysis and Mgmt* 19:4 (Fall 2000); Philip Verleger, "A Collaborative Policy to Neutralize the Economic Impact of Energy Price Fluctuations," Policy paper, June 10, 2003; "The Real Price of Gasoline: An Analysis of the Hidden External Costs Consumers Pay to Fuel Their Automobiles," Int'l Ctr for Technology Assessment, 1998; Joseph Stiglitz, *Making Globalization Work* (W.W. Norton, 2006); Laura Peterson, "Big Oil Wields Ultra Deep Influence," Ctr for Public Integrity, Dec. 2004.

Article 8.6

CLIMATE ECONOMICS IN FOUR EASY PIECES

Conventional cost-benefit models cannot inform our decisions about how to address the threat of climate change.

FRANK ACKERMAN
November/December 2008

Once upon a time, debates about climate policy were primarily about the science. An inordinate amount of attention was focused on the handful of "climate skeptics" who challenged the scientific understanding of climate change. The influence of the skeptics, however, is rapidly fading; few people were swayed by their arguments, and doubt about the major results of climate science is no longer important in shaping public policy.

As the climate *science* debate is reaching closure, the climate *economics* debate is heating up. The controversial issue now is the fear that overly ambitious climate initiatives could hurt the economy. Mainstream economists emphasizing that fear have, in effect, replaced the climate skeptics as the intellectual enablers of inaction.

For example, William Nordhaus, the U.S. economist best known for his work on climate change, pays lip service to scientists' calls for decisive action. He finds, however, that the "optimal" policy is a very small carbon tax that would reduce greenhouse gas emissions only 25% below "business-as-usual" levels by 2050—that would, in other words, allow emissions to rise well above current levels by mid-century. Richard Tol, a European economist who has written widely on climate change, favors an even smaller carbon tax of just $2 per ton of carbon dioxide. That would amount to all of $0.02 per gallon of gasoline, a microscopic "incentive" for change that consumers would never notice.

There are other voices in the climate economics debate; in particular, the British government's Stern Review offers a different perspective. Economist Nicholas Stern's analysis is much less wrong than the traditional Nordhaus-Tol approach, but even Stern has not challenged the conventional view enough.

What will it take to build a better economics of climate change, one that is consistent with the urgency expressed by the latest climate science? The issues that matter are big, non-technical principles, capable of being expressed in bumper-sticker format. Here are the four bumper stickers for a better climate economics:

- Our grandchildren's lives are important
- We need to buy insurance for the planet
- Climate damages are too valuable to have prices
- Some costs are better than others

1. Our grandchildren's lives are important

The most widely debated challenge of climate economics is the valuation of the very long run. For ordinary loans and investments, both the costs today and the resulting future benefits typically occur within a single lifetime. In such cases, it makes sense to think in terms of the same person experiencing and comparing the costs and the benefits.

In the case of climate change, the time spans involved are well beyond those encountered in most areas of economics. The most important consequences of today's choices will be felt by generations to come, long after all of us making those choices have passed away. As a result, the costs of reducing emissions today and the benefits in the far future will not be experienced by the same people. The economics of climate change is centrally concerned with our relationship to our descendants whom we will never meet. As a bridge to that unknowable future, consider our grandchildren—the last generation most of us will ever know.

Suppose that you want your grandchildren to receive $100 (in today's dollars, corrected for inflation), 60 years from now. How much would you have to put in a bank account today, to ensure that the $100 will be there 60 years from now? The answer is $55 at 1% interest, or just over $5 at 5%.

In parallel fashion, economists routinely deal with future costs and benefits by "discounting" them, or converting them to "present values"—a process that is simply compound interest in reverse. In the standard jargon, the *present value* of $100, to be received 60 years from now, is $55 at a 1% *discount rate*, or about $5 at a 5% discount rate. As this example shows, a higher discount rate implies a smaller present value.

The central problem of climate economics, in a cost-benefit framework, is deciding how much to spend today on preventing future harms. What should we spend to prevent $100 of climate damages 60 years from now? The standard answer is, no more than the present value of that future loss: $55 at a discount rate of 1%, or $5 at 5%. The higher the discount rate, the less it is "worth" spending today on protecting our grandchildren.

The effect of a change in the discount rate becomes much more pronounced as the time period lengthens. Damages of $1 million occurring 200 years from now have a present value of only about $60 at a 5% discount rate, versus more than $130,000 at a 1% discount rate. The choice of the discount rate is all-important to our stance toward the far future: should we spend as much as $130,000, or as little as $60, to avoid one million dollars of climate damages in the early twenty-third century?

For financial transactions within a single lifetime, it makes sense to use market interest rates as the discount rate. Climate change, however, involves public policy decisions with impacts spanning centuries; there is no market in which public resources are traded from one century to the next. The choice of an intergenerational discount rate is a matter of ethics and policy, not a market-determined result.

Economists commonly identify two separate aspects of long-term discounting, each contributing to the discount rate.

One component of the discount rate is based on the assumption of an upward trend in income and wealth. If future generations will be richer than we are, they will need less help from us, and they will get less benefit from an additional dollar of income than we do. So we can discount benefits that will flow to our wealthier descendants, at a rate based on the expected growth of per capita incomes. Among economists, the income-related motive for discounting may be the least controversial part of the picture.

Setting aside changes in per capita income from one generation to the next, there may still be a reason to discount a sum many years in the future. This component of the discount rate, known as "pure time preference," is the subject of longstanding ethical, philosophical, and economic debate. On the one hand, there are reasons to think that pure time preference is greater than zero: both psychological experiments and common sense suggest that people are impatient, and prefer money now to money later. On the other hand, a pure time preference of zero expresses the equal worth of people of all generations, and the equal importance of reducing climate impacts and other burdens on them (assuming that all generations have equal incomes).

The Stern Review provides an excellent discussion of the debate, explaining Stern's assumption of pure time preference close to zero and an overall discount rate of 1.4%. This discount rate alone is sufficient to explain Stern's support for a substantial program of climate protection: at the higher discount rates used in more traditional analyses, the Stern program would look "inefficient," since the costs would outweigh the present value of the benefits.

2. We need to buy insurance for the planet

Does climate science predict that things are certain to get worse? Or does it tell us that we are uncertain about what will happen next? Unfortunately, the answer seems to be yes to both questions. For example, the most likely level of sea level rise in this century, according to the latest Intergovernmental Panel on Climate Change reports, is no more than one meter or so—a real threat to low-lying coastal areas and islands that will face increasing storm damages, but survivable, with some adaptation efforts, for most of the world. On the other hand, there is a worst-case risk of an abrupt loss of the Greenland ice sheet, or perhaps of a large portion of the West Antarctic ice sheet. Either one could cause an eventual seven-meter rise in sea level—a catastrophic impact on coastal communities, economic activity, and infrastructure everywhere, and well beyond the range of plausible adaptation efforts in most places.

The evaluation of climate damages thus depends on whether we focus on the most likely outcomes or the credible worst-case risks; the latter, of course, are much larger.

Cost-benefit analysis conventionally rests on average or expected outcomes. But this is not the only way that people make decisions. When faced with uncertain, potentially large risks, people do not normally act on the basis of average outcomes; instead, they typically focus on protection against worst-case scenarios. When you go to the airport, do you leave just enough time for the average traffic delay (so that you would catch your plane, on average, half of the time)? Or do you allow time for some estimate of worst-case traffic jams? Once you get there, of course, you will experience additional delays due to security, which is all about worst cases: your *average* fellow passenger is not a threat to anyone's safety.

The very existence of the insurance industry is evidence of the desire to avoid or control worst-case scenarios. It is impossible for an insurance company to pay out in claims as much as its customers pay in premiums; if it did, there would be no money left to pay the costs of running the company, or the profits received by its owners. People who buy insurance are therefore guaranteed to get back less than they, on average, have paid; they (we) are paying for the security that insurance provides in case the worst should happen. This way of thinking does not apply to every decision: in casino games, people make bets based on averages and probabilities, and no one has any insurance against losing the next round. But life is not a casino, and public policy should not be a gamble.

Should climate policy be based on the most likely outcomes, or on the worst-case risks? Should we be investing in climate protection as if we expect sea level rise of one meter, or as if we are buying insurance to be sure of preventing a seven-meters rise?

In fact, the worst-case climate risks are even more unknown than the individual risks of fire and death that motivate insurance purchases. You do not know whether or not you will have a fire next year or die before the year is over, but you have very good information about the likelihood of these tragic events. So does the insurance industry, which is why they are willing to insure you. In contrast, there is no body of statistical information about the probability of Greenland-sized ice sheets collapsing at various temperatures; it's not an experiment that anyone can perform over and over again.

A recent analysis by Martin Weitzman argues that the probabilities of the worst outcomes are inescapably unknowable—and this deep uncertainty is more important than anything we do know in motivating concern about climate change. There is a technical sense in which the expected value of future climate damages can be infinite because we know so little about the probability of the worst, most damaging possibilities. The practical implication of infinite expected damages is that the most likely outcome is irrelevant; what matters is buying insurance for the planet, i.e., doing our best to understand and prevent the worst-case risks.

3. Climate damages are too valuable to have prices

To decide whether climate protection is worthwhile, in cost-benefit terms, we would need to know the monetary value of everything important that is being protected.

Even if we could price everything affected by climate change, the prices would conceal a critical form of international inequity. The emissions that cause climate change have come predominantly from rich countries, while the damages will be felt first and worst in some of the world's poorest, tropical countries (although no one will be immune from harm for long). There are, however, no meaningful prices for many of the benefits of health and environmental protection. What is the dollar value of a human life saved? How much is it worth to save an endangered species from extinction, or to preserve a unique location or ecosystem? Economists have made up price tags for such priceless values, but the results do not always pass the laugh test.

Is a human life worth $6.1 million, as estimated by the Clinton administration, based on small differences in the wages paid for more and less risky jobs? Or is it worth $3.7 million, as the (second) Bush administration concluded on the basis of questionnaires about people's willingness to pay for reducing small, hypothetical risks? Are lives of people in rich countries worth much more than those in poor countries, as some economists infamously argued in the IPCC's 1995 report? Can the value of an endangered species be determined by survey research on how much people would pay to protect it? If, as one study found, the U.S. population as a whole would pay $18 billion to protect the existence of humpback whales, would it be acceptable for someone to pay $36 billion for the right to hunt and kill the entire species?

The only sensible response to such nonsensical questions is that there are many crucially important values that do not have meaningful prices. This is not a new idea: as the eighteenth-century philosopher Immanuel Kant put it, some things have a price, or relative worth, while other things have a dignity, or inner worth. No price tag does justice to the dignity of human life or the natural world.

Since some of the most important benefits of climate protection are priceless, any monetary value for total benefits will necessarily be incomplete. The corollary is that preventive action may be justified even in the absence of a complete monetary measure of the benefits of doing so.

Average Risks or Worst-Case Scenarios?

You don't have to look far to find situations in which the sensible policy is to address worst-case outcomes rather than average outcomes. The annual number of residential fires in the United States is about 0.4% of the number of housing units. This means that a fire occurs, on average, about once every 250 years in each home—not even close to once per lifetime. By far the most likely number of fires a homeowner will experience next year, or even in a lifetime, is zero. Why don't these statistics inspire you to cancel your fire insurance? Unless you are extremely wealthy, the loss of your home in a fire would be a devastating financial blow; despite the low probability, you cannot afford to take any chances on it.

What are the chances of the ultimate loss? The probability that you will die next year is under 0.1% if you are in your twenties, under 0.2% in your thirties, under 0.4% in your forties. It is not until age 61 that you have as much as a 1% chance of death within the coming year. Yet most U.S. families with dependent children buy life insurance. Without it, the risk to children of losing their parents' income would be too great—even though the parents are, on average, extraordinarily likely to survive.

4. Some costs are better than others

The language of cost-benefit analysis embodies a clear normative slant: benefits are good, costs are bad. The goal is always to have larger benefits and smaller costs. In some respects, measurement and monetary valuation are easier for costs than for benefits: implementing pollution control measures typically involves changes in such areas as manufacturing, construction, and fuel use, all of which have well-defined prices. Yet conventional economic theory distorts the interpretation of costs in ways that exaggerate the burdens of environmental protection and hide the positive features of some of the "costs."

For instance, empirical studies of energy use and carbon emissions repeatedly find significant opportunities for emissions reduction at zero or negative net cost—the so-called "no regrets" options.

According to a long-standing tradition in economic theory, however, cost-free energy savings are impossible. The textbook theory of competitive markets assumes that every resource is productively employed in its most valuable use—in other words, that every no-regrets option must already have been taken. As the saying goes, there are no free lunches; there cannot be any $20 bills on the sidewalk because someone would have picked them up already. Any new emissions reduction measures, then, must have positive costs. This leads to greater estimates of climate policy costs than the bottom-up studies that reveal extensive opportunities for costless savings.

In the medium term, we will need to move beyond the no-regrets options; how much will it cost to finish the job of climate protection? Again, there are rival interpretations of the costs based on rival assumptions about the economy. The same economic theory that proclaimed the absence of $20 bills on the sidewalk is responsible for the idea that all costs are bad. Since the free market lets everyone spend their money in whatever way they choose, any new cost must represent a loss: it leaves people with less to spend on whatever purchases they had previously selected to maximize their satisfaction in life. Climate damages are one source of loss, and spending on climate protection is another; both reduce the resources available for the desirable things in life.

But are the two kinds of costs really comparable? Is it really a matter of indifference whether we spend $1 billion on bigger and better levees or lose $1 billion to storm damages? In the real-world economy, money spent on building levees creates jobs and incomes. The construction workers buy groceries, clothing, and so on, indirectly creating other jobs. With more people working, tax revenues increase while unemployment compensation payments decrease.

None of this happens if the levees are not built and the storm damages are allowed to occur. The costs of prevention are good costs, with numerous indirect benefits; the costs of climate damages are bad costs, representing pure physical destruction. One worthwhile goal is to keep total costs as low as possible; another is to have as much as possible of good costs rather than bad costs. Think of it as the cholesterol theory of climate costs.

In the long run, the deep reductions in carbon emissions needed for climate stabilization will require new technologies that have not yet been invented, or at best exist only in small, expensive prototypes. How much will it cost to invent, develop, and implement the low-carbon technologies of the future?

Lacking a rigorous theory of innovation, economists modeling climate change have often assumed that new technologies simply appear, making the economy inexorably more efficient over time. A more realistic view observes that the costs of producing a new product typically decline as industry gains more experience with it, in a pattern called "learning by doing" or the "learning curve" effect. Public investment is often necessary to support the innovation process in its early, expensive stages. Wind power is now relatively cheap and competitive, in suitable locations; this is a direct result of decades of public investment in the United States and Europe, starting when wind turbines were still quite expensive. The costs of climate policy, in the long run, will include doing the same for other promising new technologies, investing public resources in jump-starting a set of slightly different industries than we might have chosen in the absence of climate change. If this is a cost, many communities would be better off with more of it.

A widely publicized, conventional economic analysis recommends inaction on climate change, claiming that the costs currently outweigh the benefits for anything more than the smallest steps toward reducing carbon emissions. Put our "four easy pieces" together, and we have the outline of an economics that complements the science of climate change and endorses active, large-scale climate protection.

How realistic is it to expect that the world will shake off its inertia and act boldly and rapidly enough to make a difference? This may be the last generation that will have a real chance at protecting the earth's climate. Projections from the latest IPCC reports, the Stern Review, and other sources suggest that it is still possible to save the planet—if we start at once. ❑

Sources: Frank Ackerman, *Can We Afford the Future? Economics for a Warming World,* Zed Books, 2008; Frank Ackerman, *Poisoned for Pennies: The Economics of Toxics and Precaution,* Island Press, 2008; Frank Ackerman and Lisa Heinzerling, *Priceless: On Knowing the Price of Everything and the Value of Nothing,* The New Press, 2004; J. Creyts, A. Derkach, S. Nyquist, K. Ostrowski and J. Stephenson, *Reducing U.S. Greenhouse Gas Emissions: How Much at What Cost?,* McKinsey & Co., 2007; P.-A. Enkvist, T. Naucler and J. Rosander, "A Cost Curve for Greenhouse Gas Reduction," *The McKinsey Quarterly,* 2007; Immanuel Kant, *Groundwork for the Metaphysics of Morals,* translated by Thomas K. Abbot, with revisions by Lara Denis, Broadview Press, 2005 [1785]; B. Lomborg, *Cool It: The Skeptical Environmentalist's Guide to Global Warming,* Alfred A. Knopf, 2007; W.D. Nordhaus, *A Question of Balance: Economic Modeling of Global Warming,* Yale University Press, 2008; F.P. Ramsey, "A mathematical theory of saving," *The Economic Journal* 138(152): 543-59, 1928; Nicholas Stern *et al.,* *The Stern Review: The Economics of Climate Change,* HM Treasury, 2006; U.S. Census Bureau, "Statistical Abstract of the United States." 127th edition. 2008; M.L. Weitzman, "On Modeling and Interpreting the Economics of Catastrophic Climate Change," December 5, 2007 version, www. economics.harvard.edu/faculty/weitzman/files/modeling.pdf.

Article 8.7

CLIMATE CHANGE AND ECOSOCIALISM

AN INTERVIEW WITH JOEL KOVEL
March/April 2009

Joel Kovel is co-editor of the journal Capitalism Nature Socialism, *author of* Enemy of
Nature *(Zed Books, 2007), and co-producer of the 2007 video "A Really Inconvenient
Truth." D&S collective member Larry Peterson interviewed Kovel in October. This is
the third article in our series on the economics of climate change. A longer version of this
interview is available at dollarsandsense.org. —Eds.*

DOLLARS & SENSE: Many people are confused by the range of estimates of the
extent of the problem of climate change. In your view, how dire is the threat, and
how much time do we have to confront the problem in a serious way?

JOEL KOVEL: To me, the overall problem—not simply of climate change, but the
whole ecological crisis of which climate change comprises a major part—is the grav-
est threat ever faced by humanity. We had better learn to recognize that the world as
it has been known has been fundamentally changed, and act accordingly. Even if the
tendencies that have given rise to this are reversed tomorrow—actually quite incon-
ceivable—we will be suffering the consequences for generations. At the other end,
my best guess is that we have ten years to begin to make basic changes. Otherwise,
tipping points will be passed, and civilization will go downhill very rapidly.

The basic principle is that everything in nature exists interconnectedly,
something that humanity in the modern era has largely forgotten. A sign of that
forgetting is the habit of reducing everything to the costs of everything, i.e.,
economic reductionism. I would argue that this is a manifestation of our whole
estrangement from nature.

D&S: Some people claim that earlier predictions of environmental crisis have been
shown to be remarkably wrongheaded. Couldn't emerging technology resolve the
climate crisis, as it has seemed to head off ones people have predicted before?

JK: First of all, those predictions were not "remarkably wrongheaded"; they were
only somewhat premature. Today, virtually all of the major predictions are being
borne out. Julian Simon, a flamboyant believer in the sustainability of our society
(he predicted that it could last seven billion years!) crowed in the '70s and '80s about
winning bets that prices of raw materials would drop over time. You don't see people
making that claim any more, especially in the energy sector. Here a positive feedback loop emerges, as the perception of "peak oil" drives warfare, social unrest, and
intensified ravaging of the environment: see what's happening in Northern Alberta

to the oil sands; or what Chevron is doing in Ecuador; or the story in Niger, with uranium extraction, and so on. And the most comprehensive study, the U.N.'s "Millennium Assessment Report" of 2005, concluded that the majority of planet Earth's ecosystems were in rapid decay.

The point about technology pulling us out of this dilemma deserves special emphasis. Of course we can always benefit from better technology; but that doesn't mean that the technology now available is inadequate to address this problem. What's missing are the social conditions for contending with ecological crisis. I'm afraid that speaking of state and market as leading the way is all too often a reshuffling of the same old deck. We need to confront the really salient issue. Consider this: since 1957, society has tripled its output of atmospheric carbon. In the same period population has increased by a factor of 2.3—a serious problem, to be sure, but a substantially lesser one; from another angle, we can say that the average person is "responsible" for 1.3 times as much carbon per capita as was the case fifty years ago. Clearly, the responsibility for the increase lies with the economic system; indeed, it would take two billion more people consuming at 1957 rates to throw the same amount of carbon into the atmosphere as we do today. So the question is, really, what induces the insane and uncontrollable "growth complex" of material goods, which by any rational assessment is driving this crisis? And this points us in the direction of the capitalist system.

D&S: So will living standards have to fall? Will dyed-in-the-wool consumerist societies—not to mention resource-hungry developing ones—be able to make such a rapid and thorough transformation?

JK: We cannot begin to approach this question except through a confrontation with capitalism, since consumerism is strictly the reflex of capitalist overproduction. We need to change the "need structures" that are induced through mass culture and undergird consumerist addiction. In addition, ever-growing inequalities of wealth introduce widespread envy and material cravings into society. All of these tendencies of capitalism make it impossible for society to respect ecological limits.

Living standards as now constructed in the industrial countries will have to fall. However, the notion of "living standard" is relative to one's worldview and mode of social existence. From the earliest days people have been able to live remarkably integral and spiritually advanced lives with a drastically lower level of "things" than now obtains in the so-called advanced societies. And it should not be forgotten that we are spending more and more just to reverse the effects of previous consumption and its associated waste. Our challenge is to see if lives can be reconstructed within the context of overcoming ecological crisis. This is why I argue that building toward a society beyond capitalism is the necessary condition for sustainability.

D&S: How have you and others at *Capitalism Nature Socialism* developed an ecologically conscious version of Marxism?

JK: Jim O'Connor's idea of the Second Contradiction made an "Eco-Marxism" possible by allowing the categories of Marxism to be applied in a rigorous way to our interactions with the external, natural world. Following Karl Polanyi, Jim integrated these with traditional crisis theory, showing both the essential unity of all forms of capitalist exploitation, and also their crisis-ridden character. The Second Contradiction postulated that the drive toward surplus value and profit caused capital to discount, hence degrade, the "conditions of production," which were defined by Jim as nature, the workers themselves, and infrastructure. An unintended yet necessary consequence of this was to depress the rate of profit, just as exploitation of workers reduced their ability to buy the commodities they made.

My focus has been on the expansive dynamic of capital, which accounts for its unsustainability, and immediately for the phenomena of climate change. I see this as rooted, first of all, in the fundamental shift outlined by Marx between an economy centered about use values, and the capitalist alternative centered in exchange value. People in pre-capitalist markets sell commodities for money in order to obtain other commodities they can use. Those in capitalist markets advance money to produce commodities to exchange for more money. Marx makes the profound observation that the second circuit has no limit, because money, as pure number, has no limit, in contrast to commodities produced for use—a person can consume only so much. Hence the capitalist economy is disconnected from nature at its root, and is "free" to mutilate the ecosphere. That this concretely happens is due to associated features of capitalism, such as competition driven by private ownership of the means of production, the complicity of the capitalist state, and the lawless character of a society grounded in exploitation.

Capitalism Nature Socialism also gives major emphasis to ecofeminist work because of the centrality of gender in our relations with nature; and finally, to an openness to radical and ecologically rational alternatives to capitalism: ecosocialism.

D&S: What about the international geopolitical realities? How can we expect Western governments, with all their historical baggage regarding pollution (and so much else), to seriously engage with the developing world, much of which is ruled by authoritarian governments, and beholden to foreign and domestic elites?

JK: The international dimension is crucial insofar as the ecological crisis is manifestly planetary, in both its causes and its effects. The rate of change of key ecosystems quite precisely follows the path of what has been called "globalization," one of the chief features of which is expansion in trade. While capitalism is the root problem, the present neoliberal period of capitalism, which began in the 1970s, is the setting for the heightened and globalized exploitation of nature (and also of labor) that surfaces as ecological crisis, with climate change as a principal but by no means exclusive manifestation.

What we call "imperialism" is deeply implicated in the ecological crisis. Throughout history, ecological events, at times catastrophic as in pandemics, have been interwoven with the rest of the fabric. The epoch of Western domination was ushered in by the spread of European diseases that eliminated 90% of the indigenous population of the Americas. Hence the uneven distribution of ecologically induced suffering is anything but new. Nor should it be read as absolute, since what characterizes the current ecological crisis is the "globalization" of hazards as well as of finance and trade—that is to say, if the seas rise six meters, a great deal of very valuable property will be destroyed along with that of commoners.

One of the most ominous implications of the present crisis is a survivalist mentality, manifest from gated communities, to vicious crackdowns on "illegal aliens," to fundamentalist wars. Anything that severs the interconnections of an ecosystem hastens its disintegration; this is bound to be the fate of a humanity disintegrating into fragments according to the logic of imperialism and its associated splittings.

But the ecological crisis affords another path as well, which increasing numbers of people are taking. This involves finding and adopting a universalist ethic stemming from perception of our common fate and our unity with nature. It requires overcoming all forms of chauvinism, including those that hold the human species over the rest of nature. Its practical foundation, however, is in anti-imperialist politics.

D&S: A few months back the senior science advisor to the British government claimed that he would "lose credibility" with the very government that—with much fanfare—commissioned his group's study if he insisted that the government commit itself to acknowledging its policy implications. Is this emblematic of the politics of climate change worldwide?

JK: Unfortunately, yes. There are of course even more lurid stories that came out of the Bush administration, where climate officials circulated in and out of Exxon-Mobil, and reputable scientists were routinely threatened and punished for speaking the truth about climate change.

There is a basic lesson to be learned: The ecological crisis poses a bigger threat to humanity than fascism. During World War II, in Britain and the United States, the ruling classes and the state collaborated in the biggest mobilization in human history to defeat the Axis. In that case the capitalists could see that a degree of suspension of the normal operations of the market, as through planning, rationing, price controls, etc., would gain them the prized control over the global economy once the war crisis was over; from another angle, they could see their way clear of the seemingly intractable depression that had haunted the 1930s.

In this case, resolution of climate change (not to mention the other features of ecological crisis) will require such deep and permanent cuts in the processes of accumulation as to bring the capitalist era to a close. For example, a young economist, Minqi Li, has recently demonstrated ["Climate Change, Limits to Growth, and the Imperative for Socialism," *Monthly Review*, July/August 2008] that all scenarios that hold down global warming below the threshold of positive feedback loops that accelerate climate change will require sustained contractions in world domestic product—in other words, an end to "growth," which means the end of capitalism. The big bourgeoisie knows this, which is why they act irresponsibly, typically sacrificing the future to the accumulation of wealth. If they behaved differently, they wouldn't have control over accumulation, and others would step forward to take control. As Marx wrote, the capitalist is the personification of capital.

D&S: What about the coverage of the issue in the media? More of the same?

JK: Absolutely the same principle holds for the corporate media, which have during the neoliberal era become absorbed into ever-greater conglomerations of capital. This has necessarily stifled the independent voices of the press, as we see in reporting of political races, the war in Iraq, and much else. Here, once more, the context is a threat to the capitalist system itself, and therefore the behavior is more extreme. Watch the Weather Channel or the robotic weather correspondents on news programs. Will they ever, in reporting the increasingly bizarre weather patterns that accompany climate change, suggest that these correspond to an ever-gathering crisis, much less suggest that there might be a structural dynamic driving that crisis?

Virtually every sane adult (and many more children than one would suspect) knows that something very fishy is going on in the sphere of climate. People tend to be understandably worried about this. Imagine what a threat to the system would result if they became at all enlightened, which is to say, able to recognize just how profound is the threat to their future and even more, to the future of their children—and also that there is a coherent explanation as to why this is happening, one implicating the very centers of capitalist power.

To secure capital's rule, it is necessary to keep people in the dark, or to be more exact, confused, distracted, and vaguely reassured. The media tends, therefore, to meet people halfway, then move them in the wrong direction. False prophets like Al Gore are praised for calling attention to the threat posed by the carbon economy, and the fact that Gore does not attend to the role played by the accumulation of capital is never brought forward. At the same time, the corporate image machine is geared up for greenwashing.

Unhappily, the job of mass deception is relatively easy, since with the stakes so high and given the inherent complexities and level of fear, it takes only a little uncertainty to slow down necessary action. The media system is very effective in doing this.

D&S: What about carbon trading/taxes, the switch to renewables, and nuclear power? Can they help even in the short term?

JK: There is a simple and effective touchstone for evaluating proposed solutions to the climate change crisis: do not look at the technical details but at the class forces in play, and always act so as to weaken the forces of capital. From this standpoint, some schemes are doomed from their inception, while the fate of others depends on the politics of their implementation.

In the first category belongs emissions trading, including the Kyoto Protocols and their so-called "Clean Development Mechanisms" in which projects in the Global South are used, like Papal indulgences, to permit the industrial North to keep putting CO_2 into the atmosphere. This sounds odd, and it is. To be blunt: Kyoto is set up to fail, except from the standpoint of a "success" that is also a failure, namely, the making of money from the licensing of pollution credits (because such money becomes capital, which must be invested to make more capital, which is to say, made to enter a fresh cycle of throwing carbon into the atmosphere). What dooms Kyoto is transparently that of being the scheme of climate control entrusted to capital. I am not sure whether capitalists know consciously that an effective program of containing climate change will bring down their system, but they certainly act on this basis.

(When I refer to "Kyoto," I follow a common practice of including both the formal documents and the mass of practices undertaken in their wake. The written protocol is vague about a lot of details and implications. However, the total regime signified by Kyoto is one in which the actors are exclusively allied with capital. Hence everything is interpreted to create credits rather than taxes and to allow these to become subject to new forms of wealth generation through speculation. The architects of the Kyoto Protocols rationalized this as necessary to induce capitalists to get on board. They have done so—on a vessel headed toward the rocks.)

Carbon taxes belong to the second category. In principle they have the potential to reduce carbon emissions. In practice, this depends on how they are written, who is made to pay, and who stands behind them. As is pretty much the case for all kinds of taxation, politics are the decisive factor.

Alternative energy is an absolute necessity, and also a political football. The reader had better disabuse her or himself of the notion that nuclear power will solve this crisis, despite all the cheerleading for it. Intractably dangerous, enormously destructive, and expensive to build and operate, nuclear power is also basically inadequate. An MIT report from 2003 [S. Ansolabehere et al., "The Future of Nuclear Power," Massachusetts Institute of Technology, July 2003] says that 1,000 to 1,500 new 1,000-megawatt reactors would have to be built by 2050 just to displace 15–25% of the expected growth in carbon emissions from electricity generation over that time.

Similar considerations hold for genuinely renewable energies like solar, wind, geothermal, tidal, etc., despite their clear superiority from an ecological perspective. The point deserves the utmost emphasis: there is no technological or administrative fix for the ecological crisis. An effective resolution requires social transformation, one overriding criterion of which must be to keep carbon in the ground in the first place, and whose overall goals include reducing the burden of society on nature and promoting the healing and restoration of damaged ecosystems.

This requires radically anti-capitalist ecopolitics, some goals of which in the case of climate would be:

• solidarity with popular struggles to block the extraction of carbon and uranium; these occur worldwide, from Nigeria to Ecuador to Australia to California, and they need to be coordinated as well as extended;

• free and universal public transportation (just like schools and health care);

• nationalization of the oil, coal, and gas industries;

• total mobilization to force worthy climate protocols in Copenhagen in December 2009, by direct action if necessary—as is almost certainly going to be the case. This may require as many as a million people in the streets.

These measures can be seen as the prefiguration of the World Social Forum movement's slogan, "Another world is possible."

D&S: How can we deal with other environmental issues—nanotechnology, and pollution of the oceans and of space, for example—when all our efforts would seem to have to be focused on climate change?

JK: We need the notion of an ecological crisis to grasp that there are a number of ecosystemic crises, each of which can wreak major havoc and all of which are interrelated and share the same susceptibility to the accumulative pressure of capital. This is why, by the way, it is better to think in terms of ecology than environment, since the notion of an environment does not carry an assumption that its parts are interrelated. Within an ecological way of looking at things, things are differentiated but internally related. The climate crisis is one cause of the increasingly grave and lethal water crisis, just as terrestrial water flows shape climate. The same goes for increasing food crises, where the diversion of crops for biofuel production is causing incipient famine, while biotechnology becomes a potentially deadly instrument of capital by recklessly interfering with the evolved checks and balances by means of which nature introduces a degree of stability and equilibrium.

The ecological perspective requires that we see ourselves as part of nature, including as organic bodies subject to disease. Pandemics are themselves ecological events, co-determined by pollution-induced immune system disturbances, and increasingly likely. This perspective demands a complete rethinking of human existence. It cannot be grasped by a purely economic analysis.

D&S: What if a socialist movement becomes viable—perhaps due in part to the social and economic breakdown that would inevitably accompany the rapid climate change some are forecasting only a few decades hence—and takes power only to find itself unable to meet basic needs due to the effects of climate change?

JK: Today, any viable socialist movement has to be ecologically rooted, or else it is irrelevant. I would define ecosocialism as the movement toward a society of freely associated labor animated by ecocentric values, that is, by an ethic that foregrounds the healing of nature. In contrast to earlier socialisms, which often sought to perfect capitalism while redistributing the social product, ecosocialism advances the notion of limits on growth, not as a restriction upon life but as the flourishing of ecosystems in a state of balance and vibrant evolution.

Any actual socialist movement that comes to a degree of power in the interim would obviously be only a partial realization of this goal. There is no use in lamenting this prospect. One simply does the best one can and accepts the result stoically. Of course a degree of coercion would be required, especially of residual capitalist class forces. At some point, for example, the government will just have to decree strict rationing, or redirect production by fiat, without letting "market forces" do it. This is what happened in the World Wars, and the ecological crisis is their equivalent in terms of emergency. That's what states are for, and in any predictable scenario short of complete chaos, we will not be able to immediately dispense with state power. Everything here depends on how deeply ecosocialist principles have been internalized, that is, on how democratic/nonviolent means and ends have been integrated.

Rosa Luxemburg said a century ago that the real choice was between "socialism and barbarism." This remains the choice, except that socialism has become ecosocialism; while barbarism now comes into focus as ecocatastrophe, fascism, and endless war, with the nuclear option stronger than ever. That is simply the history into which we have been thrown, and we have no option except to make the best of it. ❏

Chapter 9

THE POLITICAL ECONOMY OF WAR AND IMPERIALISM

Article 9.1

WHY THE EMPEROR HAS NO CLOTHES
America's Spiraling External Debt and the Decline of the U.S. Dollar

BY ANDRE GUNDER FRANK

January 2005 — Centre for Research on Globalisation

Uncle Sam has reneged and defaulted on up to 40% of its trillion-dollar foreign debt, and nobody has said a word except for a line in *The Economist*. In plain English, that means Uncle Sam runs a worldwide confidence racket with his self-made dollar based on the confidence that he has elicited and received from others around the world, and he is also a deadbeat in that he does not honor and return the money he has received.

How much of our dollar stake we have lost depends on how much we originally paid for it. Uncle Sam let his dollar fall, or rather through his deliberate political economic policies drove it down, by 40%, from 80 cents to the euro to 133 cents. The dollar is down by a similar factor against the yen, yuan, and other currencies. And it is still declining, indeed is apt to plummet altogether.

True, as the dollar has declined, so has the real value that foreigners pay to service their debt to Uncle Sam. But that works only if they can themselves earn in currencies that have increased in value against the dollar. Otherwise, foreigners earn and pay in the same devalued dollars, and even then with some loss from devaluation between the time they got their dollars and the time they repay them to Uncle Sam.

Uncle Sam's debt to the rest of the world already amounts to more than a third of his annual domestic production and is still growing. That alone already makes his debt economically and politically never repayable, even if he wanted to, which he does not. Uncle Sam's domestic, e.g. credit-card, debt is almost 100% of gross domestic product (GDP) and consumption, including that from China. Uncle Sam's federal debt is now $7.5 trillion, of which all but $1 trillion was built up in the past three decades, the last $2 trillion in the past eight years, and the last $1 trillion in the past two years. Alas, that costs more than $300 billion a year in interest, compared with, for example, the $15 billion spent annually on the National Aeronautics and Space Administration (NASA). But no worries: Congress just raised the debt ceiling to $8.2 trillion. To help us visualize, $1 trillion tightly packed up in $1,000 bills would create a pile 100km high.

But nearly half is owed to foreigners. All Uncle Sam's debt, including private household consumer credit-card, mortgage debt, etc., of about $10 trillion, plus corporate and financial, with options, derivatives and the like, and state and local government debt comes to an unvisualizable, indeed unimaginable, $37 trillion, which is nearly four times Uncle Sam's GDP. Only some of that can be managed domestically, but with dangerous limitations for Uncle Sam noted below. That is only one reason I want you to meet Uncle Sam, the deadbeat confidence man, who may remind you of the film *Meet Joe Black*; for as we get to know him better below, we will find that he is also a Shylock, and a corrupt one at that.

The United States is the world's most privileged nation for having the monopoly privilege of printing the world's reserve currency at will and at a cost of nothing but the paper and ink it is printed on. Additionally, his is also the only country whose "foreign" debt is mostly denominated in his own world-currency dollars that he can print at will; while most foreigners' debt is also denominated in the same dollar, but they have to buy it from Uncle Sam with their own currency and real goods. So he simply pays the Chinese and others in essence with these dollars that have no real worth beyond their paper and ink. So especially poor China gives away for nothing at all to rich Uncle Sam hundreds of billions of dollars' worth of real goods produced at home and consumed by Uncle Sam. Then China turns around and trades these same paper dollar bills in for more of Uncle Sam's paper called Treasury Certificate bonds, which are even more worthless, except that they pay a percent of interest.

In an earlier essay, I argued that Uncle Sam's power rests on two pillars only, the paper dollar and the Pentagon. Each supports the other, but the vulnerability of each is also an Achilles' heel that threatens the viability of the other. Since then, Iraq, not to mention Afghanistan, has shown confidence in the Pentagon not to be what it was cracked up to be; and with the in-part-consequent decline in the dollar, so has confidence in it and Uncle Sam's ability to use it to finance his Pentagon's foreign adventures. So far relations with other countries, in particular with China, still favor Uncle Sam, but they also help maintain an image that is deceptive. Consider the following:

> A $2 toy leaving a U.S.-owned factory in China is a $3 shipment arriving at San Diego. By the time a U.S. consumer buys it for $10 at Wal-Mart, the U.S. economy registers $10 in final sales, less $3 import cost, for a $7 addition to the U.S. GDP.

Moreover, ever-clever Uncle Sam has arranged matters so as to earn 9% from his economic and financial holdings abroad, while foreigners earn only 3% on theirs, and among them on their Treasury Certificates only 1% real return. Note that this difference of 6 percentage points is already double what Uncle Sam pays out, and his total 9% take is triple the 3% he gives back. Therefore, although foreign holdings and Uncle Sam's are now about equal, Uncle Sam is still the big net interested winner, just like any Shylock, but no other ever did so grand a business.

But Uncle Sam also earns quite well, thank you, from other holdings abroad, e.g. from service payments by mostly poor foreign debtors. For from his direct investments in foreign property alone, Uncle Sam's profits now equal 50%, and including his receipts from other holdings abroad now are a full 100% of profits derived from all of his own domestic activities combined. These foreign receipts add more than 4% to Uncle Sam's national domestic product.

The productivity hype of president Bill Clinton's "new economy" in the 1990s was limited to computers and information technology (IT), and even that proved to be a sham when the dot-com bubble burst. Also, not only the apparent increase in "profits" but also that of "productivity" were, at the bottom, on the backs of shop-floor, office and sales-floor workers working harder and longer hours and, at the top, the result of innovative accounting shams by Enron and the like. Such factors still compensate for and permit much of Uncle Sam's $600-billion-and-still-rising trade deficit from excess home consumption over what he himself produces. That is what has resulted in the multi-trillion-dollar debt. Exactly how large that debt is Uncle Sam is reluctant to reveal, but what is sure is that it is by far the world's largest, even as net debt to foreigners, after their debt to him is deducted.

How Has All This Come About?

The simple answer is that Uncle Sam, who is increasingly hooked on consumption, not to mention harder drugs, saves no more than 0.2% of his own income. The Federal Reserve's guru and now you see it, now you don't doctor of magic, Alan Greenspan, recently observed that this is so because the richest 20% of Americans, who are the only ones who do save, have reduced their savings to 2%. Yet even these measly savings (other, poorer countries save and even invest 20%, 30%, even 40% of their incomes) are more than counterbalanced by the 6% deficit spending of the government. That is what brings the average saving rate to 0.2%. To maintain that $400-plus-billion budget deficit (more than 3% of national domestic product), which is really more the $600 billion if we count, as we should, the more than $200 billion Uncle Sam "borrows" from the temporary surplus in his own Federal Social Security fund, which he is also bankrupting.

So with this $600-billion-plus budget deficit and the above-mentioned related $600-billion-plus deficit, rich Uncle Sam, and primarily his highest earners and biggest consumers, as well as of course the Big Uncle himself, live off the fat of the rest of the world's land. Uncle Sam absorbs the savings of others who themselves are often much poorer, particularly when their central banks put many of their reserves in world-currency dollars and hence into the hands of Uncle Sam and some also in dollars at home. Their private investors send dollars to or buy dollar assets on Wall Street, all with the confidence that they are putting their wherewithal in the world's safest haven (and that, of course, is part of the above-mentioned confidence racket). From the central banks alone, we are looking at yearly sums of more than $100 billion from Europe, more than $100 billion from poor China, $140 billion from super-saver Japan, and many 10s of billions from many others around the globe, including the Third World. But in addition, Uncle Sam obliges them, through the good offices of their own states, to send their thus literally forced savings to Uncle Sam as well in the form of their "service" of their predominantly dollar debt to him.

His treasury secretary and his International Monetary Fund (IMF) handmaiden blithely continue to strut around the world insisting that the Third- and ex-Second, now also Third-World countries of course continue to service their foreign debts, especially to him. No matter that with interest rates multiplied several times over by Uncle Sam himself after the Fed's Paul Volcker's coup in October 1979, most have already paid off their original borrowings three to five times over. For to pay at all at interest rates that Volcker boosted to 20%, they had to borrow still more at still higher rates until thereby their outstanding foreign debt doubled and tripled, not to mention their domestic debt from which part of the foreign payments were raised, particularly in Brazil. Privatization is the name of the game there and elsewhere, except for the debt. The debt was socialized after it had been incurred mostly by private business, but only the state had enough power to squeeze the greatest bulk of back payments out of the hides of its poor and middle-class people and transfer them as "invisible service payments" to Uncle Sam.

When Mexicans were told to tighten their belts still further, they answered that they couldn't because they had already had to eat their belts. Only Argentina and for a while Russia declared an effective moratorium on debt "service," and that only after political economic policies had destroyed their societies, thanks to Uncle Sam's advisers and his IMF strong arm. Since then, Uncle Sam himself has been blithely defaulting on his own foreign debt, as he already had several times before in the 19th century.

One piece of practical advice came from the premier military strategist Carl von Clausewitz: make the lands you conquer pay for their own conquest and administration. That is of course exactly what Britain did in and with India through the infamous "Home Charges" remitted to London in payment for Britain administering India, which even the British themselves recognized as "tribute" and responsible for much of "The Drain" from India to Britain. How much more efficient yet to let foreign countries' own states administer themselves but by rules set and imposed by Uncle Sam's IMF and then effect a drain of debt service anyway. Actually, the British therein also set the 19th-century precedent of relying on the "imperialism of free trade" with "independent" states as far and as long as possible, using gunboat diplomacy to make it work (which Uncle Sam had already learned to copy by early in the 20th century); and if that was not enough, simply to invade, and if necessary to occupy—and then rely on the Clausewitz rule.

After I wrote the above, I received by e-mail an excerpt from the Democracy Now! website, titled "Confessions of an Economic Hit Man: How the U.S. Uses Globalization to Cheat Poor Countries Out of Trillions":

> We speak with John Perkins, a former respected member of the international banking community. In his book Confessions of an Economic Hit Man he describes how as a highly paid professional, he helped the U.S. cheat poor countries around the globe out of trillions of dollars by lending them more money than they could possibly repay and then take over their economies ...

> **JOHN PERKINS:** Basically what we were trained to do and what our job is to do is to build up the American empire. To bring—to create situations where as many resources as possible flow into this country, to our corporations, and our government, and in fact we've been very successful. We've built the largest empire in the history of the world ... primarily through economic manipulation, through cheating, through fraud, through seducing people into our way of life, through the economic hit men. I was very much a part of that ... I was initially recruited while I was in business school back in the late '60s by the National Security Agency, the nation's largest and least understood spy organization ... and then [it] send[s] us to work for private consulting companies, engineering firms, construction companies, so that if we were caught, there would be no connection with the government ...

> I became its chief economist. I ended up having 50 people working for me. But my real job was deal-making. It was giving loans to other countries, huge loans, much bigger than they could possibly repay. One of the conditions of the loan— let's say a $1 billion to a country like Indonesia or Ecuador—and this country would then have to give 90% of that loan back to a U.S. company, or U.S. companies ... a Halliburton or a Bechtel ... A country today like Ecuador owes over 50% of its national budget just to pay down its debt. And it really can't do it. So we literally have them over a barrel. So when we want more oil, we go to Ecuador and say, "Look, you're not able to repay your debts, therefore give your oil companies your Amazon rain [forests], which are filled with oil." And today we're going in and destroying Amazonian rain forests, forcing Ecuador to give them to us because they've accumulated all this debt ... [We work] very, very closely with the World Bank. The World Bank provides most of the money that's used by economic hit men, it and the IMF.

Last but not least, oil producers also put their savings in Uncle Sam. With the "shock" of oil that restored its real price after the dollar valuation had fallen in 1973, ever-cleverer-by-half Henry Kissinger made a deal with the world's largest oil exporter, Saudi Arabia, that it would continue to price oil in dollars, and these earnings would be deposited with Uncle Sam and partly compensated by military hardware. That deal de facto extended to all of the Organization of Petroleum Exporting Countries (OPEC) and still stands, except that before the war against Iraq that country suddenly opted out by switching to pricing its oil in euros, and Iran threatened do the same. North Korea, the third member of the "axis of evil", has no oil but trades entirely in euros. (Venezuela is a major oil supplier to Uncle Sam and also supplies some at preferential rates as non-dollar trade swaps to poor countries such as Cuba. So Uncle Sam sponsored and financed military commandos from its Plan Colombia next door, promoted an illegal coup and, when that failed, pushed a referendum in his attempt at yet another "regime change"; and now along with Brazil all three are being baptized as yet another "axis of evil").

After writing this, I found that the good (hit) man Mr. Perkins was in Saudi Arabia too:

> Yes, it was a fascinating time. I remember well ... the Treasury Department hired me and a few other economic hit men. We went to Saudi Arabia ... And we worked out this deal whereby the Royal House of Saud agreed to send most of their petrodollars back to the United States and invest them in U.S. government securities. The Treasury Department would use the interest from these securities to hire U.S. companies to build Saudi Arabia—new cities, new infrastructure—which we've done. And the House of Saud would agree to maintain the price of oil within acceptable limits to us, which they've done all of these years, and we would agree to keep the House of Saud in power as long as they did this, which we've done, which is one of the reasons we went to war with Iraq in the first place. And in Iraq we tried to implement the same policy that was so successful in Saudi Arabia, but Saddam Hussein didn't buy. When the economic hit men fail in this scenario, the next step is what we call the jackals. Jackals are CIA-sanctioned people that come in and try to foment a coup or revolution. If that doesn't work, they perform assassinations. Or try to. In the case of Iraq, they weren't able to get through to Saddam Hussein. He had—his bodyguards were too good. He had doubles. They couldn't get through to him. So the third line of defense, if the economic hit men and the jackals fail, the next line of defense is our young men and women, who are sent in to die and kill, which is what we've obviously done in Iraq.

To return to the main issue and call a spade a huge spade, all of the above is part and parcel of the world's biggest-ever Ponzi-scheme confidence racket. Like all others, its most essential characteristic is that it can only continue to pay off dollars and be maintained at the top as long as it continues to receive new dollars at the bottom, voluntarily through confidence if possible and by force if not. (Of course, the Clausewitz formula result in the poorest paying the most, since they are also the most defenseless: so that the ones sitting on/above them pass much of the cost and pain down to them.)

What If Confidence in the Dollar Runs Out?

Things are already getting shakier in the House of Uncle Sam. The declining dollar reduces the necessary dollar inflows, so Greenspan needs to raise interest rates to maintain some attraction for the foreign dollars he needs to fill the trade gap. As a quid pro quo for being reappointed by President George W Bush, he promised to do that only after the election. That time has now arrived, but doing so threatens to collapse the housing bubble that was built on low interest and mortgage—and re-mortgage—rates.

But it is in their house values that most Americans have their savings, if they have any at all. They and this imaginary wealth effect supported over-consumption and the nearly as-high-as-GDP household debt, and a collapse of the housing price bubble with increased interest and mortgage rates would not only drastically undercut house prices, it would thereby have a domino effect on their owners' enormous second and third re-mortgages and credit-card and other debt, their consumption, corporate debt and profit, and investment. In fact, these factors would be enough to plummet Uncle Sam into a deep recession, if not depression, and another Big Bear deflation on stock and de facto on other prices, rendering debt service even more onerous.

Still lower real U.S. investment would reduce its industrial productivity and competitiveness even more—probably to a degree lower than can compensated for by further devaluing the dollar and making U.S. exports cheaper, as is the confident hope of many, probably including the good Doctor. Until now, the apparent inflation of prices abroad in rubles and pesos and their consequent devaluations have been a de facto deflation in terms of the dollar world currency. Uncle Sam then printed dollars to buy up at bargain-basement fire-sale prices natural resources in Russia (whose economy was then run on $100 bills), and companies and even banks, as in South Korea. True, now Greenspan and Uncle Sam are trying again to get other central banks to raise their own interest rates and otherwise plunge their own people into even deeper depression.

So, far beyond Osama bin Laden, al-Qaeda and all the terrorists put together, the greatest real-world threat to Uncle Sam is that the inflow of dollars dries up. For instance, foreign central banks and private investors (it is said that "overseas Chinese" have a tidy trillion dollars) could any day decide to place more of their money elsewhere than in the declining dollar and abandon poor ol' Uncle Sam to his destiny. China could double its per capita income very quickly if it made real investments at home instead of financial ones with Uncle Sam. Central banks, European and others, can now put their reserves in (rising!) euros or even soon-to-be-revalued Chinese yuan. Not so far down the road, there may be an East Asian currency, eg a basket first of ASEAN + 3 (China, Japan, South Korea)—and then + 4 (India). While India's total exports in the past five years rose by 73%, those to the Association of Southeast Asian Nations (ASEAN) rose at double that rate and sixfold to China. India has become an ASEAN summit partner, and its ambitions stretch still further to an economic zone stretching from India to Japan. Not for nothing, in the 1997 East Asian currency and then full economic crisis, Uncle Sam strong-armed Japan not to start a proposed East Asian currency fund that would have prevented at least the worst of the crisis. Uncle Sam then benefited from it by buying devalued East Asian currencies and using them to buy up East Asian real resources, and in South Korea also banks, at bargain-basement reduced-price fire sales. But now, China is already taking steps toward such an arrangement, only on a much grander financial and now also economic scale.

A day after writing the above, I read in *The Economist* (December 11-17, 2004) a report on the previous week's summit meeting of ASEAN + 3 in Malaysia. That country's prime minister announced that this summit should lay the groundwork for an East Asian Community (EAC) that "should build a free-trade area, cooperate on finance, and sign a security pact ... that would transform East Asia into a cohesive economic block ... In fact, some of these schemes are already in motion ... China, as the region's pre-eminent economic and military power, will doubtless dominate ... and host the second East Asia Summit." The report went on to recall that in 1990, Uncle Sam shot down a similar initiative for fear of losing influence in the region. Now it is a case of "Yankee Stay Home."

Or what if, long before that comes to pass, exporters of oil simply cease to price it in ever-devaluing dollars, and instead make a mint by switching to the rising euro and/or a basket of East Asian currencies? Since selling oil for falling dollars instead of rising euros is evidently bad business, the world's largest oil exporters in Russia and OPEC have been considering doing just that. In the meantime, they have only raised the dollar price of oil, so that in euro terms it has remained approximately stable since 2000. So far, many oil exporters and others still place their increased amount of dollars with Uncle Sam, even though he now offers an ever less attractive and less safe haven, but Russia is now buying more euros with some of its dollars.

So also many countries' central banks have begun to put ever more of their reserves into the euro and currencies other than Uncle Sam's dollar. Now even the Central Bank of China, the greatest friend of Uncle Sam in need, has begun to buy some euros. China itself has also begun to use some of its dollars—as long as they are still accepted by them—to buy real goods from other Asians and thousands of tons of iron ore and steel from Brazil, etc. (Brazil's president recently took a huge business delegation to China, and a Chinese one just went to Argentina. They are going after South African minerals too.)

So what will happen to the rich on top of Uncle Sam's Ponzi scheme when the confidence of poorer central banks and oil exporters in the middle runs out, and the more destitute around the world, confident or not, can no longer make their in-payments at the bottom? The Uncle Sam Ponzi Scheme Confidence Racket would—or will?—come crashing down, like all other such schemes before, only this time with a worldwide bang. It would cut the present U.S. consumer demand down to realistic size and hurt many exporters and producers elsewhere in the world. In fact, it may involve a wholesale fundamental reorganization of the world political economy now run by Uncle Sam.

Uncle Sam's Paper Dollar Tiger Poses A Mad Geo-Political Catch 22

Of course, crashing the dollar would also in one fell swoop wipe out, that is default, the Uncle Sam debt altogether. Thereby, it would simultaneously also make all foreigners and rich Americans lose the whole of their dollar asset shirt. They are still desperately trying to save as much of it as possible by not going for the crash, that is for broke. That is, they are trying to protect the remainder of their dollar investment shirt by keeping their dollar life sustaining pump going. The whole business of maintaining the Uncle Sam Ponzi Scheme poses the world's biggest and craziest Catch-22 since MAD, and it is just about as mad.

This dissolution of the Uncle Sam Ponzi Scheme will be costly and the greatest costs will as usual probably be dumped on the poorest who are least able to bear these costs, but who are also least able to protect themselves from being forced to do so. And the historically necessary transition out from under the Uncle Sam run doughnut world can bring the entire world into the deepest depression ever. Only East Asia is in a relatively good position to save itself from being pulled—or pushed—to the bottom, but even then also after paying a high cost for this transition—toward itself!

However, the world is facing an even MADer global geo-political and military Catch 22. It remains the great unknown and perhaps unknowable. How will Uncle Sam react as a Paper [money] Tiger that is wounded by a crash of the Ponzi Scheme Confidence Racket from which he and millions of un-knowing Uncle Sammies have lived the good life? To compensate for less bread and civil rights but more "Patriotic" acts at home, a more chauvinist Uncle Sam can provide a World War III circus abroad. A crash of the dollar will pull the financial rug out from under, and discourage his foreign victims from continuing to pay for new Pentagon adventures abroad. But some more wars may still be possible with the weapons he would still have and some more Military Keynesian government deficit spending at home. That could well—nay horribly—be the cost to the world of the current policies to "defend Freedom and Civilization." The Super Catch 22 is that almost nobody other than Osama bin Laden wants to run that risk.

Recall how much the transition to Uncle Sam cost: a 30 Year War from 1914 to 1945 with the intervening second Great Depression in a century that cost 100 million lives lost to war, more than in all previous world history combined, not to mention the literally [hundreds?] of millions who suffered and died from unnecessary starvation and disease. Or that the previous transition to the British Major Bull cost the Napoleonic Wars, the Great Depression of 1873-95, colonialism and semi-colonialism and their human costs. The latter coincided with the most pronounced El Niño climatic changes in two centuries, which ravaged Indians, Chinese, and many others with famines. But these were in turn magnified by the Imperial Colonial powers who used them in their own interests, e.g. increased export of wheat from India especially during years of famine.

The parallels with today, including even taking advantage of renewed El Niños a century later, are too horrifying and guilt generating for hardly anybody to make. They include Uncle Sam's IMF imposed "structural adjustment" that obliges Mexican peasants to have already eaten the belt that the IMF wants them to tighten still further. Three million dead and still counting in Rwanda and Burundi, and then some in neighbouring Congo, came after IMF imposed strictures and the cancellation primarily by Uncle Sam of the Coffee Agreement that had sustained its price for these producers. And now—nay since the CIA murder of Lumumba and the elevation of Kosavubu in Katanga in 1961, indeed since the King of Belgium's private reserve of the Congo in the 19th century, we get the scramble for and production and sale there of gold for Uncle Sam's Fort Knox, and now also titanium so that we can communicate by mobile cell phone, diamonds for ever, and so on.

Uncle Sam also took advantage of yet another strong El Niño event that ravaged South East Asia, and especially Indonesia, simultaneously with the post 1997 financial crisis that Uncle Sam deliberately parlayed into an economic depression. It was so great that it swept out of office President Suharto whom Uncle Sam had installed there thirty years earlier with his CIA coup against the popular father of Indonesian independence, Sukarno. That had cost at least half a million but also an estimated up to one million lives that Suhartu took directly plus the poverty generated by the infamous "Berkeley Mafia" that he installed to run the Indonesian economy into the ground.

The parallels with the past also include environmental degradation, and the shift of ecological damage from the rich who generate it to the poor Third World who bears its greatest burden. And of course we should not forget World War III [the third after the second *and* fought in the Third World] that Daddy Bush began against Iraq in 1991

Yet there are also others in the world who do not (yet?) feel all that caught up in the Catch 22. Calculatedly just before this year's 2004 Uncle Sam election, one of them said so out loud in a video broadcast to the world. It seems to have been least publicly noted by its principal addressee Uncle Sam, who should have been the most interested party: For it was none other than bin Laden himself who announced that he is "going to bankrupt the Uncle Sam!" In view of the deliberate Uncle Sam blindness to the shakiness of his real world foundation abroad, so massive a collapse abroad may not be more difficult to arrange than it was to topple its Twin Tower symbol at home. ❑

Sources: "Blaming 'Undervalued' Yuan Wins Votes," Asia Times Online, February 26, 2004; "Yankee Stay Home," *The Economist*, December 11-17, 2004; Gerard Dumenil and Dominique Levy, "The Economics of Uncle Sam Imperialism at the Turn of the 21st Century" *Review of International Political Economy*, October, 2004.

Article 9.2

U.S. IMPERIALISM, MILITARISM, AND THE U.S. LABOR UNIONS

BY BILL FLETCHER, JR.

March 2005—WorkingUSA

Organized labor in the United States has had difficulty interacting with the global justice movement. Not only are they different labor-market sectors with different traditions, but more importantly they have no strategic agreement on the nature of the enemy. While there are many critical remarks one can make about the global justice movement, this article focuses on the challenges facing organized labor in addressing not simply the global justice movement, but also the issue of global justice as such by building international working-class solidarity.

To its credit, organized labor in the United States, beginning with the demonstrations against the World Trade Organization (WTO) in Seattle in 1999, paid greater attention to what can broadly be defined as global justice than it had in the past. The specific focus, however, was on trade-related issues and their impact on the United States. The growing interest in the global justice movement—here defined as those forces united in their opposition to neoliberal globalization—stumbled when the American Federation of Labor-Congress of Industrial Organizations (AFL-CIO) chose to mount a campaign against China's inclusion in the WTO.

This campaign was a mistake in many ways, not the least of which is that the focus of the campaign was, by definition, on China as the problem. By any objective measure, China is not the principal problem in terms of global economic development. The problem is the WTO, the trade regime of which it is a part, and the manner in which global capitalism is restructuring itself. The current conditions of restructuring are actually the essence of what activists, scholars, and progressive labor leaders call "globalization," and are precisely the issue which U.S. organized labor had difficulty grasping. In fact, in the days leading up to the Seattle demonstrations, the notion of challenging the existence and *raison d'être* of the WTO was ridiculed by some in the AFL-CIO who held that because the international community needs a mechanism for regulating trade, the WTO is what is on the table, driving the global agenda, and therefore, we must reform it to serve the interests of working people.

That the WTO was a Clinton-supported project presented apparent difficulties for many union leaders, fearing that open opposition to the WTO would mean undercutting labor's alleged friend in the White House. Few people wanted to acknowledge that the WTO was as rotten in its essence as raw meat sitting in the hot sun. At the same time and in a more progressive direction, in 2000 the AFL-CIO and some of its affiliates became increasingly interested in educating their members to some of the issues of global justice.

Educating the American Working Class

Elements of what had been called the "Common Sense Economics Education Program" (originated in 1997) were utilized to create a union member-oriented "global fairness" education effort. There were two problems that emerged. First, as with Common Sense Economics, there was and remains a faltering commitment both within the AFL-CIO and most of its affiliates to developing a truly comprehensive educational program. This is something that haunts the U.S. trade union movement. The trade union movement often confuses *education* with *information provision* and does not realize what is necessary if we truly wish to interact with our members on the questions of ideas and analyses. Education is about critical reasoning skills, dialogue *plus* the addition of new information. It fundamentally concerns providing a frame of analysis in order for the "student" to look at an issue—or the world for that matter—and understand it in its complexities. An uneducated membership is a membership that cannot lead. It is a passive membership that will continue to view the union as a third-party institution, rather than its own organization.

The second problem with the program was that the conceptualization of global justice and global fairness by the trade union movement was somewhat restricted to concerning itself with the activities of multinational corporations and trade agreements. While this is certainly part of neoliberal globalization, it is not the whole story. This became much clearer in the aftermath of the September 11, 2001 terrorist attacks and the response of most of U.S. organized labor to them. The September 11, 2001 terrorist attacks were in part a right-wing response, by Muslim clerical fascists, to U.S.-led globalization. In a sweeping analysis of America's quest for dominance in the post-World War II period, Noam Chomsky argues that the U.S. "imperial grand strategy" is an effort to gain global hegemony as the world's only superpower. However, Chomsky notes, the American pursuit of global dominance at any cost leads to the decline of U.S. legitimacy throughout the world, while it threatens the future of human survival.

The U.S. trade union movement had carried out no work to discuss with its members the broader features of globalization, including the military aspect of it. There was limited internal discussion regarding the nature of the various forms of opposition to neoliberal globalization. While rank-and-file members might hear or learn something about organized labor protesting neoliberal governments, there was little discussion of more reactionary responses to neoliberal globalization both within the United States—for example, the Oklahoma City bombing and the right-wing militia movements at home—and clerical fascism and anti-immigrant xenophobia overseas.

War and the Erosion of Worker Rights

In the wake of Sept. 11, the U.S. trade union movement tended to revert to a "World War II paradigm"—to the policy of assuming that national unity could be built in response to the crisis. The World War II paradigm suggests that organized labor in the United States decided during World War II that the fight against fascism trumped virtually everything else, including worker rights in the United States. Thus, during World War II, leaders of organized labor generally accepted the no-strike pledge and wage and price controls.

There was national unity against fascism. Organized labor expected that at war's end, capital would depart from its regular assortment of attacks on the working class, including strike-breaking and union-busting. The extent to which capital retreated from its aggressive stance against labor is another question, but that image was driven very intensely into the minds and memories of leaders of organized labor, including those who were not even active at that time.

Following the Sept. 11 attacks, there seemed to be the expectation on the part of many union leaders that Bush would change his spots, recognize the importance of workers and unions, and refrain from his vehemently anti-worker/anti-union approach toward domestic issues. Things did not work out that way. Instead, the Bush administration chose to wage a war on two fronts: against Iraq and against the American working class. As JoAnn Wypijewski asserted in 2003: "For workers, there is always a war at home and a war abroad, and it is not enough—it will never be enough—to oppose one without the other."

The deeper problem, however, is that the U.S. trade union movement is and has been caught in a ferocious bind. This labor movement, over the last 120 years, has developed within the context of a capitalist country with imperial ambitions that have now translated into foreign policy adventures. The U.S. government has justified the rise in foreign interventions in the name of patriotism and the defense of American lives and property. With certain exceptions, the official trade union movement, as opposed to, for example, the Industrial Workers of the World (IWW) that emerged a century ago, tended to support U.S. foreign policy almost without question. Labor's historic support for U.S. war policy is an expression of what it believes to be its patriotic duty. Organized labor's unconditional support for U.S. intervention has proved ineffective in building a strong labor movement because this approach fails to recognize the connection between U.S. foreign policy and the actions and plans of U.S. corporations.

During the Cold War, support for U.S. foreign policy was again seen as a patriotic step within much of organized labor. Yet, with the various actions of the AFL-CIO in particular, but most of organized labor generally, the credibility of U.S. organized labor came to be questioned internationally. First the AFL, and then later the AFL-CIO either created pro-Cold War institutions to support the struggle against "communism" and the Left, or it collaborated with institutions set up or supported by the U.S. government that had the same purpose. Among the most infamous of such institutions was the American Institute for Free Labor Development (AIFLD), which oversaw AFL-CIO-backed trade unionism in Latin America. Similar institutions were also established that worked in Europe, Africa, and Asia.

The work of the AFL-CIO's foreign labor operations usually targeted left-led worker organizations, including through the establishment of rival worker organizations (including unions) that were well resourced. This work also went beyond traditional trade union activity. To the extent to which the AFL-CIO—and I am using this to refer to the officialdom of U.S. organized labor, as most unions supported the policies of the institution known as the AFL-CIO—supported or assisted in coups and disruptions. The AFL-CIO's mischief includes disruption in British Guiana in 1964, Vietnam in the 1960s and 1970s, Chile in 1973, and South Africa during the 1980s. The AFL-CIO's actions were seen around the world, not as an expression of the interests of the U.S. working class, but rather as an arm of the U.S. state, thus the notion of the AFL–*CIA*—a reference often heard in the global South when speaking of the "old days."

To summarize at least part of the problem: organized labor in the United States has refused to acknowledge, or in the worst cases has supported, the imperial ambitions of the U.S. government. Labor's foreign policy legacy has left an inability to identify a broad front against neoliberal globalization within its ranks and the working class as a whole. The residue of labor's past has dampened progressive sentiment and encouraged right-wing populism. Organized labor's inconsistent response to neoliberal globalization has produced a strategic paralysis within the labor movement to respond to the specifics of U.S. foreign policy that undermines workers.

Corporate Neoliberalism and Global Justice

Organized labor has been unable to speak with rank-and-file members about how to understand the connections between U.S. foreign policy and the growth of the multinational corporations. Labor's inconsistency has produced a faint response to the North American Free Trade Agreement (NAFTA), the WTO, and other neoliberal policies of both the Clinton and Bush administrations. Moreover, organized labor has not resolutely responded to U.S. war policies. Ultimately, U.S. foreign military intervention has cleared the ground—as if with a political daisy cutter—of all opposition to neoliberal globalization.

In order for the union movement to understand the question of global justice, organized labor must understand the problem of *empire*, or if one prefers, *imperial ambitions*. There is simply no way to avoid it, particularly in today's world. The reason? One, the American working class resides in a world where corporate/government connections are strengthening, and with them increased repression of progressive and democratic forces in the face of unfolding globalization.

The linkage between corporations and government, at first glance, seems to contradict neoliberal ideology, but that is largely because neoliberal ideology exists to obscure the reality. As evident during the Reagan administration—a time when the world came to understand the growth of neoliberalism—the government more openly served the interests of the corporations. This was through various mechanisms, including but not limited to privatization schemes, tax policies, the choice of personnel for elected government positions and administrative positions, and expansion of the scope of international trade agreements.

In the aftermath of the Cold War, American imperial ambitions have become more blatant as the United States attempts to lead or direct the reorganization of global capitalism. That reorganization is linked not only to trade deals, but also to changes in the production process, wealth polarization on a global scale, and, as noted, repression to enforce neoliberal globalization. Understood more broadly, globalization comes to be seen as the reorganization of capitalism, accomplished through trade agreements *as well as* military operations. U.S. foreign policy, then, is not a side note to globalization, but the instrument for spreading, strengthening, and enforcing neoliberal globalization. If organized labor continues to ignore neoliberal globalization in its entirety, including U.S. foreign policy, the result will continue to produce ineffective, if not outright bad strategy that harms working people in the United States and throughout the world.

The period after World War II has been characterized—in the North, Midwest, and West Coast—as having relatively stable union/business relations. To be sure, there were periods of militant strikes and other upsurges, but the record demonstrates that unions were largely accepted as part of the scene. Labor activist and critic Stan Weir demonstrates that workers have constantly engaged in rank-and-file action, in most cases against the practices of employers and business unions. Unions in the U.S. South and Southwest, of course, were never accepted, and contrast with this picture of labor/capital compromise that is now undermined. Nevertheless, labor unions played a major role in the Democratic Party at both the national and local level, although in general they functioned more like interest-group trade associations than representatives of a workers' movement. In the international realm, particularly during the height of the Cold War, organized labor in the United States was useful to the American government, and to U.S. capital as well, in opposing left-wing labor movements around the world. After all, the AFL-CIO had labor credentials.

Social peace on the basis of some level of a *modus vivendi* between capital and organized labor was needed not only in the United States, but also around the world. This largely reflected the demands of the post-World War II period and the Cold War. The immediate need for reconstruction in the aftermath of the war, and the prospect of competition with the then-Soviet Union, as well as the rise of domestic left-wing forces in various countries, have driven capital and its allies in government toward two simultaneous approaches. One, crush domestic dissent— including in the United States (such as the creation of "Red Clauses" that had to be inserted into union constitutions prohibiting "communists" from attaining or retaining union office, as well as the expulsion of unions representing more than one million workers from the Congress of Industrial Organizations)—via the mechanism of "anticommunism." Thus, opposition forces that seemed to push the limits on capitalist democracy were challenged as being allegedly subversive, and therefore subject to repression.

The second approach was one of accommodation with the official trade union movement, and to some extent, their cooptation into some sections of the state apparatus. This approach of semi-accommodation was not directed at the official trade union movement alone, but toward most of the working class. The aim was to win it away from any appeal of working-class radicalism. The drive toward some semblance of social peace was also advanced by sections of capital that recognized that trade unions were useful in terms of keeping other sections of capital "honest," so to speak, that is, keeping wages out of capitalist competition. That day is gone. We should have no illusions. The capital–working class compromise is in tatters. The union movement is as useless to capital and the U.S. state as a bicycle is to a fish, to borrow from an old feminist expression.

Here, however, is the challenge: when one has built a labor movement on the basis of an incorrect assessment of reality, and based on the provision of incomplete and often inaccurate information to its members and supporters, it is problematic to shift gears. How does one correct the inaccuracies? How does one explain ways to build new alliances, such as with the so-called "Teamsters and Turtles"? How does one explain that those once condemned overseas a decade or more ago must now be embraced, whereas those once supported have often turned out to be our staunchest opponents? How does one explain U.S. capital's unpatriotic stance in abandoning the American worker, and policies of naked aggression and implied genocide that this same U.S. capital encourages in U.S. foreign policy?

How does one respond to questions continuously raised during the delivery of the AFL-CIO's *Common Sense Economics* education program of the 1990s? Participants would respond very favorably to the trainings and to the workshops themselves, but they would inevitably ask the following: *"Can we get more for this?"* That is a great question, and one that an educator always wants to hear. They would also ask: *"Why did we not know this before?"* The answer to that latter question goes to the heart of the history and culture of organized labor in the United States.

U.S. Military Intervention and Working-Class Patriotism

What is needed within U.S. organized labor is an understanding of how other trade union movements outside of the United States (and other social movements more generally) understand the operations of U.S. foreign policy and its implications for workers on a global scale. This is a very difficult discussion because it runs up against the assumptions upon which the U.S. trade union movement has been built. It is an uncomfortable discussion because it also challenges the way organized labor thinks of itself and how labor thinks it is viewed overseas. Nevertheless, a discussion of labor's troubled relationship with U.S. foreign policy is a discussion that must take place, without which there will be no international solidarity.

The second point is that the union movement must fuse the discussion of global justice—with a critique of multinational corporations, the U.S. imperial state, and a critical examination of American foreign policy. Such a discussion is especially difficult because it forces an examination of the manner in which the conception of patriotism has been manipulated by both capital and political leaders to advance their unsavory business. Such a discussion also compels a reexamination of how labor has been so often seduced by appeals to patriotism.

Let us look, for instance, at the U.S. intervention in Iraq. The American people were sold a bill of goods. The allegations of weapons of mass destruction and imminent threats were fabrications, pure and simple, by the U.S. government's own admission. The desire to invade Iraq dates back at least to 1991 when differences emerged in the context of the Gulf War over whether the United States should take the war to Baghdad and overthrow Saddam Hussein. Those differences simmered, and some conservatives began shortly thereafter to envision the resolution of the Saddam Hussein question, so to speak. Iraq became a virtual obsession among conservative hawks that made their way to leadership positions in the George W. Bush White House.

Supporters of U.S. invasion of Iraq included individuals who went on to help form the Project for a New American Century, a conservative think-tank which advanced a proposal for a more aggressive U.S. foreign policy. The George W. Bush administration adopted this obsession with Iraq, and it has subsequently been revealed in testimony by Richard A. Clarke that immediately following Sept. 11, 2001, the search was on for an alleged Iraqi connection, even though intelligence sources demonstrated no evidence.

The U.S. Labor Movement and the Iraq War

Although the AFL-CIO raised questions about the war somewhat late in the game, once the war started the federation felt compelled to issue a statement supporting the troops, and by implication, supporting the war. The AFL-CIO statement implied that supporting the troops was identified with workers' patriotic duty. In a cover letter on March 20, 2003, John Sweeney, the AFL-CIO's president, said: "When our nation is at war I strongly believe that we need to come together in support of our troops on the front lines." In all fairness, it should be stated that Sweeney did criticize "President Bush's insistence on military action rather than further diplomatic efforts" and there were, in effect, two statements (see below). One was a cover letter, while the other was the official statement. The different tone reflects the struggle over the message, particularly given the politics of the Bush era. The contradictory tone of the AFL-CIO is reflected in the statement on March 20, 2003:

> History will judge whether the actions taken by the United States will be seen as just and necessary. And Americans will judge if the foreign policy of the Bush administration is one that keeps the United States more secure in a dangerous world. While our fellow citizens are in harms' way, we are united in support of them and their families.

Yet on the very same day, John Sweeney noted in his cover letter "On the War with Iraq" that:

> The AFL-CIO stands firmly behind our troops. These brave men and women are America's best. The Iraqi regime is a brutal dictatorship that is a threat to its neighbors and its own citizens. We support fully the goal of ridding Iraq of weapons of mass destruction. . . . Now that a decision has been made, we are unequivocal in our support of our country and America's men and women on the front lines as well as their families here at home.

For the Bush administration to suggest—and for the U.S. trade union movement to implicitly accept—that Americans in opposition to the war do not support the troops is the height of insult. The notion that opponents of the war should be silent because the troops have already been deployed is ludicrous.

Opponents of the U.S. military intervention in Iraq have supported the troops by stating that they should be brought home. The U.S.-led invasion of Iraq violated international law by launching an assault on a sovereign nation that demonstrated no evidence of presenting a threat to its neighbors, let alone to the United States. International law and precedent only recognizes the notion of preemptive strike when there is a provable, imminent military threat, which was not the case in Iraq. Instead, a sham case for aggression was established. To borrow from the terminology used by former Marine Corps general and two-time Medal of Honor winner, Smedley Butler, "the U.S. military thus is used as a gang by the powers-that-be." Yet the trade union movement has been all-too-cautious about calling things as they are. Can we look forward to the day when our movement will even entertain a discussion in which today's version of General Butler's warning is heard? Consider General Butler's own words from over 60 years ago:

> War is just a racket. A racket is best described, I believe, as something that is not what it seems to the majority of people. Only a small inside group knows what it is about. It is conducted for the benefit of the very few at the expense of the masses. . . . I helped make Mexico, especially Tampico, safe for American oil interests in 1914. I helped make Haiti and Cuba a decent place for the National City Bank boys to collect revenues in. I helped in the raping of half a dozen Central American republics for the benefits of Wall Street. The record of racketeering is long. I helped purify Nicaragua for the international banking house of Brown Brothers in 1909–1912 (where have I heard that name before?). I brought light to the Dominican Republic for American sugar interests in 1916. In China I helped to see to it that Standard Oil went its way unmolested.

Organized labor in the United States has been held in check by its interpretation of patriotism and by its failure to critically evaluate U.S. foreign policy. Thus, we have on the one hand the surprise and support that greeted AFL-CIO President

John Sweeney at the 2000 International Confederation of Free Trade Unions (ICFTU) World Congress in Durban, South Africa with his strong denunciation of neoliberal globalization, contrasted with the general inability or unwillingness of organized labor in the United States to speak with union members about the nature of U.S. foreign policy, not to mention the difference between patriotism versus culpability in a crime.

Solidarity and Shared Objectives

Is there any hope? The answer is "yes," but it depends entirely on the willingness and ability of the U.S. trade union movement to cross a line into what has hitherto been a forbidden zone for U.S. trade unionism. This forbidden zone is a political space where the U.S. trade union movement begins to look at the interconnections among multinational corporations, U.S. capital, and U.S. foreign policy. It is a space where labor begins to question the motives and actions of the U.S. government, particularly the role of the U.S. government in crushing progressive social movements around the world. It is a space where labor dares to ask whether there is a role the U.S. trade union movement can play, not simply in a partnership with unions in other countries. The U.S. trade union movement must seek to be a champion of *consistent democracy*, both at home and abroad. Consistent democracy, *the demand for obliteration of privilege*, is the real core of a genuine global justice movement. And that global justice movement desperately needs organized labor advancing a program of international *solidarity* against neoliberal globalization.

It is worth concluding this essay with a note on the concept of solidarity. Some unions no longer use the word solidarity—whether with respect to domestic or international working-class struggles. Union leaders apparently believe that it is antiquated and unrecognized by their memberships, and therefore should be dropped from trade union lexicon in favor of the word *unity*. Although there is certainly no problem with the word unity, expunging the word solidarity is a major mistake.

Solidarity is something akin to unity but by no means conveys the equivalent. Unity often assumes a similar context or environment. The beauty of the word and concept of solidarity is that it suggests the active bridging of the gap between the *known* and the *unfamiliar*. In that sense, solidarity is a clear step toward a higher level of unity. Some may think of solidarity as a rhetorical exercise. The late leader of Mozambique, Samora Machel, put it best: "Solidarity is not an act of charity, but mutual support in pursuit of shared objectives."

Solidarity is the process of bridging that gap with the unfamiliar—whether on the basis of geography, industry, race, ethnicity, or gender, to name a few. Solidarity is a process of building a linkage where one does not exist; a linkage tied to a common project or opposition to a common enemy. Cross-border solidarity develops when there is mutual respect and no sense of one domination, privilege, or elitism by the outsiders. Solidarity means a coming together of partners—voluntarily—but with shared objectives, as suggested by President Machel.

Thus, global unionism does not or should not be seen as resulting from the expansion of U.S.-based so-called "international unions," but rather by creating a new international partnership of workers. The initial developments of U.S.-based international unions nearly always contained a bias in favor of the American perspective. A genuine, global unionism, and its corresponding institutions, cannot afford to have such a bias. International working-class solidarity may result in a reformation of existing international bodies, and/or it may result in the creation of new bodies. In either case, this solidarity must represent a voluntary coming together, rather than the imposition of *unity* on someone by someone else who thinks they know better. That is not solidarity, but rather imperial arrogance. Thus, when thinking about renewed trade unionism and global justice, the concept of genuine solidarity must be at the core. ❑

Sources: AFL-CIO, *Common Sense Economics*, www.aflcio.org/issuespolitics/education/, 2004; Smedley Butler, "On Interventionism," excerpt from a speech delivered in 1933 by Major General Smedley Butler, USMC, www.fas.org/man/smedley.htm; Daniel J.Cantor and Juliet B. Schor, *Tunnel Vision: Labor, the World Economy and Central America*, South End Press, 1987; Noam Chomsky, *Hegemony or Survival: America's Quest for Global Dominance*, Henry Holt and Company 2003; Richard A. Clarke, *Against All Enemies: Inside America's War on Terror*, Free Press, 2004; Nelson Lichtenstein, *Labor's War at Home: The CIO in World War II*. Temple University Press, 2003; Samora Machel, *Samora Machel: An African Revolutionary, Selected Speeches and Writings*, St. Martin's Press, 1985; Beth Sims, *Workers of the World Undermined: American Labor's Role in U.S. Foreign Policy*, South End Press, 1991; John Sweeney, "AFL-CIO statement on the war in Iraq to National and International Unions, State Federations and Central Labor Councils, Trade and Industrial Departments, and Allied Organizations," aflcio.org, March 20, 2003; John Sweeney 2003, "On the war with Iraq," aflcio.org, March 20, 2003; Gore Vidal, *Perpetual War for Perpetual Peace: How We Got to Be So Hated*, Thunder's Mouth Press, 2002; Stan Weir, *Singlejack Solidarity*, ed. George Lipsitz. University of Minnesota Press, 2004; JoAnn Wypijewski, "History is Not Frozen in the Past: Labor in the Dawn of Empire," *Counterpunch*, May 10, 2003; Michael D. Yates, *Naming the System: Inequality and Work in the Global Economy*, Monthly Review Press, 2003.

Article 9.3

WAR ON THE EARTH

BY BOB FELDMAN
March/April 2003

In this era of "permanent war," the U.S. war machine bombards civilians in places like Serbia, Afghanistan, and Iraq. It also makes "war on the earth," both at home and abroad. The U.S. Department of Defense is, in fact, the world's largest polluter, producing more hazardous waste per year than the five largest U.S. chemical companies combined. Washington's Fairchild Air Force Base, the number one *producer* of hazardous waste among domestic military bases, generated over 13 million pounds of waste in 1997 (more than the weight of the Eiffel Tower's iron structure). Oklahoma's Tinker Air Force Base, the top toxic waste *emitter*, released over 600,000 pounds in the same year (the same amount of water would cover an entire football field about two inches deep).

Just about every U.S. military base and nuclear arms facility emits toxics into the environment. At many U.S. military target ranges, petroleum products and heavy metals used in bombs and bullets contaminate the soil and groundwater. And since the Pentagon operates its bases as "federal reservations," they are usually beyond the reach of local and state environmental regulations. Local and state authorities often do not find out the extent of the toxic contamination until after a base is closed down.

Active and abandoned military bases have released toxic pollution from Cape Cod to San Diego, Alaska to Hawaii. In June 2001, the Military Toxics Project and the Environmental Health Coalition released the report "Defend Our Health: A People's Report to Congress," detailing the Pentagon's "war on the earth" in the United States and Puerto Rico. The contaminants emitted from military bases include pesticides, solvents, petroleum, lead, mercury, and uranium. The health effects for the surrounding communities are devastating: miscarriages, low birth weights, birth defects, kidney disease, and cancer.

Even the Defense Department itself now acknowledges some of the environmental destruction wrought by the U.S. military worldwide. The Pentagon's own Inspector General documented, in a 1999 report, pollution at U.S. bases in Canada, Germany, Great Britain, Greenland, Iceland, Italy, Panama, the Philippines, South Korea, Spain, and Turkey. Again, since even U.S. military bases abroad are treated as U.S. territory, the installations typically remain exempt from the environmental authority of the host country.

Activists worldwide have called attention to the scourge of toxic pollution, target-range bombardment, noise pollution, abandoned munitions, and radioactive waste unleashed by U.S. bases. The International Grassroots Summit on Military Bases Cleanup in 1999 brought together 70 representatives of citizen groups affected by U.S. military contamination. The gathering adopted an "Environmental Bill of Rights for Persons, Indigenous Peoples, Communities and Nations Hosting Foreign and Colonial Military Bases," declaring that past and present military bases "threaten health, welfare, and the environment, [as well as] future generations." The document emphasizes that the burden of environmental destruction has fallen disproportionately on "economically disadvantaged communities, women, children, people of color and indigenous people." And it demands that the "foreign and colonial" armed forces responsible for the contamination bear the costs the cleanup."

Yet until the era of "permanent war" and global U.S. militarism gives way to an era of world peace, the U.S. military machine will likely remain above the law. And the Pentagon will continue its "war on the earth."

Military Pollution in the United States

Alaska   U.S. military land fills, drum storage areas, fuel spill areas, and leaking underground storage tanks have polluted communities surrounding Cape Romanzof Long Range Radar station in Hooper Bay, Alaska. While fishing near Fort Greeley, Alaska, members of local indigenous tribes have found canisters of mustard gas left over from the 1950s and 1960s—when the U.S. military tested biological and chemical weapons at the site.

Lassen County, California   The Sierra Army Depot—where the military burns and detonates munitions—ranked as California's top source of air pollution in 1999, releasing 17% of all the toxic air emissions for the entire state. Increased cancer rates have been reported in both the surrounding county and the nearby Pyramid Lake Indian Reservation in Nevada.

San Diego, California   The largest polluter in San Diego is the U.S. Navy, which has created 100 toxic and radioactive waste sites in San Diego Bay over the last eighty years. The National Oceanic and Atmospheric Administration found that the bay had the country's second-most-toxic estuary sediments, with the pollution concentrated around Navy and Navy-contractor sites. Fish in San Diego Bay contain high levels of mercury and radioactive compounds. The Navy also spilled over 11,000 gallons of oil into the bay in 1998.

Makua Valley, Hawaii   In the Makua Valley, the U.S. Army's live-fire assault training has caused fires and erosion and introduced alien plants and animals. These activities have threatened over 40 endangered plant and animal species, including the elpano bird. Homes and churches have also been destroyed by the fires and erosion. In addition, heavy metals and other pollutants from the base have contaminated the soil and groundwater.

Cape Cod, Massachusetts   Toxic pollution from the Massachusetts Military Reservation, former site of Otis Military Base, has contaminated drinking water in the nearby town of Falmouth. Over the years, the military "recycled" old ammunition and hazardous wastes at Otis by openly burning them. It also dumped 6 million gallons of aviation fuel directly on the ground. By 1986, Falmouth's cancer rate was 38% higher than the state average.

Concord, Massachusetts   Starmet, a company that manufactured depleted uranium ammunition for the U.S. military, contaminated Concord's groundwater and soil with uranium. Local residents have contracted some cancers at rates up to twice those of other Massachusetts residents.

Colonie, New York   A plant which manufactured 30mm depleted uranium rounds for the U.S. military contaminated a nearby residential community, where the soil was found to contain 500 times more uranium than normal.

Oklahoma City, Oklahoma   The Agency for Toxic Substance and Disease Registry found the average birth weight in the Kimsey neighborhood near Tinker Air Force Base to be about two ounces lower than in other Oklahoma City neighborhoods. It attributed the low birth weights to Kimsey residents' greater exposure to chemicals released from the base.

Isla De Vieques, Puerto Rico   After fifty years of U.S. Navy target practice, Isla de Vieques has more craters per square kilometer than the moon. The Navy's use of bombs, depleted uranium, and Agent Orange on Vieques has produced a cancer rate 26% higher than in the rest of Puerto Rico. Vieques's children also show high levels of mercury and lead. The Navy, which occupies 26,000 of the island's 33,000 acres, has also contaminated the soil, destroyed its coral reefs, and emitted toxic heavy metals into the marine environment.

Memphis, Tennessee   The Pentagon's Defense Distribution Depot began operating as a chemical-weapons dump in the heart of Memphis' African-American community in 1942—and didn't warn residents of the danger. The depot contaminated the soil and groundwater. People who live nearby suffer a disproportionate number of miscarriages, birth defects, childhood cancers, and kidney ailments.

San Antonio, Texas   Kelly Air Force Base ranked as the county's fifth-largest air polluter before its 2001 closing. Metals, solvents. and fuel from the base also contaminated the local groundwater. Over 70 former Kelly Air Force Base workers have developed Lou Gehrig's Disease in recent years. The U.S. Agency for Toxic Substance and Disease Registry found elevated levels of cancer, low birth weight, and birth defects in the San Antonio neighborhood closest to the base.

Washington State The U.S. Navy is the leading cause of oil spills off the Washington coast. The Navy spilled over 10,000 gallons of oil into Puget Sound in 1998. It also tests depleted uranium weapons in prime fishing waters nearby.

Military Pollution Worldwide

Afghanistan Following the Pentagon's 2001-2002 military campaign in Afghanistan, the Uranium Medical Research Center (UMRC) sent two scientific teams to Afghanistan to examine the effects of U.S. bombing on Kabul. Many residents, the UMRC teams found, had symptoms consistent with uranium exposure (joint pains, flu-like illnesses, bleeding mucous membranes, etc.). One fourth of the Kabul newborns examined had health problems consistent with uranium, including lethargy, skin rashes, and enlarged heads.

Canada The U.S. military built a network of radar sites in Northern Canada between 1953 and 1958. Cancer-causing agents were used in the construction and maintenance of the sites, which are now contaminated.

Colombia Large-scale herbicide spraying under the "Plan Colombia"—ostensibly for coca eradication—has caused "serious human health effects; large-scale destruction of food crops; and severe environmental impacts in sensitive tropical ecosystems," according to a 2002 report of the *Aerial Spraying Review*, an environmental publication. There is also evidence that the Pentagon-sponsored fumigation campaign has caused a "loss of agricultural resources, including fish kills and sickness and death of livestock." Border areas of Ecuador have also been contaminated.

Greenland In 1968, a B-52 carrying four nuclear bombs crashed near the Pentagon's Thule Air Force base in northern Greenland, causing severe plutonium contamination of the area.

Indochina Nearly 30 years after the end of the U.S. war in Southeast Asia, many of the affected ecosystems have still not recovered, according to the Environmental Conference on Cambodia, Laos and Vietnam (Stockholm, 2002). Ten percent of southern Vietnam's forests (including one-third of the coastal mangoes, which play a vital role in the coastal ecosystem and fish habitats) were destroyed by the 72 million liters of herbicide the U.S. military dropped during the Vietnam War era. Arsenic and dioxin in the herbicides are expected to pose a health threat long into the future. Since 1975, 50,000 civilians have been killed by the landmines and other weapons the U.S. military left behind. The U.S.'s vast bombing campaign also left millions of large bomb craters.

Iraq U.S. bombing of oil facilities in January 1991 caused spills of 6 to 8 million barrels of crude oil, killing about 30,000 marine birds. For nearly a year afterwards, oil well fires spewed toxic soot. The bombing also poisoned Iraqi water supplies. In addition, according to Iraq's Ministry of Health, depleted uranium from U.S. weapons has contaminated the soil and plants in southern Iraq, causing cancers and deformities associated with uranium exposure.

Okinawa   U.S. military exercises with live artillery have caused forest fires, soil erosion, and earth tremors—leaving sections of Okinawa barren and shell-ridden. Toxins emitted by the U.S. military have infiltrated Okinawa's land, water and air, and have been linked to low birth weights and elevated rates of leukemia and other cancers. Noise pollution at Kadena Air Base may also be a cause of low birth weights.

Panama   The U.S. military left firing ranges in the Panama Canal Zone littered with thousands of unexploded rounds. A July 1998 Pentagon report found that the U.S. Army Corps of Engineers dumped tons of soil from a project to widen the canal onto 92 acres in Panama's Empire Range, damaging the rainforest ecosystem. A 1997 study for the U.S. Army also discovered the carcinogen TCI in the ground water at Fort Koblhe—at twenty times the level acceptable under U.S. federal law.

Philippines   The former site of Clark Air Base has contaminated the groundwater. The U.S. military also dumped hazardous waste in a municipal landfill in a residential area of Mabalacat. The power plant at the Subic Bay Naval Base emitted untreated pollutants directly into the air. Toxic waste from the destruction of excess bombs and ammunition were poured into local streams. In addition, most of the sewage generated at the Subic Bay base was discharged each day, untreated, directly into the bay.

Serbia   After the U.S. military bombed a petrochemical complex in the suburbs of Belgrade in 1999, the destroyed plastics factory and ammonia production unit released toxins such as chlorine into the air.

South Korea   Oil from the Yongsan 8th garrison's base has contaminated the soil and water. Asbestos has been found around the Camp Indian base. In May 1998, a ruptured pipeline at the Mt. Rackun military base polluted a large section of a South Korean forest conservancy area. U.S. military drills and maneuvers have also damaged farmlands and destroyed crops. Oil discharged by the U.S. Army has polluted the Sankogos River, contaminated farmland, and destroyed crops. Off the coast of South Korea, the U.S. military has used small islands as bombing ranges, creating noise pollution for nearby villages. The ammunition left behind has also injured residents. ❑

Sources: Safety Forum Research/Safetyforum.com <www.safetyforum.com>; Military Toxics Project and Environmental Health Coalition, "Defend Our Health: A People's Report to Congress," (June 2001); Greenpeace <www.greenpeace.org>; East Asia/U.S. Women's Network Against Militarism <www.apcjp.org/womens_network/skorea.htm>; Okinawan Peace Network of Los Angeles <www.uchinanchu.org>; Organization for the Prohibition of Chemical Weapons Technical Assistance Visit, Final Report, 8/14/01; *Financial Times*, 9/7/01; Ecocompass/IslandPress; Fellowship of Reconciliation Panama Campaign <www. forusa.org/program/panama>; *Coastal Post* newsmonthly <www.coastal-post.com>

Dollars & Sense would like to acknowledge and thank the Military Toxics Project (MTP) for much of the information in this article. The MTP seeks to "unite activists, organizations, and communities in the struggle to clean up military pollution, safeguard the transportation of hazardous materials, and to advance the development and implementation of preventive solutions to the toxic and radioactive pollution caused by military activities." For more information readers can write to Military Toxics Project, P.O. Box 558, Lewiston, ME 04243, call 207-783-5091 or visit www.miltoxproj.org.

Article 9.4

IN VIEQUES, PUERTO RICO, *LA LUCHA CONTINUA*

BY LIV GOLD
November/December 2006

L ast spring, I came across an article in *Caribbean Edge* magazine on Vieques, a small island seven miles off the coast of Puerto Rico. According to the article, Vieques' "lush green rainforest, pristine beaches, and crystal clear waters" are "the perfect place to relax and experience the quiet charms of a truly unspoiled Caribbean island."

They must have mistaken a different island for Vieques, I thought. "Pristine" and "unspoiled" could not possibly describe the Vieques I knew of, a U.S. aerial weapons testing ground for over 50 years whose residents had a 30% higher cancer rate than Puerto Ricans do, a 381% higher rate of hypertension, and a 95% higher rate of cirrhosis of the liver. And phrases like "perfect place to relax" and "quiet charms" hardly seem apt to describe a place that has been the site of demonstrations and arrests, and whose future continues to be contested terrain.

Of course I could have been wrong—and there was only one way to be sure. In June, I packed my bags and headed to Vieques.

Sixty Years of Bombing

The U.S. Navy's occupation of Vieques began on December 10, 1941, three days after Japanese bombs struck Pearl Harbor, when Congress authorized $30 million to build military installations in Puerto Rico, including a dual-use target range/amphibious exercise base in Vieques. Between 1941 and 1947, the Navy expropriated two-thirds of the island and displaced 10,000 Viequenses. It compensated possessors of legally titled land—a small number of mostly white, mostly wealthy plantation owners. Almost overnight Vieques was rebuilt to serve as one side in a defensive triangle, made up of Puerto Rico, Florida, and Panama, that would protect the Panama Canal and hold European fascism at bay.

But by the time construction was completed, the base was already obsolete. The Panama Canal was calm and the Caribbean Sea, initially expected to be a theater of war, had hosted only one minor battle. At the end of World War II the largest base on the Puerto Rican mainland was placed on maintenance status. Some tracts of land were leased back to the Puerto Rican government, but in Vieques the Navy remained planted. It kept Viequenses in the center of the island and poured more capital into munitions storage facilities in the west and weapons testing grounds in the east, all the while insisting that its maneuvers on Vieques were vital to national security. The service members who trained there fought the wars on fascism, on communism, on drugs, and later on terror. During the Navy's 60-year residency,

18,000 tons of bombs fell on the island; napalm and Agent Orange rained from the sky.

Nonetheless, in an official "Vieques White Paper," the Navy asserted that it "has been a good steward of the land and water entrusted to its care at Vieques. It has protected and nurtured the wildlife, forests, plants, and resources. … Its use of a very small part of the island for a live impact area has not harmed the health of its neighbors on Vieques or the environment in which they live. … To date, the Navy has seen no credible evidence that its activities pose a risk to human health."

That was in 1999, six months after two 500-pound bombs were accidentally dropped on a civilian Viequense named David Sanes. Four years later, a solidarity movement worldwide in reach was conducting large-scale demonstrations and civil disobedience actions to force the Navy off of the island. Over 1,500 people were imprisoned, including some of Puerto Rico's most esteemed religious and political leaders. The mayor of Vieques himself served four months in a federal penitentiary. Finally, in 2003, the Navy deactivated the base. The press stopped reporting on "the struggle in Vieques." In the *New York Times*, Vieques slid seamlessly from social justice talking point to hot tourist destination.

This Is Not Wilderness

When the Navy closed its base, it transferred land administration to the U.S. Fish and Wildlife Service, which applied the term "wilderness area" to 900 acres of the eastern portion of the island. The 1964 Wilderness Act defines "wilderness" as [a place] where the earth and its community are untrammeled by man … retaining its primeval character and influence … and that generally appears to have been affected primarily by forces of nature, with the imprint of man's work substantially unnoticeable.

It seemed to me that the imprint of man's work would be rather pronounced on an ex-Navy bombing range; that a site with more craters than parts of the moon could only loosely be termed "wilderness." This is more than just semantics. Engaging in an Orwellian name game allows the Navy to evade its decontamination responsibilities. Suppose the land was classified as residential or commercial rather than as "wilderness." Or better yet, imagine that it must one day accommodate an elementary school. Environmental standards and corresponding clean-up processes enjoy a reciprocal relationship with future land use plans. So whether the land must be made suitable for sea turtles or school children makes a big difference. By designating much of the land as wildlife refuge and wilderness area, the U.S. government has reduced the Navy's financial and environmental responsibility to the lowest possible level.

For evidence of the Navy's financial evasion, consider Kahoʻolawe, Hawaii. Like Vieques, Kahoʻolawe was used for conventional and non-conventional military operations for over 50 years. Unlike Vieques, however, Kahoʻolawe was uninhabited. Yet Kahoʻolawe received $400 million for decontamination, while Vieques, with a population above 7,000, received less than half that.

This Is Not Clean-Up

The environmental repercussions of such parsimony are everywhere. The Navy and its contractors say they are "removing" unexploded ordnance and munitions scrap debris. But safe, complete removal requires the use of controlled detonation chambers to explode live ordinance. "Operational limitations" preclude such methods, says the Navy. As a result, 20 tons of explosives have been blown up in place recently, including 1,046 munitions of up to one-ton size, 495 of which were classified as "high explosives."

While I was in Vieques I attended a meeting of the Restoration Advisory Board, which lasted more than four hours and brought together members of the Viequense community with representatives from the Navy, EPA, U.S. Fish and Wildlife Service, and the Vieques municipal government. But most Viequenses do not trust the federal government; they feel angry and alienated and betrayed. "This is still a matter of life or death," shouted Bob Rabin, a long time resident of Vieques. "*Bombs are being detonated.*"

Naval contractor CH2M Hill has begun testing for background levels of inorganics (metals) in soil samples from areas on Vieques identified as "not impacted by past Navy activities." These data will be compared with soil tests from sites where Navy activity is a concern. During discussions about background sampling, a resident named Mike Diaz expressed concern that areas "not impacted by past Navy activities" may simply not exist on his small island. "If you can envision a volcano distributing material over the islands," he asked, "why can't you envision the same distribution by bombs?"

Rabin's assertion that lives are at stake is not overstated. Study after study shows that toxic substances from Navy activity have entered the food chain, contaminating surface vegetation like squash, peppers, and pigeon peas, as well as fish. A research group from the University of Puerto Rico School of Public Health examined the dust in residents' homes and found it laced with cadmium, arsenic and lead. Yet until the Navy's own team of contracted experts executes *its* contamination study, the Navy denies any responsibility.

This Is Not Control

The struggle in Vieques was many things, but it was never solely an expression of anti-militarism. It was more about control, or more specifically, about putting control of their land and economy back into the hands of Viequenses.

Consequently, the Navy's 2003 departure was bittersweet because since then, land administration has gone from the U.S. Department of Defense's Naval Facilities Atlantic Command to the U.S. Department of Interior's Fish and Wildlife Service, and ongoing clean-up efforts, though aided by private contractors, are overseen and regulated by the EPA. In each case, the governing body—the body determining the fate of the island—belongs to the U.S. government, not to the people of Vieques.

The economic sub-plot is similar. During the Navy's occupation of the island, Viequenses lost access to their ports, both marine and air, which effectively halted foreign investment and stalled domestic production in industries like sugar, fishing and agriculture. While unemployment soared among Viequenses, the U.S. government took in close to $100 million annually by renting the eastern Live Impact Area to allied militaries. Now that the bombing has stopped, Vieques has a chance to restore its faltering economy. But in the absence of regulatory controls and a sustainable land use plan, Viequenses risk losing control yet again.

Already gentrification has displaced a large segment of the Viequense population. As one local realtor explained, "When the Navy left, land on Vieques was cheap and plentiful, at least from the perspective of foreign investors." Those investors had business experience and capital to front; in just a few years they cultivated a tourism industry that put the island in demand.

As more people come to Vieques, the cost of living rises and the real estate market becomes inflated. "Nobody forces Viequenses to leave," insisted the realtor. "They get offered a hundred thousand dollars for their concrete house and soon they're gone."

Nilda Medina, a Viequense woman, has watched foreign capital displace her friends. "It's like a ghost community has taken over," she said. Absentee owners with bank accounts in Boston are coming into possession of beach-front properties, hotels, and shops. Only they can swallow the sort of land speculation that makes previously untitled properties rapidly triple and quadruple in value. And all of these purchases by foreign investors, renters, and second-home buyers are happening while 600 homeless or underhoused Puerto Rican families bide their time on a waiting list for Section 8 housing assistance.

"After decades of resistance," Nilda told me, "American capital might accomplish what American bombs never could—the erosion and eventual eviction of Viequense population and culture."

Vieques needs a land use plan that will moderate the power of both the real estate and tourism industries and the federal government, a plan that can restore agency to the Viequense people. It needs a plan that will mandate the quick and complete decontamination of the island and pave the way for future economic growth—growth that is not just sustainable, but also endogenous. Given its history, this is a tough task for Vieques. The task is complicated further by the fact that Vieques has not just one, but three official land use plans: one applies to the municipality, one applies to all of Puerto Rico, and one was specially designed for Vieques by a group of Puerto Rican academics. Testing the legal fortitude of each plan has already proven challenging. It may be some time before a stable land use plan is adopted.

The Struggle Continues

For over half a decade, the struggle in Vieques was described in mythic terms, as a battle between David and Goliath, the Viequenses and the Navy. Now that the Navy is gone, the challenges facing Vieques are less clear-cut; instead of bombs and mortars, residents confront poorly regulated markets where absentee ownership and staggering foreign investment threaten wholesale displacement of the native people and culture.

Bob Rabin is one of the founding members of the Committee for the Rescue and Development of Vieques (CRDV), formed in 1995 to articulate a vision of a Navy-free Vieques. He and his colleagues advocate the four Ds: demilitarization, decontamination, devolution, and (community-based, sustainable) development. "Demilitarization" refers specifically to the closure of remaining radar facilities and telecommunications centers that still occupy 200 acres on the island. "Decontamination" broadly demands that the Navy leave Vieques as clean as it was found in 1940, including the complete cleanup of heavy metals, napalm, Agent Orange, depleted uranium, and other land, marine, and aerial contaminants. "Devolution" speaks to the return of all land to Vieques, as opposed to the Fish and Wildlife Service. "Development" urges sustainable economic development by the Viequenses for the Viequenses, which respects the cultural and natural resources of the island.

"You might laugh at this," said Rabin, "but in some ways it used to be easier. The themes and issues were more straightforward. And there was consensus—we all believed there was something fundamentally correct about what we were doing." Today the issues are complicated; each proposal, each plan, and each initiative is controversial.

The same can be said for the solidarity movement that once rallied around the island. The Navy's presence was a unifying force; now the support network is frayed. Many people assume that with the base deactivated, the struggle is over. And those still attuned find it hard to stay informed and difficult to get involved. However, at the core of the struggle are familiar themes—respect for Vieques' land and waters, dignity for its people—and strategies—civil disobedience, town meetings, and referendums.

In the United States, I hope that our solidarity can shift with the circumstances to fight the U.S. military's "war on the earth" and support Vieques' efforts to achieve self-determination. In Vieques, *la lucha continua*. ❑

Article 9.5

CONSCRIPTED BY POVERTY

BY ANNA SUSSMAN
November/December 2007

Providing economic alternatives has been key to the successful demobilization of nearly 30,000 child soldiers in eastern Congo.

Ronaldo is covered with a thin layer of sawdust. As the sun sets over a hilltop woodshop in eastern Congo, the 16-year-old takes a moment to rest, wiping his brow with a cloth. He's been sawing all day, cutting wood for chairs, tables and shelves. The work is hard and physically demanding, but it's better than his last job: child soldier.

Two years ago, at the age of 14, Ronaldo, whose name has been changed to protect his identity, joined a local armed rebel group.

"I thought it would give me a better life," he said. He says he joined voluntarily. But advocates here say that Ronaldo's recruitment was not exactly voluntary: while he was not forced with a gun or knife, Ronaldo, like thousands of other child soldiers in the Congo, was compelled to join an armed group by extreme poverty. "My family didn't have enough food or money," he says. "That's why I decided to join."

In the Democratic Republic of the Congo, more than 33,000 young people have been associated with armed groups in recent years, mostly in the troubled eastern Congo region. UNICEF officials and international aid agencies operating here say the child soldier epidemic in eastern Congo can be traced largely to economics. Across the globe there are many reasons children join armed groups—some are forcibly abducted, for example, while others are looking for revenge or prestige. But advocates here are finding that poverty is the driving force: many children enlist for the minimal food and shelter it will provide them.

"In such a poor country as the Democratic Republic of the Congo, there are economic factors that drive children towards joining armed groups or forces," says Pernile Ironside, a protection specialist with UNICEF in eastern Congo. "Families tend to be very large, so there is a certain allure for children to join up with a military group, where they are able to get enough food to eat," she said. "Occasionally parents, as well, drive children to join [an armed group], recognizing that they can't meet the needs of their child and that the child may be better off in their view by leaving the family and joining up with a group."

That's why UNICEF, along with other international agencies, is focusing its demobilization efforts on economic solutions. "Fundamentally the reason is economic," says Murhabazi Namegabe, who directs a child soldier demobilization center in Bukavu. "Ninety-nine percent of these children come from poor families. The main problem we are dealing with is how to provide assistance for their families."

In Congo, where civil war has raged since President Mobutu Sese Seko was overthrown in 1997, young people have grown up in a climate of brutal warfare in which families are regularly slaughtered, homes burned, and villages destroyed. Although the war is officially over and the country held democratic elections last year, the fighting continues today as ethnic, political, and government factions battle along Congo's mineral-rich border with Rwanda.

The eastern Congo region is controlled by more than a dozen armed groups, many battling over the valuable mineral resources abundant in this region of the country: gold, diamonds, and coltan (short for columbite-tantalite), a mineral widely used in the manufacture of electronic gadgets like mobile phones, computer chips, and VCRs. But the billions of dollars extracted from the ground here are enjoyed by an elite few, while hundreds of warlords and soldiers on the ground vie for control over civilian territories with brutal force.

Many children, including Ronaldo, have joined local "Mai-Mai" militias, decentralized armed groups operating across the region who claim they are engaging in self-defense against the government and ethnic rebel groups. Others are conscripted by the national army, says Ironside.

But amid the fighting, UNICEF is successfully negotiating for the removal of children from armed groups. Today, nearly 6,000 former child soldiers are learning income-generating activities like sewing, woodworking, and bicycle repair. This way, children like Ronaldo will be able to survive without the patronage of an armed group, says Ironside.

Restricting Re-recruitment

The "skill-building" demobilization programs championed by UNICEF and others, like Save the Children, began several years ago and have been hugely successful. In all, 29,000 child soldiers have been demobilized in the Congo since 2002. But at the same time the financial security promised by armed groups continues to draw in poor children.

"Re-recruitment is something that is best prevented by giving real opportunities to children once they've left an armed group," says Ironside. "Opportunities could entail going back to school, learning a trade, or having a small income-generating project or business because children really need to regain their hope for the future and visualize what else they may be able to become, aside from being part of an armed group."

In a small cement building in the city of Bukavu, 300 former child soldiers have just completed a six-month training course in sewing and tailoring with the Dutch-based non-governmental organization War Child. At the graduation ceremony, students and parents sing songs, bang drums, and dance. Then, they stand up and give testimony to their newly learned skills.

"With this experience I will never go back to armed forces," says 19-year-old Papi Bijeri. "My weapon now is what I learned; that is how I will survive." Bijeri, who was orphaned at a young age, says he joined a rebel group "to earn some money and survive."

While fighting, Bijeri participated in gang-rape and killing, and eventually earned the position of bodyguard to a high-ranking commander, a job that earned him about $9 a month plus a bar of soap and food.

The War Child program takes children directly from drop-off centers, where they are left by armed rebel groups taking the steps required to integrate into the national army. During their six-month training, most of the children live with relatives or friends in the town. When the course is completed, they receive a small tool kit, including a prized sewing machine. It's a model that is repeated, with some variation, in programs across the region.

When Basic Needs Go Unmet

There are between 200,000 and 300,000 child soldiers worldwide. Many are abducted and forced into armed groups. Others "volunteer." Stating that young people require special protection because of their physical and mental immaturity, however, the U.N. Convention on the Rights of the Child prohibits military recruitment—voluntary or not—of children under 18.

Most child soldiers come from nations that have dissolved into civil war. Child soldiers are a symptom that states which lack the capacity to meet their citizens' most basic needs. "Poverty and its link to the crisis of child soldiers around the globe is inextricably linked to other antecedent factors," says Eddie Mandhry of the New York-based group Global Kids. "These factors include the deterioration of social infrastructures prior to or during times of war and the economic and political marginalization and disaffection of youth."

Just as poverty can motivate the struggle over resources that is often at the root of war, war itself amplifies poverty and the problems that often accompany it—problems like corruption, lawlessness, and limited education. Families collapse, schools stop running, work opportunities disappear, and food becomes scarce. Looking to bolster their ranks, warlords lure physically vulnerable and economically desperate children, many without families, into armed groups. Most end up being forced to do terrible things. Many former child soldiers in Congo report being forced to rape and kill villagers. Ronaldo says he was forced to work on the frontlines, walking for days on end without food.

"Children are quite easily manipulated," Ironside says. "And it doesn't take a whole lot for them to perhaps become motivated to do something, given their extreme poverty and the fact that they might not consider the consequences of a particular action."

As violent instability and war have ravaged Congo, per-capita annual income (adjusted for inflation) fell from $380 in 1960 to $100 in 2004, according to the IMF. The vast majority of households in eastern Congo have no running water or electricity, and few of the children attend school. Women report that armed groups regularly steal crops from their fields, leaving their families hungry.

Across the African great lakes region, where violent unrest spills across borders between Uganda, Burundi, Rwanda, and Congo, the vast majority of households live on less than a dollar a day. Not surprisingly, potential child soldiers are in large supply.

A Generation of Soldiers

But demobilization programs are taking hold in eastern Congo. Most of the income-generating and skill-building programs run by UNICEF and its partners here are coupled with counseling and group play-therapy, where children learn to cope with the atrocities they have seen or carried out.

In towns like Bukavu in the South Kivu province of eastern Congo where UNICEF programs work one-on-one with children to teach them job skills, most children are able to resist re-recruitment.

But farther north in the villages of North Kivu, where ethnic fighting between Hutu militants and the Congolese army continues to play out, the situation is worse. UNICEF officials estimate that hundreds of former child soldiers have been re-recruited in North Kivu in recent months. "About three-quarters of children who were demobilized have been re-recruited because of a lack of jobs," says Namegabe.

The head of U.N. humanitarian efforts in North Kivu, Patrick Lavand'Homme, says he fears the United Nations will be unable to meet the huge demand for basic supplies like food and water if the fighting continues. And the Congolese government has shown little interest in providing humanitarian help. As needs become more desperate, Ironside says, more than 5,000 more children in North Kivu are at risk of being re-recruited.

There are many reasons for the child soldier crisis, but until real economic needs are met here, children will continue to be attracted to the promises of food, money, and shelter offered by armed groups.

The conflict in this region has been called Africa's World War. Asked why his homeland has seen so much war, 16-year-old Ronaldo does not pause to think. As he picks up his saw and resumes his woodwork, he gives a simple answer.

"There are no jobs here. People want to work but there is no work to do. If everyone had a job that had a decent salary, there would be peace in the country." ❏

Sources: UNICEF, "Displaced children especially vulnerable to illness and military re-recruitment in North Kivu," 2007; Child Rights Information Network, crin.org; Human Rights Watch Child Soldiers Campaign, hrw.org/campaigns/crp; Amnesty International, "Democratic Republic of Congo: Children at War," 2003.

Article 9.6

IRAQ'S WORKERS STRIKE TO KEEP THEIR OIL

BY DAVID BACON
September/October 2007

The Bush administration has no love for unions anywhere, but in Iraq it has a special reason for hating them. They are the main opposition to the occupation's economic agenda, and the biggest obstacle to that agenda's centerpiece—the privatization of Iraq's oil. At the same time, unions have become the only force in Iraq trying to maintain at least a survival living standard for the millions of Iraqis who still have to earn a living somehow in the middle of the now four-year-old war.

This summer [2007], Iraqi popular anger over starvation incomes and oil rip-offs boiled over. On Monday, June 4, the largest and strongest of Iraq's unions, the Iraqi Federation of Oil Unions (IFOU), launched a strike to underline its call for keeping oil in public hands, and to force the government to live up to its economic promises. Workers on the pipelines that carry oil from the rigs in the south to Baghdad's big refinery stopped work.

This was a very limited job action which still allowed the Iraqi economy to function. Nonetheless, Iraqi Prime Minister Nouri al-Maliki responded by calling out the army and surrounding the strikers at Sheiba, near Basra. Then he issued arrest warrants for the union's leaders. On June 6, the union decided to postpone the strike plans for five more days. Facing the possibility that a renewed strike could escalate into shutdowns on the rigs themselves, or even the cutoff of oil exports, the source of the income stream that keeps his regime in power, Maliki blinked. He agreed to the union's principal demand—that implementation of the oil law be delayed until October, while the union gets a chance to pose objections and propose alternatives.

This will undoubtedly get Maliki in trouble in Washington, where his government will be accused of weakness, incompetence, and a failure to move on the oil law, one of the key political benchmarks it is under pressure to achieve. In Iraq, however, Maliki faces a fact that U.S. policymakers refuse to recognize—the oil industry is a symbol of Iraqi sovereignty and nationalism. Handing control to foreign companies is an extremely unpopular idea.

Some of the oil workers' demands reflect the desperate situation of workers under the occupation. They want their employer—the government's oil ministry—to pay for wage increases and promised vacations, and give permanent status to thousands of temporary employees. In a country where housing has been destroyed on a massive scale and workers often live under primitive conditions in dilapidated structures, the union wants the government to turn over land for building homes. Since 2003, the Oil Institute, a national technical training college for the industry's workers and technicians, has miraculously continued holding classes and training technicians. Yet the ministry won't give work to graduates, despite the war-torn industry's desperate need for skilled labor. The union demands jobs and a future for these young people.

Fighting for these demands makes the union popular, and enhances its nationalist credentials. Iraqis see it defending the interests of the millions of workers who have to make a living and keep food on the table for their families. On the other hand, the U.S. authorities, which imposed a series of low-wage laws at the beginning of the occupation, look to ordinary Iraqis like an enemy bent on enforcing poverty.

But one demand overshadows even these basic needs—renegotiation of the oil law that would turn the industry itself over to foreign corporations. And it is this demand that has brought out even the U.S. fighter jets, which have circled and buzzed over the strikers' demonstrations. In Iraq, the hostile maneuvering of military aircraft is not an idle threat to the people below. This standoff reflects a long history of actions in Iraq, by both the Iraqi government and the U.S. occupation administration, to suppress union activity.

Iraq has a long labor history. Union activists, banned and jailed under the British and its puppet monarchy, organized a labor movement that was the admiration of the Arab world when Iraq became independent after 1958. Iraq's oil industry was nationalized in the 1960s, like that of every other country in the Middle East. The Iraqi oil union became, and still is, the industry's most zealous guardian. Saddam Hussein later drove its leaders underground, killing and jailing the ones he could catch.

When Saddam fell, Iraqi unionists came out of prison, up from underground, and back from exile, determined to rebuild their labor movement. Miraculously, in the midst of war and bombings, they did. The oil workers union in the south is now one of the largest organizations in Iraq, with thousands of members on the rigs, pipelines, and refineries. The electrical workers union is the first national labor organization headed by a woman, Hashmeya Muhsin Hussein.

Together with other unions in railroads, hotels, ports, schools, and factories, they've gone on strike, held elections, won wage increases, and made democracy a living reality. Yet the Bush administration, and the Baghdad government it controls, has continued to enforce a Saddam-era law that outlawed collective bargaining, has impounded union funds, and has turned its back (or worse) on a wave of assassinations of Iraqi union leaders. Following the June strike, Iraq's oil minister ordered officials of the state oil industry to refuse to recognize or bargain with the IFOU.

President Bush says he wants democracy, yet he will not accept the one political demand that unites Iraqis above all others. They want the country's oil (and its electrical power stations, ports, and other key facilities) to remain in public hands.

The fact that Iraqi unions are the strongest voice demanding this makes them anathema. Selling the oil off to large corporations is far more important to the Bush administration than a paper commitment to the democratic process. And the oil workers' union has now emerged as one of the strongest voices of Iraqi nationalism, protecting an important symbol of Iraq's national identity, and, more important, the only source of income capable of financing the country's post-occupation reconstruction.

The administration and those U.S. legislators trying to impose the oil law might take note that they are requiring the Maliki government to betray one of the few reasons Iraqis have for supporting it—its ability to keep the oil revenue in public hands.

With a no-bid, sweetheart contract with occupation authorities in hand, Halliburton Corporation came into Iraq in the wake of the troops in 2003. The company tried to seize control of the wells and rigs, withholding reconstruction aid to force workers to submit. The oil union struck for three days that August, stopping exports and cutting off government revenue. Halliburton left the oil districts, and the Oil Ministry regained control.

The oil and port unions then forced foreign corporations, including Seattle-based Stevedoring Services of America and the Danish shipping giant Maersk, to give up similar sweetheart agreements in Iraq's deepwater shipping facilities. Muhsin's electrical union is still battling to stop subcontracting in the power stations—a prelude to corporate control. The occupation has always had an economic agenda. In 2003 and 2004, occupation czar Paul Bremer published lists in Baghdad newspapers of the public enterprises he intended to auction off. Arab labor leader Hacene Djemam bitterly observed, "War makes privatization easy: first you destroy society; then you let the corporations rebuild it."

The Bush administration won't leave Iraq in part because that economic agenda is still insecure. Under Washington's guidance, the Iraqi government wrote a new oil law in secret. The Iraq study commission, headed by oilman James Baker, called it the key to ending the occupation. That law is touted in the U.S. press as ensuring an equitable division of oil wealth. Iraqis see it differently. They look at the means it sets up for welcoming foreign oil companies into the oil fields, and the control it would give them over setting royalties, deciding on production levels, and even determining whether Iraqis themselves get to work in their own industry. Iraqi unions charge it will ensure that foreign corporations control future exploration and development, in one of the world's largest reserves, through so-called production sharing contracts that favor multinational oil corporations. Such contracts have been rejected by most oil-producing countries, including those of the Middle East.

In May, Hassan Juma'a Awad, president of the IFOU, which had been banned from the secret negotiations, wrote a letter to the U.S. Congress. "Everyone knows the oil law doesn't serve the Iraqi people," he warned. The draft law "serves Bush, his supporters and foreign companies at the expense of the Iraqi people." The union has threatened to strike if the law is implemented.

After Muhsin and IFOU general secretary Faleh Abood Umara toured the United States in June, Leo Gerard, president of the United Steel Workers of America, which represents U.S. oil workers, backed up the Iraqis' demand. In a July 31 letter to key Congress members, Gerard warned that "the oil privatization law now under consideration by Iraq's government is designed to benefit the multinational oil companies; not the Iraqi people. ... Iraq's oil is a national resource that should not be privatized [or] used as any kind of 'benchmark' of the Iraqi government's success or failure."

Like all Iraqi unionists, Juma'a says the occupation should end without demanding Iraq's oil as a price. "The USA claimed that it came here as a liberator, not to control our resources," he reminded Congress.

Congressional opponents of the war can only win Iraqis' respect if they disavow the oil law. Gerard told those representatives that "the views of this labor movement should be heard much more clearly in Washington than they have been to date," and noted that "they believe strongly that sectarian strife will ease, and that unions will be able to act with substantially more freedom when the U.S. military presence has ended." The steel workers, he said, wanted Congress to "oppose the privatization of Iraq's oil resources, correct the inequities present in Iraqi labor policy, and continue to support an end to the U.S. military presence in Iraq." ❏

Chapter 10

GLOBAL ECONOMIC CRISIS

Article 10.1

PUTTING THE "GLOBAL" IN THE GLOBAL ECONOMIC CRISIS

BY SMRITI RAO
August 2009

There is no question that the current economic crisis originated in the developed world, and primarily in the United States. Much of the analysis of the crisis has thus focused on institutional failures within the United States and there is, rightly, tremendous concern about high rates of unemployment and underemployment within the country. But after three decades of globalization, what happens in the United States does not stay in the United States and the actions of traders in New York City will mean hunger for children in Nairobi. We now know what crisis looks like in the age of globalization and it is not pretty.

This crisis is uniquely a child of the neo-liberal global order. For developing countries the key elements of neo-liberalism have consisted of trade liberalization and an emphasis on export growth; reductions in government spending on subsidies and public sector wages; a greater reliance on the market for determining the price of everything from the currency exchange rate to water from the tap, and last but not least, economy-wide privatization and deregulation. In each case, the aim was also to promote cross-border flows of goods, services and capital—although not, for the most part, of people.

Despite Thomas Friedman's assertions of a "flat" world, this age of globalization did not in fact eliminate global inequality. Indeed if we exclude China and India, inter-country inequality actually increased during this period. These asymmetries in economic and political power across countries were in turn reflected in the asymmetrical flows of resources globally. The globalization of the last 25 years was predicated upon the extraction by the developed world of the natural resources, cheap labor and in particular, capital of the developing world, via financial markets that siphoned the world's savings for U.S. middle-class consumption.

What could be more tragically ironic than the billions of dollars in annual flows of capital from developing countries with unfunded domestic development projects to developed countries, which then failed to meet even their minimum obligations with respect to foreign aid? For example, Africa has been a net creditor to the United States for some time, a fact both shocking and revealing of the underlying basis of the world economy. As many point out today, this dynamic reeks of age-old colonialism.

This situation arose in part because developing countries tried to ward off balance-of-payment crises by holding large foreign exchange reserves. These reverse flows of capital only exacerbated the debt bubble within the United States, helping to sustain its indebted households, corporations, and governments. Meanwhile, the global "race to the bottom" among developing county exporters ensured that the prices of most manufactured goods and services remained low, taking the threat of inflation off the table and enabling the U.S. Federal Reserve to keep interest rates low and facilitate the housing bubble.

Now that this debt bubble has finally burst, it is no surprise that the crisis has been transmitted back to the global South at record speed.

The Extent of the Impact

We currently have consistent cross-country macroeconomic data for 2008 that allow us to estimate the relative slowdown in real GDP growth by country, when compared to its average GDP growth in the preceding three years (2005-2007). Data are available for 178 developed and developing countries. Given that the financial crisis only hit in full force in September 2008, the 2009 data will give us a more complete picture of the impact of the crisis, but here is what we have learned thus far.

Overall, GDP growth for these 178 countries is down by 1.3 percentage points in 2008 compared to the average for 2005-2007. Of course December 2008, which is when the data set ends, was still early days for the crisis, and the International Monetary Fund (IMF) estimates that for the first time since World War II, global

TABLE 1: TOP TEN COUNTRIES BY RELATIVE DECLINE IN REAL GDP GROWTH		
Rank	Reporting countries	Relative decline GDP growth (percentage points)
1	Latvia	15.56
2	Azerbaijan	14.44
3	Estonia	12.26
4	Georgia	8.42
5	Myanmar	8.32
6	Ireland	8.30
7	Seychelles	7.62
8	Armenia	6.85
9	Singapore	6.66
10	Kazakhstan	6.57

Sources: Author's calculations based on data from World Development Indicators online, World Bank, June 2009.

GDP will decline in 2009. Currently, the IMF is expecting a 1.4% contraction for the year. According to the International Labor Organization, global unemployment increased by 10.7 million in 2008 with a further increase of 19 million expected in 2009 (by relatively conservative estimates). As a result, the World Bank predicts that the number of people living in poverty will increase by an estimated 46 million.

The initial impact in 2008 was greatest in Eastern Europe and Central Asia. For 2008, six of the top ten countries by steepest relative declines in real GDP were from the Eastern Europe/Central Asia region (Table 1). Joined by Ireland, this is a list of global high-fliers—countries with very high rates of growth, as well as countries that globalized rapidly and enthusiastically in the last decade and a half. Singapore of course was an early adopter of globalization, serving as a model for other small countries according to the IMF, while Seychelles has depended heavily on international tourism. Myanmar would seem to be the exception to this rule, given its political isolation. From an economic perspective, however, this was a country that experienced economic growth thanks to the rising prices of its commodity exports (natural gas and gems) until the crisis intervened.

Indeed, if we rank these 178 countries by relative declines in GDP growth, as well as by their pre-crisis shares of exports in GDP (averaged from 2005-2007), we find a strong correlation between the two. Countries with the largest relative GDP declines in 2008 tended to also be the countries that ranked high in reliance upon exports.

This pattern of globalizers being most affected by the crisis is no accident. It turns out that each of the three primary channels through which the crisis has been transmitted from the United States to other countries is a direct outcome of the policy choices countries were urged and sometimes coerced into making with assurances that this particular form of globalization was the best way to build a healthy and prosperous economy (see Fig. 1 for a summary).

FIGURE 1: THE CURRENT CRISIS AND IMF POLICIES: MAKING THE LINKS

Lowered exports, remittances ("openness")

+

Outflows of portfolio capital ("openness" + no capital controls)

=

Depreciating currencies (floating exchange rates)

=>

Worsening current account balances/debt burdens

X

Falling flows of FDI and development aid

X

"Inflation targeting" and "fiscal restraint"

Transmission Channels of the Crisis

Lowered exports and remittances. The recession in the United States and Europe has hit exports from the developing world hard. Globally, trade in goods and services did rise by 3% in 2008, but that was compared to 10% and 7% in the previous two years. Trade is expected to decline by a sharp 12% in 2009. Within the United States, the world's most important importer, imports have dropped by an unprecedented 35% since July last year. For countries ranging from Pakistan to Cameroon, this has meant lower foreign exchange earnings and employment and a slowdown in economic growth.

Meanwhile, for many developing countries, the emphasis on export promotion resulted in the increasing export of people, rather than goods and services. Remittance flows from temporary and permanent migrants accounted for 25% of net inflows of private capital to the global South in 2007. These flows are also affected by the crisis, although they have proved more resilient than other sources of private capital.

Migrant workers in construction, in particular, find that they are no longer able to find work and send money back home, and countries in Latin America have seen sharp declines in remittance inflows. However, as Indian economist Jayati Ghosh points out, women migrants working as maids, nurses and nannies in the West have not been as hard hit by the recession. This has meant that remittance flows to countries with primarily female migrants, such as Sri Lanka and the Phillipines, are not as badly affected. The Middle Eastern countries that are important host countries for many Asian migrants have also been relatively shielded from the crisis. Interestingly, the stock of migrants even in hard-hit countries has not decreased, with most migrants choosing to wait out the crisis. As a result, for the developing

TABLE 2: RELATIONSHIP BETWEENS NEO-LIBERAL "GOOD" POLICIES AND 2008 GDP DECLINE			
	Rank by share of exports in GDP, 2005-07 avgerage (1= highest export share)	Rank by share of remittances in GDP, 2005-07 average (1 = highest share)	Exchange rate regime, Jan 2008 (1=forms of fixed exchange rates, 2=managed float, 3=freely floating)
Rank of country by relative slowdown in real GDP growth in 2008, compared to average real GDP growth between 2005-2007 (1=worst off)	0.15** N=167	0.125* N=155	-0.131* N=178

* Statistically significant at 5%; ** Statistically significant at 1%.

Sources: Author's calculations based on data from World Development Indicators online, World Bank, June 2009 and De Facto Classification of Exchange Rate Regimes and Monetary Policy Frameworks as of April 31, 2008. IMF.

world as a whole, remittances actually rose in 2008. Given that other private capital flows declined sharply post-crisis, remittances accounted for 46% of net private capital inflows to the developing world in 2008.

Despite the fact that remittances were, on average, more stable than other sources of foreign exchange earnings, the ranking of countries by relative GDP decline is also highly correlated with the ranking of countries by share of remittances in GDP. Thus countries more dependent upon remittances from 2005-2007 were also more badly affected by the crisis in 2008 (Table 2).

Outflows of portfolio capital. In the boom years up to 2007, developing countries were encouraged to liberalize their financial sectors. This meant removing regulatory barriers to the inflow (and outflow) of foreign investors and their money. While some foreign investors did put money into buying actual physical assets in the developing world, a substantial portion of foreign capital came in the form of portfolio capital—short-term investments in stock and real estate markets in the developing

TABLE 3: RELATIONSHIP BETWEENS NEO-LIBERAL "GOOD" POLICIES AND 2008 GDP DECLINE, CONTINUED.		
	Rank by share of FDI in GDP, 2005-07 average (1 = highest share)	Inflation targeting, January 2008 (0=does not have inflation targeting, 1=has inflation targeting)
Rank of country by relative slowdown in real GDP growth in 2008, compared to average real GDP growth between 2005-2007 (1=worst off)	0.15** N=167	-0.207** N=178

** Statistically significant at 1%.

Sources: Author's calculations based on data from World Development Indicators online, World Bank, June 2009 and De Facto Classification of Exchange Rate Regimes and Monetary Policy Frameworks as of April 31, 2008. IMF.

TABLE 4: INDICATORS OF VULNERABILITY AND 2008 GDP DECLINE			
	Rank by share of food in imports (1= highest export share)	Rank by aid per capita (1= highest aid p.c.)	HIPC country
Rank by relative decline in GDP growth rate (1= worst off)	0.163** N=147	-0.180** N=151	0.255** N=178

** Statistically significant at 1%.

Sources: Author's calculations based on data from World Development Indicators online, World Bank, June 2009 and De Facto Classification of Exchange Rate Regimes and Monetary Policy Frameworks as of April 31, 2008. IMF.

world. This money is called "hot money" for a reason—it tends to be incredibly mobile, and its mobility has been enhanced by the systematic dismantling of various government restrictions (capital controls) that prevented this money from both entering and leaving countries at the speed it can today.

After early 2008, around the time of the collapse of Bear Stearns in the United States, various global financial powerhouses began pulling their money out of developing country markets. The pace of the pullout only accelerated after the crash in September. One consequence for developing countries was a fall in stock market indices that in turn depressed growth. Another was that as these foreign investors converted their krona, rupees, or rubles into dollars in order to leave, the value of the local currency got pushed down.

The IMF has long touted the virtues of allowing freely floating exchange rates, where market forces determine the value of the currency. In the aftermath of the financial crisis, however, this meant a sharp depreciation in the value of many local currencies relative to the dollar. This in turn meant that every gallon of oil priced in dollars would require that many more, say, rupees to buy. Similarly, any dollar-denominated debt a country held became harder to repay. The dollar cost of imports and debt servicing went up, just as exports and remittances—the ability to earn those dollars—were falling.

Once again, Table 2 tells us that countries with "floating" exchange rates (i.e., market determined exchange rates) were harder hit in 2008.

Falling flows of FDI and development aid. Meanwhile, one other source of foreign exchange, foreign investment in actual physical assets such as factories, known as foreign direct investment (FDI), is stagnant and likely to fall as companies across the world shelve expansion plans. The signs of vulnerability are evident in the fact that countries most dependent upon FDI inflows (as a percentage of GDP) between 2005 and 2007 also suffered greater relative GDP declines in 2008 (Table 3).

Developed countries are also cutting back on foreign aid budgets, citing the cost of domestic stimulus programs and reduced tax revenues. The countries impacted are likely to be among the poorest in the world. Given that the economic slowdown means that governments are losing domestic tax and other revenues, falling aid flows are likely to hurt even more. The importance of continued aid flows can be seen in the fact that higher levels of aid per capita from 2005 to 2007 were actually negatively correlated with GDP decline in 2008 (Table 4). This may be partly due to the fact that these countries already had low or negative rates of GDP growth so that 2008 declines were smaller relative to that baseline. Nevertheless, aid flows appear to have protected the most vulnerable countries from even greater economic disaster. Table 4 also tells us that HIPC countries (highly indebted poor countries) were also less affected by the crisis, for the same reasons.

Both FDI and aid work their way into and out of the economy more slowly. As a result we may have to wait for 2009 data to estimate the full impact of the crisis via this channel. One dangerous sign is the fact that the countries with the largest share of food in imports from 2005 to 2007 were also those worst affected by the crisis (Table 4).

Conclusions

The simultaneous transmission of the crisis through these three channels has left developing countries reeling. What makes the situation even worse is that unlike developed countries, developing countries are unlikely to be able to afford generous stimulus packages (China is an important exception). Meanwhile, the IMF and its allies, rather than supporting developing country governments in their quest to stimulate domestic demand and investment, are hindering the process by insisting on the same policy mix of deficit reductions and interest rate hikes. In an illustration of how ruinous this policy mix can be, countries that had followed IMF advice and adopted "inflation targeting" before the crisis actually suffered greater GDP declines once the crisis hit (Table 2).

The tragedy of course is that while the remnants of the welfare state do protect citizens of the developed world from the very worst effects of the crisis, developing countries have been urged for two decades to abandon the food and fuel subsidies and public sector provision of essential services that are the only things that come close to resembling a floor for living standards. They were told they didn't need that safety net, that it only got in the way, and now, of course, their citizens are free to fall.

For those unwilling to let this tragedy unfold, this is the time to apply pressure on developed country governments to maintain aid flows. Even more importantly, this is the time to apply pressure on the multilateral development banks, such as the World Bank, and their supporters in the halls of power so that they offer developing countries a genuine chance to survive this crisis and begin to rebuild for the future.

It is worth recalling that the end of the previous "age of globalization," signaled by the Great Depression, led to a renewed role for the public sector the world over and an attempt to achieve growth alongside self-reliance. Led by Latin America, newly independent developing countries attempted to prioritize the building of a domestic producer and consumer base. In the long run, perhaps this crisis will result in a similar rethinking of the currently dominant model of development. In the short run, however, the world seems ready to stand by and watch while the poor and vulnerable in developing countries, truly innocent bystanders, suffer. ❑

Sources: Dilip Ratha, Sanket Mohapatra, and Ani Silwal, "Migration and Development Brief 10," Migration and Remittances Team, Development Prospects Group, World Bank, July 13, 2009; Atish R. Ghosh *et al.*, "Coping with the Crisis: Policy Options for Emerging Market Countries," *IMF Staff Postion Note, SPN/09/08*, April 23, 2009; World Bank, "Swimming Against the Tide: How Developing Countries Are Coping with the Global Crisis," Background Paper prepared by World Bank Staff for the G20 Finance Ministers and Central Bank Governors Meeting, Horsham, United Kingdom on March 13-14, 2009; Jayati Ghosh, "Current Global Financial Crisis: Curse or Blessing in Disguise for Developing Countries?" Presentation prepared for the IWG-GEM Workshop, Levy Economics Institute, New York, June 29-July 10, 2009.

Article 10.2

(ECONOMIC) FREEDOM'S JUST ANOTHER WORD FOR...CRISIS-PRONE

BY JOHN MILLER

September/October 2009

In "Capitalism in Crisis," his May op-ed in the *Wall Street Journal*, U.S. Court of Appeals judge and archconservative legal scholar Richard Posner argued that "a capitalist economy, while immensely dynamic and productive, is not inherently stable." Posner, the long-time cheerleader for deregulation added, quite sensibly, "we may need more regulation of banking to reduce its inherent riskiness."

That may seem like a no-brainer to you and me, right there in the middle of the road with yellow-lines and dead armadillos, as Jim Hightower is fond of saying. But *Journal* readers were having none of it. They wrote in to set Judge Posner straight. "It is not free markets that fail, but government-controlled ones," protested one reader.

And why wouldn't they protest? The *Journal* has repeatedly told readers that "economic freedom" is "the real key to development." And each January for 15 years now the *Journal* tries to elevate that claim to a scientific truth by publishing a summary of the Heritage Foundation Index of Economic Freedom, which they assure readers proves the veracity of the claim.   But the hands of the editors of the *Wall Street Journal* and the researchers from the Heritage Foundation, Washington's foremost right-wing think tank, the Index of Economic Freedom is a barometer of corporate and entrepreneurial freedom from accountability rather than a guide to which countries are giving people more control over their economic lives and over the institutions that govern them.

This January was no different. "The 2009 Index provides strong evidence that the countries that maintain the freest economies do the best job promoting prosperity for all citizens," proclaimed this year's editorial, "Freedom is Still the Winning Formula." But with economies across the globe in recession, the virtues of free markets are a harder sell this year. That is not lost on *Wall Street Journal* editor Paul Gigot, who wrote the foreword to this year's report. Gigot allows that, "ostensibly free-market policymakers in the U.S. lost their monetary policy discipline, and we are now paying a terrible price." Still Gigot maintains that, "the *Index of Economic Freedom* exists to chronicle how steep that price will be and to point the way back to policy wisdom."

What the Heritage report fails to mention is this: while the global economy is in recession, many of the star performers in the Economic Freedom Index are tanking. Fully one half of the ten hardest-hit economies in the world are among the 30 "free" and "mostly free" economies at the top of the Economic Freedom Index rankings of 179 countries.

Here's the damage, according to the IMF. Singapore, the Southeast Asian trading center and perennial number two in the Index, will suffer a 10.0% drop in output this year. Slotting in at number 4, Ireland, the so-called Celtic tiger, has seen its rapid export-led growth give way to an 8.0% drop in output. Number 13 and number 30, the foreign-direct-investment-favored Baltic states, Estonia and Lithuania, will each endure a 10.0% loss of output this year. Finally, the economy of Iceland, the loosely regulated European banking center that sits at number 14 on the Index, will contract 10.6% in 2009.

As a group, the Index's 30 most "free" economies will contract 4.1% in 2009. All of the other groups in the Index ("moderately free," "mostly unfree," and "repressed" economies) will muddle through 2009 with a much smaller loss of output or with moderate growth. The 67 "mostly unfree" countries in the Index will post the fastest growth rate for the year, 2.3%.

So it seems that if the Index of Economic Freedom can be trusted, then Judge Posner was not so far off the mark when he described capitalism as dynamic but "not inherently stable." That wouldn't be so bad, one *Journal* reader pointed out in a letter: "Economic recessions are the cost we pay for our economic freedom and economic prosperity is the benefit. We've had many more years of the latter than the former."

Not to be Trusted

But the Index of Economic Freedom cannot and should not be trusted. How free or unfree an economy is according to the Index seems to have little do with how quickly it grows. For instance, economist Jeffery Sachs found "no correlation" between a country's ranking in the Index and its per capita growth rates from 1995 to 2003. Also, in this year's report North America is the "freest" of its six regions of the world, but logged the slowest average rate over the last five years, 2.7% per annum. The Asia-Pacific region, which is "less free" than every other region except Sub-Saharan Africa according to the Index, posted the fastest average growth over the last five years, 7.8% per annum. That region includes several of fastest growing of the world's economies, India, China, and Vietnam, which ranked 123, 132, and

ECONOMIC FREEDOM AND ECONOMIC GROWTH IN 2009	
Degree of Economic Freedom	IMF Projected Growth Rate for 2009
"Free" (7 Countries)	-4.54%
"Mostly Free" (23 Counties)	-3.99%
"Moderately Free" (53 Countries)	-0.92%
"Mostly Unfree" (67 Countries)	+2.31%
"Repressed" (69 Counties)	+1.65%

Sources: International Monetary Fund, *World Economic Outlook,: Crisis and Recovery*, April 2009, Tables A1, A2, A3; Terry Miller and Kim R. Holmes, eds., *2009 Index of Economic Freedom*, heritage.org/Index/, Executive Summary.

145 respectively in the Index and were classified as "mostly unfree." And there are plenty of relatively slow growers among the countries high up in the Index, including Switzerland (which ranks ninth).

The Heritage Foundation folks who edited the Index objected to Sachs' criticisms, pointing out that they claimed "a close relationship" between *changes* in economic freedom, not the *level* of economic freedom, and growth. But even that claim is fraught with problems. Statistically it doesn't hold up. Economic journalist Doug Henwood found that improvements in the index and GDP growth from 1997 to 2003 could explain no more than 10% of GDP growth. In addition, even a tight correlation would not resolve the problem that many of the fastest growing economies are "mostly unfree" according to the Index.

But even more fundamental flaws with the Index render any claim about the relationship between prosperity and economic freedom, as measured by the Heritage Foundation, questionable. Consider just two of the ten components the Economic Freedom Index uses to rank countries: fiscal freedom and government size.

Fiscal freedom (what we might call the "hell-if-I'm-going-to-pay-for-government" index) relies on the top income tax and corporate income tax brackets as two of its three measures of the tax burden. These are decidedly flawed measures even if all that concerned you was the tax burden of the rich and owners of corporations (or the super-rich). Besides ignoring the burden of other taxes, singling out these two top tax rates don't get at effective corporate and income tax rates, or how much of a taxpayer's total income goes to paying these taxes. For example, on paper U.S. corporate tax rates are higher than those in Europe. But nearly one half of U.S. corporate profits go untaxed. The effective rate of taxation on U.S. corporate profits currently stands at 15%, far below the top corporate tax rate of 35%. And relative to GDP, U.S. corporate income taxes are no more than half those of other OECD countries.

Even their third measure of fiscal freedom, government tax revenues relative to GDP, bears little relationship to economic growth. After an exhaustive review, economist Joel Selmrod, former member of the Reagan Treasury Department, concludes that the literature reveals "no consensus" about the relationship between the level of taxation and economic growth.

The Index's treatment of government size, which relies exclusively on the level of government spending relative to GDP, is just as flawed as the fiscal freedom index. First, "richer countries do not tax and spend less" than poorer countries, reports economist Peter Lindhert. Beyond that, this measure does not take into account how the government uses its money. Social spending programs—public education, child-care and parental support, and public health programs—can make people more productive and promote economic growth. That lesson is not lost on Hong Kong and Singapore, number one and number two in the index. They both provide universal access to health care, despite the small size of their governments.

The size-of-government index also misses the mark because it fails to account for industrial policy. This is a serious mistake, because it overestimates the degree to which some of the fastest growing economies of the last few decades, such as Taiwan and South Korea, relied on the market and underestimates the positive role that government played in directing economic development in those countries by guiding investment and protecting infant industries.

This flaw is thrown into sharp relief by the recent report of the World Bank's Commission on Growth and Development. That group studied 13 economies that grew at least 7% a year for at least 25 years since 1950. Three of the Index's "free" and "mostly free" countries made the list (Singapore, Hong Kong, and Japan) but so did three of the index's "mostly unfree" countries (China, Brazil, and Indonesia). While these rapid growers were all export-oriented, their governments "were not free-market purists," according the Commission's report. "They tried a variety of policies to help diversify exports or sustain competitiveness. These included industrial policies to promote new investments."

Still More

Beyond all that, the Index says nothing about political freedom. Consider once again the two city-states, Hong Kong and Singapore, which top their list of free countries. Both are only "partially free" according to Freedom House, which the editors have called "the Michelin Guide to democracy's development." Hong Kong is still without direct elections for it legislatures or its chief executive and a proposed internal security laws threaten press and academic freedom as well as political dissent. In Singapore, freedom of the press and rights to demonstrate are limited, films, TV and the like are censored, and preventive detention is legal.

So it seems that the Index of Economic Freedom in practice tells us little about the cost of abandoning free market policies and offers little proof that government intervention into the economy would either retard economic growth or contract political freedom. In actuality, this rather objective-looking index is a slip-shod measure that would seem to have no other purpose than to sell the neoliberal policies that brought on the current crisis, and to stand in the way of policies that might correct the crisis. ❏

Sources: "Capitalism in Crisis," by Richard A Posner, *Wall Street Journal*, 5/07/09; "Letters: Recessions are the Price We Pay for Economic Freedom," *Wall Street Journal*, 5/19/09/; "Freedom is Still the Winning Formula," by Terry Miller, *Wall Street Journal*, 1/13/09 ; "The Real Key to Development," by Mary Anastasia O'Grady, *Wall Street Journal*, 1/15/08; Terry Miller and Kim R. Holmes, eds., *2009 Index of Economic Freedom*, heritage.org/Index/; Freedom House, "Freedom in the World 2009 Survey," freedomhouse.org; Joel Selmrod and Jon Bakija, *Taxing Ourselves: A Citizen's Guide to the Debate over Taxes*, MIT Press, 2008; International Monetary Fund, *World Economic Outlook,: Crisis and Recovery*, April 2009; Peter H. Lindert, *Growing Public*, Cambridge University Press, 2004; Doug Henwood, "*Laissez-faire* Olympics: An LBO Special Report," leftbusinessobserver.com, March 26, 2005; Jeffrey Sachs, *The End of Poverty: Economic Possibilities for Our Time*, Penguin, 2005.

Article 10.3

THE GIANT POOL OF MONEY

BY ARTHUR MacEWAN
September/October 2009

Dear Dr. Dollar

On May 9, the public radio program This American Life broadcast an explanation of the housing crisis with the title: "The Giant Pool of Money." With too much money looking for investment opportunities, lots of bad investments were made—including the bad loans to home buyers. But where did this "giant pool of money" come from? Was this really a source of the home mortgage crisis?

—*Gail Radford, Buffalo, N.Y.*

The show was both entertaining and interesting. A good show, but maybe a bit more explanation will be useful.

There was indeed a "giant pool of money" that was an important part of the story of the home mortgage crisis—well, not "money" as we usually think of it, but financial assets, which I'll get to in a moment. And that pool of money is an important link in the larger economic crisis story.

The giant pool of money was the build-up of financial assets—U.S. Treasury bonds, for example, and other assets that pay a fixed income. According to the program, the amount of these assets had grown from roughly $36 trillion in 2000 to $70 trillion in 2008. That's $70 *trillion*, with a T, which is a lot of money, roughly the same as total world output in 2008.

These financial assets built up for a number of reasons. One was the doubling of oil prices (after adjusting for inflation) between 2000 and 2007, largely due to the U.S. invasion of Iraq. This put a lot of money in the hands of governments in oil-producing countries and private individuals connected to the oil industry.

A second factor was the large build up of reserves (i.e., the excess of receipts from exports over payments for imports) by several low-income countries, most notably China. One reason some countries operated in this manner was simply to keep the cost of their currency low in terms of U.S. dollars, thus maintaining demand for their exports. (Using their own currencies to buy dollars, they were increasing both the supply of their currencies and the demand for dollars; this pushed the price of their currencies down and of dollars up.) But another reason was to protect themselves from the sort of problems they had faced in the early 1980s, when world recession cut their export earnings and left them unable to meet their import costs and pay their debts—thus the debt crisis of that era.

This build-up of dollar reserves by governments (actually, central banks) of other countries was also a result of the budgetary deficits of the Bush administration. Spending more than it was taking in as taxes (after the big tax cuts for the wealthy and with the heavy war spending), the Bush administration needed to borrow. Foreign governments, by buying the U.S. securities, were providing the loans.

Still a third factor explaining the giant pool of financial assets was the high level of inequality within the United States and elsewhere in the global economy. Since 1993, half of all income gains in the United States have gone to the highest-income 1% of households. While the very rich spend a good share of their money on mansions, fancy cars, and other luxuries, there was plenty more money for them to put into investments—the stock market but also fixed-income securities (i.e., bonds).

So there is the giant pool of money or, again, of financial assets.

The financial assets became a problem for two connected reasons. First, in the recovery following the 2001 recession, economic growth was very slow; there were thus very limited real investment opportunities. Between 2001 and 2007, private fixed investment (adjusted for inflation) grew by only 11%, whereas in the same number of years following the recession of the early 1990s, investment grew by 59%.

Second, in an effort to stimulate more growth, the Federal Reserve kept interest rates very low. But the low interest rates meant low returns on financial assets— U.S. government bonds in particular, but financial assets in general. So the holders of financial assets went searching for new investment opportunities, which, as the radio program explained, meant pushing money into high-risk mortgages. The rest, as they say, is history.

So the giant pool of money was the link that tied high inequality, the war, and rising financial imbalances in the world economy (caused in large part by the U.S. government's budgetary policies) to the housing crisis and thus to the more general financial crisis.

Again, check out the *This American Life* episode for the details of how this "link" operated. It's quite a story! ❑

Article 10.4

THE SPECTER OF CAPITAL FLIGHT

How long will the power of the dollar protect the United States?

BY MARIE DUGGAN
January/February 2009

The depth and scope of the unfolding financial crisis have taken most observers by surprise. Yet there were definite warning signs. One was the United States' growing dependence on foreign capital, an issue that came to my attention in 2005 when I was preparing a lecture on Mexico's mid-1990s financial crisis. This was the so-called Tequila Crisis: foreign investors and wealthy Mexicans abruptly fled dollar-denominated Mexican bonds called Tesebonos as well as Mexican stocks, moving their money into safer U.S. assets. In hindsight, many observers point to Mexico's increased borrowing from abroad in the early 1990s, reflected in its worsening current account deficit, as a sign of impending trouble. (See sidebar, "Current Account Explained," below.)

Curious about where the United States stood, I was shocked to discover that the U.S. current account deficit in 2005, measured as a percent of GDP, was approaching the same level as Mexico's had been in 1993—and getting worse (see Figure 1). In other words, in the early 2000s the United States became as dependent on foreign financing as Mexico was just prior to its crisis.

Mexico was only the first of many emerging markets to undergo spectacular financial crises in the late 1990s and early 2000s. The list includes Thailand, Indonesia, South Korea, Malaysia, Russia, and Argentina, among others.

The typical financial crisis story in an emerging market begins with capital flight—the sudden withdrawal of money by foreign investors from an economy's stocks, bonds, and banking system. Often locals decide to move their wealth abroad as well. Stock markets crash, banks fail, the local currency drops in value, and governments face default. Interest rates rise as governments try to woo foreign investors and their own citizens back into the home currency with the promise of high returns, but then the high interest rates push domestic borrowers, whether firms or households, toward bankruptcy. Unemployment shoots up and GDP falls. In some emerging markets, the magnitude of these difficulties mirrored those the United States experienced in the Great Depression of the 1930s.

At the time, the United States and the other developed countries were widely viewed as immune from such financial crises.

Now it is clear that the United States is not immune. The current crisis began in the financial sector in the summer of 2007 and hit the real side of the economy in fall 2008, with the unemployment rate rising by more than 26% in just five months, from 5.7% in July to 7.2% in December. Since 1979, the real side of the U.S. economy has suffered (think deindustrialization) while the financial side has thrived.

With stagnant or falling real wages coinciding with a lengthy period of low interest rates, many working people went into debt in order to purchase homes and stocks so that they would be able to participate in some modest way in the rise of finance. The collapse of finance, then, is pulling working Americans down with it.

But the United States' crisis is departing from the typical pattern. For one thing, far from dropping in value, the dollar has risen against other currencies in recent months. The factors which were supposed to make the United States immune to financial crisis did not do so, but they are causing the crisis to play out in new and unpredictable ways.

Swimming Pool of Savings

The United States' dependence on foreign financing is one reason the collapse of housing prices has sparked an economy-wide financial crisis.

Imagine the pool of savings in an economy as a giant swimming pool; the water in the pool represents money available to borrowers. Everyone who saves money in a bank account, in the stock market, or in government bonds—whether a U.S. resident or a foreign investor—adds water to the pool.

In recent years an increasingly large share of the water in the United States' pool has been coming from abroad. And when foreign capital is a substantial part of the water in the pool, the sheer volume of capital that can fly in and out of a country's assets is much larger, making its stock market and other asset markets more volatile.

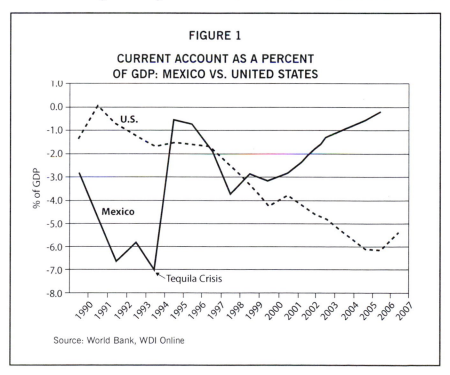

FIGURE 1

CURRENT ACCOUNT AS A PERCENT
OF GDP: MEXICO VS. UNITED STATES

Source: World Bank, WDI Online

Here we are not talking about foreign investment in factories or other economic activity on U.S. soil, termed foreign direct investment, which would take months or years to liquidate. Rather, this is portfolio investment—investment in paper assets such as stocks and bonds—and this money can fly out of a country at the touch of a computer key.

You can see in Figure 1 the moment when foreign investors suddenly stopped putting money into Mexico, forcing the nation to live within its means: Mexico's current account deficit went from 7% of GDP in 1994 to 1% of GDP in 1995. So one might think that foreign investors pulling out of the United States would be a good thing—Americans would finally be forced to live within our means.

But it's not quite that simple. Most Americans with debts—whether student loans, a mortgage, a car loan, or credit card balances—do not think of themselves as borrowing from foreigners. But part of the reason banks were willing to provide all this credit to U.S. consumers at fairly low interest rates was that foreign investors were filling the pool with plenty of water by buying U.S. stocks or bonds or putting their savings into U.S. deposit accounts. It is not only our government that borrows from foreign investors, but U.S. households and firms as well.

As a result, as large numbers of both foreign and domestic investors have pulled out of U.S. stocks and banks over the past 18 months, it has become harder for my students, for small businesses, and even for General Motors to get loans. Without access to student loans, the poorest students are dropping out of college; some colleges may close their doors. Fewer people now qualify for mortgage loans, so houses sell more slowly and at cut prices. Car loans are drying up, so dealerships are laying people off. If the credit crunch pushes credit-card interest rates up, then even consumers who stop making new purchases will be stuck with high interest rates on existing balances. In Mexico in 1995, credit card interest rates of 65% were considered on the low side.

CURRENT ACCOUNT EXPLAINED

For over 15 years, the United States has been spending more foreign currency annually on imports than the country has earned through its exports—and borrowing from foreign investors every year to cover the difference. The amount a nation's spending on imports differs from its income from exports is called the current account. If imports exceed exports, the current account is negative; in other words, the country has a current account deficit.

Specifically, in 2007 U.S. imports exceeded exports to the tune of $731 billion. That current account deficit was covered by a $774 billion "net financial inflow," i.e., the amount U.S. borrowing from abroad exceeded U.S. lending to foreigners. (The $41 billion difference between the current account deficit and the country's net borrowing is mostly a statistical discrepancy.) Note that the United States's total foreign debt is going to be much higher, the pile of net financial inflows accumulated year after year.

Until 2007, this kind of capital flight and ensuing financial crisis were widely viewed as impossible in the United States. Three factors were supposed to account for U.S. immunity:

- The dollar is the world's reserve currency, so foreign investors will always hold it.

- U.S. debt is denominated in dollars, so the exchange rate depreciation that would result from capital flight would not increase the debt burden on domestic borrowers.

- U.S. political and financial institutions are far more functional and less corrupt than those in emerging markets.

Let's look at how each of these factors has played out in the current crisis.

Dollars Are Special

Many countries around the world hold onto U.S. Treasury bonds as a so-called reserve asset.

To explore what reserves are, consider a professor suddenly faced with $30,000 in urgent home repairs she cannot cover out of her current income. This is not a problem as long as relatively cheap credit is available; for instance, she may plan to take out a home equity loan to pay for the repairs. But suppose that loan suddenly becomes unavailable. What will she do?

Many people do have other sources of financing, and in a sense, these are their reserves. They resort to liquidating the savings account and the IRA or selling off the wedding ring.

Countries, too, have reserves. Typically, they hoard gold and U.S. Treasury bonds for rainy days. The dollar has been the world's reserve currency since the close of World War II. This means that U.S. Treasury bonds (which are issued by the U.S. government to finance its debt) are the safest, most stable place for countries to park their reserves because the U.S. government has the power to print the reserve currency.

In fact, one reason the United States has been able to run so large a current account deficit has been other countries' desire to hold more reserves.

In 1997, suddenly unable to borrow from abroad, many Asian countries used up their reserves. Then they turned to the International Monetary Fund (IMF) for emergency loans. This is analogous to the professor turning to her parents for an emergency loan. Her parents may well agree to finance the repairs—but only on the condition that she never buy another caffè latte at Starbucks. Likewise, the IMF agreed to these loans, but only if the Asian nations acquiesced to certain conditions, generally much more onerous ones than giving up lattes. For example, then-Treasury

Secretary Robert Rubin basically withheld South Korea's IMF rescue package until the country agreed to sell shares of its profitable companies, like Samsung, to U.S. investors. The Asian nations agreed to the IMF's conditions, but they swore "never again," and have since hoarded vast amounts of dollars. Today, about 20% of the United States' total borrowing comes from foreign governments that are buying up dollar assets as reserves.

But it is starting to seem possible that other countries might not want to use the dollar as their reserve currency forever.

By July 2008, China, which alone holds about $1.8 trillion in U.S. assets, admitted that "it has been looking to strike deals with private equity firms in Europe as part of a strategy to reduce its dollar holdings," and "a big sovereign fund in the [Persian] Gulf has cut its dollar denominated holdings from more than 80% a year ago to less than 60% today," the *Financial Times* reported.

The euro is emerging as an alternative, as is gold. Between August 2007, when it became clear that the subprime debacle would cause widespread losses for investors, and March 2008, when fear of a U.S. financial meltdown reached fever pitch, the price of gold jumped by over 45%, breaking the $1,000/ounce mark. Investors in large numbers were evidently selling U.S. assets and buying gold as an alternative safe haven.

Debt Stable; Net Worth Down

So maybe the dollar's role as reserve currency cannot prevent capital flight from the United States. But even if it did occur, capital flight was not supposed to hurt the

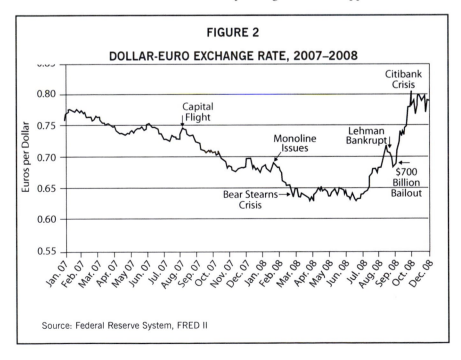

FIGURE 2

DOLLAR-EURO EXCHANGE RATE, 2007–2008

Source: Federal Reserve System, FRED II

U.S. economy the way it damaged so many emerging markets in the late 1990s and early 2000s.

When other nations borrow in a foreign currency—which is common in many emerging markets—then any devaluation of their home currency automatically swells the size of the debts owed by their citizens, governments, and businesses. Here's an example: In 1995 my landlady in Mexico City owed $1,000 on a dollar-denominated credit card. She earned her income in pesos, so this meant 3,000 pesos of debt prior to January 1995. But that turned into 12,000 pesos of debt a few weeks later, when capital flight from the peso had caused it to devalue from three pesos to the dollar to twelve pesos to the dollar. (Her income, of course, did not quadruple!) In 2001, many Argentineans had taken out mortgage loans in dollars, so that when the Argentine peso devaluated from one to three pesos per dollar, their monthly mortgage payments effectively tripled.

With the debts of U.S. households and businesses denominated in our own currency, a devaluation of the dollar does not affect the size of those debts. But capital flight can damage net worth anyway—by causing asset values to fall.

The current fall in home prices, for instance, is directly tied to the United States' dependence on foreign lending. International buyers were swelling the U.S.

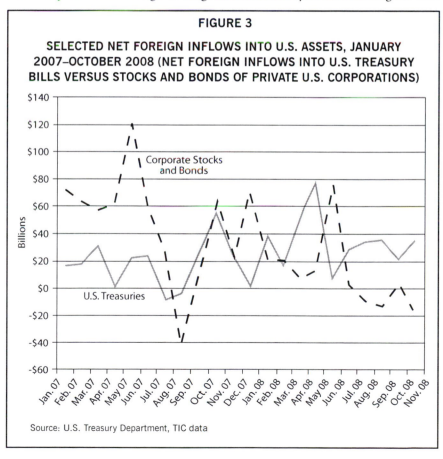

FIGURE 3

SELECTED NET FOREIGN INFLOWS INTO U.S. ASSETS, JANUARY 2007–OCTOBER 2008 (NET FOREIGN INFLOWS INTO U.S. TREASURY BILLS VERSUS STOCKS AND BONDS OF PRIVATE U.S. CORPORATIONS)

Source: U.S. Treasury Department, TIC data

housing bubble by buying up the now-infamous mortgage-backed securities comprised of bundles of individual mortgage loans. So long as there was international (as well as domestic) demand for these securities, U.S. lenders could not issue new mortgages fast enough. But once foreign investors realized that these securities were not the safe investment they'd been marketed as and dumped them, U.S. banks were much less interested in making mortgages since they could no longer sell them off. With fewer buyers able to get home loans, houses are harder to sell and their prices are falling.

It's a parallel story in the stock market, which has lost close to half its value just since last summer as both foreign and U.S. investors have pulled their money out.

Although data on household wealth trends are not immediately available, this one-two punch almost certainly means that the net worth of U.S. households has taken a big hit. In my case, until recently home equity and pension funds performed the miracle of giving me positive net worth despite my typical debt load. They are not pulling this miracle off today.

The loss of wealth that occurs when assets lose value can in itself cause problems in the real economy. Even though net worth is somewhat intangible, it is disconcerting to watch it fall. Vacations get cancelled, new car purchases delayed, and home improvements put off. This is happening on a massive scale today, resulting in significant layoffs by airlines, car dealerships, and construction firms, with spin-off

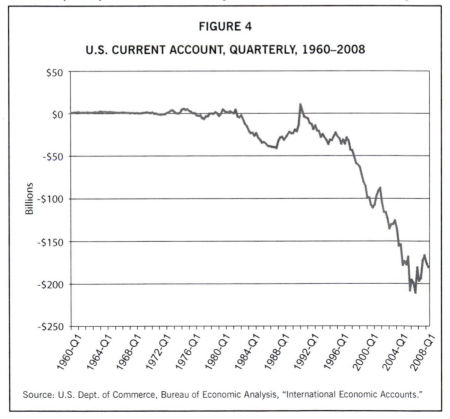

FIGURE 4

U.S. CURRENT ACCOUNT, QUARTERLY, 1960–2008

Source: U.S. Dept. of Commerce, Bureau of Economic Analysis, "International Economic Accounts."

effects throughout the economy. The pain on the real side of the economy has only just begun.

Are U.S. Institutions More Sound?

In the mid-1990s, one of the major clues that Argentina was heading for crisis was the country's high level of government debt, nearly 40% of GDP. At the time, the IMF opposed new loans to Argentina until the country got its government debt down to 34% of GDP.

By these IMF guidelines, the United States has been in the danger zone since 2003. U.S. central government debt as a percent of GDP jumped from the 30% range in 2002 to the 47% range just a year later—presumably due to the combination of Bush's 2001 tax cut and the wars in Iraq and Afghanistan. It is unusual for a nation to cut taxes while it is entering two wars.

Economist Paul Blustein's description of the Menem regime so resonates with George W. Bush's time in office that it bears repeating here:

> Former Argentine policymakers acknowledge that foreign money made the government less concerned than it should have been about its debt burden and more inclined to treat admonitions with indifference. [One Argentine advisor stated,] "You can say to the politicians 'We need fiscal balance.' But if you get the money so easily, as we did, it's very tough to tell the politicians, 'Don't spend more, be more prudent,' because the money was there, and they knew it."

George Bush is a consummate politician. Like Menem, he used money (including big tax cuts for his well-to-do patrons) to build up debts and loyalty. Throwing money around helped keep Menem (and Bush) in power, but it built up debt which hamstrings economic policy in a crunch. Had Bush maintained the surpluses of the Clinton years, the U.S. economy might be in a different place today.

Of course, as recent events have underscored, the government has no monopoly on dysfunction. At first glance, it may seem ludicrous to suggest that U.S. banks could be fragile in a way similar to the banks in, say, Indonesia. In the years leading up to the Asian financial crises, Indonesia's banks held many non-performing loans, often loans made to President Suharto's cronies that no one ever expected would be repaid. Thus, the banking system's net worth on paper was an overstatement, inflated by what were essentially political donations by the banks.

But it turns out that U.S. banks have also been claiming worthless paper as assets. As of March 2008, when U.S. banks had reported only $160 billion in losses, independent analysts argued that their losses were in fact at least $300 billion and possibly as high as $1.2 trillion, according to the *Financial Times*. Clearly, many banks had lost more than they were willing to admit.

U.S. regulatory institutions were slow to force banks to reveal the real magnitude of their losses. However, investors do not rely solely on regulators to verify the value of the financial instruments they buy or hold. They also rely on private credit rating agencies. Here too, though, a kind of institutionalized corruption has crept in. One reason international holders of mortgage-backed securities and other similarly complex investments (broadly known as collateralized debt obligations, or CDOs) began dropping them like hot potatoes in August 2007 was that they realized the AAA credit rating these investments bore was false. A triple-A credit rating was supposed to mean that these securities were a very safe investment. But credit ratings are not what they used to be. Traditionally, it was the buyers of securities who paid agencies such as Moody's to rate them, but today it is the sellers of securities who pay for the ratings. So ratings agencies now have an incentive to please the issuers of CDOs by calling them safe.

Once the credibility of the rating system was put into question, the collapse in the value of CDOs had the potential to spark capital flight from many U.S. assets. International faith in Wall Street as a place of transparent and reasonably honest institutions was shaken—and with it, at least potentially, the dollar's role as key global currency.

A Peculiar Crisis

All in all, the factors that were supposed to inoculate the United States against any threat of capital flight turned out to work not quite in the way economists and financial analysts had expected. In the summer of 2007, capital flight struck. The dramatic announcement came two months after the fact, when the data were released:

> Foreign investors slashed their holdings of US securities by a record amount… The Treasury said net sales of US market assets—including bonds, notes, and equities, were $69.3 billion in August…. The August outflow exceeded the previous record decline of $21.2 billion in March 1990. [*Financial Times*, October 17, 2007]

As in the standard capital-flight scenario, the dollar's value did fall (see Figure 2). Then, in February 2008, the dollar fell further when it turned out that U.S. firms with only $46 billion in assets had sold so-called credit default swaps—a kind of quasi-insurance against financial losses—on $2 trillion worth of securities.

The dollar depreciation that occurred between August 2007 and April 2008 had a silver lining. With foreign investors selling more U.S. assets than they were buying, U.S. borrowing from abroad declined. Plus, a devalued dollar made U.S. products cheaper abroad, so exports rose. Both factors contributed to an improvement in the U.S. current account deficit. At the time, this was hailed as an "orderly" change in trajectory. Many observers breathed a sigh of relief, believing the U.S. current account deficit would shrink gradually, allowing the United States to avoid a severe contraction such as Mexico had experienced.

But then a strange thing happened. Shortly after major investment bank Bear Stearns collapsed, and while the larger financial crisis was far from over, the dollar exchange rate bottomed out and began to rise.

This was probably not on account of foreign investors suddenly renewing their faith in the securities Wall Street was selling. Rather, global investors had fled dollar-denominated assets when they got nervous in the summer of 2007, but when they got a full-blown case of panic around March 2008, they flocked to the safest haven in the financial world: U.S. Treasury bonds. (See Figure 3.) Between January and July 2007, the monthly net inflow of foreign capital into the stocks and bonds of U.S. corporations averaged over $65 trillion, more than four times the net foreign capital flowing into U.S. Treasuries. But from August 2007 to October 2008, the average monthly net inflow from abroad to U.S. stocks and bonds fell by over 75% compared to the earlier period, while the inflow to U.S. Treasuries almost doubled. At this point, almost twice as much foreign capital is flowing into Treasuries per month as into stocks and corporate bonds.

On balance, money was now coming into the United States, so the dollar appreciated. Unfortunately, that makes U.S. exports more expensive and imports a bargain, and as a result the current account worsens. By April 2008, the current account was already beginning to dive back down (see Figure 4). Hopes for an orderly escape from dependence on foreign capital evaporated.

Capital flight has played out in the United States in an unusual, even perverse way. Capital has been fleeing from U.S. stocks and private banks for over a year now. But as the saying goes, when the United States sneezes, other parts of the world get pneumonia. The U.S. financial crisis has shaken stock markets around the world. As a result, rather than continuing to leave U.S. shores, investment capital from abroad started to be re-routed to U.S. Treasury bonds. And panicky U.S. investors are augmenting the sums flowing into U.S. Treasuries as they repatriate their money from foreign stock markets.

The stampede into Treasury bonds means that money is available to the federal government at extremely low rates, close to 0% interest. The effect is to push the U.S. government to the forefront of all financing, putting it in the driver's seat of the economy whether or not the political leadership believes in laissez-faire. No surprise then that the private sector is seeking financing from the government on a massive scale.

The key to any kind of recovery for working people is going to be persuading the government to use that money to rebuild the real side of the economy, not just the financial sector. Of course, families want to see the value of their houses and 401(k)s go back up. What they really need, though, are jobs that pay enough so they don't have to count on asset bubbles and ballooning debt to meet their expenses. Talk of rebuilding infrastructure is welcome: both the labor market and a lot of bridges need to be strengthened. Stimulus dollars would be welcome in the economy's care sector too—in child care, in education, in elder care.

And yes, the United States needs a functioning financial sector so that small businesses, students, and even GM have access to credit. But not one as large as it was before the crisis. In recent years finance has acted as a weight on the real economy. Foreign investment in U.S. assets was causing the dollar to appreciate to such levels that U.S. products were less and less affordable overseas. So yes, fix the financial sector, but don't let it get awash with cash to the extent that the dollar appreciates U.S. manufacturers out of business, and that Wall Street CEOs pay themselves tens of millions of dollars a year with which to buy political influence. Don't let the financiers use the money that the government is borrowing today to rebuild finance as the primary engine of the U.S. economy. ❏

Sources: Gerard Dumenil & Dominique Levy, *Capital Resurgent,* 2004; Nora Lustig, *Mexico: The Remaking of an Economy,* 1998; Paul Blustein, *And the Money Kept Rolling In (and Out),* 2005.

Article 10.5

TAX HAVENS AND THE FINANCIAL CRISIS

From offshore havens to financial centers, banking secrecy faces scrutiny.

BY RACHEL KEELER
May/June 2009

When an entire global financial system collapses, it is reasonable to expect some bickering over the ultimate fixing of things. Rumors of dissention and talk of stimulus-paved roads to hell made everyone squeamish going into the April summit of the G20 group of large and industrialized nations in London. French President Nicolas Sarkozy even threatened to walk out on the whole thing if he didn't get his way.

The French were perhaps right to be nervous: they were taking a somewhat socialist stand, declaring that unregulated shadow banking and offshore tax havens were at the heart of the financial crisis and had to be either controlled or eradicated. They were doing it in a city at the center of the shadow system, and at a summit chaired by British Prime Minister Gordon Brown, a man recently described by the *Financial Times* as "one of the principal cheerleaders for the competitive international deregulation of international financial markets."

But Gordon Brown had already announced his intention to lead the global crackdown on tax havens as a first step toward global financial recovery. German Chancellor Angela Merkel had long backed France in calling for regulation of hedge funds, the poster boys of shadow banking charged with fostering the crisis. And, to Sarkozy's delight, everyone kept their promises at the G20.

"Major failures in the financial sector and in financial regulation and supervision were fundamental causes of the crisis," read the summit's reassuringly clear communiqué. World leaders agreed to regulate all systemically important financial institutions, including hedge funds and those located in tax havens, under threat of sanctions for noncompliance. "The era of banking secrecy is over," they concluded, as close to united as anyone could have dreamed.

But unity that looks good on paper is always more difficult to achieve in reality. The lingering questions post-summit are the same ones Sarkozy may have pondered on his way to London: will leaders from countries made rich from offshore banking follow through to shut it down? What is at stake, and what will the globally coordinated regulation everyone agrees is necessary actually look like? Not surprisingly, there are no easy answers.

Nature of the Beast

Over the years, trillions of dollars in both corporate profits and personal wealth have migrated "offshore" in search of rock bottom tax rates and the comfort of no questions asked. Tax havens and other financial centers promoting low tax rates, light regulation, and financial secrecy include a long list of tropical nations like the Cayman Islands as well as whole mainland economies from Switzerland to Singapore.

Tax Justice Network, an international non-profit advocating tax haven reform, estimates one- third of global assets are held offshore. The offshore world harbors $11.5 trillion in individual wealth alone, representing $250 billion in lost annual tax revenue. Treasury figures show tax havens sucking $100 billion a year out of U.S. coffers. And these numbers have all been growing steadily over the past decade. A *Tax Notes* study found that between 1999 and 2002, the amount of profits U.S. companies reported in tax havens grew from $88 billion to $149 billion.

With little patience left for fat-cat tax scams, the public is finally cheering for reform. Tax havens, it seems, have become the perfect embodiment of suddenly unfashionable capitalist greed. Unemployed workers and unhappy investors grow hot with anger as they imagine exotic hideouts where businessmen go to sip poolside martinis and laugh off their national tax burden.

Reformers have tried and failed in the past to shut down these locales. But analysts say 2008, the year the global financial system finally collapsed under its own liberalized weight, made all the difference. Not only are governments now desperate for tax revenue to help fund bailouts, but a recognition of the role offshore financial centers played in the system's implosion is dawning.

Along with the G20 fanfare, economists and policymakers including Treasury Secretary Timothy Geithner have pointed to the shadow banking system as a root cause of the global crisis. They're talking about the raft of highly-leveraged, virtually unregulated investment vehicles developed over the last 20 years: hedge funds, private equity, conduits, structured investment vehicles (SIVs), collateralized debt obligations (CDOs), and other wildly arcane investment banker toys.

While most of these innovations were born of Wall Street imaginations, few found their home in New York. Seventy-five percent of the world's hedge funds are based in four Caribbean tax havens: the Cayman Islands, Bermuda, the British Virgin Islands, and the Bahamas. The two subprime mortgage-backed Bear Stearns funds that collapsed in 2007, precipitating the credit crisis, were incorporated in the Caymans. Jersey and Guernsey, offshore financial centers in the Channel Islands, specialize in private equity. Many SIVs were created offshore, far from regulatory eyes.

We now know that hedge funds made their record profits from offshore bases by taking long-term gambles with short-term loans. The risky funds were often backed by onshore banks but kept off those institutions' books as they were repackaged and sold around the world. Regulators never took much notice: one, because lobbyists told them not to; two, because the funds were so complex that George Soros barely understood them; and three, because many of the deals were happening offshore.

Beneath regulatory radar, shadow bankers were able to scrap capital cushions, conceal illiquidity, and muddle debt accountability while depending on constant refinancing to survive. When the bubble burst and investors made a run for their money, panicked fund managers found it impossible to honor their debts, or even figure out how to price them as the markets crumbled.

William Cohan writes in his new book on the Bear Stearns collapse (*House of Cards: A Tale of Hubris and Wretched Excess on Wall Street*) that it took the brokerage three weeks working day and night to value illiquid securities when two of its Cayman-based hedge funds fell apart in 2007. In the end, the firm realized it was off by $1 billion from its original guesstimate, on just $1.5 billion in funds.

Mortgage-backed securities that once flourished in offshore tax havens are now the toxic assets that U.S. taxpayers are being asked to salvage through the trillion-dollar TARP and TALF programs.

Last Laughs

This convoluted network of offshore escapades is what world leaders have vowed to bring under global regulatory watch in order to restore worldwide financial stability. To their credit, the crackdown on banking secrecy has already begun in a big way.

In February, secret Swiss bank accounts were blown open to permit an unprecedented Internal Revenue Service probe. Europe's UBS bank has admitted to helping wealthy Americans evade what prosecutors believe to be $300 million a year in taxes.

Switzerland, the world's biggest tax haven where at least $2 trillion in offshore money is stashed, has long refused to recognize tax evasion as a crime. Every nation has the sovereign right to set its own tax code, which is why regulators have had such a hard time challenging offshore banking in the past. The dirty secret of tax havens, as President Obama once noted, is that they're mostly legal.

Under U.S. law, tax avoidance (legal) only becomes tax evasion (illegal) in the absence of other, more credible perks. In other words, a company is free to establish foreign subsidiaries in search of financial expertise, global reach, convenience, etc., just so long as tax dodging does not appear to be the sole reason for relocation.

The IRS will tax individual American income wherever it's found, but finding it is often the key. To access account information in Switzerland, authorities had to have proof not merely of tax evasion but of fraud, which is what much white-knuckled investigation finally produced on UBS. In the wake of this success, and under threat of landing on the OECD's new list of "uncooperative" tax havens, all of Europe's secrecy jurisdictions—Liechtenstein, Andorra, Austria, Luxembourg, and Switzerland—have signed information-sharing agreements.

Following the blood trail, congressional investigators descended on the Cayman Islands in March to tour the infamous Ugland House: one building supposedly home to 12,748 U.S. companies. The trip was an attempt to verify some of the implicit accusations made by a Government Accountability Office report in January which found that 83 of the United States' top 100 companies operate subsidiaries in tax havens.

Many of those, including Citigroup (which holds 90 subsidiaries in the Cayman Islands alone), Bank of America, and AIG, have received billions in taxpayer-funded bailouts. But the report failed to establish whether the subsidiaries were set up for the sole purpose of tax evasion.

Offshore Arguments

Politicians are already patting themselves on the back for their success in tackling tax crime. Everyone is making a big deal of the new tax information-exchange standard that all but three nations (Costa Rica, Malaysia, and the Philippines—the OECD's freshly minted blacklist) have agreed to implement in the wake of the G20 meeting. What leaders aren't saying is that before it became a G20 talking point, tax information exchange was actually tax haven *fans'* favored reform measure.

The first thing most offshore officials claim when confronted with criticism is that their countries are not, indeed, tax havens. Since the OECD launched a tax policy campaign in 1996, many of the offshore centers have been working to clean up their acts. A hoard of information-exchange agreements with onshore economies were signed even before Switzerland took the plunge. Geoff Cook, head of Jersey Finance, says Jersey's agreements with the United States, Germany, Sweden, and others have long outpaced what banks in Switzerland and Singapore traditionally maintained. "Our only fear in this is that people wouldn't look into the subject deep enough to draw those distinctions," Cook said.

But analysts say the agreements lack teeth. To request information from offshore, authorities must already have some evidence of misconduct. And the information-exchange standard still only covers illegal tax evasion, not legal tax avoidance. More importantly, what is already evident is that these agreements don't change much about the way offshore financial centers function. Offshore centers that agree to open up their books still have the luxury of setting their own regulatory standards and will continue to attract business based on their shadow banking credentials.

The G20 decided that shadow banking must be subjected to the same regulation as onshore commercial activity, which will also see more diligent oversight. Financial activity everywhere will be required to maintain better capital buffers, they said, monitored by a new Financial Stability Board; and excessive risk-taking will be rebuked. But the push for harmonized regulation across all finan-cial centers revokes a degree of local liberty. Big ideas about state sovereignty and economic growth are at stake, which is probably what made Sarkozy so nervous about taking his regulatory demands global.

"People come here for expertise and knowledge," argues head of Guernsey Finance Peter Niven, and he may have a point. Many in finance think it's wrong to put all the blame on private funds and offshore centers for a crisis of such complex origins. Havens say stripping away their financial freedoms is hypocritical and shortsighted. "It's really not about the Cayman Islands, it's about the U.S. tax gap— and we're the collateral damage," said one frustrated Cayman Island official, adding: "Everybody needs liquidity and everyone needs money. That's what we do."

Predictably, reform critics warn that responding to the global crisis with "too much" regulation will stifle economic growth, something they know world leaders are quite conscious of. "International Financial Centres such as Jersey play an important role as conduits in the flow of international capital around the world by providing liquidity in neighbouring (often onshore) financial centres, the very lubrication which markets now need," wrote Cook in a recent statement.

Overall, attempting to move beyond paltry information exchange to implementing real regulation of shadow banking across national jurisdictions promises to be extremely difficult.

Real Reform

Part of the solution starts at home. Offshore enthusiasts might be the first to point out that the Securities and Exchange Commission never had the remit to regulate *onshore* hedge funds because Congress didn't give it to them. Wall Street deregulation is often cited in Europe as the base rot in the system.

But demanding more regulation onshore won't do any good if you can't regulate in the same way offshore. A serious aspect of the tax haven problem is a kind of global regulatory arbitrage: widespread onshore deregulation over the last 20 years came alongside an affinity for doing business offshore where even less regulation was possible, which in turn encouraged tax haven-style policies in countries like Britain, the United States, Singapore, and Ireland, all fighting to draw finance back into their economies.

President Obama has long been a champion of both domestic and offshore financial reform, and a critic of the deregulation popular during the Bush years. But for global action to happen, Obama needs Europe's help (not to mention cooperation from Asia and the Middle East) and no one knows how deep Gordon Brown's commitment runs. It is only very recently that Brown transformed himself from deregulation cheerleader as chancellor of the exchequer under Tony Blair to global regulatory savior as Britain's new prime minister.

In an interview late last year, Tax Justice Network's John Christensen predicted Britain could become a barrier to reform. "Britain, I think, will become increasingly isolated, particularly in Europe where the City of London is regarded as a tax haven," he said. Even if Gordon Brown is on board, Britain's finance sector hates to see itself sink. Moreover, some say the UK's lax financial regulatory system has saved the wider economy from decay. When British manufacturing declined, the City of London became the nation's new breadwinner. It grew into the powerhouse it is today largely by luring business away from other centers with the promise of adventurous profit-making and mild public oversight.

The City now funnels much of its business through British overseas territories that make up a big faction in the world's offshore banking club. Many offshore officials have accused Britain of making a show of tax haven reform to deflect attention from its own dirty dealings onshore.

Other obstacles to reform could come from Belgium and Luxembourg, which each hold important votes at the Basel Committee on Banking Supervision (a leading international regulatory voice) and the EU. Neither country has shown much enthusiasm for Europe's reform agenda. And no one will soon forget that China nearly neutered the G20 communiqué when it refused to "endorse" an OECD tax haven blacklist that would allow Europe to chastise financial activities in Hong Kong and Macau.

Still, the regulatory tide is strong and rising; even global financial heavyweights may find it unwise or simply impossible to swim against it. For perhaps the first time since the end of World War II, the world appears open to the kind of global cooperation necessary to facilitate global integration in a socially responsible way.

But the tiny nations that have built empires around unfettered financial services will surely continue to fight for their place in the sun. Some may go the way of Darwinian selection. Declining tourism is already crippling economies across the Caribbean. But many more are optimistic about their ability to hang on. Guernsey is pursuing Chinese markets. Jersey claims business in private equity remains strong. Bermuda still has insurance and hopes to dabble in gambling. Many offshore say they welcome the coming reforms.

"We look forward to those challenges" said Michael Dunkley, leader of the United Bermuda Party, noting that Bermuda, a tiny island with a population of just 66,000 people, is not encumbered by big bureaucracy when it comes to getting things done. Whatever new regulations come up, he said: "Bermuda would be at the cutting edge of making sure it worked."

Accusations of capitalist evil aside, one can't help but admire their spirit. ❑

Sources: Willem Buiter, "Making monetary policy in the UK has become simpler, in no small part thanks to Gordon Brown," *Financial Times*, October 26, 2008; G20 Final Communiqué, "The Global Plan for Recovery and Reform," April 2, 2009; Tax Justice Network, taxjustice.net; Martin Sullivan, Data Shows Dramatic Shift of Profits to Tax Havens, *Tax Notes*, September 13, 2004; William Cohan, *House of Cards: A Tale of Hubris and Wretched Excess on Wall Street*, March 2009; U.S. Government Accountability Office, "International Taxation: Large US corporations and federal contractors in jurisdictions listed as tax havens or financial privacy jurisdictions," December 2008; Organisation for Economic Co-operation and Development. "A Progress Report on the Jurisdictions Surveyed by the OECD Global Forum in Implementing the Internationally Agreed Tax Standard," April 2, 2009; Geoff Cook, Response to *Financial Times* Comment, mail. jerseyfinance.je; March 5, 2009; William Brittain-Catlin, "How offshore capitalism ate our economies—and itself," *The Guardian*, Feb. 5, 2009.

Article 10.6

NO BAILOUT FOR AIDS
Are cuts to health care a necessary part of "fiscal reform," or the continuation of decades of neglect?

BY MARA KARDAS-NELSON
July/August 2009

Despite trillions being spent on bank bailouts, the world's AIDS programs are facing billion-dollar deficits in order to continue lifesaving prevention, care, and treatment initiatives. Both domestic and donation governments cite the global financial downturn to explain the significant decrease in funding for AIDS and other health programs in the past year. While a fall-off in government revenue is undeniable, activists condemn the justification of the likely illness and death of millions in the name of "fiscal reform." Some even claim that the economic crisis is simply an excuse for governments to continue decades of AIDS neglect.

Nearly 40 million people are living with HIV worldwide, with 2.7 million new infections and two million people dying of AIDS-related illnesses every year. Sub-Saharan Africa is the hardest-hit region. According to the African Union, the region "faces a grim scenario with respect to the health of its people. [It is]... home to 12 percent of the world's population [yet] accounts for 22 percent of the total global disease burden, and more than 68 percent of the people living with HIV/AIDS. [This] poor health status is mirrored by crises in health financing and human resources for health. With only 2% of the global health workforce and only 1% of the world's health expenditures, Sub-Saharan African countries are ill-equipped to adequately address their health problems."

In light of the global economic downturn, such indicators will only get worse. The World Bank has gloomily predicted that "the global economic crisis will cause an additional 22 children to die per hour, throughout all of 2009... it's possible that the toll will be twice that: an additional 400,000 child deaths, or an extra child dying every 79 seconds."

Unequal Cutbacks

Government-funded health care programs will no doubt be cut during the recession. Such cutbacks are seen as an unfortunate side effect of fiscal reform. According to a recent World Bank report: "Governments tend to expand social expenditures during times of economic expansion and decrease them during times of economic recession." Regardless of whether some cutbacks are necessary, the proportional cuts in funding for social programs historically have not reflected actual decreases in government revenues, thus undermining the argument that governments are "forced" to cut back on health spending. Data from Mexico between 1994 and 1996 show a

4.9% fall in GDP met "by a 23.7% fall in targeted spending per poor person." More damning is the example of Argentina where, "from the end of 2001 to the middle of 2002, preventive health care for children dropped 38% in the general population, but 57% in the poorest households." The World Bank report goes on to point out: "general strategies to maintain government social spending have often failed to protect poor people's access to essential social services during financial emergencies and ended up helping better-off groups in society instead."

These decreases in health spending come at a time when public health programs are most in need. As a statement issued by the South African non-profit Treatment Action Campaign puts it, "reduced income makes people less likely to seek medical attention when they are sick as they can no longer afford to travel. It also forces people to buy cheaper, less nutritious food which leads to an increase in malnutrition.... Despite the fact that clinic visits may contract in times of economic recession, the actual demand for these services increases as people face greater difficulties in accessing adequate food and housing."

One Step Forward, Two Steps Back

Since the beginning of the AIDS epidemic, governments worldwide, with a few notable exceptions, have inadequately funded prevention and treatment efforts. This is true for both domestic funding and for large donor countries like the United States and Britain which, because of their immense political and economic power, have been expected to help fund programs for countries far less economically or politically stable. Until recently, governments did not recognize the urgency or financial support that the epidemic requires.

OBAMA AND AIDS FUNDING:
CHANGE, OR MORE OF THE SAME?

AIDS activists have high expectations for President Obama, hoping that he will not only live up to a long-anticipated increase in prevention and treatment funding, but also that he will reverse the harmful policies propagated by his predecessor, George Bush.

Bush's creation of the President's Emergency Plan for AIDS Relief (PEPFAR) was hailed by many as a brief moment of sanity during eight years of reckless reign. Despite PEPFAR's $15 billion contribution from 2003-2008, AIDS activists were appalled by the program's stipulation that one-third of prevention funding go to abstinence-only programs. To add insult to injury, the program required that all funded organizations sign an "anti-prostitution pledge," stating that they would not give aid to sex workers. They were also not allowed to openly work with intravenous drug users. Although PEPFAR is "the largest commitment by any nation to combat a single disease in history," Bush handicapped the program by discriminating against some of the people who need treatment most.

Furthermore, the United States' global gag rule "prohibited organizations receiving U.S. money for family planning from performing abortions, making referrals for safe abortion services, and supporting safe abortion laws and policies, even with funding from other sources," according to a report from Physicians for Human Rights. Though the gag rule did not apply to PEPFAR, the Bush administration's ambiguity on the issue

Finally, in the early and mid-2000s, after decades of campaigning and millions of deaths, domestic and foreign governments began to recognize the importance of funding a variety of programs. Most significantly, the Global Fund to Fight AIDS, Tuberculosis, and Malaria was founded in 2001 as a public-private partnership to direct funding, provided by wealthy countries, foundations, and the private sector, to poorer countries. In 2007, after years of chronic under-financing, the Fund's board voted to triple the size of the effort from $2-3 billion per year in aid to $6-8 billion per year.

In the wake of the economic crisis, the Fund has reneged on this promise. It now faces a $5 billion funding gap, and the board has already responded by delaying the next round of funding applications by six months and cutting budgets for projects currently underway by 10%, warning that it may have to cut their future years' funding by 25%.

A decrease in foreign donations could substantially affect AIDS programs, especially within Africa. According to the World Bank, 28 African states are dependent on external sources for over 11% of their health expenditures; of these, six depend on foreign spending for 41-60% of their health funding. Such "highly donor dependent countries" are "especially vulnerable to aid cuts." Therefore, the sustainability of these countries' AIDS programs, including the critically important provision of antiretroviral treatment to those already infected, depends on their ability to find alternate sources of funding, primarily internal sources.

But countries are already reporting domestic funding cuts for AIDS programs, again blaming the economy. In March of this year, the Botswana government warned that it "may have to cut or completely withdraw its HIV/AIDS funding, despite the rising number of people needing treatment, as the...crisis takes a toll on

---

prevented recipient organizations from effectively integrating HIV and family planning services.

Within days of his inauguration, Obama repealed the global gag rule. A change in PEPFAR policy is less likely, however: although candidate Obama promised that "best practice, not ideology" would determine his AIDS policy, a great deal of red-tape-hacking and hand-shaking is required before there is any real change. Considering the virulent opposition by many conservative members of Congress, this may take longer than the president may have expected.

On a more optimistic note, Obama recently picked Dr. Eric Goosby, heralded as a "pioneer in the fight against AIDS," to be the State Department's global AIDS coordinator and ambassador at large. Further, the United States is expected to give $51 billion over the next six years to HIV, malaria and tuberculosis prevention and treatment. Despite the apparent grandiosity of this figure, AIDS activists are disappointed: Obama originally pledged to expand PEPFAR by $1 billion each year for the next five years and provide $50 billion over the next five years, instead of six, to fight HIV. Activists responded to the announcement by calling the pledge "meagre." Dr. Paul Zeitz, executive director of Global AIDS Alliance, stated that reneging on such promises was "a betrayal of trust." Activists estimate that "one million people worldwide could go without AIDS treatment due to the shortfall, and some 2.9 million fewer women could receive assistance to prevent mother-to-child HIV transmission."

the vitally important diamond-mining sector….[the country's] most important revenue source." Government funding provides 80% of the cost of Botswana's AIDS programs, with donors making up the remainder. The country's treatment program is considered one of the best in Africa, with the U.N. AIDS agency (UNAIDS) estimating that 94% of those in need have access to antiretrovirals.

Recession, or Continued Neglect?

While the World Bank asserts that the current funding crisis for the Global Fund and other international and domestic AIDS programs can be attributed to the global recession, others are more skeptical. Regarding the Global Fund's current $5 billion shortfall, U.S.-based AIDS non-profit Health Gap contends: "The increase in the size and quality of proposals was exactly in line with what the Board had voted for in 2007. But, the tripling of demand from poor countries [coincided] with a global financial crisis. It's important to note that the…funding gap was not caused by the … crisis."

While the crisis may affect governments' willingness to give to the Fund and other AIDS programs, it does not necessarily affect their ability to do so. As Jeffrey Sachs of Columbia University argues: "There is no shortage of funds at the moment when in three months the rich world has found…$3 trillion of funding for bank bailouts and in which there have been $18 billion of Christmas bonuses for Wall Street supported by bailout legislation." Health Gap agrees: "The total amount of money that went to bail out banks from all the rich countries in the world is 1,000 times more than the amount needed to fill the gap in funding for the Global Fund." Furthermore, "the Global Fund has been successful, whereas banks failed and caused this crisis."

For many, such a gap is simply a continuation of chronic under-funding of health systems, especially AIDS programs. In 2007, before the crisis hit and when most developed economies were booming, "the difference between UNAIDS' estimates of resource needs compared to resources available…was at least $8 billion."

The Global Fund especially has been shortchanged, most notably by the United States. Each contributing country is supposed to donate according to its percentage of the global economy. Thus, the United States should fill one-third of the current funding gap, since it accounts for one-third of the global economy. Such a stipulation is also written into U.S. law. But according to Health Gap, "the United States has historically not contributed its fair share to the Global Fund. After the Fund announced it intended to distribute $10 billion per year, President Bush made the paltry first contribution of $200 million. As a result, the Global Fund has been smaller than anticipated and has had to grow over time instead of starting out large." Today the United States continues to fail its one-third commitment. If the Fund is to keep its pledge to increase funding—a pledge the U.S. government agreed to—then the country must give $2.7 billion for 2010. For 2009 it has given only $900 million to date, $1 billion short of its fair share.

The legitimacy of domestic cuts is also in question. While the Ugandan government has blamed severe shortages of AIDS and tuberculosis drugs in the Gulu region on "delays in the disbursement of money from the Global Fund," according to the online HIV/AIDS news service PlusNews, observers point to mismanagement and, at times, corruption as factors. When the parliament's budget committee recommended cutting funding for antiretroviral drugs nearly in half next year, one local AIDS activist pointed out that the government is still finding plenty of money for the defense ministry and for politicians' perks.

Paula Akugizibwe of the AIDS and Rights Alliance of Southern Africa says that while a decrease in government revenue must be taken into consideration, it does not diminish governments' responsibility for public health. "We need to ensure that African lives do not become a silent casualty of the global financial downturn. Our lives are not cheap or expendable. The crisis does not absolve governments of the responsibility to fund essential programmes that they've promised. They must look at how they can re-allocate the money that they do have. We expect health to be prioritised over weapons, sports and lavish politics." Rebecca Hodes of the Treatment Action Campaign adds, "HIV and TB are not in recession." ❑

Sources: "2008 Report on the Global AIDS Epidemic," UNAIDS; African Union Paper (CAMH/EXP/13a(IV)), AU Ministers of Health Conference, Ethiopia, May 2009; Nicholas D. Kristof, "At Stake Are More Than Banks," *New York Times*, April 1 2009; The World Bank's Human Development Network, "Averting a Human Crisis During the Global Downturn," The World Bank, March 2009; "TAC statement on new cabinet appointments and resources for health," The Treatment Action Campaign, May 12, 2009; "Fact Sheet on Global Fund $5 billion shortfall," Health GAP; "Botswana: Bleak Outlook for Future AIDS Funding," PlusNews, February 20, 2009; Rosanne Skirbel, "Economic Downturn Threatens Global Fund for AIDS, TB, Malaria," VOA News, February 4, 2009. "About Pepfar," from pepfar.gov; Neil MacFarquhar, "Obama Picks Leader for Global AIDS effort," *New York Times*, April 27, 2009; Amanda Cary, "Repealing the Global Gage Rule: Obama takes Action to Combat AIDS," Physicians for Human Rights, January 23, 2009; "A New and Improved Pepfar Under Obama?" South African Business Coalition on HIV/AIDS, January 21, 2009; Sheryl Gay Stolberg, "Obama Seeks a Global Health Plan Broader Than Bush's AIDS Effort," *New York Times*, May 5, 2009; Derek Kilner, "AIDS Activists Criticize Obama Budget for HIV," VOA News, May 19 2009.

CONTRIBUTORS

Frank Ackerman, a founder of *Dollars & Sense*, is Director of Research and Policy at the Global Development and Environment Institute at Tufts University.

David Bacon is a journalist and photographer covering labor, immigration, and the impact of the global economy on workers.

Dean Baker is co-director of the Center for Economic and Policy Research (www. cepr.net) in Washington, D.C.

Ricky Baldwin is a labor and anti-war activist and organizer whose articles have appeared in *Dollars & Sense, Z Magazine, Extra!, In These Times,* and *Labor Notes.*

Arpita Banerjee is a graduate student in economics at the University of New Hampshire and a member of the *Dollars & Sense* collective.

Madeleine Baran is a freelance writer and a graduate student at New York University's Graduate School of Journalism.

Drucilla K. Barker is professor of economics and women's studies at Hollins University. She is co-author of *Liberating Economics: Feminist Perspectives on Families, Work, and Globalization.*

Frida Berrigan is a Senior Research Associate at the Arms Trade Resource Center of the World Policy Institute, located in New York City.

Ravi Bhandari (co-editor of this volume) is the Chevron Endowed Chair of Economics and International Political Economy at Saint Mary's College of California, visiting professor at Tribhuvan University and Kathmandu University's School of Management (KUSOM) and Senior Fulbright Scholar in Nepal, 2009.

Faisal Chaudhry, a member of the *Dollars & Sense* collective, is a lawyer and Ph.D. candidate in history at Harvard University.

Ben Collins is a member of the *Dollars & Sense* collective and a research analyst at a sustainable investment research company.

Felicitas Contreras is an activist with the Center for Workers and Communities in Nuevo Laredo, Mexico.

Paul Cummings is a software engineer with a long-standing interest in environmental and social issues.

Han Deqiang is an economist at the Economics and Management School, Beijing University of Aeronautics and Astronautics.

Maurice Dufour teaches political science and humanities at Marianopolis College in Montreal.

Marie Duggan is an associate professor of economics at Keene State College in New Hampshire.

Mark Engler is an analyst with Foreign Policy In Focus.

Susan F. Feiner is professor of economics and women's studies at the University of Southern Maine. She is co-author of *Liberating Economics: Feminist Perspectives on Families, Work, and Globalization.*

Bob Feldman is an anti-war and anti-corporate writer-activist based in the Boston area.

Bill Fletcher, Jr. is a long-time labor and international activist and writer. He is the former president of the Washington, D.C.-based organizing and educational center TransAfrica Forum.

Ellen Frank teaches economics at the University of Massachusetts-Boston and is a *Dollars & Sense* Associate. She is the author of *The Raw Deal: How Myths and Misinformation about Deficits, Inflation, and Wealth Impoverish America.*

Andre Gunder Frank, the father of world system theory and the older dependency theory, was a pioneer in the global analysis of history and social science. He died in 2005 at the age of 76.

Liv Gold is a former *Dollars & Sense* collective member.

Mara Kardas-Nelson is a freelance writer currently based in Cape Town, South Africa. She has written on health, the environment, and human rights for the *Globe & Mail* and the *Mail & Guardian*.

Rachel Keeler is a freelance international business journalist. She holds an MSc in Global Politics from the London School of Economics.

Marie Kennedy is professor emerita of Community Planning at the University of Massachusetts-Boston and visiting professor in Urban Planning at UCLA. She is a member of the board of directors of Grassroots International.

Joel Kovel is co-editor of the journal *Capitalism Nature Socialism*, author of *The Enemy of Nature*, and co-producer of the 2007 video "A Really Inconvenient Truth."

Gawain Kripke is a senior policy advisor at Oxfam America.

Alex Linghorn has spent the last two years closely engaged with the land rights movement in Nepal. He is currently a postgraduate at the School of Oriental and African Studies (SOAS), University of London.

Arthur MacEwan is professor emeritus of economics at the University of Massachusetts-Boston and is a *Dollars & Sense* Associate.

John Miller is a member of the *Dollars & Sense* collective and teaches economics at Wheaton College.

Anuradha Mittal is a co-director of Food First/The Institute for Food and Development Policy in Oakland, California.

Dena Montague is a Senior Research Associate at the Arms Trade Resource Center of the World Policy Institute, located in New York City.

Vasuki Nesiah is a senior associate at the International Center for Transitional Justice and co-editor of *lines* magazine (www.lines-magazine.org), an online magazine that engages with the political spaces of Sri Lanka and South Asia more broadly.

Immanuel Ness is a professor of political science at Brooklyn College-City University of New York. He is author of *Immigrants, Unions, and the New U.S. Labor Market* and editor of *WorkingUSA: The Journal of Labor and Society*.

Martha Ojeda, a former *maquiladora* worker, is the executive director of the Coalition for Justice in the Maquiladoras.

Thomas I. Palley is an economist who has held positions at the AFL-CIO, Open Society Institute, and the U.S.-China Economic and Security Review Commission.

James Petras is an advisor and teacher for the Rural Landless Workers Movement in Brazil and an activist-scholar working with socio-political movements in Latin America, Europe, and Asia.

Robert Pollin teaches economics and is co-director of the Political Economy Research Institute at the University of Massachusetts-Amherst. He is also a *Dollars & Sense* Associate.

Kenneth Pomeranz is a professor of history at the University of California at Irvine and author of *The Great Divergence: China, Europe, and the Making of the Modern World Economy.*

Tarso Luís Ramos is director of Political Research Associates in Somerville, Mass., and a member of the board of directors of Grassroots International.

Smriti Rao teaches economics at Assumption College in Worcester, Mass., and is a member of the *Dollars & Sense* collective.

Alejandro Reuss, an economist and historian, is a former editor of *Dollars & Sense* and a current member of the *D&S* collective.

Peter Rosset is a co-director of Food First/The Institute for Food and Development Policy in Oakland, California.

Katherine Sciacchitano is a former labor lawyer and organizer. She currently teaches at the National Labor College in Silver Spring, Maryland.

Devinder Sharma is a food and trade policy analyst. He chairs the New Delhi-based Forum for Biotechnology & Food Security. Among his recent works are *GATT to WTO: Seeds of Despair* and *In the Famine Trap.*

Dariush Sokolov is an activist and independent journalist based in Argentina. He writes about political philosophy, anarchist economics, and global finance.

Chris Sturr (co-editor of this volume) is co-editor of *Dollars & Sense.*

Anna Sussman is a freelance print and radio reporter.

Alissa Thuotte is a former *Dollars & Sense* intern.

Chris Tilly is a *Dollars & Sense* Associate and director of the Institute for Research on Labor and Employment and professor of urban planning at UCLA.

Yolanda Treviño is a former Sony *maquiladora* worker whose testimony against NAFTA is included in the book *NAFTA from Below.*

Marie Trigona is an independent journalist based in Buenos Aires. She is also a member of Grupo Alavío, a direct action and video collective.

Mark Weisbrot is co-director of the Center for Economic and Policy Research (www.cepr.net) in Washington, D.C.

Jessica Weisberg is a former *Dollars & Sense* intern.